The Walkabout Chronicles

Epic Journeys by Foot

with Tor and Siffy Torkildson

Introduction by Sir Ranulph Fiennes

Sacred World Explorations
Alaska

This edition copyright © 2016 by Sacred World Explorations, USA All rights reserved. No part of this publication may be reproduced, stored in a retrieval system, or transmitted, in any form or by any means, without the prior written permission of the publisher or authors, except by a reviewer who may quote brief passages in a review to be printed in a newspaper or magazine or broadcast on radio or television.

First edition, Sacred World Explorations, 2016.

Credits and copyright notices for previously published material are at the end of each essay. In the event of any question of ownership, we can make the correction in future printings. Contact Sacred World Explorations. sacredworldexplorations.com

Text © 2016 Tor Torkildson and authors
Cover art: Candace Rose Rardon
Maps: Siffy Torkildson
Page layout and design: Siffy Torkildson

ISBN 978-1533269744

Sacred World Explorations
Alaska

Dedication

We dedicate this book to our grandmothers, Evelyn Gagne Torkildson and Myrrl Trueblood Houle, both prolific walkers who inspired us.

Evelyn (Tor's grandmother)

Myrrl (Siffy's grandmother)

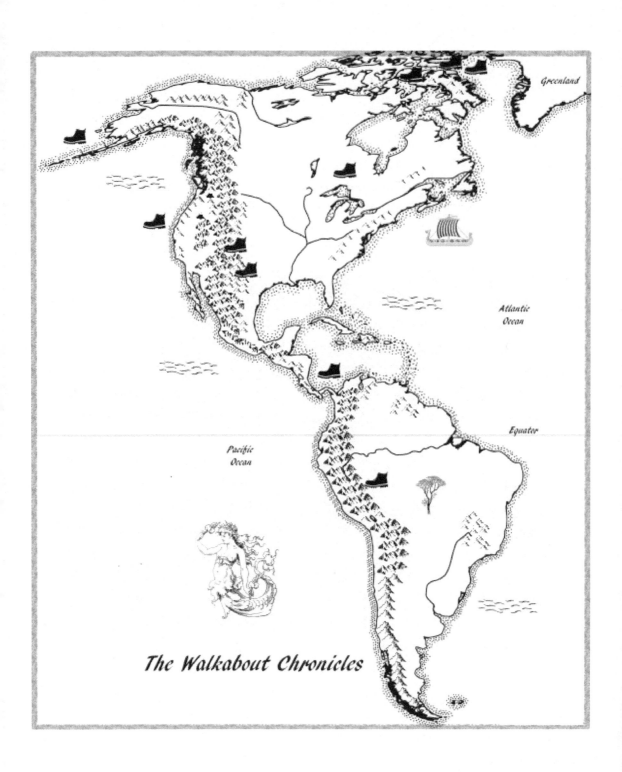

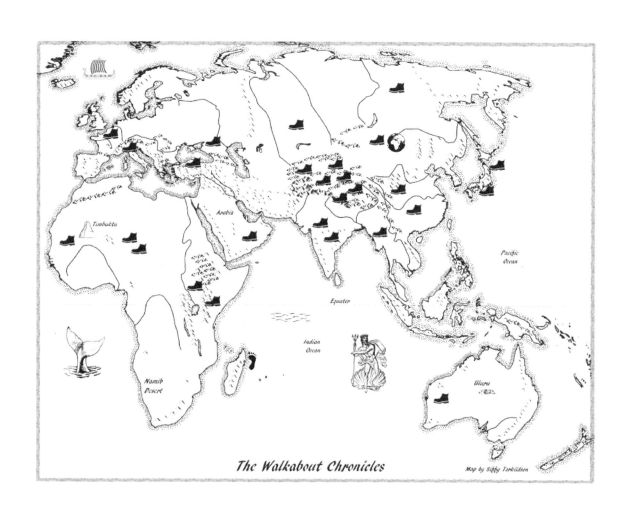

We'd like to give a special thank you to the Walkabout tribe. You know who you are.

Keep on Keeping on!

with Tor and Siffy Torkildson

TABLE OF CONTENTS

Steven Newman: *India* 1
Don George: *Karakorum Highway–Pakistan* 11
Sophie Ibbotson: *Wakhan Corridor–Afghanistan* 17
James Dorsey: *The Great Rift Valley* 31
Jon Turk: *Siberia, Ellesmere Island* 37
Jeff Fuchs: *China Tea Caravan Routes* 45
Lorie Karnath: *Burma* 59
Francis O'Donnell: *Marco Polo Route* 77
Tor Torkildson: *Japan* 93
Siffy Torkildson: *Madagascar* 109
Dhawa Gyanjen Tsumba and Phunjo Lama: *Tsum Valley–Nepal* 117
Angela Maxwell: *Mongolia, Georgia, Australia* 127
David Downie: *France* 141
Baiba and Pat Morrow: *Sikkim–India* 155
Tony Mangan: *Southwestern U.S.A.* 173
John Francis: *Northern California* 179
Ariane Alzhara Kirtley: *Niamey–Niger* 193
Michael and Aubine Kirtley: *Ayr Mountains–Niger* 221
Candace Rose Rardon: *Turkey* 245
Robb Saunders: *Japan* 255
Edwin Bernbaum: *Nepal* 271
Moataz Bonser: *Mauritania* 281
Levison Wood: *Himalayas* 285
Pierre Delattre: *New Mexico–U.S.A.* 291
Mikael Strandberg: *Yemen* 299
Colin Monteath: *Mongolia* 305
Dan Rubinstein: *Quebec–Canada* 315
Maria Coffey: *Kenya, Himalayas* 327
Helen Thayer: *Magnetic North Pole* 345
Brandon Wilson: *The Alps, Mount Everest, Tibet* 355
Erin McKittrick: *Aleutian Islands–Alaska* 385
Polly Letofsky: *India* 393
Jerry Kobalenko: *Ellesmere Island* 401
Wade Davis: *Darian Gap–Colombia/Panama* 405
Johan Reinhard: *Peru* 413

"The Walkabout Chronicles is likely to become
a classic in adventure and travel literature."

An Introduction by Sir Ranulph Fiennes

The Walkabout Chronicles: Epic Journeys by Foot is the brainchild of Tor and Siffy Torkildson. This unique collection of essays, interviews and photography share contemporary and inspiring journeys around the world on foot, an exercise with which I am quite familiar and can appreciate both the effort and the end results!

What is most distinct about this anthology is the diversity of walkers and landscapes they have travelled. There are extreme expedition walkers, humanitarian workers walking for water, artists seeking inspiration, a Nepalese trekking guide, around-the-world walkers, Arctic explorers and those who seek to travel the world's many pilgrimage pathways.

These walkabouts take the reader across ice caps, over soaring mountain ranges, along the great river-ways, into the heart of jungles and searing deserts, through war zones and across sacred landscapes. Here the reader will find great writing and epic journeys from lesser-known walkers, as well as some very well-known explorers. Such adventures are taken on for many reasons, some of which may not be fully understood at the time and with retrospection but that there is an inner urge to explore is undeniable.

The Walkabout Chronicles is likely to become a classic in adventure and travel literature. This book should interest anyone that has ever set out on a walk in their own neighborhood or across a distant and remarkable landscape somewhere beyond their horizon.

Sir Ranulph Fiennes

Preface
Tor Torkildson, series editor

Meandering leads to perfection.
~Lao Tzu

This book was born out of a dream. I never imagined my dream would lead to such an amazing outcome; it is a dream I have nonetheless been developing all my life. I'd like to share this dream with you.

When I was sixteen years old, I read two books that would change the direction of my life. The first book was *On the Road* by Jack Kerouac, which set into motion a yearning to get out of my hometown and see the world. The second book was *The Man Who Walked Around the World*, by David Kunst. Between 1970 and 1974, David Kunst walked 14,450 miles, becoming the first person documented to have walked around the world. Reading about this epic walk by a fellow Minnesotan planted a seed deep inside me that would continue to grow as the years and my travels passed by. There hasn't been a day since I read about David Kunst's journey that I wasn't planning my own world walk in my head. Unfortunately, the responsibilities of life kept this dream at bay. I often daydreamed that I would be like a Hindu, fulfilling my worldly obligations, until the day I could renounce everything and hit the road as a wandering *bhikkhu*. I kept this dream to myself and rarely shared it with anyone. I knew my day to tramp would come: I never stopped believing I would live the life I imagined.

In the mid-1980s, after completing a journey around the globe by plane, train, bus, camel, and boat, I discovered that another man had circumnavigated the world under his own power: Steven Newman had written a mesmerizing account of his walk, entitled *Worldwalk*. Admittedly, this account rattled my cage, and I seriously began to take stock of my life and my dreams. The pace and extent of my travels increased substantially, but so did the weight of my obligations. I was on a razor's edge. In the meantime, I began to research long-distance walkers, historical figures such as George Matthew Schilling and the Romanian geographer Dumitru Dan, who had both made undocumented walks around the world. Dumitru Dan had supposedly walked across 76 countries, visited 1,500 cities, and worn out 497 pairs of shoes on his venture.

Several years ago, in the midst of my blossoming relationship with Siffy, who soon became my wife, I decided to test the waters: I asked her if she'd be interested in walking around the world with me.

"Absolutely, how exciting! I have always wanted to do something adventurous like that," came her quick reply.

I was relieved to know that I would have a partner to share my childhood dream with. Later, I would learn that Siffy's grandmother, like mine, had been a serious walker.

When my grandmother, Evelyn Torkildson, was a young girl, she was diagnosed with polio. Her doctor told her she would need to walk to survive the disease. And walk she did, three times a day, after each meal.

My father also became an obsessive walker when he decided he needed to shed a few pounds to keep up with his athletic wife. It did not matter if there was a blizzard raging and it was minus forty degrees, he would be out hiking with a backpack full of rocks. (At age 62 he climbed Mount Kilimanjaro.) Siffy's grandmother walked several miles a day into her mid-nineties.

I only went out for a walk and finally concluded to stay out till sundown, for going out, I found, was really going in.
~John Muir

There have been many great walkers throughout history: luminaries, who have fueled their creativity by wandering about on foot. One was Aristotle, the Greek philosopher, empiricist, and pupil of Plato. While conducting his lectures, Plato would walk the grounds of his school in Athens. Over his lifetime, William Wordsworth walked nearly 175,000 miles. It has been said that he walked to find meter in his poetry. Charles Dickens often walked 20 to 30 miles during the middle of the night. Many of his friends felt his walking habit bordered on pathological. Philosopher Soren Kierkegaard said that he walked himself into a state of well being, and far away from every illness. Ludwig Van Beethoven walked several times a day, "like a bee swarming out to collect honey," to inspire his creativity.

Between 1983 and 1987, Steven Newman completed his solo round-the-world walk, covering 15,000 miles. I can still remember the day I spotted his fantastic book, *Worldwalk*. The book cover showed the black silhouette of a backpacker walking across the planet earth. After five years of preparation, Newman had managed to save $25,000 from roustabouting on small drilling rigs in Wyoming. Then after poring over hundreds of maps and visiting public libraries and embassies, he set off on his epic trek, with a backpack he named Clinger. His would be recognized as the first documented solo walk around the world. I elatedly consumed his book, and I continue to read it annually. Steven Newman continues to share his experiences with thousands of people, and his excitement and compassion are inspiring. Siffy and I will be connecting with this legendary walker soon, to do a bit of tramping up Mount Kilimanjaro.

With the dream of our own world walk coming into focus, Siffy and I are taking walking very seriously. We have embarked on long treks in the Himalayas and North Africa, across the Alps and Pyrenees, and to the outback of the western United States. We continue to research great walkers and long distance trails.

In the process, we stumbled upon two obscure female characters, Mildred Lisette Norman ("Peace Pilgrim") and "Grandma" Gatewood. "Peace Pilgrim" was an American vegetarian and peace activist. Starting in 1953, she walked back and forth across the United States for 28 years until her death in 1981. "Grandma" was an epic hiker, starting at age 67. She was the first woman to hike the full length of the Appalachian Trail.

As our library of famous walkers filled up, two naturalist writers, Henry David Thoreau and John Muir, inspired us with their beautifully written prose and their reflective tramping. Thoreau was a famous saunterer. In his appropriately titled essay,

Walker, he said that for him walking through nature was a kind of pilgrimage without a destination. Siffy and I admire his Zen-like approach to life and nature. John Muir was a naturalist who helped preserve Yosemite and other natural areas. He was an eccentric guy who climbed mountains and hiked incredible distances, to whoop and howl, from flower to flower. He said that walking was often the only way to access the subject of his writing and passion.

> *Me thinks that the moment my legs begin to move my thoughts begin to flow.*
> ~Henry David Thoreau

In 2013, we learned about Rosie Swale Pope, who, at the age of 57, ran around the world in five years. When her husband, Clive, died of cancer, Rosie decided to run around the world to raise money for the Prostate Cancer Charity. She ran across the northern hemisphere hauling a specially designed cart that carried her supplies, and that she slept in. She would go on to write a book about her experiences, *Just a Little Run Around the World: 5 years, 3 packs of wolves, and 53 pairs of shoes*. Her book had my heart pumping all the way through, especially the night she spent in frozen Siberia, surrounded by wolves. Rosie is one tough lady, and is currently running and walking across the United States. We recently talked to Rosie and found her positive worldview absolutely inspiring. She excitedly told us that she is planning to walk and run around the world again!

Walk, ramble, stroll, wander, saunter, travel (on foot), march, parade, tramp, hike, tread, amble, hoof it, perambulate, peregrinate, prance, roam, stagger, stride, trot, circumambulate, go on a pilgrimage. Call it what you will. When you walk, you slow down and see things, learn about the environment you are passing through, improve your health, and free up religious and creative energy. There seems to be no better way to clear one's mind from the dust and calamity of life. Take Brandon Wilson, for example. Wilson has walked more than 8,000 miles along the world's greatest pilgrimage trails, from the Camino de Santiago in Spain to Norway's St. Olav's Way, from Lhasa to Kathmandu, from England to Rome, and the Templar Trail from France to Jerusalem. Wilson finds great joy in these journeys, and soaks up the spirituality in large sacred doses. Or Jeff Fuchs, whose relentless passion is to find great tea, and walk ancient trade routes along the way. Others, such as Pierre Delattre and Moataz Bonser, walk to fuel their creativity.

Many walkers wish to push themselves to the limits of human endurance. Some walk for humanitarian reasons, or to bring awareness to the environment. Walking can even be a profession, as it is for guides and tour operators. Walking can be for whatever reason you want it to be. There is no age limit for walking. And walking is free.

One night, with my head full of walking motifs, I had a dream that I'd brought together all the amazing walkers in the world. In the morning, I mentally listed walkers I knew and the books I had read that involved epic walks. I made a list of potential people to contact and pondered my library for a day with Siffy. The next night a title came to me: *The Walkabout Chronicles: Epic Journeys by Foot*. In April 2016, this book began to transpire as I reached out to friends, created a closed Facebook group for walkers, and started to conduct serious research into all things involved with walking.

What an adventure! Along this journey, I have met so many interesting people, read dozens of amazing essays and books, and made many lifelong friends. Each and every person represented in this book has inspired me to live the life I imagined. Their collective positive energy will make the world a better place. This book represents not only extreme walkers, but the entire range of people who walk, each for their own amazing reasons. I have learned that each time we step out, there is the potential to step within, and the chance to become better people.

As you will soon find out, the *Walkabout Chronicles* is like attending a wonderful festival, with award-winning writers, world-renowned explorers, artists and scientists, extreme athletes, guides, pilgrims, anthropologists, dreamers, and ordinary people who have gone out and done extraordinary things with their lives. In this book you will find refined essays, short interviews, photographic essays, and journeys to the far corners of the planet. I encourage you to read this book with an open mind and an adventurous soul. Our hope is that this book will inspire you to keep your face in the sun and to head out on a walkabout with wide open eyes and hearts.

The seed that was planted in my soul, all those years ago will soon blossom. The time is drawing near when Siffy and I will set out to wander this sacred planet as purely and as in tune with nature as possible. Yes, that day is drawing near, very near. This book has been a labor of love, our way of paying tribute to the great walkers who have inspired us through their stories, books, examples, and friendship. We are honored to present *The Walkabout Chronicles: Epic Journeys by Foot* to the world.

Keep on walking on!!!
Enjoy the journey,

Tor and Siffy Torkildson, Sacred World Explorations

"It all changes, everything, and walking illustrates that elemental condition of our lives. Nothing else so completely clears our minds or lays bare the soul of place. This monumental book, full of graceful prose by writers and explorers, walks us through the familiar, the unfamiliar and downright strange. Highly recommended."

~Tim Cahill, author of *Pass the Butterworms: Remote Journeys Oddly Rendered*

An amazing and monumental book that provides firsthand accounts of what it is to explore and why. It takes us through many remote as well as familiar places around the world, at the same time each story shares a similar experience of learning something fundamental about the human condition.

~Lorie Karnath: Co-founder of The Explorers Museum and served as the president of The Explorers Club

"The history of walking and writing is almost as old as culture: every step is a story, and every path *tells*. This marvelous collection adds a new mile to the written way, a new stride to the literature of the leg."

~Robert Macfarlane, author of *The Old Ways: A Journey on Foot*

"*The Walkabout Chronicles*—It is likely to become a classic of the genre as this group of explorers and authors will most likely never be together again."

~James Dorsey, author of *Vanishing Tales from Ancient Trail*

"This book is quite an undertaking and only my friends Tor and Siffy could have pulled off such an adventure extravaganza. Whether you're a serious long distance trekker, a weekend rambler, a fellow pilgrim, or never get further than your sofa, this compilation is bound to fuel your wanderlust."

~Brandon Wilson, author of *Yak Butter Blues*

THE WALKABOUT CHRONICLES

Steven in South Korea. *Photograph courtesy of Steven Newman.*

Steven Newman

Two roads diverged in a wood, and I—I took the one less traveled by,
And that has made all the difference.
~Robert Frost

Excerpt from Worldwalk

I would never forget the roses. So large and regal as to be from the pages of a tale, each flower seemed a perfect sculpture of Nature.

Nor would the kindly Baba—the elder—be easily dismissed from my mind. He had guided me to those roses. And to the special gift of love they watched over.

It was in a jungle that I first encountered him. At the time I was over seven hundred miles into India and should have been advancing toward my final destination of Calcutta, almost an equal number of miles to the east. Instead, I was hopelessly lost.

Foolishly, I had left the G. T. Road to follow the banks of a small river channel that seemed to parallel the road. The crowds of people along the road had become thicker with each day since my departure from New Delhi, and I wanted to follow a path that was more quiet and private. Those in the towns had a frightening habit of massing around me in unruly crowds of hundreds and even thousands. They would crush against me from all sides and scream for my attention: Twice I had almost fainted from the heat and jostling. I had not realized how overwhelming the reaction to my sudden appearance in those towns and villages would be. Sometimes in the rural villages so many yelling schoolboys and young men swept over any shop I entered that the outside sunlight was blocked out, and the badly shaken shop owner would have to strike up his oil lamps. They even climbed onto each other's backs to get their faces closer to the doorway or the window bars. More than once, a squad of police charged into the crowds to find the cause of the sudden mass "riot," then led me to the edge of the town and made me leave. My presence was causing too much danger, they said. It didn't matter that no one knew who I was, what I was doing, or even where I was from (most didn't have the faintest idea what country the flag on Clinger was from). I had a feeling that as many were drawn to me by the hope of finding out what the unusual contraption of metal and straps and slick cloth was as they were by my red hair.

So simply for my physical safety, I needed to find more peace of mind, and quickly. Furthermore, with Dad's death still weighing heavily on my mind, the need to be alone and with my own thoughts was very strong.

Yet even during the earliest moments of the mornings, when I was wavering between sleep and waking in the chilliness of my tent, I knew little peace. Many mornings I was abruptly awakened by some big-eyed brown head poking unannounced through the tent's flaps. Even more common was having the entire populace of a village crowd around me while I shaved and bathed at the local well. Slowly and surely, the constant stares began to wear me down, and in one farm village, when I cut myself shaving and could not get the blood to stop pouring out of my wound, I felt something snap in my brain. Screaming and cursing furiously, my blood running down my front and soap lather all over my face, I chased my visitors with my disposable razor, threatening death a million times over to anyone who should be so unlucky as to be caught.

By following the river, I was sure there would be far fewer people seeing me, since the river meandered almost out of sight through the farm fields and behind the road's towns. But after a few hours of following the almost empty foot trails along the river, I sensed that I was no longer paralleling the distant roadway. The sun, my only compass, was not setting behind me, where it should have been. By all indications I was heading south, rather than east, as I should.

Though it was nearly dusk, I had little choice but to plunge into a thick forest of bamboo shoots and banyan tentacles and head in the direction I hoped the road still lay. Soon I was stumbling among the vine and root cords of the leafy net draped around me, worried by the approaching night and the unseen wild cries. I was in the state of India known as Uttar Pradesh, the home of deadly cobras and man-eating tigers. Just the day before, I had read of a veteran British guide being killed in the bush of "U.P." by one of those fearsome striped cats. And as dusk grew thicker and every trail led only to more fleeting shadows and deeper swamps, I began to wonder if this maze might be my last vision of the world.

Then, suddenly, as composed as a monk and looking as if he'd been patiently awaiting me, there stood the little, wiry, baldheaded man of about fifty I would later know as Baba. To my relief, a glint of recognition shone in his peaceful eyes at my mention of the elusive G. T. Road. Uttering not a single word, he turned and glided away down the footpath, having simply nodded that I should follow.

I raced toward his fading back. Teetering from my pack's weight, tripping over the roots of trees, and slipping along in the greasy mud, I kept my eyes on the steady form always just ahead and out of reach.

Finally, we were out of the jungle. Before us stretched an enormous checkerboard of inlaid sky mirrors and squares of golden rice speckled with snow-feathered herons. We splashed our way over the paddies to a distant vine of asphalt and broad shade trees—the missing G. T. Road. There a divine scent reached me—and I looked across the still road to see magnificent red roses hanging over a front wall.

Leading me past the roses, through a tall double gate, and under an inconspicuous hand-painted wood sign that read THE INTERNATIONAL GUEST HOUSE, Baba guided me up onto the columned veranda of a beautiful yellow brick home that could have been on a seaside cliff in the south of Europe. I stared at it, then at Baba. How could someone as poor as he be living in such a modern home—probably the quietest and cleanest one I'd seen in all of India?

With a key that he seemed to have picked right out of the air, he opened the front door and waved me to continue following him. I did so, filled with all sorts of expectations about how the dark inside would be decorated. What I saw, when he lit a candle, left me more puzzled than ever. The house's three rooms were nearly empty. The only furniture was a bed, a writing desk, and a wicker chair. Even on the wall shelves, there was little more than a speck or two of dust. The rich, fresh smell of newness still clung stubbornly to the shut-in air.

My host set the candle in a small holder and placed it on the desk. Its light was soaked up by his white shirt, white turban, and white sheetlike wrappings covering his thighs. In the darkness, the white cloths gave off a supernatural glow.

"Your house?" I asked, trying to induce an answer by keeping my question as simple as possible. I even pointed to the smooth plaster walls and then at him with a telltale shrug and arched eyebrows.

He did not answer, just set the key on the desk by the candle holder and turned and left. I was all alone for the first time in weeks. I sat on the edge of the bed, feeling a thousand pounds of frustration slip from my shoulders like a dead weight. I'd almost forgotten how refreshing lonesomeness could be. I wanted to explore the house more intimately, but I was just too worn out. All the hiking on the narrow, demanding footpaths along the river, then being lost in the middle of tiger country, and then trying to make sense out of this house and its owner had been too much for one day. I leaned back to rest for a minute, and promptly fell asleep. When I awoke again, the morning was slipping sunbeams through the slats on the windows, and what seemed a million birdsong notes. The candle had burned down to a wax puddle.

I propped myself on my elbow and glanced at the desk. The key was still there. My situation was just too good to be true. I had needed just this very sort of refuge more than anything. It couldn't have come at a better time.

The sixteen days since I had learned of Dad's death had been some of the hardest in all my life. I didn't know if I was more tired physically or emotionally. Never had I experienced such a mixture of beauty, fascination, and mystery with ugliness, brutality, and banality. I felt that I was on a constant roller coaster that one day had me screaming, the next laughing, then shocked, then inspired. . . .

The Taj Mahal, sitting on the banks of the Yamuna River like an enormous pearl, had given me a glimpse of heaven itself. But only a few days before I saw it, I had searched for a forgotten old palace I had been told by a Hindu priest was high above a village in the jungle far from the G. T. Road, and there I had been as close to hell as I ever cared to be again. My heart had almost pounded itself right out of my chest.

For inside the crumbling ruins of that hilltop fortress of some former Muslim warlord, I had discovered enough homeless poor to fill a town. With a stormy late-afternoon sky rumbling overhead and vultures silhouetted along its ramparts, all that was needed to make it some scene from a demented novel were some skewered heads.

After perhaps an hour, the hundreds of ragged poor, who had crowded about me tightly, began suddenly to scream at each other for some strange reason, and I knew it was time to dash for safety. But it was too late. Turning upon me like dogs on the flank of a fleeing deer, they grabbed at my gear, trying to rip it away. Some threw stones that hit me on the legs and head. Then, inexplicably, and just as suddenly as their frenzy had started, they became silent after chasing me only perhaps a hundred yards and retreated back to the hill with its circling vultures. It was as if something deep in the bowels of that fortress had commanded them not to venture out of sight of its walls. Even when I was back at the G. T. Road, my nightmare wasn't over. For the first person I encountered was a totally naked man, striding past me as if I weren't there.

Now, I rose from my bed feeling more refreshed and alive than I had in weeks, but still not without some trepidation. I was sure that when I opened the house's door, I would find the walled grounds filled with waiting people. But I didn't—only sunshine and the perfume of those roses again. There was a pail beside the well outside, and I gleefully took a bath in the same manner I had all across India—by emptying pails of icy water over my loudly protesting bones. Still, I had good reason to celebrate. It was the very first time I had no large crowds of gawking villagers for bathmates.

It was the first bath in a long time that I came away from feeling totally cleansed. Awash in perfumed mist, warmed by the sun's rays, and with the sparkle of watery diamonds dripping from petals all around me, I set out to see who was responsible for the secret little paradise I had been led to. My answer lay but three strides away, around the nearest corner of that house in a little garden of gold roses.

Beneath the sheltering branches of an old mango tree stood two headstones. The one on the left was etched in the flowing script of Hindi, the one on the right in the stoic characters of English. I read its special message:

The divine souls of an extremely simple couple of this area, who symbolized the ideal of love, compassion, and selfless service to mankind are resting here in peace.

This place has been constructed by their son in the memory of his most ideal parents, as an expression of his extreme devotion and love towards them. Having founded this memorial he has made a meek effort to give concrete form to his parents' feelings of `welfare of all.'

What an honor to have been invited into a home built entirely from love and devotion! And what a strange coincidence that the one man who held its keys had been there in the jungle when I'd needed shelter the most. I picked two wildflowers and gently placed one on each grave.

That day stretched into three, and never a single rupee of payment was wanted, or even accepted. To the Hindus, one of the saddest tragedies anyone can suffer is to be separated from one's family, particularly one's parents. And so it was that many farmers and villagers, some with small gifts of fruit or vegetables, visited me at the guest house to let me know in their own subtle way that I was still among a family of sorts. Some stopped by just long enough to ask where I was from and where I was going (as if they didn't already know), while they puffed on their crude and bitter-tasting *bitas*—cigarettes. Others stayed for hours and took their turn trouncing me at chess, deftly capturing all the pebbles we had standing in for pawns and rooks. Usually, in the background there were children, playing their unusual badminton games in which marigolds were substituted for shuttlecocks and hands became rackets.

Eventually, I learned about the man who had built the guest house. He lived in West Germany, having gone there many years before as a young man from a nearby village, and had been fortunate enough to land a good job with the government. But though he had found the material riches he'd hoped for, he was still plagued by homesickness. Acutely aware of how it felt to be alone and in a strange culture, he'd had the home built to shelter and provide comfort to any foreigner who should need it.

The night before my departure, I sat up late reading the messages of gratitude contained in the house's guest book, which Baba had brought to me from his own bamboo hut in the woods. Since the house was but three years old, and unknown to any except the occasional foot or bicycle traveler who chanced upon it, there had been only a few guests inside its walls. I was the thirteenth, a very lucky number in India, where many associated with it the meaning "giving to all." I was also the first American.

Excerpt from Chapter 37 of Steven Newman's book *Worldwalk*. Reprinted by permission of the author.

Questions and Answers

1. *What compels you to walk?*

I am compelled by two powerful forces to explore the world using my feet as my principal mode of transportation. The first force is curiosity. I have always been interested in the world and, despite all the disaster headlines, have been convinced there are good people throughout it. I have wanted to meet those good people up close, and I can think of no more intimate means to do so than on foot. Just think of it this way: when you are on foot, you can see, hear, smell, taste, and touch the world a thousand times more vividly than when there is a door or window between you and the environment you are passing through.

I love the fact that not only can I touch the world at will, but the world can do likewise to me! The second force is adventure. Yes walking is slow and even tiresome at times, but because I have no car or motorcycle or bicycle to worry about I can wander anywhere I fancy. On my world walk, that freedom to head down any road, or foot path, or alleyway I chanced upon was to lead me to literally millions of people who had never met a traveler from another country. Indeed, in most of the poor rural areas I was shocked at how few were the numbers who had ever seen an American. When you are walking, there is no sense in being overly concerned with schedules and obligations; you can be more attuned to the actual pulse of the surrounding people and nature.

2. *Do you experience instances while you are walking when your mind is somewhere off the trail and on its own journey?*

Because my walking projects sometimes involve great distances, and vast expanses of unfriendly terrain, and even extreme social and natural challenges (such as wars and droughts and diseases), it has been vital to my mental and physical health that, from time to time, I "escape" mentally to some place or time less threatening and painful. A perfect example was during the many months I traversed the endless dead centre of Australia's outback region. There, day after day after day, the emptiness and the horizon vied for my sanity, and I kept my wits largely intact by intermittently placing images of forests and snow-capped mountain peaks in my mind. I even replayed in my thoughts my idea of what it would be like to finally rendezvous with that continent's southern coastline where the sands and the desert were kissing even as I was trudging from dune to dune. It was a survival tactic that I had had years to refine already on that walk, and even then, I found myself one blistering afternoon carrying on a conversation with myself that would have definitely qualified me for a psyche ward.

3. *How do you manage to stay physically and emotionally healthy during long and arduous journeys?*

One of the chief reasons I have been able to do a four-year-long solo walk around the world, and ascend to dizzying heights in the Himalaya and Andes and Rocky and Atlas mountain ranges, as well as stumble and crawl over miles and miles of the Great Wall's ruins, is that I have entered into each endeavor with a strong mind and the right attitude. If there is one thing I took away from my days (long ago) as a champion marathon runner, it was that our greatest challenges are always more mental than physical. And so I go into each walking/hiking project with my mind even more prepared than my body. I know I must be uber patient, tremendously open minded, as relaxed as a bowl of Jello, and as fearless as possible. It is fear—especially of the unknown—that wears one down—surely, insidiously, totally. If my mind is healthy, so more likely will my body be. I have developed a mind that is forever childlike and, thus, where others see only ugliness or things to complain about, I see wonderment—perhaps even miracles of sorts. Inspire the mind, and the body will always somehow find the energy to go a little farther. Still, the greatest mystery of my world walk was that I never caught any debilitating illnesses from all the thousands of times I had to eat and drink the foods and waters of the locals in the exact same manner as they did. It was the 1980s, and diseases and polluted drinking water was the norm in those hundreds of poor rural households I stayed, sometimes for weeks at a time. I had no iodine, no filters, no bottled water.

And yet, even as I drank from irrigation ditches and ancient wells and even rivers choked with human corpses and feces, I seemed to have continued to my final destination unscathed. Was I lucky? Had my walking so slowly and in a rambling way allowed my body to adapt to the new legions of germs that awaited me in each place?

4. Please share a high and a low period that you experienced during your walkabouts.

The lowest period in all my walks is unquestionably when on Christmas night in 1984. I was in India, halfway along my walk around the world, and I had one of those rare opportunities to call home—this is before cell phones and laptops, when two-thirds of the world had no access to phones—only to find that my father had died of a heart attack a month earlier. Of course, no one could have told me earlier of his death, for not only was I unreachable but no one could have known where I was in any given day or week. Unlike today, communication was crude in places like India. Most villages had no land lines running to them, and again, worldwide wireless phones were few and mostly in the hands of the military. At any rate, my father's death hit especially hard because he alone had believed that I would survive such a journey. As to my highest period, that was when I reached my world walk's start/finish point of my hometown of Bethel, Ohio. When I had started my journey on April 1, 1983, there had been only a couple dozen villagers who had said goodbye, even though I had as a child told many in the village I would some day walk around the world. But now, on a snowy April 1, 1987, they came by the hundreds to welcome me back. And there in the colorful shouting mix of flags, balloons, and handwritten signs, was someone very dear I hadn't seen in such a long time: my mother.

5. *Have you experienced an important Encounter that somehow changed the direction of your journey?*

So many people had warned me that it was impossible for a lone American to walk around the world. Paramount among their worries was that much of the world's peoples—Muslims in particular—were mostly anti-America. I was too simplistic and naïve about just how much hatred would be awaiting me in places like North Africa, Turkey, Pakistan, and India, they said. Also, the roads in many places would surely be thick with armed thieves.

And it didn't help that the Pakistan embassy in Washington, DC, had warned me during my pre-walk research that I would definitely be killed by bandits if I tried to cross that nation on foot. ("You will not walk there!" the vice-consul had shouted, flinging his eyeglasses to his desk. "There are too many bandits. You will be killed, that I'm certain of. You must take a train or a bus.") So, out of curiosity as to how I would handle myself in a dangerous setting, I was to include on my world walk what was then the USA's most dangerous neighborhood: the Bronx in New York City. And it was there, in the middle of the night in a decrepit setting of abandoned buildings and burnt-out cars, I would find myself befriended—not attacked—by a gang of thugs replete with knives and leather jackets and innumerable scars. Though they thought me stupid for being in such a place at such an hour, they were to find my stories of the people I had met while walking from Ohio to their neighborhood both fascinating and entertaining enough to send one off one of their own to steal a trophy. For, they reasoned, did not someone who had the courage to follow his dream deserve an honor (even if it turned out to be a bowling trophy)?

As you may guess, the insights I gained from that encounter were invaluable in helping me to keep on my original world route, even though it would be leading me into some of the most poor and war-torn regions on our planet. Key among the lessons I learned from that encounter was to just be myself, and to let everyone I met know I was as interested in them as they were in me. Had that encounter been tragic, I would likely have changed my mind about crossing places like North Africa. Instead, it gave me hope.

Steven in China. *Photograph courtesy of Steven Newman.*

Biography

Steven M. Newman (born May 31, 1954) is an American world trekker who earned a spot in the Guinness Book of World Records for being the first person documented to have walked around the world alone. And he was truly on his own: no sponsorship, limited funds, his total luggage a backpack he named Clinger. It took him four years to complete his journey of five continents, twenty-one countries, over twenty-four thousand kilometers. A journalist by trade, he was popularly known to his one million newspaper readers as "The Worldwalker," and the bi-weekly stories he penned during the duration of his world walk became the basis for two popular books, *Worldwalk* and *Letters from Steven*. Given a hero's welcome at the conclusion of his world walk in 1987, Steven has gone on to give over 2,300 speeches, author or co-author three books, and ink multiple shoe and sportswear endorsement contracts. The longest hiking trail in the Ohio state park system has been permanently renamed the Steven Newman Worldwalker Perimeter Trail, and he has been honored with a doctorate degree in humanities by Capital University.

In the years since his solo backpacking trek around the world, Newman has hiked the entire lengths of Japan, South Korea, and Taiwan, as well as 322 kilometers of the original Great Wall in China, the entire El Choro Inca Trail in Bolivia's Andes Mountains, the Himalayas of far western China, and the 1,674-kilometer Shikoku Pilgrimage, the world's longest circular pilgrimage. He and his wife, Darci, reside on more than 10 hectares alongside the Ohio River on a heavily forested hillside known as Worldwalker Hill

THE WALKABOUT CHRONICLES

Don George

Finding My Way on the Karakoram Highway

When the pressures of the world become too intense and the spring of life threatens to uncoil wildly into the stratosphere, I transport myself back to an adventure I took three decades ago in northern Pakistan—specifically, to a stretch of the wild, gritty, avalanche-threatened, pothole-punctured Karakoram Highway between Hunza and Gulmit, not far from the Chinese border.

My tour group was bumping by van along the Karakoram when we came to a road-closing avalanche about 10 minutes from Gulmit. The avalanche had buried the road long enough ago that a plow had already cut a corridor through its twenty-foot-deep drifts, but our steel-nerved driver, Ali Muhammad, feared the van would lose traction on the icy path and sit there, sandwiched in the snow, a fat target for a second avalanche.

So Asad Esker, our Pakistani guide, set out on foot for Gulmit to get a tractor that could pull the van through, and Ali backed the van up to a point on the road that looked reasonably secure. And we sat and waited.

Waiting for an avalanche or rockslide to sweep us into oblivion quickly lost its appeal, so after a while I decided to set out on foot for Gulmit, too. There wasn't much chance of making a wrong turn—the nearest intersection was about four hours away.

Scrunch, scrunch, scrunch went my feet, quickly along the snow-plowed path, then slowly when I reached the other side. There, beyond sight of the van, the notion of solitude took on a whole new, almost otherworldly dimension. It was just me and the mountains, and I tried to imagine what the traders and missionaries and adventurers who had wandered this way before me had felt.

Scrunch, scrunch, scrunch.

If I walk long enough, I thought, I'll reach the Chinese border. And if I keep walking after that, eventually this same road will take me to Kashgar, where right now wild-eyed mountain men are sizing up camels and crockery, bartering for boots and broadcloth.

Scrunch, scrunch, scrunch.

This is one of the most remote and desolate places I've ever been, I thought. If I were traveling alone, I would probably think I had come to the end of the Earth.

I took out my tape recorder and said, "It's not just that it's an inhospitable environment—which it certainly is—but also that you sense the forces of nature and time grinding on all around you, and you feel like a grain of sand on the slopes of one of the mountains."

My voice seemed like an intruder, and I stopped—and listened. The silence was so overpowering, so absolute, that it was almost like a vacuum of sound. Instead of sound, enormous waves of energy emanated from the mountains all around, so strong that I had to sit down.

Perhaps Marco Polo felt these same waves, I thought. Perhaps he called his fellow adventurers to a halt in this very spot, and sat on this very rock, and pondered—just like me—what an insignificant piece he was in the world's vast puzzle, how easily he could be bent, or lost, or simply worn away.

On I walked, as alone as I have ever been, into an awesomely uncompromising landscape: a rocky, gray-brown world of sere, monumental mountains, boulders looming by the side of the road, and—whenever I stopped to listen—that absolute, ear-ringing silence.

As I walked, my footsteps feebly scrunch-scrunch-scrunching into the implacable air, I thought about nature and time, about how my life was like one grain of sand on the slopes of one of those mountains.

Scrunch. Scrunch. Scrunch. I imagined straying off the path and scrambling crazily up a scree-slippery peak; I tried to absorb the silence; I strained a handful of pebbles through my fingers.

Scrunch. Scrunch. Scrunch. I considered the clouds, a scraggly tree, a boulder twice as big as me.

I listened to my own breath coming in and going out; I listened to the pounding of my frail and all-too-human heart.

In one sense, nothing much happened: Eventually I reached the warm waiting room at the Silk Route Lodge, and the others arrived by van a half-hour later.

But in another sense, everything had changed: I had seen the strangeness of the world, the rawness and beauty and sheerness of it; the age of the Earth; and our essential solitude—how we are born and die alone. I had seen the smallness of man and the largeness of the human spirit that dares to create and to love.

I had realized just what a precious gift life is, as are the people with whom we share it; and I knew that one day in the future, when life became too harassed, I would stop and say: "Savor the world one step at a time, just like you did on the Karakoram Highway."

Excerpt from Don George's book *Wanderlust*. Reprinted by permission of the author.

Question and Answers

1. What compels you to walk?

Whether I'm in the city or the country, I love the slow pace of walking and the fact that it allows you to observe things closely and to experience the surrounding world using all your senses.

2. Do you experience instances while you are walking when your mind is somewhere off the trail and on its own journey?

Yes, absolutely. In fact, I did on the Karakoram Highway as described in my essay in this book. Walking liberates the imagination.

3. How do you manage to stay physically and emotionally healthy during long and arduous journeys?

Eating well, keeping a journal, and being mindful of the little miracles around me.

4. Please share a high and a low period that you experienced during your walkabouts.

I simultaneously experienced one of the most memorable high and low periods of my life on one of my first epic walks, to the top of Mount Kilimanjaro. Reaching the summit should have been a gloriously triumphant experience, with all of Africa spreading beneath me. But instead, I was in such pain from the lack of oxygen that I spent most of my time on the summit doubled over, my stomach churning and my head pounding. I managed to force myself to look at the view a couple of times, for a few precious seconds, but when I think of that journey, I remember the overwhelming pain and the triumphant view in equal measure.

5. Have you experienced an important Encounter that somehow changed the direction of your journey?

Whenever I first encounter a city, I love to get to know it by roaming about. On my first visit to Cairo, I was wandering in this way and I got completely lost. I finally ended up in a visibly impoverished, claustrophobic neighborhood where I was almost stepping over people who were sitting surlily in their stoops and eyeing my watch and wallet. When I'd just about relinquished hope of getting out intact, a young boy appeared out of nowhere, and without a word took me by the hand and guided me back to a main square I recognized. I turned away from him in my exultation and when I turned back to thank him, he'd disappeared into the crowd.

Biography

Don George is a travel writer and editor who has won numerous awards for his work. He has been travel editor at the *San Francisco Examiner & Chronicle*, founded and edited the Wanderlust section of Salon.com, and most recently was Global Travel Editor at Lonely Planet Publications. He is the author of *The Lonely Planet Guide to Travel Writing* and the editor of seven literary travel anthologies, including *The Kindness of Strangers, Tales from Nowhere, By the Seat of My Pants*, and his new book, *A Moveable Feast*. Read Don's column, "Bookshelf," in *Traveler*.

In addition to his writing and editing, Don appears frequently on NPR, CNN, and other TV and radio outlets, is a highly sought-after speaker, and hosts a national series of onstage conversations with prominent writers. Don is also co-founder and chairman of the annual Book Passage Travel Writers and Photographers Conference.

Before becoming a travel writer, Don worked as a translator in Paris, a teacher in Athens, and a television talk show host in Tokyo. He currently lives with his wife in the San Francisco area.

DON GEORGE

Wakhan Corridor. *Photograph by Sophie Ibbotson.*

Sophie Ibbotson

Curiosity is the one thing invincible in Nature.
~Freya Stark

Afghanistan: Beyond the Wars

If you cast your eye across a map of Central Asia and zoom in to the north eastern corner of Afghanistan, you will spy a little sliver of territory, a pan handle that juts out between Tajikistan and Pakistan, just touching China at its eastern end. At its narrowest the territory is only 19km (12 miles) wide. Any of these countries might have a reasonable claim on the Wakhan, you would think, but it was given to Afghanistan for a very important reason: so that the Russian and British Empires would not touch. The River Panj (the famous River Oxus of antiquity) was a natural barrier, itself trapped between the Pamirs to the north and the Hindu Kush to the south, and so the Corridor became the tiny but politically significant buffer between the two great imperial rivals.

In 2010 I first arrived in Ishkashim, Afghanistan's border post with Tajikistan and one of only two points between the two countries where foreigners are permitted to cross. The four men in our party had spent the preceding weeks carefully growing their beards so that properly attired in *shalwar kamiz* and their skin darkened in the sun, at least from a distance they'd not stand out from the crowd. We crossed the border and entered the town, and heads began to turn: clean shaven men in dark blazers and slacks looked up from their stalls and laughed. Here, it seemed, beards were a thing of the past, in fashion only for old men and mullahs.

This first visit was fleetingly short but, as you'll frequently hear people say, Afghanistan gets under your skin. One visit is never enough. When the mountains start to call, I know now it is time to pack, and though the journey to get there is invariably long and arduous, the excitement of what awaits me helps the hours fly by.

The most obvious draw of the Wakhan is its mountains: in every direction, majestic, ice-capped peaks rise strikingly up to meet the sky. Before the Soviet invasion it was a popular training spot for professional mountaineers, particularly those from Russia, and there are plenty of challenging climbs. Noshaq, the highest mountain in Afghanistan, lies on the southern side of the valley, though there are so many passes, so many peaks, that in spite of its towering height of 7,492m (24,580'), it remains invisible until you have reached base camp and are making the final ascent.

Of all the routes through the Wakhan, be they meandering alongside the river in the valley floor, or climbing steeply up into the passes, one sticks forever in my mind. It takes you beyond the road, beyond humanity, into the great wilderness where the sky, the mountains and, very occasionally, a nomad or marmot, are your only company.

There is, along the way, a little something for everyone who thrives in the great outdoors.

Our journey began again at Ishkashim: it is the only place to start. For 150 years the Broghil Pass, the route into Chitral, Pakistan has been shut to foreigners, and the Chinese are equally disinclined to open their border anytime soon else it become a back door for troublemakers entering Xinjiang. The core of the town is a single street lined on either side with low-rise shops. The merchants are men, and so are most of their customers, but there's no feeling that a woman is unwelcome.

The goods on sale are basic: life in northern Afghanistan is hard and there is little disposable income. In addition to fruits and vegetables, rice and occasional packeted goods, there are cheap imports from China (plastic buckets, children's toys and the like), 'army surplus' that may or may not have been let go with its original owner's permission, and occasional, so-called fashion stores. The mid-blue *burqas* synonymous with Taliban oppression are in evidence, on the rails and on the back of an occasional passer-by, but this was the realm of the Northern Alliance—the Taliban had no power this far north—and so the decision to wear one or not is less about politics and more about older family traditions.

In the early evening each day we would walk from the bazaar through the lanes to our guesthouse, soaking—up the ambience, enjoying the warm, dusky air. While teenage boys played cricket down by the river, their younger siblings (both girls and boys) chased us and giggled, like a large clutch of chicks behind a hen.

Nearly every house in Ishkashim is in a compound. Unlike in Kabul, it is not a security feature. Extended families live, raise livestock and tend their cottage gardens within the confines of the perimeter wall. The wall keeps the chickens and the toddlers from wandering out on to the street, and the women of the family can go about their business unveiled, without concern about who is looking in.

A sign of Ishkashim's relative prosperity, and the important role that tourism is already playing in the local economy, is the number of guesthouses that have sprung up. Year-round they host visiting aid workers and an occasional academic, and in the summer months the trekkers and climbers. Around 200 foreign tourists came to the Wakhan last year.

It's a pleasant stroll from the centre of the town up the hill to the Juma Guesthouse where we tend to rest our heads. Opening the small door in a much larger double door allows you to enter a lush, green haven. Brightly coloured flowers compete for space with fruit and vegetables and help the local bee population to thrive. We enjoy their sweet, sticky honey come dinnertime.

Rooms in the guesthouse are simple, laid out in the traditional Pamiri architectural style known as *chid*. The design of the building is deeply symbolic. The main room is square with a pitched roof, and light enters through a skylight made from four concentric squares, one each for the earth, wind, air and fire. Five long, tapered pillars, often from finely carved wood, support the roof, and they represent the Prophet Mohammed and four other members of his family, as well as the five principles of Islam. The *Khasitan Shokhsutun*, the pillar representing the Prophet, lies to the left of the entranceway and is traditionally carved from juniper, a sacred wood thought to have healing properties. Above the pillars are two transversal supporting beams, one each for universal reason and the universal soul, and then groups of smaller beams in total numbering 49 (the number of Ismaili Imams) or 72 (the number of soldiers killed in Ali's army).

As the daylight turns to dark, the quiet of the dusk also gives way to the cranking of the diesel generator outside. A handful of light bulbs glow brightly and, for half an hour or so until dinner arrives, an old television set wired up to a satellite dish and a car battery blares out something akin to Afghanistan's Got Talent, interspersed now and then with the cricket scores. We snack on nuts and sweets, stomachs rumbling whilst we wait. In the mountains, dinner can never come too soon.

Unlike in neighbouring Tajikistan, where the food is heavy and often greasy, Afghan cuisine has much in common with that of Persia. Fresh, flat bread, sometimes as much as 40 cm (16") in diameter, boiled white rice and gently curried potatoes are the staples, and there is always plenty of yoghurt, jam and tea. In wealthier homes, or on a special occasion, there is succulent roasted lamb, with pistachios, almonds and mint leaves, and otherwise simple vegetables, stewed and spiced, grown in the compound garden. The food is tasty, organic and healthy, though you might find it repetitive at times.

As pleasant as Ishkashim is, I always have an impatience to leave: adventure awaits and it can't properly start until we've left the town behind.

A single road winds its way from Ishkashim east along the Wakhan Corridor, but it only goes half way along the valley's total length, to the village of Sahad-e Broghil. I call it a road—that's a very generous term—for it is wholly unmade and, in some places where the river has swelled and swallowed it, it no longer exists at all. A handful of bridges, all recently constructed but some still rather rickety, criss-cross the river to link together villages that would otherwise be cut-off from the road.

We drove out of Ishkashim in our 4x4, a 15-year-old Land Rover Discovery that we'd driven out to Central Asia two years before and was consequently showing a few signs of wear and tear. It was, however, a lion amongst lambs as far as the other motorists were concerned: it is estimated that there are six cars in total in the Wakhan, two of them semi-permanently off road for lack of replacement parts, and the other four are barely clinging on to life.

Even in a Land Rover, the drive was never going to be comfortable. We were five trekkers plus a guide, and all of our camping gear to boot. We bounced and shook as we crawled along, and there were plentiful streams to ford. There were horrible crunches as rocks scraped away the undercarriage of the vehicle, and the plastic trim, footboards and tow bracket pretty soon worked their way loose, even though we drove with care. A mixture of ratchet straps, elastic bungee cords and cable ties kept the most essential parts in place.

We stopped for the night at Baba Tangi, a small village beneath a mountain of the same name that has only been recently climbed. It is a distinctive, triangular peak, almost a caricature of how a mountain should be. It was early September, the harvest was in full flow, and every man, woman and child was out in the fields, bringing in crops or threshing the grain underfoot. A young boy, probably no more than 10, drove his team of donkeys round and round across the ears of wheat, trampling it to separate out the chaff, which then blew away in the wind.

Baba Tangi, like all the villages along the valley floor, is a Wakhi village: it is from the Wakhi people that the Wakhan Corridor takes its name. Speakers of the Wakhi language, there are thought to be around 70,000 Wakhi people worldwide, though outside of the Corridor they are frequently referred to as Pamiris. Though the population originated here, today there are far more Wakhi living in Pakistan, China and Tajikistan than remain in Afghanistan itself.

The Wakhi are Isma'ili Muslims, that is they are a Shi'ite sect who follow the hereditary Aga Khan. *Forbes* magazine describes him as one of the world's 10 richest royals, and he is unique amongst hereditary rulers in that he does not rule across a specific geographical territory. His wealth comes from a mixture of religious tithes and successful enterprises, including hotels, telecommunications and stud farms. An estimated US$600m of his wealth is channelled philanthropically through the Aga Khan Development Network (AKDN) each year, and it is used to build schools, health care facilities and community centres. He espouses a relatively liberal, progressive form of Islam and is on good terms with other world leaders.

The most immediately obvious influence of Isma'ilism in the Wakhi villages is on the women. They work outdoors alongside their husbands and brothers, and they readily approached us to chat. There are no full face vein or *burqas* here, but rather embroidered headdresses with coloured veils that cover just the back of the head and leave their beautiful, delicate faces on show. The women are animated, engaging and wanted to show us their homes and what they were doing. In exchange they wanted to see our cameras, to learn how they worked, and to see photographs of themselves. Their laughter when they see their own solemn expressions on the camera screen was infectious, and then we took the best pictures of all.

Sarhad still beckoned, however, so we left Baba Tangi behind and drove on to the end of the road. The way petered out into nothing; a striking, seemingly almost vertical wall of mountains blocks the way.

We left the car at the guesthouse, a gift to the village from the Aga Khan, and engaged two horsemen with their stocky, long-suffering ponies to help us on our way. Porterage charges are fixed for trekking parties at US$20 per horse per day; it is a small fortune in an area where a labourer might earn one seventh of that, and a teacher takes home US$60 per month. Each of our rucksacks was carefully weighed, and smaller items piled in a sack. The baggage was balanced on the back of each horse and securely tied with rope. The horsemen and guide led the way.

And so we began to climb. Straight away there is a steep ascent from the valley floor to the Dahliz Pass (4,267m; 14,000'), a barren, rocky place that is bitterly cold when the cloud comes down and cloaks it. Looking back towards Sarhad you can just about pick out the river glinting silver in the sunlight, and the patchwork of harvest-ready fields in varying shades of gold.

The light at the top of the pass is soft, muted by the cloud. The air is thin due to the altitude, and so you find yourself puffing and panting with every step. The horsemen and their horses strode out with ease—they were born in these mountains—and it is only us poor, unfit low-landers who were struggling.

We camped for the night at Borak on one bank of the Wakhan River. There is no permanent settlement here, just a simple stone hut where shepherds take rest when driving their flocks down to Sarhad in the weeks before the winter snows. It had certainly been several days since somebody stopped here: the remains of their fire was long cold.

We pitched our domed tents, their glaring orange fly sheets incongruously bright against the dusty landscape. The two horses, now freed of their burdens, were released to find grass and take a long, well-earned drink by the river. We joined them for a quick splash, washing away the dust and the sweat from our skin. Though we had a multi-fuel burner for cooking, nothing beats the glow of an open fire, and so we gathered up bracken and brushwood, then sat round, mugs of tea in hand, as the flames made it crackle into life.

When darkness fell, the air temperature dropped, and the warmth of the fire was welcome. We wrapped up ourselves in fleeces and coats, warm gloves and woolly hats and tucked in to a much-anticipated hot meal. Rather than put pressure on the meagre supplies available locally, we always bring our camp food in: spaghetti bolognaise and lamb hotpot slip down particularly well; the guide and horsemen were in awe, and tucked in with predictable gusto.

I always rise early in the mountains, as soon as the first light penetrates the tent. Whereas at home a lie-in appeals, here there is far too much to do. I crawled from my sleeping bag, and any doziness was washed away instantly with a handful of near-freezing water from the stream. I lit the stove, put the kettle on, and awoke the campers with steaming mugs of tea.

They say that breakfast is the most important meal of the day, and when trekking it is certainly true. Whether or not you like porridge, you will eat it, with a handful of nuts or jam. We packed up our gear, loaded it onto the horses, and again we were ready to go.

It's a pattern that soon becomes familiar, but each day retains its distinctive charms. Remarkable geological formations catch the eye and spark a conversation on plate tectonics; fat, gold-brown marmots poke their heads from their burrows, curious and completely unperturbed by our presence.

Now and then we passed by a *mazar*, a shrine, some of hundreds of years old, weathered by the elements to the point they seem to have grown organically from the earth. Although most people in the Wakhan are Muslim, Islam has never entirely replaced the older religious traditions and so you'll see piles of stones, animal horns and tiny ribbons tied to trees, each symbolising someone's prayer.

The horns are of Siberian ibex or, occasionally, Marco Polo sheep. Marco Polo is said to have traversed the Wakhan when he journeyed east to the court of Kubla Khan, and the *Ovis ammon polii*, with their impressive, spiralled horns commemorate his visit in their name. Though shy of humans and hard to spot, it is thought that as many as 1,500 of these rare, imposing-looking sheep still live in the upper reaches of the Wakhan. Illegal poachers do threaten their long-term survival, but so far the difficulty of getting here and the dangerous reputation of Afghanistan as a whole have provided a degree of protection. Long may that continue.

Although much of the joy from this journey comes from being in the wilderness, far away from the maddening crowds, our destination was in fact a man made one: the settlement of Bozai Gumbaz. The Wakhi are a sedentary people, who have made their homes in villages along the valley floor, but up here in the mountains, where the earth touches sky, their neighbours are the nomadic Kyrgyz.

No one knows exactly where the Kyrgyz here came from: they may or may not share ancestry with the Kyrgyz of Kyrgyzstan, the post-Soviet republic to the north. Their physical features are distinctly more Mongol than those of the Wakhi, and their clothing is unique too.

What we do know is that the Kyrgyz have driven their flocks of sheep and goats back and forth across the Pamir range for centuries, climbing to the high mountain meadows in summer so that their livestock can graze, and then retreating to lower lands in winter when the high passes are under snow. This way of life came to an abrupt halt in the early 20th century when national borders solidified: no one cared for their way of life, and the Kyrgyz were stuck permanently in the Wakhan. Some members of the community subsequently emigrated *en masse* to eastern Turkey; the rest remain here in limbo.

Our first glimpse of Kyrgyz habitation came some miles before Bozai Gumaz, when we stumble upon Kashch Goz. Two *yurts*, the traditional nomad tents, appeared on the horizon, and it took us an hour or so to reach them. The family here raise yaks for a living; they have a herd nearly 100 animals strong. The yaks are reliable pack animals, their milk is rich in nutrients, and the thick, warm fur makes excellent winter clothes. We were ushered inside for tea and bread, and enjoyed the break from the wind.

Rested and refreshed, we trekked on in eager anticipation until finally we reached the crest of one last hill, and a plateau opened up below. From here each one of the collection of grey-white *yurts* appears scarcely larger than a thumbnail, but as we descended the gravelly goat track, they came properly into view.

There are perhaps a dozen *yurts* at Bozai Gumbaz and, miraculously given the location, the settlement also includes a school. Children whose families live in the surrounding valleys come here for the season, board, and then return home for the holidays. There are three teachers, all from elsewhere in Afghanistan, and their work really is a calling. The construction of the school, built against all odds, is described in Greg Mortenson's book *Stones into Schools*, and its very existence is a triumph over adversity.

We stumbled, exhausted but elated, into Bozai Gumbaz in the late afternoon. Smoke was rising from the chimney in each *yurt*; the smell of something tasty cooking on a stove lingered in the air. A gaggle of small boys, ruddy cheeked and grinning, came out to welcome us and try out their few words of English. We were invited inside their guesthouse *yurt*, a storehouse when no guests are here, and the place bustled with boys and an occasional mother, serving tea and lighting our fire inside.

It was fairly dark inside the *yurt*, the door having been fastened shut to keep the cold air out. There was a hole in the roof to let out the firewood smoke, but as the fire was still getting going, a fair amount billowed around the room, making our eyes smart. With so many small, inquisitive visitors, I feel a little like an animal in a cage at the zoo, but it only took one stern word from Bill, our party's octogenarian trekker, and they scampered back outside, contenting themselves with taking turns to stare at us through a gap in the wall.

Even then, though, we were not alone, as once the noisy boys had gone, two young girls silently slipped inside. They had been sent by their mother to bring in some food, but once it was delivered they stayed put, crouching on their haunches, watching and whispering to each other, hands across their mouths. All Kyrgyz women wear red. It is a vibrant, blood red that stands out dramatically from everything in the grey-brown landscape around them and, as in China and India, the colour has connotations of prosperity, fertility and good fortune. Until a girl is married, her filmy veil too is red, but when she finds a husband, she takes a white veil instead. I wondered what the girls were saying, what it is that they were waiting for. And then a hand was proffered, the palm upturned: "School pen?" I bit my lip and, for the only time during the trip, felt a little uncomfortable: I'd unthinkingly given all my supplies to the boys.

The night was cold and crisp; a full moon lit up the sky and cast a bluish-white light across the peaks. I scurried away from the *yurts* to relieve myself and wash, then hurried back with quite a turn of speed, my breath hanging like a fog in the air. Inside the yurt it was still smokey and it made my throat a little dry, but the space had warmed up quite noticeably, and the smoke's no price at all to pay for that. We had our sleeping bags and a pile of rugs and curled up side by side. As we drifted off to sleep a single yak was snorting and lowing; there was no other sound to be heard.

There is an idyllic side to life in Bozai Gumbaz; it's charming when you first arrive. The romantic landscapes, warm welcome and colourful costumes are only one side of life, however; and the other side is very, very hard indeed. Afghanistan is one of the world's poorest countries, and these are its poorest people. Life expectancy here is somewhere between 35 and 40 years, and many children never reach their fifth birthday. Those who fall sick have no chance of medical care, and if the winter is particularly harsh and the livestock die, a similar fate awaits many of their owners a few months along the line. Some income is derived from cross-border smuggling of opium, strapped on the backs of donkeys, but it is relatively little, and opium addiction has itself become a real problem amongst Kyrgyz adults. There is regular, heated discussion amongst the community's elders as to whether the last Kyrgyz families in the Wakhan should emigrate and join their relatives in Turkey, but I doubt very much this is a viable proposition: they have no money, would be unlikely to get visas and, having been isolated so long in their time warp, would find integrating with a new society tough.

And so our story comes full circle: I announce I will be spending my summer holiday in Afghanistan (again). It is the third time now, so my colleagues and friends just roll their eyes and smile. Several of them have even been convinced to join me this year. My mother knows I'm going. She doesn't necessarily like it, but she expects me to come home again safely. I tell all of them that Afghanistan needs tourism. The people in the Wakhan need tourism. It is a message I believe in passionately.

In countries where peoples' lives and livelihoods have been torn apart by war, tourism has a vital role to play, and for almost a decade, we've been trying to encourage people to look beyond the sensationalist headlines and see something of the real people and real places where life goes on regardless of the news. Long before the Foreign and Commonwealth Office and State Department lift their travel restrictions, small numbers of tourists can and do make their way into ravaged communities, helping them to rebuild their lives. The Wakhan Corridor may not have suffered direct attack during the past four decades, but the conflicts raging elsewhere in Afghanistan have had far-reaching consequences. The government in Kabul is able to exercise little power; its influence cannot spread this far. Economic development in Afghanistan's hinterland is understandably low on the state's list of priorities when even the survival of the government has a question mark.

The most obvious impact of tourism in the Wakhan is a financial one: experienced trekking guides can earn as much as US$50 per day, porters make US$10 per day, and tourists pay guesthouse owners US$30–35 a night for bed and board. Hence, the visit of a single trekking party can double a village's annual income; every tourist counts. Places with high unemployment, extreme poverty and low aspirations are fertile breeding grounds for extremism and violence, and the taking up of arms is often motivated by economic factors. Religion and politics may feature heavily in official rhetoric, but they matter little to ordinary men who simply see an opportunity to feed their families and send their children to school. If opportunities arise closer to home and without the threat to life, they will take them, as the successful take-up of micro-enterprise projects and the impact of increased food-crop prices in reducing the occurrence of militant attacks have frequently shown.

Tourism also changes the perception of a country. This applies both on the international stage and, critically, at a local level. Tourists returning home inevitably talk about what they've seen: the good things and the bad. I can say with authority that Afghanistan is not a lost cause, that there are pockets of hope, and that small economic investments, such as the training of guides, have a huge, positive impact that is valued by the communities who receive the gift. I can also broadcast loud and clear that in the 21st century children should not be dying at such a rate for lack of medical facilities, and maybe someone will hear and fund a permanent health clinic in the Wakhan. If no one goes and no one sees, the message can't get out.

Whenever I go to the Wakhan, the people I meet tell me they feel proud: they're proud that the beauty of their country is such that its fame has travelled all the way to England; they are proud of their village guesthouse and that the Aga Khan gave it to them; and they are proud that their son (or daughter) has not only had the opportunity to go to school, but they can practise the English they have learned on a native speaker. For once they feel that their far, forgotten corner of Afghanistan is not forgotten at all, but somewhere unique and to be treasured. Tourism can bring with it hope for the future where there was very little hope before.

Questions and Answers

1. What compels you to walk?

Walking is pretty much the only opportunity which modern life affords to completely escape from the rat race. When I head into the wilderness, beyond the reach of WiFi and cellphone coverage, there's just me. It usually takes a couple of days to clear my head of detritus, and then I can properly observe my environment, reflect on and analyse important issues, and make decisions. I find that when I am walking I have my most innovative ideas, seemingly out of nowhere, and also come up with the best solutions to problems. I'm not someone who can happily sit still, so meditation is out of the question, but a long walk to nowhere in particular, ideally in crisp, clean air up in the mountains, gives me the chance to take stock of what's been going on and make plans for the future.

2. Do you experience instances while you are walking when your mind in somewhere off the trail and on its own journey?

Last year in Ladakh, I hadn't properly acclimatised before I started trekking in the Hemis National Park. That was a rookie mistake. I found the climb to Ganda La (4,900m) exceptionally slow and painful; every single step was an effort. But what I realised that day was that normally when I walk, my body and my mind are completely detached from one another. Physically I am moving, mostly in the right direction, but my limbs are on auto-pilot. I don't have to tell them what to do, and I am barely aware of the exertion.

My mind is in an entirely different place, wrangling with complex problems and twisting and turning them around as though they were a Rubik's cube waiting to be solved. The squares of the cube might be people's faces, or snippets of conversation, or products. They could be real, or not even in existence yet. I am loosely aware of my surroundings—the temperature, the colours, the views—but it is my thoughts which preoccupy me and are most immediate; the natural world is a dream-like bubble one-step removed.

3. How do you manage to stay physically and emotionally healthy during long and arduous journeys?

Walking is essential to my psychological and emotional wellbeing. It's a chance to reset the system, and no matter how long or tough the journey, I'm happy in my own thoughts. If I'm trekking with others I might engage in conversation, but it's unlikely that they have my full attention.

Keeping physically fit on the trail can be more of a challenge. I've had my fair share of heat exhaustion and sunburn, bruises and grazes, and vomiting and shitting myself many days' walk away from proper toilets. There are a few things I've learned to keep sickness to a minimum, and I'd advocate all new walkers follow them.

Firstly, keep drinking. It doesn't matter whether you feel thirsty or not, when you walk you will be sweating, and you need to replace not only the fluids but the salts and sugars as well. I discovered the LifeStraw last summer, which is a superb option anywhere where the water might be questionable, and its inbuilt filter means you can drink straight from a stream or pond. Of course you will still want to carry some water with you, but this option certainly cuts down on the weight. Adding a sachet of rehydration to the water now and then is a good idea, and makes the taste more interesting.

Secondly, beware of the sun, even when it doesn't feel hot. In the mountains in particular, it'll burn your skin, crack your lips, and give you an almighty headache. Drinking helps, but wearing suncream, sunglasses, and a wide brimmed hat or headscarf is also essential.

For the sake of your stomach, eat simple food. Carbs are the easiest. Wash your fruit and veg properly, and if you have porters or a cook and think their hygiene standards are questionable, wash it again. Alcohol gel is a lifesaver for sanitising your hands before eating, and it is well worth squirting some on anyone else around you too, as if one person gets sick you'll probably all go down with it soon enough. Pack more packets of Imodium than you ever expect to need, plus rehydration salts and a broad spectrum antibiotic for serious bouts of stomach trouble. I always have a reserve stash of digestive biscuits (too boring to snack on in general circumstances) in the bottom of my rucksack because if you do get sick as a parrot, they're probably the most likely thing to stay down.

4. Please share a high and a low period that you experienced during your walkabouts.

Physical high-points are always the highlights of my treks. When you reach the top of a pass which you've dreamed of, and been walking towards for days, and suddenly the entire world is stretched out in a panorama about your feet, it's an intensely moving experience. I can see, crystal clear in my mind, the view from the top of Khardung La back towards Leh; the border post atop the Khunjerab Pass between Pakistan and China; and the view along the Wakhan Corridor when I climbed up the cliffs overlooking Ishkashim.

For me, low periods are almost always caused by the weather. My ascent to Noshaq Base Camp in Afghanistan was overshadowed, literally and metaphorically speaking, by cloud cover, so the long-awaited views of the Hindu Kush never materialised. That was a huge disappointment. In spite of my love of the mountains, I'm also someone who hates the cold with a passion. And so on those nights when temperatures have plunged and I'm lying shivering in my tent, unable to sleep because I can't get warm, then I'm very miserable indeed.

5. Have you experienced an important Encounter that somehow changed the direction of your journey?

The encounters I have when I walk may not change the course of the physical route I'm on, but certainly they've caused me to rethink the bigger journey of life. More I've been inspired by a person I've trekked with to make a major u-turn in my personal and professional life, in spite of the upheaval it causes, and touch-wood the results so far have been overwhelmingly positive. I don't believe in guardian angels, but I do think people appear in our lives now and then to make us change our path, and when we're walking it opens our minds, making us more amenable to such unanticipated interventions.

Photograph courtesy of Sophie Ibbotson.

Biography

Sophie Ibbotson is a British entrepreneur, explorer, and writer who has lived and worked in more than 40 countries. She has led three expeditions to Afghanistan, two of which were on foot; trekked in the Hindu Kush, Pamirs, and Himalayas; written about trekking and hiking trails in the *Bradt Travel Guides* to Kashmir, South Sudan, Sudan, Tajikistan, and Uzbekistan; and regularly publishes trekking stories and clothing and equipment reviews in the international press. She has lectured about her journeys on foot and by various other transport means at the Royal Geographical Society, the Royal Asiatic Society, and the Royal Society for Asian Affairs, as well as onboard Celebrity Cruises and Golden Eagle Luxury Trains.

Wakhan Corridor. *Photograph by Sophie Ibbotson.*

Wakhan Corridor. *Photographs by Sophie Ibbotson.*

Photograph courtesy of James Dorsey.

James Dorsey

The world is a book and those who do not travel read but the first page.
~Saint Augustine, first century Christian mystic

Walking With Markus

The view from my tent is a panorama of the Great Rift Valley; the immense rock wall in the distance rising slowly from the highlands of Manyara, and creeping northward to terminate in the massive caldera of Ngorogoro Crater.

The weight of history on this land is a physical presence. Evidence of earliest man keeps revealing itself to archeologists, each find pushing back the count of years that my own ancestors have tread where I now stand. I am less than 30 miles from the last nomadic clans of the Hadzabe, East Africa's stone-age Bushmen, and one of three distinct genetic groups from which all of mankind is descended. The valley before me is literally the cradle of humanity. It was from this land that man first walked away to populate the earth and has never stopped walking.

It is a land of nomads where the bomas, both permanent and temporary, of 300,000 Maasai surround me, filling the Manyara Valley like so many brown mushrooms, and early morning cooking fires coat the land with a low flat mist pushed down by the lingering cool night air. These are the places that call me, places that lighten a traveler's heart and fill the soul.

Many Maasai are transitioning from a nomadic lifestyle into agriculturalists or even assimilating into cities, but walking is in their DNA. In the Manyara it is not unusual to pass a person walking on the side of the road when you are 50 miles from nowhere. That is how I met Markus.

A figure walks slowly uphill through the mist, robes billowing wraithlike in the morning chill. It is a Maasai from one of the bomas I drove past late last night; he is alone. This is the time of morning when the boys and young men escort the village cattle out to graze so I assume by his being here that he is above such menial labors. As he draws near I see that his shuka is a deep magenta and he carries an ebony walking stick that identifies him as an elder, a title of respect rather than age. He walks with the grace of one used to authority. His pace is slow and steady, *polepole*, as they say here. He stops just downwind from my tent and with a broad smile addresses me in Swahili, the lingua franca of east Africa; "Jambo Papa," he says; referring to my white hair. In Africa I am almost always older than the most ancient man in the village and in this land age commands respect as it does nowhere else. Papa is a common greeting here for an elder of any race. "I welcome you," he adds in heavily accented English.

I share my morning coffee with him as he squats in front of my tent, in that local way my knees no longer allow me to do. His name is Markus and he emphasizes that it is spelled with a K. It is common in Africa for tribal people to adopt a western name to protect their own from being butchered by English speaking visitors.

Markus smiles broadly at me over our coffee, showing off the gap where his front tooth has been removed to allow the insertion of small food particles, an aging custom from when lockjaw once decimated his people.

After our coffee, Markus stands and begins to walk slowly up the hill behind my camp; a simple gesture is enough to beckon me. I follow him silently. Above the morning clouds we reach a flatland full of thorny acacia trees and Markus disappears into a thicket. The interior is a much used campsite and we sit on a fallen tree trunk to examine the bony remnants of previous hunts. The trunk is notched to show the number of days the Moran; (Newly initiated warriors) have spent here. It is where they come to eat meat privately, no women allowed, in a sort of testosterone fueled man-cave in the forest, and it is an honor that Markus has revealed it to me. His pantomime of a hunt soon has me laughing out loud and he lifts his shuka to proudly reveal all the scars that come with being a Maasai warrior.

Before a Maasai boy is considered to be a man he must hunt a lion with a spear and shield. He does not have to actually kill the lion, but he must participate in the hunt. This is a tradition whose origins are long lost and lion hunting has officially been banned in much of East Africa because of the terrible loss to poachers but the Maasai still practice it in remote areas.

Now the Maasai hunt a lion by surrounding it with a circle of warriors who slowly advance, tightening the circle until it is so small the lion has no choice but to attack to fight its way out. The warrior the lion attacks will fall to the ground, cover himself with his shield, and hope his brother warriors slay the great beast before it kills him. The bravest of the hunters will attempt to grab the lion's tail while this is going on, and doing that gives the holder immense face.

We continue our walk up the hill, Markus padding silently in his rubber sandals made from old truck tires, the Maasai equivalent of Crocs, until we stand on a steep slope, our necks craning backwards to take in the towering immensity of the largest Baobab tree I have ever seen; its spreading boughs most likely home to hundreds of varied creatures. Numerous small branches have been hammered into the side of the baobab in an alternating pattern and Markus uses them to begin climbing. Twenty feet above me he points out a large bee hive I would not have noticed without him. Sitting on a massive branch he tells me how the Maasai trail a small black and white bird called a honeyguide that brings them to such trees where they make a torch to smoke the bees out in order to steal the honey, a rare delicacy in these parts.

As we retreat back down the hill Markus points out a dozen different plants and bushes that provide the Maasai with medicine, meticulously explaining how each is harvested and utilized. He shows me old wounds that the plants have healed. There is a grace to his movements, a flow that expresses harmony with his surroundings. Maasai believe that ancestors watch over them as part of the land and Markus seems an organic part of the whole.

We have walked for hours and when we are almost back at my tent he stops and just stands silent, taking in the view. He is smiling, but then he has been smiling all day. I stand next to him and whisper, "Enkai," referring to the Maasai equivalent of a deity that is beyond the comprehension of most western city dwellers. Enkai encompasses all of nature if I have listened correctly, but a more detailed explanation of the meaning is beyond my abilities and probably beyond understanding by anyone not born a Maasai. "Yes, Enkai," he quietly says with great satisfaction. We stand shoulder to shoulder as the sun disappears behind the great rift wall and I have never known a more intense moment of peace.

Arriving at my tent I invite him to sit with me for coffee once more but he politely refuses. I extend my hand for a farewell shake and he reaches inside his robe to produce a small gourd, meticulously decorated with beadwork, a hall mark of Maasai culture. The gourd is half the size of a tennis ball and has a cork stopper in the top hole. It is a snuff carrier, one of the only true vices of Maasai men, who seem addicted to it. It is the sort of gift only given to a friend. He places it in my palm and closes my fingers around it. With that he turns to walk back down the hill, calling to me that we will walk again tomorrow and so we did for the next four days, just the two of us, in the cradle of mankind.

I never asked him why he stopped to see me or why he spent the better part of the day sharing esoteric knowledge with me. Perhaps he was simply curious about this lone traveler in his land, when my kind usually arrives in large groups of safari vehicles with cameras clicking. Perhaps he sensed that I was different and would understand in a way that most visitors never can. I like to think that I do.

If I have learned one important lesson from my travels across Africa it is that tribal people occupy a separate reality than I do. For them there is no distinction between the material and spiritual worlds, and they move between them with alacrity. Markus gifted me with a taste of both worlds and that is the kind of gift all travelers pray for.

Questions and Answers

1. What compels you to walk?

I have an unknowable inner need to walk. Even at a young age I walked wherever I could even if it was miles away. I believe it is something in human DNA that goes back to when our ancestors walked out of Africa. Humans have always needed to know what is beyond the next mountain or across the next river. This need has evolved with the times in that it has advanced from exploring our local environment to visiting new worlds beyond our own planet. Without such a need the world never would have become populated. With it, the universe will become smaller as we venture further and further from home. Space exploration comes from the same need to walk, it is just made easier now through technology.

2. Do you experience instances while you are walking when your mind in somewhere off the trail and on its own journey?

All the time. For me walking is a form of meditation. Keeping a steady cadence with controlled breathing is the same as many forms of Yoga. It is a vehicle that allows my mind to interact with all that is around it on a different level. The repetition of motion is important to reach an altered state of consciousness. I have had some of my finest journeys on walks where my mind went to a totally different place than my body but the act of walking was the vehicle that allowed it to happen.

3. How do you manage to stay physically and emotionally healthy during long and arduous journeys?

Strangely enough I have always been at my best when the going is rough. I guess I have always equated visiting the people and places that interest me the most with arduous travel and that is a price I am more than willing to pay. Where some require comfort, I thrive on a primitive environment.

4. Please share a high and a low period that you experienced during your walkabouts.

My greatest high was seeing my vehicle again after walking 26 miles in 24 hours while climbing a 600 foot volcano in that time. The low was collapsing on the volcano, unable to breathe and finding out two weeks later that my lungs were filled with blood clots. This condition has hit me twice on expeditions.

5. Have you experienced an important Encounter that somehow changed the direction of your journey?

I have met countless people on these journeys that fascinated me enough to plan entire future trips just to see them again, especially a Tuareg nomad in Mali and a Bobo tribesman in Togo. I travel to learn and everyone I meet along the way becomes a future possible journey.

James with Mursi gunman, Ethiopia. *Photograph courtesy of James Dorsey.*

Biography

James Michael Dorsey is an award winning author, explorer, photographer, and lecturer who has traveled extensively in 47 countries. He has spent the past two decades researching remote cultures around the world.

He is a former contributing editor at Transitions Abroad and frequent contributor to United Airlines and Perceptive Travel. He has also written for *Colliers, The Christian Science Monitor, Los Angeles Times, BBC Wildlife, Wend, Natural History,* and *Geo Expeditions.* He writes for numerous African magazines, and is a travel consultant to Brown & Hudson of London and correspondent for Camerapix International of Nairobi.

His latest book, *Vanishing Tales from Ancient Trails* is available from lulu.com. His stories have appeared in 11 travel anthologies. He is a 13 time Solas Award category winner from Travelers Tales, and a contributor to their *Best Travel Writing, Volumes Ten, and Eleven.* He is a fellow of the Explorers Club and former director of the Adventurers Club.

Oleg. *Photograph by Jon Turk.*

Jon Turk

The moral imperative of humanism is the endeavor alone, whether successful or not, provided the effort is honorable and the failure memorable.
~E.O. Wilson

You are a Lousy Traveler in the Spirit World

The following is an excerpt from: *The Raven's Gift: A Scientist, a Shaman, and their Remarkable Journey through the Siberian Wilderness.* As the story unfolds, the old shaman, Moolynaut, invited me to eat the hallucinogenic mushroom, mukhomor, so I could journey to the Spirit World and talk with Kutcha, the Raven. But I failed to make the journey. The following day, Oleg, the hunter, asked my partner Misha and me to go fishing. For more about the book, check out my website or the Amazon page.

Despite a slow start, the fish began biting by mid-morning and we filled a second gunny sack by lunch time. After the mid-day sun melted the overnight ice, we loaded our catch and gear into the boat and headed downstream, toward town. The motor purred, the hull planed gracefully over the mirror smooth river, and Oleg guided us adroitly past underwater shoals. Then he cut the engine and the boat drifted with the current. A small cloud of exhaust floated away with the breeze and the tundra silence overtook us.

After a few moments Oleg looked at me, "Jon. Do you know why you were afraid to enter the Spirit World?"

I looked into his weather-beaten face, lined by hardships of the land and the economic and political world he lived in. Oleg was a pragmatic man, a hunter, "Duck Devil." He could keep an engine running, without spare parts, for a decade after most people would have sung its requiem, but he seldom talked about emotional or spiritual matters. He smiled softly.

"No," I answered. "I don't know why I was afraid. But the fear was real. I couldn't force myself to walk through the door into the Spirit World."

Oleg nodded. "I understand."

The boat drifted in the current, spun slowly in an eddy, and then caught the downstream current again. The tundra drifted by, gold and red with autumn colors.

Oleg continued. "Every person is born with a certain amount of power. The Gods have given you great power to travel in the Real World. But because you have channeled so much energy in this direction, you don't have enough energy left over to travel in the Spirit World. You were smart not to walk through the door into the Spirit World. Maybe you would never have found your way home. You are a lousy traveler in the Spirit World, like me. I am a good hunter. But I do not travel into the Spirit World."

I almost cried with relief. There was no plot against me, no shrunken heads warning me to retreat. I was among friends and limited only by myself. No, I wasn't limited; I was empowered—as long as I understood the source of that power. And now quiet, taciturn Oleg, my adventure partner—not Moolynaut or the *mukhomor*—was the teacher I had longed for yesterday. I didn't know how to explain all this to Oleg; so I smiled, certain that he would see across the gap in our cultures, language, and heritage, and accept the heartfelt thanks in my silence.

Oleg continued, "You obviously came here because you are seeking something. But you will not find it in the *mukhomor*. Kutcha lives in the Spirit World, but you can also find him on the tundra. Wait and watch. Kutcha will understand and he will visit you in the Real World. Then you can thank him. Do you understand me?"

I nodded and Oleg continued, "You and Misha must return one more time. You must make a long, hard trek on foot across the tundra, in the Real World. You will be cold, tired, frostbitten, and strung out. Maybe you will die out there." Oleg grinned. "But maybe, if you are lucky, you will find what you are looking for."

Excerpt reprinted by permission of the author.

Journey to Talovka

The next morning the temperature was twenty below Fahrenheit and the north wind raged. We donned goggles, pulled our hoods tightly around our faces, and headed toward Pevek, 800 miles away, on the Arctic coast. In some ideal, but nonexistent never-never land of Arctic travel, there must be a smooth, undulating field of spring-hardened snow, where sleds slide effortlessly across the vastness. But here, we never encountered joyous, unfettered travel, muscles stretching in long-strides, the mind drifting in the vastness because it wasn't needed in the practiced repetition of walking. Instead, we bashed through shoulder high thickets of willow and elfin cedar and then scraped our sleds across exposed grass, dirt, and rocks. It was impossible to talk because the wind blew the words back into our throats and then chased them down our alveoli, like a junkyard dog making sure they'd never climb over the fence. Misha and I walked side-by-side, close but isolated, each nesting inside the few centimeters of tenuous warmth that lay between our bodies and our clothing.

We were headed toward the Arctic Ocean, or toward a rendezvous with Kutcha the Messenger Raven— both destinations seemed about equally obtuse.

A whirlwind swept snow into a small funnel cloud that washed our faces in swirling whiteness before it raced off, dancing erratically across the empty plain. The spindrift melted against my face, carrying some of my urban, left-brain rationality off to that distant land where urban left-brain rationality resides. Whatever happened, or didn't happen, that day when I stood on one leg and the old shaman Moolynaut spit on my pubic hairs, I saw a glimmer of the potential of an unencumbered right brain. I saw it again in the labyrinth, and I had seen it in the avalanche—roiling in the mayhem between life and death. Those experiences changed my life, forever, and for the better.

Now I was out here—ostensibly to thank Kutcha, but really to open my mind by "suffering through hunger and suffering through cold." But that wasn't really right, either. It seems strange that in an urban world, with a warm house and the assurance that there will be food on the table tomorrow, I frequently fill my head with worry. Out here on the tundra, where life is so fragile, surrounded by cold, hardship, hunger, and immensity of space, I find it easy to sweep the cobwebs out of the brain with Lydia's magic broom and exorcise them with her incantation, "Evil Spirits, go away. Go to your Mother. She lives in the darkest place in the North." And when the fur-clad, hunched over, Evil Spirits trudge off through the snow, what is left is a peaceful oneness with all that space.

Many of my Koryak friends had assured me that I could never experience the world as Moolynaut does, because I hadn't grown up on the tundra. But insight isn't binary, on or off. Moolynaut's gift wasn't merely that she healed my pelvis. Maybe her largest gift was that she brought me back to this frozen Siberian landscape repeatedly, where I learned to accept, cherish, and follow that right brain, non-verbal voice that was always inside. And now, as I shivered against the cold and the sled harness chaffed against my shoulders, I was reaching for a power within me that is released by wild landscapes—even though I was absolutely certain I would never grasp it as firmly as Moolynaut had.

We followed a narrow streambed into the mountains and then climbed a U-shaped swale leading toward a low pass. Late in the afternoon, we stood at the summit looking northward at a broad system of river valleys and swamps that stretched largely unbroken for 350 miles until it collided with mountains that guarded the Arctic Ocean. Our bodies were vibrating in the intense wind, like twigs and grasses poking out of the snow, waiting for summer.

The landscape below us was glorious in its immensity, but sobering in the details. Wind had blown almost all the snow off the tundra, leaving a broad, dun-colored plain. There was no way we could drag our sleds over bare dirt.

But, with no other alternative, we turned our sleds around and lowered them, stern first, down a steep brushy hillside to a tributary of the Talovka River. It was nearly dark. Wind-deposited snow had collected in the lee of the riverbank, so we dug a cozy nook into the drift and pitched our tent.

The next morning, we loaded our sleds and climbed the bank to plot a course toward the town of Talovka. For the next few hundred yards, there was no snow on the tundra. None. Zero, zip, zilch. Wind rustled two-inch tall birch trees and shook the freeze-dried seed pods that clung tenuously to the grasses and sedges. Frostbite nipped my chin and cheeks. The tundra was snow-covered to the west, against the mountains, and I suggested that we make a long detour to find easy traveling. Misha shook his head. "That is not the Russian way. In Russia we go straight. We do not travel west just to find an easy way. You are in Russia now." It seemed silly to me, trudging over bare ground, pulling a reluctant sled, in a wintry wind. But I was in Russia now.

This story is a brief excerpt from *The Raven's Gift, A Scientist, A Shaman, and their Remarkable Journey Through the Siberian Wilderness*. Excerpt reprinted by permission of the author.

Embrace the Crawl

As the story unfolds, Erik Boomer and I are dragging our sea kayaks across the Polar Ocean on the remote and dangerous north coast of Ellesmere Island.

June 23: *"Woke at 2:30 AM and looked out of tent. Snowing. Felt like going back to sleep. My turn to cook and the stove quit. That sort of morning. Followed a convenient ice toe around the next cape, then we went back onto sea ice. Smooth ice, then rubbly. Traveling over the rough, angular ice, Boomer's ski breaks, for about the third or fourth time, I can't remember, so we move the bindings around again, until the set-up looks downright silly. Over pressure ridge ice and then onto smooth ice. All this involves a lot of huffing and puffing. Boomer announces, 'This is fun. Finally I feel like I'm really on the North Coast. When it was easy, back there, I felt that we were cheating.' I smile and agree—halfheartedly—because I am too tired to really agree but because it would be too much work to disagree. In the afternoon, Boomer's ski breaks yet again and we decide that skis are sort of useless in this terrain anyway—jagged blocks of ice, interspersed with melt-water pools."*

...

With the skis behind us, and ragged, tilted, slippery ice ahead, we strapped on lightweight crampons and forged onward.

June 24: *"Travel into heavy rubble ice early in the day. At times, there is just too much resistance to pull the loaded boats forward while standing on two feet. So we crawl. There's more power that way. Both of us do it. Even Boomer. When you've got 750 miles to go and you're crawling through saturated slush and frigid melt-water pools, soaked to the skin, you've got to shut the mind off. Stop thinking, stop calculating miles versus food remaining. Don't even suffer. Just crawl. It's clean. Fundamental. Cathartic. Then we find smooth ice right against the shore and we stand up and walk again, as if we have just evolved from knuckle-walking apes to humans. Most of the snow has melted off the land and in the afternoon we find purple flowers lying low to the ground. No, I don't know what species they are; it is just wonderful that they are purple... My small toes are quite gnarled and bloody. They hurt with every step. Throb when I go to sleep."*

...

June 27: *"At one point during the day I dragged my kayak onto the top of a chunk of ice, and then walked down into the melt-water pool below. My kayak slid down, speared me in the left calf, and knocked me into the icy water. Splash. Full, spread eagled immersion. Now I'm wet from head to toe. I strip naked, wring out my garments so they will dry faster against my skin, dress again, and continue onward, doggedly. My calf aches and I am limping. When I catch up to Boomer, he is cheery, oblivious to what happened. 'Hey buddy, if you just drag your boat onto that pressure ridge, over there, even though it is out of your way, I'll got a great photo. It's all set up.' We laugh about it in the evening, but at the time I wasn't amused."*

...

June 29: *"I got nailed hard in the right calf today when the boat slid out of control. A moment of carelessness. This is the foot with the bad toe. I'm limping on both legs now, which should cancel into a non-limp, but it doesn't. I sit down on an ice block and cut a bigger chunk out of my boot to relieve pressure on my toe. But it doesn't seem to do any good. I have to leave some remnants of boot on my foot or the boot will simply disintegrate."*

July 2: ... My toe looks and feels horrible, mangled and showing the meat that lies beneath the thin and fragile layer of skin. I make a conscious decision today not to pretend that I am above the pain. Just endure. I am good at enduring; I've done it before. Count the miles. Open your heart to this pain. Accept it. Embrace it."

... That day there was no energy left in my brain for subterfuge or posturing. I did what was necessary to drag my kayak across the ice. The first of the Four Noble Truths in Buddhism starts with the observation that in life, pain is unavoidable. We stub our toe when walking into the bathroom, get old, watch loved ones pass away, suffer economic setbacks, and eventually each and every one of us, dies. No one escapes this reality. But suffering, which is an emotional response to pain, is a decision we allow ourselves to make, and is absolutely and unequivocally avoidable.

I'm not a Buddhist acolyte or scholar. But, from my own experience, suffering occurs when that pesky think-too-much-know-it-all brain takes a simple event—which started out maybe slightly negative, or maybe even positive or neutral—it doesn't matter—and twists that event up into knots, invents side-plots and intrigue, runs it around and around in feedback loops, like a puppy chasing its tail, until it grows, explodes, matures, overruns the castle, and emerges triumphant as true misery. Suffering. We've all done it. But out there on the ice, there is no room for that bullshit. No energy. Life is on too thin a line to allow the brain to indulge in its favorite pastime—the luxury of extraneous emotional misery. So a sore toe is just a sore toe. It hurts. Nothing more and nothing less. So simple. So liberating.

Jesus, Moses, and Buddha all wandered off into the desert to fast and find awakening. Most, perhaps all, aboriginal cultures embrace some intentionally induced pain, such as fasting or self-mutilation, as part of their religious and cultural rituals. The great Inuit shaman Igjugarjuk, once said, "All true wisdom is only to be learned far from the dwellings of men, out in the great solitude, and is only to be obtained through pain."[1] I would disagree that this is the "only" way, but agree that it is one way.

Thus, counterintuitive as it may seem, pain can lead to ecstasy, not suffering.

Excerpt from *Crocodiles and Ice: A Journey into Deep Wild*. Reprinted by permission of the author.

---

[1] As quoted in, Joan Halifax, *Shamanic Voices*. New York, Arkana Press, 1979, 266 pp, quote found on page, 6.

Questions and Answers

1. What compels you to walk?

For me, walking is the journey into Deep Wild, in remote landscapes and in the mysterious labyrinths of my own mind.

2. Do you experience instances while you are walking when your mind is somewhere off the trail and on its own journey?

Yes, of course, sometimes my mind is on its own journey, but that is not always desirable. I feel most content when my feet are on a journey but my mind is silent.

3. How do you manage to stay physically and emotionally healthy during long and arduous journeys?

If the journey is arduous enough, you can't remain physically healthy. If you push hard enough, your body breaks down. To understand the emotional journey read my entry, "Embrace the Crawl."

4. Please share a high and a low period that you experienced during your walkabouts.

Read my entry, "Embrace the Crawl."

5. Have you experienced an important Encounter that somehow changed the direction of your journey?

The answer is, yes, I have experienced Encounters. These Encounters frame my lifelong passage from suburban Connecticut into Deep Wild. But I refuse to reduce these Encounters into a sound-bite. If you want to understand, you'll have to take the time to read my books, *The Raven's Gift*, and *Crocodiles and Ice*. Explaining an Encounter takes time, just as you need to take time for your own journeys on long multi-week or multi-month walks.

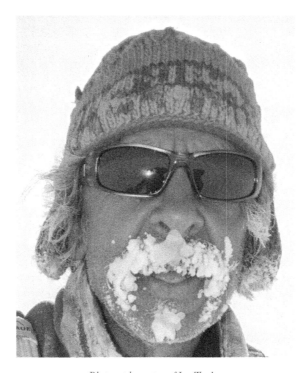
Photograph courtesy of Jon Turk.

Biography

Jon Turk received his Ph.D. in chemistry in 1971 and wrote the first environmental science textbook in North America. He has since engaged in extreme outdoor expeditions, many of them involved in walking, skiing, bicycling, or kayaking long distances across remote environments. Jon's circumnavigation of Ellesmere with Erik Boomer was nominated in 2012 by National Geographic as one of the world's "Top Ten Adventures of the Year" and was also awarded "Expedition of the Year" by *Canoe and Kayak Magazine*. Jon's newest book, *Crocodiles and Ice: A Journey into Deep Wild* tells the story of Jon's lifelong journey from suburban Connecticut into a passion for Deep Wild, an ancient passage, repeated—in one form or another—countless times, and ignored just as often.

Photograph by Jeff Fuchs.

Jeff Fuchs

There are no straight lines through the mountains.
~Tibetan muleteer Dawa about travel through the Himalayas.

No Straight Lines Through The Mountains

"Caravans would be completely engulfed, and bodies lay unfound for months. Some still lie buried in the earth". The old crinkled face of one of the last muleteers of the Tea Horse Road was deep in memory as these words came out of his mouth recounting a time along one of the great trade routes of the world.

It is hard to imagine the daunting risks along the path that we follow given the calm sky of bolt blue above us. Warm winds, cactus (called 'ghosts hands' to local Tibetans), and soft air embalm us. The path that we make our way along is little more than a strand of dirt and stone that arcs along an extended cliff. We are entering into the region known to traders as 'the land of the mountains' breath' and the mountains in this case are the Himalayas. Here beauty staggers and hides risk under layers of stone, constant winds and the odd waft of snow off of nearby snowcaps.

We follow what is left of one of the great adventures of the globe that is rarely acknowledged, the Tea Horse Road (called Gya'lam or 'wide road' to the Tibetans). An ancient corridor and series of routes that pre-dated the Silk Road, it was as daunting a journey as it was spectacular ushering all manner of commodities to and from the mountains through the heartlands of over a dozen cultures. Known to many traders as the 'Eternal Road' the risks were as utterly grand as the rewards: nothing less than everything was required to travel this highway through the sky. The risks remain to my own team as we have just begun a journey that will take almost a year to complete and take in well over 5000 km. Coursing from China's sub-tropical southwest onto the Tibetan Plateau and beyond it was a journey that qualified as a kind of odyssey.

Sand, blown by the winds up from the river valleys, has settled in ridges along the mountainsides making the nearby specters of nearby hulking snow peaks seem strange. Slivers of barley fields tucked into rocky slopes bend in the winds. We are close to the old trading town of Benzilan heading north in northwestern Yunnan. The Yangtze River coils beneath us, coursing along its ancient route out of the Himalayas. Here, even now, we are in a bastion where Mother Nature's every mood still rules. The elements of sun, wind, and snow are unpredictable and time has changed none of this.

Ahead of me on the trail Dorje and Dakpa sing Tibetan songs to our team, to themselves, and to the skies. The lean and tough Sonam and powerful Norbu are behind, while our cook and force of calm Nomè is not to be seen. Notions of self-consciousness and false humility had never been popular among Khampa men, meaning the singing is belted out unapologetically. Rugged Dorje sings with the earnest effort of the tone-deaf, while the more elegant Dakpa's vocal skills inspire and sooth.

We are making our way through golden particles of dust that are whipped high into the air by the winds and towards an 'ancient'; one of the last of the remaining muleteers who remembers a time of ushering tea by foot into the great spires and the land of snows and onto the great Himalayan capital of Lhasa.

Two dusty days later we find this legendary trader tucked away in the small village of Melixui. Some places exist as entrances, as introductions to greater places; they are associated with something vast and formidable. The little village of Melixui with mule caravans and traders in its DNA was such a place leading to the vast spires to the Himalayas, to its people, and to its deities.

Dawa's cavernous home of dark corners is in need of the presence of others. Perhaps we too are in need of him. Meeting this legend amidst winds, our entire teams bows involuntarily. For me, Dawa is the embodiment of the traditional muleteer. In Tibetan the word for muleteer is 'la'do' and hints at the qualifications. 'La' meaning 'hand' and 'do' meaning 'stone' points to will, physical power, and perhaps desperation in equal measures.

Calm, deliberate, and understated, Dawa is gentle in the formidable way that truly tough men are. All of this is brought into focus by a pair of sad eyes; eyes that had witnessed, and felt much. He speaks in a steady voice of himself, of the people, of the geography, and of the informal ways of the lado's and remarkably he seems not at all surprised that strangers have shown up to listen and speak of his exploits along the Tea Horse Road.

We have woken him from a Himalayan version of a siesta, though he remains magnificent in his disheveled state. His 'home' is a simple earthen structure with a bedroom adorned with very little. Bolts of light come through tiny windows catching Dawa's eyes as old memories stir him.

He speaks of not simply a route of risks and snow but of a route that "opened up worlds of people and land".

As we share a dinner with him, our talk turns to Sho La, the snow pass we will ascend in the morning. Dawa's voice drops as he looks at each of us in turn. He warns us that Sho La sometimes remained impassable for months during the winter. Its danger was "its ability to change instantly, becoming unrecognizable—even to those of us who knew it."

Both pilgrims and traders passed over it with trepidation; it was believed that ascending Sho La cleansed the mind and body of negative energy—that is, if it didn't demand the ultimate sacrifice of life. He finishes off his warning with a metaphor. "The Pass is capable of charming with sweet words and destroying with bad words". He smiles though at one point shaking his head.

"As much as this route took, it gave so much…", he trailed off.

Questions and Answers

1. What compels you to walk?

Texture, grinding pleasure, and time sums the motives up for me. Walking still offers up the hint of some kind of autonomy which I crave above most things. It allows a sense that one—given will, fortune, and some gratitude—might reach any space and people. From an exploratory point of view, there is no better way for the mind and body to be complicit than in walking.

Textures are the waves of sound and light that in themselves assist the transition for the mind. For me the impact of surroundings or textures affects my every breath and intensifies what the senses take in. When the senses and physiology are affected, one is truly in that zone of a humble high.

There is a kind of gentle aspect when one walks, arriving and departing with effort and intention in the natural 'old' way, with leagues of choice and a soft approach rather than a race.

There is too, the all-important grinding effort that is something utterly simple and pure (and perhaps every-so-slightly masochistic) in that it takes a commitment to walk and trek somewhere. Walking seems too, to be the most egalitarian and graceful method of travel. It is timeless and eternal.

Time allows one to look and listen twice and in that time, transitions filter in through being affected Mother Nature's every little whim. It also gives the mind and blood time to alter and transition out of one sphere and into another. Time is the one ultimate vital in all of this.

2. Do you experience instances while you are walking when your mind in somewhere off the trail and on its own journey?

Usually, I'm right 'here' in the moment, though in the rests and breaks and times of camp, my mind flutters away for little flights. Where I walk—the Himalayas—the wind and impact of the culture keep me very much fixed in the now. The elements literally demand that one be in the now, and though that present tense can be delusional, desperate, and pained in the mountains, it is elements that hold me fixed. When the body relaxes is when the edges of the mind soften and the head (and heart for that matter) tend to wander and surge everywhere. It is there that I suppose little journeys begin and end, but I always return to the very vital 'present'. It is for that reason that I so enjoy the wandering and roving in the mountains. There is a wonderful kind of narcotic feeling when the body is nearing the 'beyond repair' stage, and is simply functioning of its own accord. It is then, with the mind just barely complying with the lungs and quads that there is a kind of clarity and humility that I find solace in. Inevitably I'm in the gorgeous 'now'.

3. How do you manage to stay physically and emotionally healthy during long and arduous journeys?

Tea, sleep, and eating local for as much as I can manage. I don't travel anywhere without a gluttonous amount of tea. It is the one 'need'. I sleep well and pretty much anywhere. Local foods (and faith in the very necessary digestive organs) allows for one to simply go. As for emotion, I think that comes with the body's high and with the blood flowing of being engaged. If you need too much of anything on any journey, that kind of goes against the flow of a journey in general…in my view at least. I'm also devoted to consulting locals at any and every turn, even though there may be hyperbole, there are no better guardians and guides than those who live and breathe the land. In my own experiences it is they who can counsel better than any graph or diagnostic and allow me a comfort of simply being there.

4. Please share a high and a low period that you experienced during your walkabouts.

Almost as a rule, my low points come at an 'end' point or a transition period, for it inevitably seems as though in those moments when this notion of rest and processing takes hold, I'm temporarily overwhelmed and almost panicked.

After one 52 day, 1500 km portion of walking between Shangri-La in northwestern Yunnan and Lhasa, Tibet, our team of Tibetans and I had arrived in Lhasa. We collectively were staggered by the arrival, anti-social to a man, and I had the very manic desire to simply bolt out of this marvelous historical capital of the mountains, back into the hinterlands of wind, wool tents and my own spaces. I had lost faith in myself in such environments. It took me days to get my head back and I'd felt as though I'd abandoned the simplicity for something entirely too much for me. There was a residue and feeling of loss somehow that gripped my body and I couldn't even begin to hide it. I go through lulls often post expedition, where the senses are lonely and pining to be fully engaged again. I also crave and miss that intensity between trek partners that one shares in a daunting joint collaborative effort…it isn't something one finds very often in the course of life, but once it is in the system it is a difficult element not to miss.

High points often occur randomly in waves of time rather than a single moment for me. One such 'wave' occurred in northeastern Tibet one morning with an 11-year old nomadic shepherd. I had been staying with his family, and during my departure on a brutally cold morning, a wolf pack could be seen flowing across this snow and mustard coloured landscape like a graceful fog. It was across a valley but the shepherd knew what we were watching and mentioned the "junke" (wolf in nomad-speak). Though I knew that these creatures were the one true—but respected—enemy of the nomads, the site riveted me with their off-white forms flowing in a streak. The wolves were making an early morning attack on a nearby nomadic sheep flock and I could see that there was a very definite plan within their minds. The young nomad himself streaked down our hill towards the wolves with a leather sling and rock (called an "ordo") in his own fearless attack…and me with him. The wolves though, were thoroughly strategic and seemed to know exactly how much time they had and gorged and evaporated before we and other nomads reached the site. Riveting, brutal, and utterly fluid, the event was staggering in its intensity and I could only watch in wonder. It is only in such environments I've found that such an event can be witnessed in its own natural frame and speed with little of human intervening. The high was one of being entirely impacted by nature's stunning simplicity and epic disregard for expectation.

Of course, another high on any given day is simply being offered a cup of tea on the road, and particularly in a nomad's tent, as it is in this simple gesture for me that I find a kind of brief home with bowl in hand. It is one of the wonderful informal laws of the mountains that no being (besides a wolf perhaps) is turned away. Though it may seem mundane, this offering of tea never ever ceases to give me a warm rush and 'high'.

5. Have you experienced an important Encounter that somehow changed the direction of your journey?

Not so much the direction literally but certainly the way in which I viewed a journey and its absolute impact for locals. During a month long walk to trace what is left of a nomadic route of salt in Amdo, Tibet, a sit down with a family of nomads impacted. An elder woman of the family spoke at great length and with passion of how vital the route was. She mentioned something that stays in the mind still…she spoke of how the nomads would have no other way of "meeting the outside world" were it not for these vital 'highways through the sky'. She spoke as she fed a fire and the words had to do with how nomad's life was eternal movement, and without movement there was nothing. She spoke about how the routes were terrifying and life-giving, and how there wasn't really a choice for the mountain people. One moved and travelled if one wanted to survive and thrive. A combination of shriveled dehydration, giddiness, and joy with a cup of tea in hand might have been contributing to my interpretation, but I felt her words almost as a plea to make me see that there was so very much more than simply trade along these vital pathways…it was nothing less than life-giving and life-taking journeys for these people.

Her words, the moment, and the whole evening in that smoke-filled enclave with winds burrowing into every sliver of space was etched into me for the remainder of the journey and indeed every journey and expedition since. It was a powerful moment of dimming my own subjective view and being given in very a tangible perspective, a local's interpretation, which in many ways, was so very much more important than my own. Her verve remains with me still.

Biography

Award-winning Himalayan explorer and author Jeff Fuchs decided that to make the oral narratives and legends of the Himalayan trade and pilgrimage routes more intimate and historically tangible, he needed to walk them with its remaining participants. Living for a decade in the eastern Himalayas, he became the first documented westerner to walk and document the Tea Horse Road, which took 7.5 months to trace. He then documented the Nomadic route of salt (Tsa-lam) in Amdo and the 'Hor'lam' (Pashmina Route) in Ladakh and Himachal Pradesh. He has since led clients including universities, academics, and water legislators into the mountains and onto glaciers to promote the mountain environments and culture. An upcoming documentary film will follow Jeff's feet and empty cups as he traces the Tea Horse Road. A North Face ambassador, he was once described by climber and producer Bill Roberts as a "charmingly volatile mix of Anglo-Hungarian genes," and a "languid hard man with a soft touch."

He never travels without tea, and rarely without "my right knee, Sonam Gelek," his Tibetan trek partner. His journeys by foot were motivated by a fierce Hungarian grandmother, and a desire to "feel the wind for as much of my days and nights as I can."

Most of the greatest journeys through the Himalayas were fuelled—and in many cases motivated—by tea. Tea simmers in a Tibetan nomad's tent upon a hand-made clay stove and it is still one of the first things offered to travellers, as it was here to me upon my arrival to a tent at 4800 metres.

One of the last of the great muleteers and tea traders Ngawang, who traded tea, salt, and resin between northwestern Yunnan and Lhasa along the Tea Horse Road. The name in Tibetan of these traders "La'do" means 'hands of stone' and their great tales were of journeys that took up to half of a year to complete.

Tea in one its first compressed forms devised for travel along the trade routes. Dried teas, steamed and forced into bamboo husks by the minorities of Yunnan would travel (and age) on its long journeys becoming fermented and flavoured on its way.

Some of the most epic foot travellers of the Himalayas were simply plying trade or wandering pilgrims. Up until the mid-1950s most of the Himalayas were still only accessible by foot and will. He is one of the great unsung storytellers and travellers of the mountains who in his day thieved, traded, and fled along the great mountain routes.

A nomadic woman feeds her charges a treat of yak milk. Nomads remain some of the world's great travellers, moving their entire homesteads up to six times annually. Omu from the Ganzi region of western Sichuan, who is a great inspiration to me, assesses cloud formations, winds, and sun in seconds knowing what they mean and what they will bring. Readers of the elements and of the great mountain routes, nomads are told tales through the oral narrative tradition which acts as their history and science classes.

Bowls of fresh tea leaves sit awaiting a sampling. Southwestern Yunnan's indigenous hotbed is one of the planet's original DNA zones of all tea. For the indigenous who traded tea and used it as a panacea and medicine, the green leaves are no less than everything. Sacred and treated as a kind of living deity, the leaves have long been a fluid link with the outside world. Leaves have for more than two-thousand years been transported out of southern Yunnan. Many minorities refer to tea not simply as a beverage but rather as a fuel and medicine.

Puerh tea from southern Yunnan gets hand-sorted. So vital a commodity was tea, that up until the mid-20th Century it was often referred to as 'green gold'. The best teas are still to this day cultivated, harvested, and produced entirely by hand, and generally come from trees that are centuries old. For much of the past thousand years, if one had tea to trade, one had a commodity and currency that could be used for bartering.

A Hani tea harvester within a forest that is entirely ancient tea trees. Such trees often must be climbed in order to pluck harvests. Teas from such regions were prepared and sent to all points of the compass and acted as one of the ancient world's great stimulants.

Plucking season in Yunnan and Myanmar amongst the Akha people is a time where the forest divinities must be appeased and thanked for great harvests. Teas within many local communities are used in ceremonies and as the base for medicinal composts and mixes. Amongst the indigenous locals, tea is an anti-inflammatory, anti-bacterial stimulant that is good for the heart and pancreas.

"A good traveler
Has no fixed
Plans and is not
Intent on arriving."
~Lao Tzu

Photograph by Lorie Karnath.

Lorie Karnath

We shall not cease from exploration, and the end of all our exploring will be to arrive where we started and know the place for the first time.
~T. S. Eliot

Through Dark Forests Wandering–Burma Trails

To truly see and understand this mystical land, identified by many names over the millennia and experience its wide range of cultural traditions and rituals, it must be walked. In numerous cases this is still the only means to journey to many of the isolated habitats that have been peopled, only perhaps by the happenstance of a river flow, the opportunity of an open plain, or the largess of the intrinsic bounty of a fecund forest. For intermittent periods spanning two decades, I have traveled many of these oftentimes little known or non-existent routes throughout much of Burma's tableau of resplendent jewel-toned landscape, exploring its myriad of rivers, following their tributaries, walking their banks, traversing the thicket of the jungle or its arid expanses of crusted earth. As one of the least reconnoitered places on the planet, these journeys have offered a unique perspective both in terms of piecing together the fabric of where this country came from as well as through witnessing the beginnings and evolution of a newly emerging Burma.

While it was in the late 1800's that Rudolf Kipling wrote that Burma was "quite unlike any place you know about", arguably his description of this inimitable realm applies even more so today. Burma as a country represents a mesmeric, beguiling, anomaly. Despite the recent opening of the country's borders that has engendered a rapid advance towards modernization, the genesis of Burma is still deeply steeped in a magical, otherworldly realm. On the cusp of modernity, it remains a unique amalgam of its history, tribal cultures, natural assets, religious beliefs and of superstitions that are all so complexly intertwined straddling both reality and the supernatural, as to be virtually impossible to unravel. In fact to try to disentangle the fictional from the factual narrative would leave little of what actually comprises the foundations of Burma, its peoples and its cultures. It is frequently the country's oral narrative in the form of legends, stories and circumstance, oftentimes unique to each region and township that weaves a link to the numerous tribal origins and ethnic mores in a way that Burma's factual history never could. Should one embark on the monumental task of unraveling the real from the illusory in Burma the results might ascertain the original cause, but would consequently loose the effect. And in Burma it is rather the effect and subsequent outcome that are attributed to the cause. Instead this enchanting journey of incalculable pieces should be undertaken step by step with a suspended disbelief, each encounter or revelation providing another scintillating jewel to contribute towards the overall emerging panorama unveiling the true hues of Burma's portrait.

In the rural regions, walking, animal transport or traveling by some form of mostly man-propelled water medium is still the manner in that these communities go about their daily lives. Many villages are still only attainable via these means. Until the time of the British rule over Burma, roads were virtually non-existent and when necessary waterways served as the primary means of journeying. Subsequent to the British period, which was followed by over a century of a virtual closing off of the country, very few additional thoroughfares were constructed primarily as a dearth of vehicles, little commerce, in addition to restrictions on travel, did not provoke any such need. It is only in the last few years that thoroughfares are now being built in earnest and that maps detailing many a previously unknown tenancy are being created. The first of these based on the template of the British routes and river soundings from the 1850's and have now expanded to enhance important trade opportunities. As such bypassing many of the small villages that remain for the majority inaccessible, very much as they always have. However it is worth seeking out these isolated pockets as among these, tribal traditions, rituals and storytelling continue to evolve and flourish. Perhaps this is in part the result of the culmination of generations without access to formal education attempting to add contours to the mysteries of the world that surrounds them, or possibly these enclaves as yet unencumbered by modern civility, provide for a greater range of imagination and creativity.

Long before Burma confirmed its current outline, for centuries much of the region had already served as advantageous crossroads both in terms of geography and trade, connecting diverse and far ranging lands, civilizations and cultures. For trading purposes the area was fortuitously embedded between two of the most historically prolific commercially driven partners, as to the north and east lies China, while India fronts a portion of its western border. Furthermore the country's strategic coastline allowed for access by sea towards much of the rest of the world. It was the country's enviable positioning coupled with a profusion of treasured natural assets that has since early times attracted many of the varied ethnic origins that have sought this region to stake out both commerce as well as territorial conquests propelling a melding of a unique and multifaceted historical blend of beliefs, customs and traditions. It has been the course of both demise and redemption of tribal powers in Burma that are reflected and woven within this country's long, habitually fractious, albeit storied history. One that remains punctuated to this day by a tapestry of ethnic tribal conflicts and conjoins.

To begin to know this nation one needs to appreciate the intricate patchwork of its ethnic regions ensconced amidst a fairly condensed expanse of numerous topographically distinct regions. In order to really do this one needs to journey to the secluded corners that many of these have taken refuge in, to peer across the centuries of history, sense firsthand their tides and flows and absorb the nature of their change. Across many regions of the land a complex lattice of watercourses spreads, providing significant tactical persuasion in mode and methods of inhabitation. These have served both as a primary access, as well as a barrier segregating the numerous tribal dominions. It was, and to a large extent still is, these variables that have allowed for so many diverse cultures to continue to resiliently subsist without significant outside influences or interference.

If one wanders towards the hard won passages of Burma's northern territory, one is rewarded with a realm encapsulated by glistening beauty that soars snow-capped towards the sky, the seemingly impermeable Himalayan mountain ranges these guarding the uppermost periphery of the land from outside intrusion. From far flung glaciers flow two rivers that at their confluence form the mighty Ayerawaddy, this sinuous artery that meanders through what are known as the river valleys, linking the country from north to south before eventually voiding to the Andaman Sea. It is from this river that courses the lifeblood of the country, it is for many a primary form of transport, a means to exchange produce for much needed supplies, a place to bath and for spiritual replenishment. With each languid undulation, the next valley is welcomed heralding another climatic disposition, from the dry arid dustiness of the country's central regions, where many an ancient kingdom first laid stake, to the luxuriant sweltering tropics of the river delta. To the east one encounters an extended plateau and progressing further south there is a lengthy slip of coral strewn sandy shoreline nestled between Thailand and the Andaman Sea. The individual features and scintillating beauty and breath of these landscapes have each played a role in Burma's direction and tribal persuasions.

The country's remarkably divergent, proximal variations present a collage of landscape including a myriad of naturally forged obstacles and defenses that has served not only towards engendering a scarcity of ethnic fusion, allowing for the plethora of distinctive cultures and traditions to take form unencumbered from outside pressure, but has in a similar manner provided a miscellany of habitat for a number of the planet's least known flora and fauna. Although very little research has been as yet conducted, a number of critically endangered as well as previously unknown species have been spotted in a number of the especially remote regions, many of these remaining essentially still "closed". It is in part the mysteries of these and the terrain that envelops them that many of the Burmese tales, mystical happenings and rituals have arisen. Even the very early Western visitors to the regions were impressed with the tenacity of the country's wilderness, the astonishing tribal configurations, along with the variety of unusual creatures that frequented these parts. In 1278 when Marco Polo journeyed to the area he chronicled in his notes a remote and little known region with unfathomable, impenetrable jungles, where ethnic peoples lived "in sites so wild and strong" that to reach such areas one had to negotiate with forests "abounding in elephants and unicorns and numbers of other wild beasts".

Every aspect of nature is believed by the Burmese to have a purpose and a story. For many the connection with the natural world is so strong that most frequently even in the metropolitan settings, the planning of structures in Burma will have a close consideration of nature. In particular Burmese religious edifices while conceived in pursuit of the otherworldly, are mindful of the natural world and retain a close affinity to this, in keeping with the tenets of Buddhism. Oftentimes organic characteristics are incorporated (integrated) within their design. When one wanders the countryside one will see unusual vagaries, wonders and happenstance of nature in the form of mountainsides, trees, water configurations, rocks as well as other of nature's living materials and formations that have provided inspiration and were assimilated within a construction. Despite the otherworldly ends of Buddhism, it serves also to foster an awe and respect of the natural environment and its mysteries. Although the intent of a place of worship reaches towards the ethereal, in Burma these retain and build upon their connection to nature seeking to acknowledge and extend the connection between nature and the spiritual melding of the beauties of the physical world. There is little attempt to order or control the natural sphere. Instead there exists a respect and harmony as in the daily habits of nature in all of its forms and contexts. The correlation of nature's provision of earthly needs, without which there could be no existence in the pursuit of spiritual grace, is recognized. It is in this context that the more earthly dominion of animism reigns. In particular a type of spiritual being referred to as Nat are known to dominate the animist belief system. Although considered part of the spirit world, many Nats are known to possess considerable foibles and often demonstrate behavior of a less than exemplary nature. For the Burmese these deities are more approachable and more immediate than Buddha's direction for a noble path towards enlightenment and can offer a less lofty and more practical venue for help especially when seeking less spiritual goals.

It is especially throughout the Burmese woodlands where many mystical happenings take form. It is in these forests that it is believed alchemists, hermits, princely creatures and a variety of spirits of all authority, benevolent and fractious roam. It is believed that it is there where boys, sometimes destined to be kings, can be born from Naga dragon eggs, where future queens may be the offspring of deer, where hermits seeking pious existence confer with Buddha and other luminaries, many of these the provenance of an otherworldly realm. It often to the forest that many of today's Burmese denizens will still turn for solace, for blessings, to seek out a direction devoid of the detrimental forces that will thwart a devout path. Oftentimes my wanderings in Burma have for one reason or another also led me towards these.

Recently on my way towards the woods of the Karen regions in search of a group of autonomous peoples known as the "forest dwellers", I was invited inside a local home to receive the spirits blessing. I find over and over that the Burmese are truly among the most welcoming of societies, exceedingly kind and guileless in their generosity. It was the time of the water festival leading up to the New Year in Burma, which takes place each April. This year portends to be especially propitious as serendipitously the dates for both the Western calendar as well as the Burmese add up to 9, considered to be a powerful and spiritual number. The Karen tribes unusually to most other tribal traditions pay homage to the spirits of their grandmothers, as it is these that are believed to protect the family. Each family has a spirit house outside of their main dwelling where they keep a plate, glass, pan at the ready and every year a meal is prepared using these same accouterments.

In preparation for the asking of blessing for the New Year celebration the extended family had gathered in the home. All were in the best of their traditional hand woven costumes, a less elegant version of which they still wear daily. For the ceremony the woman dressed me in traditional garb as well, a long white robe with layers of colorful fringes and embroideries of their own hand.

To begin, a chicken was sacrificed and prepared which consisted of chopping the carcass and boiling the pieces for a number of hours with nothing more than a pinch of salt and hot chili added to the pot. This, along with many of the other rituals that have derived from animist practices are at odds with Buddhism, particularly relating to the sacrifice of animals. Animism was firmly entrenched in Burma by the time Theravada Buddhism began to be methodically introduced to the country under King Anawrahta who took the throne in 1244 representing for the majority the formal accounting of the beginning of Burmese history. However to help ensure acceptance of the religion the King tactically instilled a number of concessions to allow room for animist observances as well as for the remnants of other beliefs. Along with the integration of Buddhist principles concludes an understanding of an interrelation between humans and other animal species, inherently necessitating respect for all living creatures and significantly at odds with the concept of animal sacrifice used for animist ritual. Over time animist practices have also provided leeway so as to not interfere with Buddhist beliefs and those families wishing to present animals slaughtered by third parties are permitted to do so. Despite this, many families will still conduct or at least observe the slaughter to examine the animal's innards. If the liver or any other organ is not in perfect order as determined, by shape, size and color, it cannot be employed as an offering and must be discarded.

The family's great uncle, who was also a known communicator with the spirit world, presided over the ritual. We all crouched along the petroleum-stained teak floor, the use of petroleum a practice gained from the British as a way to protect the wood from bug infestation but one that has proven a significant detriment in the case of fire. As is customary for most Burmese village houses there was little furniture or decoration besides a curved shield that looked like something like a large turtle shell, tightly woven from bamboo that could be worn over one's head covering the length of a back when the heavy rains came. The medium began the formalities by judiciously measuring out and cutting a length from a skein of fine red hand-spooled thread. This he swung to and fro while chanting, calling out for the protective spirits asking these to provide shelter and protection while beseeching these to prohibit any evil specters and their erroneous ways that might be lurking. A plate of rice was placed on a thin mat along the floor between the medium and myself. Next the thread was laid across the rice, the string symbolizing the spirits and this act serving to invite these to partake in the offering. The cooked chicken's head, feet, legs and wings were then carefully arranged around the thread. After the spirits had been properly appropriated, it was our turn to partake in the meal, each taking a bit of the rice and chicken in one's hand and then eating this. Traditionally it is the father, mother, followed by any son in the family, who in this order would each serve themselves from the offering. Three scoops of rice and chicken pieces also divided into three are segregated to demonstrate respect for the Buddha, his teachings and the monks as his followers. The rest of the plate must be entirely consumed. At the end of the meal the medium tied the thin red string around my wrist with the instructions to not remove it and to let it disintegrate and fall off naturally. However the string is crafted it is an amazing example of workmanship. After several months it is still around my wrist and has shown no signs of degenerating.

While the meal is dedicated to the grandmother, the grandfather is not entirely ignored during the ceremony. Once the food has been fully dispersed, the medium smokes a corn cigar wrapped in newspaper and presents a portion of peppery stimulant, the betel nut (which neither a nut nor betel, but rather areca berry) to placate the grandfather spirit. Once all the surrounding spirits are believed to be accordingly satiated, the medium opens a string purse replete with popcorn interspersed with money folded into triangular shape which he proceeds to sprinkle over our heads, body and floor. All those present grab for the deltoid-shaped currency and the remaining popcorn is swept away. Some of the money is fixed to your hair or hat as this is the body's highest position and therefore closest to the spirits. The rest is to be kept in your wallet for the remainder of the New Year to help to ensure prosperity, success, good health and protection of the family.

From there I continued on in search of the "forest dwellers" a community reputed to be especially self-sufficient living off the land and whom encourage little communication outside of their own. They are known to worship the Monkey King and such is their autonomy that even their closest neighbors had seemingly no idea how to reach them. Having asked a number of people that we encountered along the way without success we eventually came across a pair of elderly Karen women in long flowing brightly colored dresses. They seemed to live in this part of the woods; the rest of whatever family lived with them perhaps out tending fields. The elder of the pair, her long grey hair fixed in a tightly coiffed bun, indicated that she could lead us to their settlement. Encouraged we set off behind this diminutive woman who despite the steamy heat surprised us with a tempered yet purposeful gait that greatly belied her years. At one point we crossed a long narrow bridge flanked on one side by watercress and the other by rice fields and entered the boundary of a dense and primordial forest region. The woman walked for a distance in the woods bringing us to a bit of a clearing where a man stood before the most rudimentary of huts. In regional dialect our newly enlisted Karen guide explained to the man where we wished to go and from his expression it seemed that he was willing to direct us along the next segment of forest, however not before trying to enlist our help to take down the largest of beehives that I have ever seen. It seemed that somehow he thought that being from the West I might have had some special knowledge relating to high altitude beehives. As an incentive for helping him he was prepared to provide 10 jars of the resultant nectar. The region is especially renowned for the honey that it produces and the floral scent emanating from the many hives we had noticed throughout the area permeated the air. This hive, however; was easily the size of a large car rocking back and forth over 30 feet in the air, the waxy construction banding together the tops of several trees overshadowing the hut, the man's living quarters considerably smaller than the bustling hive. It took a while to convince him that trying to fell the home of thousands of bees was not a good idea especially without any tools or protective gear, and it was only after he was absolutely sure that we could not assist him in this effort did he agree to take us deeper into the forest.

It was oppressively hot as we traversed the woodlands and the density of the closely set trees and other jungle flora eliminated any chance of a relieving breeze. As we were not too sure about our honey seeking trailblazer to begin with, we began to think about turning back for the day as it began to seem unlikely that we would ever find these illusive inhabitants. However just as we had difficultly persuading him that I could not take down his beehive, we did not fare much better in convincing him that we should turn around. Fortunately it was not long after these first inklings of doubt that we came across a small number of mostly raised bamboo structures well cloaked amidst the foliage. The residents of these were all dressed in humble woven yet pristine white robes. The looms for the crafting of these were present on each of the outside platforms of the residential dwellings. Many of the women sat before these, their legs extended to steady the frame, weaving additional white garments. The men as well as the woman wore their hair long and uncut. The men covered their heads and much of their hair with pointed hats. The people of this special community choose to dress in the simplest manner possible and wear their hair this way to stay as closely correlated with nature as possible. They are all vegetarian living solely off of the forest's natural abundance. The largest of the bamboo edifices present represented a place of worship where effigies of the Karen spirit, Pa O and of the Money King were evident. The "forest dwellers" live a peaceful and mystical existence in tangent with the nature they live to serve. They continuously honor the other residents of the woodland in which they live and are especially dedicated to the monkey who is known to have given honey to the Buddha, however also pay homage to the elephant who is said to have presented the Holy One bananas as well as to the birds which are said to have offered fruit. After spending some time with these unassuming people who had much to teach us about remunerations far greater than any one could ascribe a monetary value to, I could not help but think of the recent discoveries of vast amounts of rare earths that had been found in the region, already begetting an institute of technology and numerous foreign interests in this far away, sparsely habited part of the land and could not help but wonder how long this pristine and primal existence could continue without intrusion.

From the Kayin State heading in a northeasterly direction leads eventually to Burma's most eastern state, today known as Kayah State and referred to in earlier times as the Karenni State. It is flanked by Burma's Shan State towards the north, whereas the Kayin regions skirt its westerly and southern border. To the east fronts the Mae Hong Son Province of Thailand. Aside from the capital of Loikaw, the region is very sparsely populated. The majority of the far-flung residents are ethnic Karenni also known as Red Karen of Sino-Tibetan origin. It is a fiercely independent tribal territory, so fervently resistant to relinquishing sovereignty that it managed to evade becoming part of British Burma during the Colonial period. After efforts to assimilate this land within the overall framework of the British intentions had proven futile, the colonist government recognized, as well as guaranteed, the Karreni their independence drawing up a treaty in 1875 with King Mindon Min, penultimate of the Burmese kings. The treaty proclaimed that the Karenni States were not part of the British conquest nor would they constitute part of Konbaung Burma, which was to be the country's last royal dynasty. As a result, the Karenni territory was provided sanction to operate in virtual isolation. Animist worship in this particular region was especially allowed to thrive unhindered, without significant tempering from Buddhism, which continued to gain foothold elsewhere in surrounding regions.

It was here in my walkabouts that I experienced an especially unusual forest foray. The region is mountainous, sliced by the rapid currents of the Salween River, one of the world's lengthiest free-flowing rivers. This slender watershed courses along steep rocky ravines serving to collect the runoff and split the Dawna Mountain Range from the Karen Hills. Only a small portion of the river is navigable and solely in the rainy season, as a result the people of this region are virtually cut off from the rest of the world. Limited parts of the territory have recently opened to travel both to outsiders as well as to natives living in other parts of Burma: however, the area we had targeted was in parts mostly unknown. To access these remote regions not included among the open sections, required months of negotiating special permits. During this same period a long-term Burmese friend and her network were also in touch with the head Shaman of one of the most remote tribal townships. The motivation for the permit requests had stemmed from knowledge that we had received of a specific animist ritual and related ceremonies that would soon be conducted amongst these peoples: one that had never before witnessed by outsiders from within or without Burma.

Historically animist practices in Burma has involved animal sacrifice, whereas in some regions this form of appeasing the Nats and other spirits has diminished, in Kayah State it is still very much in evidence where it is both widely prevalent and ritualized. The offering of animal sacrifices and other favors seeks to placate or to curry favor with the various spirits and enlist their help in a particular matter. Properly redressing these spirit beings is especially important amongst rural denizens of the Kayah State where it is believed that it is a number of Nats who actually serve as the administrators to their region, superseding official governmental channels. In particular the remote regions lend towards a preponderance of protector Nats designated to guard and oversee the natural world, a designation of particular import to those that survive due to the manifestations of nature.

The ritual that was to be conducted was to involve the felling of a number of trees, one for each of the tribal villages that were seeking a special blessing, for bountiful harvest, prosperity, and health for the villagers and their livestock. However before the cutting of any trees could take place, a tree had to be chosen and to do this the forest spirits and later once selected, the specific tree spirit also needed to be addressed. Any initiator of such an act must first petition the spirits to help in the selection of a tree as well as to help find ways to appease an individual tree's Nat resident; in part, this usually requires reserving the best of the wood from any given tree or the building of a shrine or Nat house for the spirit to reside in once the tree has been felled. Oftentimes, a new seedling is planted as a further means to assuage any Nats involved and to replenish nature's gift. As a result, the widespread clearing of trees has been traditionally eschewed by the Burmese so as not to raise the ire of forest or tree Nats and as such has historically helped to prohibit significant environmental destruction. Similarly, such beliefs, so as not to exacerbate and fall afoul of the mountain Nats, have assisted in the preservation of natural landscapes.

Over the course of months the complex process involved in the tree selection was conducted by the Shaman and his followers, which required extensive consultation with a number of spirits. To communicate with these a slew of animals were sacrificed over this period. Each time that a sacrifice was made a series of pins were inserted into the animal's bones and examined for messages. At times the bones were thrown and were also analyzed for information dependent upon how these landed. The indicators of these various sessions were tallied and the accrued information prophesied when and where to cut down a tree. In this case the tree that was eventually selected through the spirit sessions designated a tree that was just beyond the parameters of the Shaman's village township, heralding a whole new set of sacrifices and additional queries from the neighboring tribe. This was because the expanded territorial domain now trespassed on another set of spirits who now had to be engaged and assuaged to ensure that the prospective tree sacrifice would not incur their wrath. This again took quite some time and careful consideration and analysis. Once it had been ascertained that all the sets of spirits would condone the cutting of the tree at this specific location, an auspicious timeframe within which to do this had to be determined. Each night the Shaman consulted a set of chicken bones until again the arrangement of these indicated that the time was favorable.

With all permissions spiritual, tribal and in our particular case, governmental granted we were finally able to head towards our destination. It was already late evening by the time we reached the vicinity of the village only to receive notice by someone sent by the Shaman that the bones had aligned that evening in such a manner that we would have to set out several hours before daybreak the next morning. The Shaman requested that we meet at a specific place at 4 AM, meaning that we would have almost no sleep that night if we were to arrive in time for the encounter. Part of the ritual required that the tree be felled and transported in darkness so that all the power that it possessed would arrive intact. We were instructed not to carry any light so as not to frighten the spirits. We followed the Shaman's directives and made our way to the designated spot a bit in advance of the designated time. Aside from a faint glimmer from a partial moon we were enveloped by a thick mantle of darkness, making it difficult to distinguish what lay ahead more than a couple steps in advance. To our great disappointment there was no Shaman or anyone else waiting for us. We later learned that in a last throwing of the chicken bones the spirits had mandated that the Shaman leave immediately a couple hours earlier than originally intended.

Not sure what to do we stumbled along a bit in the dark until we found a small enclave of huts. Despite the searing heat of the day, at this time in the morning amongst the hills it was still cool and we could see some bright embers being stirred behind the bamboo partition of the communal kitchen area. I gently pulled this back and saw two women crouching low to the ground stirring a large pot of grain over some residue of hot burning wood. The light from the glowing coals outlined their shocked faces seeing for the first time a light-skinned Western face, especially startling at this early hour in the morning. However without knowing who we were or why we were there they went about rousing their neighbors in hopes that someone would be able to understand how to help us. When these still a bit sleepy from having been awoken so abruptly had gathered, we did our best with hand gestures and drawings in the dirt to explain what it was that we were seeking. I wondered that night and have since contemplated how someone in a rural location in another part of the world might have reacted had several people of unknown origin entered their house uninvited during the night.

A couple of the younger males seemed to grasp what it was that we wanted and indicted that we should follow them. In the dark and dense forest with hardly any illumination the muddy, rock-strewn path proved extremely treacherous. On the left we could hear and sometimes see when the tree covering opened enough for the moon to reflect upon this, a bit of the river's outline quite a long way down from the boulder-edged embankments. Under these conditions the group's progress was extremely slow and we knew that the rituals had to take place and the tree felled before dawn, only a few hours away. By then word must have spread that some unusual visitors were in the vicinity as a few more young male villagers, seemingly out of nowhere joined the group. I stayed towards the front with the two original men who had first been enlisted to show us the way; it was clear that the way that they were picking through the terrain that they were not sure of where to go. There had been several trees under consideration and apparently the spirits final choice was not information that was shared with many. After the first few hundred meters into the forest, there was no longer any semblance of a path and we were doing our best not to trip over large rocks or woodlands debris or slip into the river precipice. The lead men started picking up pace through the trees, probably to gain some traction from the others for some time to determine in which direction we should be heading. I stayed close to these as one had a light colored longhi, serving to reflect a bit of the moonlight and I could follow in this manner. We soon had a considerable lead over the rest of the group and eventually as we continued to negotiate the dark and unfamiliar terrain, began to become aware of a low, metered, reverberating sound. We turned towards the sound and followed this. As we drew closer it became apparent that it was caused by the beating of several drums and cymbals which rang out in ominous cadence. Some distant flickers of light amongst the trees added to the mystical tenor of the instruments. After surmounting a last uneven crest we came upon the Shaman and the others in his party who were chopping away at the very large tree. Candles had been lit and placed in a circle around the area, a few small fires interspersed amidst these. A number of drummers were keeping a continuous rhythmic beat disseminating across the dense forest, hanging low to the ground. A number of crouched figures barely discernable outside the range of the feint flare of the candles were rocking back and forth and chanting. I took my place without being noticed towards the back. As I began to gradually make out some of the different figures around me I realized that at least until my team arrived I was the only female at the site.

    I could see a few yards away the head Shaman his brown face deeply-lined as he prayed beside the tree; he wore a pink silk scarf around his head the end of which was extended resembling a cock's comb or a large feather. I sat in this way without moving, afraid almost to breathe hoping to avoid detection for over an hour as the chopping and chanting progressed. It was a strange feeling to be there and to know that no one else there aside from the two men who had accompanied me and had quickly again disappeared, even knew that I was there amidst the darkness. There was still no sign of anyone in my group. I began to become concerned that they may have encountered some harm. Beyond this, of additional consternation was that I had noticed that the chopping of the enormous tree was only taking place on the side closest to all those crouching along the forest floor. There was an incline to the terrain and the tree listed a bit towards the higher ground where those observing the proceedings were positioned. As the fissure grew, the Shaman and the others were actively preparing for the tree to fall forward into a shallow chasm; however, living in the Hudson Valley and seeing many a tree cleared, it was apparent to me that this tree would fall towards all those who were squatting behind it. I started to cautiously move up the incline and gestured to those around to do the same. Initially shocked to see this foreigner amongst them they began to follow me. Just then the tree started its fall directly towards us; it toppled with a seemingly interminable crashing sound, taking down several smaller although still good-sized trees in its perimeter. The smaller trees helped to slow down and cushion the requisitioned tree's fall and it dropped as though in slow motion. It was this delay that allowed all to escape unharmed from its trajectory. Perhaps this was indeed a sign that the spirits were sanctioning the trees removal after all.

Once on the ground the Shaman studiously measured the length of the tree that had been sacrificed and after numerous calculations indicated that it met the conditions and was large enough. A number of the Shaman team then began to completely remove the bark and branches. Offerings of candles, money and food were made to the tree and another chicken was sacrificed and gutted to again read the bones. Several Shaman members' deliberated for quite some time over the bones before confirming that the offerings would be accepted although the tree spirit considered these to be on the somewhat meager side. The Shaman who appeared a bit shaken had been duly warned by the spirits to offer greater appeasement to any future felled trees. Around this point the rest of the team wandered in to the scene and while they had missed the actual descent of the tree, they had been accompanied as they traversed the forest by the sounds of the mystical chants and drum beating, punctuated by the chopping sounds, an eerie and unforgettable experience on its own. The women of our group were requested not to approach the tree too closely now that it was down, as it was believed that females could distract and taint the fallen tree. The trees branches were removed and the entire bark was skimmed by machete and when this was finished the heavy and cumbersome tree post was picked up by all the men present from the village and these embarked on the arduous trek towards home over slippery and uneven ground. The carrying of the trunk could only take place through the difficult terrain of the forest in the same manner as we had journeyed there, as the tree was not allowed to pass any structure on its way to the village. Without a tree to transport we were able to make our way back more quickly than the carriers.

Just before the first rays of light began to crest the horizon, the new post arrived in the village where a feast for those who had worked on the cutting, preparing and transporting of the tree was awaiting. In the coming days the various villages would undergo several days of feasting, drinking of copious amounts of rice wine and dancing. The best of indigenous costumes were donned for the occasions, among these those of the long neck tribes who wear stacks of brass rings around their neck, arms and legs, whereas the neck decorations from another of the tribes were English silver coins from the 1800's that they had strung into necklaces. Abstract elaborate crowns from pieces of each tree's branches were crafted for the new posts and following another set of numerous spirit consultations and the examination of yet more chicken bones, the crown crested posts were raised to stand alongside the others culled in past rituals, etching a unique silhouette along the skyline. This raising of the newly acquired protective post cumulated the many days of festivities and following this the tribal groups headed once again towards their fields assured that the spirits had been appeased and that good crops and prosperity lay ahead. We also returned to our callings, assured that we had experienced some special magic, a glimpse of a mystical ancient past that still exists deep in the Burmese woodlands.

Questions and Answers

> *I go to nature to be soothed and healed, and to have my senses put in order.*
> ~John Burroughs

1. What compels you to walk?

Growing up in the place where many of the early naturalists made their home, Concord, Massachusetts, I was exposed early on to their writings. For most of these authors walking was an integral portion of their work. Not only did this daily discipline serve as a means to clear one's thoughts, a walk surrounded by the pristine nature of the region provided a seemingly endless, ever-changing, source of inspiration. As a young girl I could read the writings of Thoreau, Emerson and others who had lived nearby and venture upon the same pathways that they had written about. In this manner experiencing the natural world through the observations of centuries past and upon this template, incorporate my own interpretations of the beauty and mysteries of the realm that surrounded me. Most importantly for those who had the wonderful chance to grow up in this manner, nature was always a familiar place, and by extension, walking the easiest and least intrusive manner to frequent it. Within the context of nature there are five words I seek to live by. Explore, Discover, Share, Preserve, Sustain. To achieve this it is important to foster the concepts of originality and creativity leading to the discovery process, and then consider how such discovery can be harnessed for sustainable use. The most important thing is not to stop questioning…. it is only through inquisitiveness and thought, imagination and creativity that we acquire the tools needed to advance.

It is in fact the process of "discovery" which probably best links all those who willingly wander. However while discovery by definition has always required a willingness to confront the untried or unfamiliar, these days the volatility of global circumstances has propelled the uncertainties relating to venturing into the unknown…. to new levels. If we consider the human quest for exploration it is a deep rooted one, fostered by our innate instinct to learn. It is only partially about the adventure and mostly about the experience. It is the search for the unknown and the unveiling of beauty amongst the mysteries of nature's untamed wilderness. Oftentimes, particularly in urban scenarios, one can become detached from nature. Part of the motivation for walkabouts is to remind oneself that it doesn't matter if you live in an apartment in a high-rise or in a jungle, nature still surrounds, it is this that sustains us. We should heed the call of the unknown path and cannot live in isolation from the natural world.

2. Do you experience instances while you are walking when your mind is somewhere off the trail and on its own journey?

Among the greatest benefits of the trail is that walking as an innate pursuit, allows for your mind to embark on a journey of its own, providing a freedom of contemplation and observation difficult to duplicate in any other context. Even a walk well travelled allows for a means of seeing familiar things in a new and different way. This opportunity provides the door that opens to understanding, conceiving or discovering new things. It serves to break down the confines of judging or interpreting things founded on what one already knows, enabling a new perspective and oftentimes can result in new understandings quite peripheral to the original journey. The physical transit is oftentimes only the periphery to the voyage that the mind takes.

3. How do you manage to stay physically and emotionally healthy during long and arduous journeys?

For those that consider walking as an essential part of their existence, it is this pursuit in itself that enables one to remain both physically and emotional healthy. It is the ability to engage as well as to disengage the mind, rather than one's physical abilities that best enable one to overcome challenging conditions and emotional travails of a long walk.

As Thoreau indicated, "I think that I cannot preserve my health and spirits, unless I spend four hours a day at least—and it is commonly more than that—sauntering through the woods and over the hills and fields, absolutely free from all worldly engagements."

4. Please share a high and a low period that you experienced during your walkabouts.

The question that I am most often asked about my journeys is what was the most harrowing or unexpected experience that I encountered while on a walkabout. As often expeditions offer circumstances or discoveries quite unforeseen in a wide range of contexts, it is quite difficult to pick out one specific story. However included among the highs of the many places in which I have spent time exploring and conducting research, some of the most memorable instants include my first steps in Antarctica, where the landscape from the cracked ice below one's feet to the white sky above that sparkles like glittering crystal, or alone 100 miles deep in the jungles of Borneo, a face to face encounter with an orang-utan, its crinkled grin leading to an immediate appreciation of why they are referred to as the "old men of the forest", to note that he was perhaps even more astounded to see me than I was to see him, or to witness a flock of white storks as they seamlessly gather, gliding in unison along their migration route, a perilous journey representing up to 20 thousand kilometres, guided only by instinct.

Lows are often punctuated by extreme adverse weather conditions. Such as the challenges of trying to descend a slippery granite face along a Malaysian mountainside when the monsoons had unexpectedly arrived early, this while towing a larger colleague who was suffering the effects of altitude sickness. However embedded within the lows are often highs to be serendipitously unveiled. A journey to Canada's Grand Prairie region represented one such experience where within minutes of arriving at our chosen excavation site after a fairly treacherous and chilling traverse, I had already uncovered a relic, a portion of a fossilized dinosaur bone, a message from millions of years before.

It seems that over the course of time that it is the high moments of a journey that become ever more vibrant in one's memory while the low periods dim over time. Perhaps it is our biology that serves to help to protect us in this way, not only to overcome some of the difficult physical and emotional challenges that we at times experience but also to ensure that our desire to explore remains intact.

5. Have you experienced an important Encounter that somehow changed the direction of your journey?

Encounters, expected or unintended, will often change the course of one's journey. One such example was the first time that I journeyed toward the bonebeds of Pipestone Creek, which over 70 million years ago was steamy tropical rainforest, amply populated by a number of dinosaur species. However, any of the region's erstwhile tropical characteristics have been long ago extinguished, similar to the enormous creatures that used to roam the sultry lush terrain. It was under a relentless and frigid rain that we worked our way over steep and rocky topography through virtually impenetrable scrub that filled the spaces between the massive conifers that characterize the landscape today. The wet earth of the forest bed anchoring the dense vegetation was of a sludge-like consistency that served to at times perilously fix one's feet, further hindering forward progression.

Having finally arrived at the projected destination, the angle of the rugged cliffs that flank the water exacerbated by the resolute downpour, proved to present an even greater test to find a secure foothold than the journey to reach these. Although little was known at this time about what lay below the surface, recent findings had indicated that the area represented a massive dinosaur burial site, predominantly Pachyrhinosaurus. Early excavations indicated that there were potentially numerous fossilized remains of both mature and young specimens along these banks suggesting that there had been some sort of cataclysmic occurrence that had hastened their demise. Chilled and wet through my raingear I cautiously positioned myself along the steep and slippery precipice to begin carefully scrutinizing the clinging mud for evidence of these ill-fated inhabitants of long ago. Within my first handful there was a smaller sized rock but I knew immediately from its consistency and concentration that it was much more than it appeared. It was eventually confirmed as a part of Pachyrhinosaurus rib. Later in the day I was to help uncover several near complete ribs as well as a skull of one of these ancient creatures and many more during the expedition as well as in following visits. However it was the touch of that first bit of fossilized bone that would change the perspective of my journeys then and now. The discovery of this vestige from an ancient landscape, emphasizing both the greatness and eternalness of the savage power of nature's wilderness as well as the ephemeral aspect of man's contributions. An ardent reminder of how short our time on the planet has been…

Photograph courtesy of Lorie Karnath.

Biography

Spending her childhood years in Concord Massachusetts, writers like Emerson, Thoreau and others helped to inspire Lorie Karnath's love of nature from an early age. A family move to Europe at age 10 instilled a fondness for travel and exploration that has taken her to the ends of the earth in search of answers to some of the planet's most elusive questions. Lorie is the co-founder of The Explorers Museum and served as the president of The Explorers Club, the second woman to hold this position in the organization's 107 year history. Much of her work has been focused on efforts to foster the realm of science and education. She has conceived and implemented many programs around the world which foster creativity, discovery and the sciences. Lorie also participates on numerous international scientific and educational boards. She is a fellow of the Royal Geographic Society and a founding member of the RGS Hong Kong branch. She has led several Explorers Club flag expeditions including one that followed the migration of the white storks, and following this helped to establish a sanctuary for these animals in Northern Germany. Lorie is a lecturer and author of many international articles and books.

"...the place to observe nature is where you are; the walk you take today is the walk you took yesterday. You will not find the same things: both the observed and the observer have changed..."
~John Burroughs *Signs and Seasons*

Photograph by Denis Belliveau.

Francis O'Donnell

Travel is fatal to prejudice, bigotry, and narrow-mindedness, and many of our people need it sorely on these accounts. Broad, wholesome, charitable views of men and things cannot be acquired by vegetating in one little corner of the earth all one's lifetime.
~Mark Twain

Note: This excerpt is from my upcoming fantasy adventure book series, entitled *The Untold Adventures of Marco Polo*. This chapter is based on true-life events and circumstances-that I personally experienced during my walkabouts.

Descent Over Dead Woman Pass

We put the land of Bolor and its frozen horrors behind us, but we had yet to escape the snow, which was falling heavily as we approached a place of great height. Dead Woman Pass would take us to the other side, and down into another world: Chinese Turkestan. There, we would face another endurance test, the fearsome Taklamakan desert, a realm known to be so harsh that it made you want to turn back and face almost certain death in the snowstorm. By chance, we had run across, and were now traveling with, a merchant caravan that had come via the Fergana Valley, north of the Pamirs. They had had an easier time of it than we. At the pass, we all checked into the last tea house, before crossing between the mountains of Boma-alam and Sankretuyu. From there it would be many days until we reached the Machakalichi Valley. After bedding down the animals, we rested in a typical low-slung stone hut which clung to the side of a mountain precipice. The whole structure was laden with snow.

Our innkeeper Mr. No-Whang and his two adult sons kept coming and going—just enough to let the little bit of warmth that had built up inside escape. He told us he was expecting other travelers to arrive that evening, and was trying to keep the route as clear as possible under these conditions. Slumber came quickly to the others, but I fell into an uncomfortable malaise. My stomach rumbled and churned as if it were cooking up something evil. I heard my mates snoring and our host greeting some newly-arrived guests. I went into a dazed, half-conscious state, when I was swarmed upon by a pack of field mice. They ran across my bed, burrowing under my pile of blankets, trying to get close to me in order to steal my body heat. My head began to throb; and even though I was covered with a mountain of blankets, I was cold and shivering like a leaf. I could swear I called out for help, but no one heard me.

Sometime later, our host came in, to re-stoke our fire. He noticed my condition and was immediately distressed. He roused some of my Mongol companions, who assisted him in dragging me outside into the face of the bitter cold and howling wind, so that I could reach the outdoor privy; I made the last twenty meters or so on my own. The outhouse was built on an overhanging ledge, part of a cantilevered structure that extended into space. The frozen snow and ice that enveloped it served to make it stronger and held the rickety structure together. I really didn't care. My business exploded violently out of my bared bottom; and I squatted there for a long time, my guts spilling out, hanging on to—I don't know what. I stood up and peered through the opening in the floor, into the stygian emptiness below. Suddenly I felt a hot rush of blood and fear course madly through my veins. Here I was, suspended in space, thousands of feet up, with my ass hanging out. I felt small and vulnerable.

The weather didn't improve much throughout the night. Though still weak, I began feeling much better. Mr. No-Whang had nursed me back to health with endless bowls of piping hot garlic soup, which he assured me would do the trick. "You, you drinka one mo' bowl a 'dis 'garic' soup," he insisted. "It bery, bery good for you when you are too much high in mountains. You too much high in mountains. Head hurts, here, here, drinka' da soup Mr. Marco. You feeling better." No-Whang had some strange ideas. He seemed to think my illness had something to do with the altitude, which was ridiculous, because I had been much higher in the mountains before without getting sick. Everyone knows that there is no such thing as altitude sickness; it was a preposterous theory.

Short and thin, crooked over to one side, No-Whang always had a big toothless smile slapped across his face. He was a powerhouse of non-stop energy; he was always happy, always moving, and always doing something—cooking, melting water for tea, caring for his lodgers and their animals, relentlessly fighting what seemed a futile battle against the never-ending snow, in order to keep his little stretch of mountain trail open.

By mid-morning the weather had broken. Although I was a bit reluctant, I agreed with the party's consensus that we should push on. We wouldn't make much distance, but with any luck we would clear the pass, be out of the mountains and into the valley below. I watched the late-night arrivals depart and round the bend, fading from sight. I then informed No-Whang of our decision and that I would like to settle up our account. "No, no, no, Mr. Marco. You no can be going today," he declared. "You rest one more time. No good time for you to go. You stay here. I make you 'garic' soup. Have nice sleep. Staying good; going bad." I tried paying him. He declined: "Ok, ok, no money, you no paying No-Whang. No money for to staying, it's ok, you just staying now, ok, Mr. Marco? Ok?"

I was perplexed by his enthusiastic insistence, but we all agreed to reconsider. After all, we had been pushing hard during the last few weeks; one day more or less was of little importance.

The night passed uneventfully. The storm had begun to strengthen again; No-Whang—who, I'm sure, never slept—kept his boys, Yo-Whang and Mo-Whang, busy throughout the night, letting the cold air into our little hovel as they tended to their mountain pathway. Rested and refreshed, we awoke to blue skies and invigorating crisp clear mountain air. While we said our goodbyes, No-Whang spoke through his toothless smile: "Mr. Marco, ereyting is ok. Ok for you now. Ok you save to go. Save to pass." I patted him on the back and replied, "Thank you, very good my friend." I thought to myself, No-Whang is a funny little guy!

It seemed we had left too soon; after three hours the skies darkened and the wind picked up dramatically, as we approached Dead Woman Pass. A heavy, wet, icy snow began to fall. Our fur clothing became encrusted and frozen stiff. We had gone too far to turn back; yet we couldn't go forward. There was no "forward"—the trail was completely obliterated; it no longer existed. We stumbled on for hours, only to realize to our consternation that we were back where we had begun! An unspoken foreboding settled like a fog over our group; I could even sense that it invaded our pack animals, who stirred fretfully.

My mind started wandering, as if possessed. I heard the most bone-chilling sounds ever—in my imaginings the wind whispered, "Dead Woman Pass, Dead Woman Pass," over and over, with each gust it blew. I lost control and screamed out "Stop!" In the midst of my raving, my father appeared and grabbed me by my sleeve; he looked me in the eye and shook his head. "Listen Marco, listen!" he yelled, "the wind carries the Dead Woman's warning!" A shiver went down my already frozen spine. We all were terrified by the message of doom! With daylight fading, we stood in a circle, debating our options. I felt something; someone staring at me. I turned around and there stood a huge black dog.

The dog looked at us intently, and then started slowly walking away, as if beckoning us to follow. Both dismayed and vigilant, we tried to decipher what to make of this unexpected apparition. He reappeared and glared at us, and then darted off in the direction whence he had come. It was clear he wanted us to follow. Perhaps he would be our savior and lead us out of this icy maze. Or, was he a hound from hell, sent by the Dead Woman to do her bidding? Hour after hour he led the way. Big and strong, our furry phantom powerfully made a path through this trail-less wasteland, as if he had done so a thousand times before. When we faltered or fell behind, he waited for us.

The few times he came close enough to engage, it was clear that he wasn't interested in human contact. He needed neither encouragement nor petting. He was missing part of his left ear, and looked to be blind in his left eye. It seemed that to be fulfilled he needed a mission, a purpose—and at this moment we were it. Suddenly he led us into an extremely treacherous area. Giant, slippery shards of ice stood all around us, mimicking sheets of glass which had tumbled down from above and shattered. At that point I began wondering if this seemingly benevolent animal had betrayed us towards our doom.

We all hesitated and refused to make any further attempt to follow him. Calmly, as nimbly as a ballet dancer, this canine devil crossed the first section of the barrier. Looking back, he urged us forward, but not one of us budged. He disappeared amongst the crags, and then, minutes later he returned. He looked at us quizzically and barked wildly. His thunderous barking made the mountains come to life and rumble.

We realized he had led us into an avalanche zone; we had to move again or die.

At last, we realized that forward, led by our strange companion, was the only way towards possible escape. Within minutes, we came upon a terrible sight: it was the caravan of late night travelers who had left No-Whang's lodge the day before—the entire party of twenty or more people lay dead, their bodies crushed under the ice and snow. It was a gruesome scene. A leg stuck out here; an arm there; a severed head—bloody, smashed, and flattened—sat on the edge of the cliff, as if peering over the edge. Horse and camel entrails were splattered everywhere. The snow was stained brown and red.

Obviously, these poor souls had been the victims of an avalanche, caught up in the falling ice and snow. The mountain had wrought its fury upon them—or was it the ghost of the Dead Woman? Were they just hapless fools or had they deserved their fate? Had they done something to bring this wrath down upon them?

We increased our pace; the mountains continued to groan, and the wind continued to sing its ghoulish song of the Dead Woman, over and over. After a while we seemed to have passed the danger; thank God for our furry guide. Who was this weird being who appeared out of nowhere and came to our rescue? What's more, what kismet had compelled No-Whang to insist that we stay on one more night? Dumb luck? Divine intervention?

Just as quickly as our canine ghoul appeared, he disappeared, unceremoniously, without a goodbye—just as we began to think we were safe, we rounded a corner and he was nowhere to be seen! We were elated that the ice and snow gave way to cloud forest and jungle. We were still deep in the mountains, but now we were surrounded by green plants and living things; we knew we had put the worst behind us.

We could hear music and celebrations in the distance, emanating from a small settlement. As our party approached it, we were cheered boisterously and escorted to the town's courtyard, which was surrounded by fifteen or twenty small buildings with banners and flags flapping from atop them. The townspeople gave each of us a big bowl of chang and encouraged us to drink heartily.

The women watched from the sidelines, serving alcohol and keeping an eye on things, while the men made fools of themselves, dancing and singing, drinking and clapping their hands to the beat of the musicians' drums. Some men shot off fireworks, others beat on pots and pans—anything to make noise and join in. It was a rousing event!

I wasn't sure if the villagers realized that we were not part of their tribe; perhaps they believed we were strange-looking kinfolk from the next mountain over. A trio of insistent chaps invited me to join the dance circle. I feigned reluctance, but at that point I was feeling no pain. I was fully recovered from my illness, and the chang was working its magic. We had survived the Roof of the World, the horrors of the Yeti, the Crystal Cave, and a mountain avalanche. I was flying high! I felt as though I were one with the world—and, as my father always said, "When in Rome, do as the Romans!" I danced the Cosmic Dance and thought of Rumi as I whirled—as my old Sufi friend Melena had taught me to do. God Bless that old man!

Late at night the festivities started to wane, and I was able to steal away to our encampment. My father, Uncle Matteo, the Mongol triplets, and a few others were keeping warm around the fire. Out of the darkness came a woman with a child on her hip. She looked too old to be the child's mother, but it was hard to guess the age of people who suffered such hard lives in these mountains. She was obviously from the village—although it was unusual that she would approach us unescorted, alone, and without a man.

Calmly, yet with an urgent insistence, she thrust her child's hand towards us, emphatically raising it as high as possible for all to see. Her son, perhaps two years of age, had what looked like a bloody clump on the end of his wrist. Quickly my father jumped into action and ordered Monkusie to bring him some freshly-boiled hot water and candles, in order to light the table where he laid the boy. "Marco" he said, "Go to my tent and get my medical kit; make sure that my scissors and tweezers are both inside of it, and check for fresh dressings."

All the while, Uncle Matteo was spinning in circles saying, "Oh no, don't touch the child, don't do it! What are you doing? Oh no!" After soaking the little guy's hand in the warm water, my father said, "It is hard to tell; perhaps he has had a bad burn or something. Whatever it is, it is clearly infected."

My Uncle chimed in once again: "Oh no, Niccolo, I told you to leave the child alone. Please leave the child alone!"

Oblivious to Matteo's entreaties, my father continued, "You can see someone tried to bandage the wound; the dressing became enmeshed in the puss and scab as it was trying to heal, only increasing the damage and the infection."

"Oh no… No, No, No! Marco, tell your father no, just leave that child alone. What if he dies? They will blame us!"

All the while, the mother stood at a distance, away from us. She seemed uninterested in the commotion swirling around her infant son. I looked at her more closely; she looked blind in her left eye, and was missing part of her left ear. She was as aloof as Marguerite of Provence, Queen of the Franks, in a parade of peasants. This I could not understand; had it been my child I would have been in as much the same panic as my Uncle Matteo, or as concerned as my father Niccolo.

My father worked diligently on the child's hand; layer-by-layer he gently cut, separated, and pulled away the infected mass, until the image of a hand re-emerged. He cleaned the wound thoroughly, covered it with ointment, and replaced the dressing with one that would neither meld with the wound nor interfere with the natural healing process.

"Forgive me, brother," my father told Matteo. "Of course you are right, but by the will of God, the child will be all right and no one will be upset with us. You understand; I just couldn't let the boy die. I mean, knowing that I could help."

At that moment I was so proud of my father that my chest could have burst open. I had a tear in my eye as he handed the infant back over to his mother, giving her instructions on how to care for the wound and prevent future complications. Noticing the emotion on my face, he smiled and laid his hand on my shoulder. We stood there on that mountainside, together, in silence, for quite a while. Exhausted and rejuvenated at the same time, we looked beyond the peaks, into the starry heavens.

A few days later, after the long descent over Dead Woman Pass, I asked my father about the mother's seemingly nonchalant attitude. He responded, "Marco you will come to understand the true facts of life and realities outside the civilized world. The hardship, disease, and privation which most people on earth have to endure, is monumental. They truly have the odds stacked against them. The short of it is this: rural farming folk have many children. This ensures helping hands and loved ones to care for them in their old age. But in the beginning when children are very young, it is too emotionally expensive to invest one's heart and soul into loving a child, who the odds say will die. A woman may have as many as ten or fifteen children; oftentimes only three or four will survive."

Trying to wrap my mind around such mysteries, I soon fell into a deep sleep. Tomorrow would be another day. I would enjoy another adventure to recount.

Questions and Answers

1. What compels you to walk?

The Sufi, the searcher, the seeker, the teacher. They wander and travel without a care in the world, knowing that the universe will fill their bowls. Curiosity, growth, wanderlust, the love of people, art, and history is a must. Learning about cultures, past and present, and what inspired their faith, their beliefs, their religion; this is why I walk. Without movement you atrophy. Without learning and growth, you die and fade away, little by little, day by day. I am endlessly curious about the world and all it contains. This curiosity keeps me young and engaged. The word boredom is unknown to me; I keep myself entertained. Great wonders wait at every turn. That is the magic for which I yearn. I love to experience new things; seeing vistas of which I have only dreamed. A waterfall, lake, mountain stream, or rainbow, refreshes body, mind and soul. I learned this wise lesson early in my life from a woman. To walk and get lost in an endless hectic crowd is a joy of communion with the human race. But to get lost in those empty spaces, off the map, is the true escape. The truth of life, the nature of the divine, exposed, bare, sublime. If I find paradise behind the eternal veil, I will plant my flag and no longer roam.

2. Do you experience instances while you are walking when your mind is somewhere off the trail and on its own journey?

I believe all of us who walk must experience these instances. It is our way of fighting off the monotony and pain that often comes on demanding journeys. It is natural when deprived of food to think of a juicy hamburger, slice of pizza, or other favorite dish. When deprived of fellowship, to think of home, friends, loved ones, and a soft bed. When lonely, to think of wives and girlfriends, past and present. I have relived countless events over and over in my head, be they successes or failures, to see if I could have had a different outcome. Words to obscure songs, held deep in the subconscious, long forgotten, come flooding forth. Scenes from beloved movies fill my mind, as deserts and mountain vistas fill my eyes. I meditate while walking, on goals, hopes and dreams; sometimes on how to overcome an obstacle that lies ahead, such as nature or logistics. Inspired by the moment and the journey, I muse on what mode of creation might express it best. Should I execute a sculpture or painting, write a story, or, as I often do, write a poem? The poem I share below was inspired by a walkabout.

Capricious is the Desert

Capricious is the Desert, its fickle sands flow like an ocean down to the sea
It promises nothing but death and desolation, arriving mercifully quick
Heat, cold, and starvation, a constant companion held closely like a long lost friend
Silence, so deafening nothing can be heard but the searing sun, the rotating moon, and twinkling stars
Day after day, the endless expanse retreats, moving mountain ranges on a mobile horizon

Capricious is the Desert, unyielding, ever-changing, sands shifting, growing dunes recede
Routes plied by caravans lost and gone, footprints covered up by time
Sun-bleached bones tell the tale, of trading missions failed,
Capricious is the Desert that holds out the promise of untold riches
One needs just to cross it, to reap its profit, armies that once paroled the road, too, were consumed

Capricious is the Desert, who hides lost civilizations below its surface
Scuttled in its sandy depths, a crystalline ocean without liquid, its torrents rage like stormy waters
Whirlwinds, cyclones, hurricanes, all spin and live,
Capricious is the Desert, an indiscriminate killer, sweeping life and signs away,
Its vengeance complete for those who dare to trespass within,
Capricious is the Desert though it lets others pass in safety

Capricious is the Desert, it holds no love for man nor beast, yet ghosts and memories, haunts persists
Sandstorms obliterate the light of day, bringing night to this indifferent wasteland world
That gives life to life, yet unknown, change comes slowly, unperceived, yet change it does, as does all things,
Bugs, snakes, and lizards, too, find shelter, residing side by side, rodents, deer, and eagles, all food for jackal or vulture

The desert, as a conduit, connects thorough corridors of faith, art, and cultures spread
Religions flourished, painting and sculpture merged, transformed, forming new ideas of the ideal
Peoples intermingled, changed, assimilated, binding separate worlds together, they found in themselves one another,
Who with joy and communion, picked and smelled the rains seldom gift of wildflowers
How Capricious is the Desert? Very, yet it holds kindness and God if you look close enough to love.

3. How do you manage to stay physically and emotionally healthy during long and arduous journeys?

I try to eat well, get plenty of sleep, and not over indulge in alcohol. This is difficult when you are constantly on the move and often don't know where you will be sleeping or where your next meal is coming from. During "In the Footsteps" we almost never slept in the same place twice. The myriad of accommodations were varied. We were on a low budget, and one of our goals was to immerse ourselves in the diverse cultures we encountered. Flee-infested shit holes were the norm.

Sleeping rough under the stars was a joy. I say this with one caveat; we froze every second of every day, for five months straight, from the time we entered northern Afghanistan in early October, until we reached Beijing in February. All the high tech clothes in the world did little to protect us against the winter cold of the Taklamakan Desert and the high Pamirs. We resorted to donning native garb. Heavy felt socks, huge sheepskin coats, and fur hats helped somewhat. We were still cold, even if we were indoors standing by a raging Bukhari stove. We lived and slept in our clothes. During one stretch we didn't bathe for six weeks.

We found ourselves curled up on frozen dirt floors of one room shacks in the Wakhan Corridor of Afghanistan, or sprawled out on a couch in the lobby of some no-name Chinese hotel that would not rent rooms to foreigners. We slept on park benches or in the backseats of cars and trucks. Bouncing along in third class bunks during endless train rides was a favorite place to sleep. We always slept with one eye open, to guard against having our camera gear and other possessions stolen. New friends put us up in barns or on living room floors. While riding horses along the edge of the Taklamakan Desert, in China, we had the pleasure of stepping back in time and lodging in a true caravanserai, a medieval motel that Marco would have still recognized and felt at home in.

For months we ate only one meal a day. While crossing much of Afghanistan, we ate little more than rice, potatoes, and onions. Much of central Asia was in serious economic turmoil. The Soviet Union had just collapsed and there wasn't much food. There were basic staples, and the ubiquitous borscht, with bread so stale that you needed a hacksaw to cut it. Every single part of a sheep or goat was known to us: eyeballs, tongue, brain, fat, and liver. Fortunately, the desert oases of Uzbekistan served up a cornucopia of fruit. We reveled in the refreshing clusters of grapes and melons of all types and shapes.

Staying emotionally healthy is perhaps even tougher than staying physically healthy. In China, for instance, there is no word for privacy. The key to your hotel room door means nothing. The floor matron, or the police, barge in anytime it suits their fancy. Every day you are an oddity and attract curious locals. They don't realize the gawking, staring, pointing of fingers and outright insults are something you have to endlessly endure.

Ironically, whenever possible, you find yourself seeking refuge in things that you have so desperately tried to get away from, such as McDonald's, or other Western-style establishments. Making new friends with expats and other travelers brings a moment of normalcy. Worst of all, perhaps, is the affliction of homesickness. It plagued my colleague more than I. This created some tension, and traveling with a partner is not always easy; compromise is necessary. We had an expression that we shared to motivate each other to continue the journey when we were down, "We will sleep when we are dead."

4. Please share a high and a low period that you experienced during your walkabouts.

This piece first appeared January, 2015 in "Mongol China and the Silkroad" blog, which in my opinion is the finest clearinghouse of information concerning these regions.

The dream was to be the first expedition in history to retrace the entire route of Marco Polo; however, we came to find there are many gray areas, places lost forever in the annals of time. The Smithsonian staff wrote after we returned, "They are almost certainly the first to approximate Polo's steps through Eurasia, entirely by land and sea, without resorting to helicopters or airplanes." We had informed the Smithsonian of our intentions before leaving, and stayed in contact with them through our liaisons back home. When they heard we had successfully completed the Afghan leg of our journey, they asked us to write an article for their magazine.

When we reached Beijing in late February 1994, it was cold and gray, so we hunkered down in the Chinese capital for two weeks. We locked ourselves away in our room and wrote the article for Smithsonian. Several weeks later we got word that they had rejected our article. "There is too much action in it and it reads like something from 'Soldier of Fortune'." This was a blow for us; there would be no money for the article. Rejection is never a good feeling, but in the past we had always been able to use the negativity of others, to harden, motivate, and inspire ourselves. "We will show them," was how we handled naysayers.

I can't tell you how many people, scholars, and other so-called "experts" told us, "It can't be done, and if it can, it isn't going to be by you two!" This time was different. I was let down, but it took the wind out of my partner's sails, as he felt somehow perhaps his photos were not up to par. I assured him that was nonsense; that he was an excellent photographer. I continued, "We have nothing to worry about; we need to stay focused on the expedition; that is what counts." I told him that when we got home, having been successful, things would be different.

High: In the town of Ishkashim, which is split and divided by a branch of the Oxus River, I stood looking out at the mighty spires guarding the entrance to the Wakhan Corridor. The Hindu Kush to the south and the Pamirs, the Roof of the World to the north. Marked on our map, which we first plotted at home, the corridor was one of the obstacles, if crossed, would separate us from all the failed attempts before us. There I asked the universe why, why me? Why am I so blessed, knowing that soon I would traverse that mythical corridor, the Wakhan, a lost and all but forgotten secret passage into the backdoor of China?

Being allowed to cross borders was a challenge, from Iran, to Afghanistan, as well as political instability. We were captured in a firefight, ironically, by the descendants of the same tribe that Polo described as almost capturing him, and killing and enslaving many of his companions. We came under the protection of an Afghan warlord, and crossed the bulk of the country with our own heavily armed contingent of bodyguards.

We encountered fierce, strong, proud, and handsome people, friendly, and giving. They ached for peace and an end to war.

Upon returning home, the response we received from the major media players was "Isn't that nice; well congratulations but we are so sorry, Americans aren't interested in that part of the world … now if you had something on national parks?" However; soon thereafter, the tragedy of 911 occurred. Now Americans were interested, as was the Smithsonian. They finally published our article.

5. Have you experienced an important Encounter that somehow changed the direction of your journey?

The Hero's Journey

We have not even to risk the adventure alone
for the heroes of all time have gone before us.
The labyrinth is thoroughly known …
we have only to follow the thread of the hero path.
And where we had thought to find an abomination
we shall find a God.

And where we had thought to slay another
we shall slay ourselves.
Where we had thought to travel outwards
we shall come to the center of our own existence.
And where we had thought to be alone
we shall be with all the world.
~Joseph Campbell

My favorite quote is, "The Hero's Journey," by my mentor and guru-of-sorts, Joseph Campbell. In 1983, "The Power of Myth," a six-part series of interviews, conducted by Bill Moyers, and the author and scholar of comparative mythology, Joseph Campbell, aired. I thought I was well-travelled and educated, but the series left me dumb-struck. I was mesmerized by their conversation, most of which I didn't understand, but I knew it was important and I was determined to learn. I watched the series over and over. I bought Joe's books and read them voraciously. I read books on all the subject matter and topics they discussed, delving into the philosophy, mythology, folklore, and religions of the world's cultures. I knew, I knew nothing, therefore, I knew.

While preparing for our two year expedition "In the Footsteps of Marco Polo" there were some frightening moments of realization. We had constructed a "War Room" full of pertinent materials, books, maps, contact numbers, supplies, and information. We hung inspirational quotes on the wall, and repeated the quotes as we practiced basic words and greetings in a half-dozen languages.

It was the map that held the terror; I would stare at it in horror, and break out in a cold sweat. We were proposing to cross the world's largest landmass and follow the fabled Silk Road. A journey which offered up the promise of crossing the world's harshest mountain ranges, endless barren desert wastelands, and tropical jungles, mysterious dark and deep. Our route would take us through twenty two countries and territories, as well as eight war zones. Many of the areas we needed to cross had been shut tight for years. Visas and politics aside, we faced bandits, militias, and Islamic extremists. During times like these, when the fear of the unknown wanted to take hold, I would take refuge and solace in Campbell's words written in "The Heroes Journey," knowing I was not alone. I thought of the explorers who had gone before; explorers of old, standing on the edge of the known world, who had set out on voyages of discovery knowing the odds were they may never return. I knew I had to throw the knife up into the air. My reward for that risk is being able to share my story with others. Sadly, Campbell died shortly after his series of interviews with Moyers was completed. Years later, when "In the Footsteps" finally came to fruition and was produced by PBS, we were honored beyond all measure to have Bill Moyers write this review about our venture.

"It was the best-documented journey of its time, inspiring the imaginations and ambitions of countless adventurers, including Christopher Columbus. Now we, too, can follow in the footsteps of Marco Polo, with guides as vividly exciting and engaging as Marco himself. With both their film and this book Denis and Francis have recreated what Joseph Campbell would have applauded as 'The Hero's Journey.' Come take it yourself—and you'll never turn back."
(Bill Moyers)

Francis and Denis Belliveau on the route of Marco Polo. *Photograph courtesy of Francis O'Donnell.*

Biography

After a tour of duty in the Marines, Francis studied sculpture at the School of Visual Arts in Manhattan. When not exhibiting his work or lecturing on his numerous expeditions to the four corners of the world, he can be found working on his series of fantasy novels, based on his expedition following Marco Polo's route. This trip was the first expedition to trace Marco Polo's journeys. He is a speaker for the World Explorers Bureau.

Photographs by Denis Belliveau.

Photograph by Denis Belliveau.

Yamabushi ritual in Japan. *Photograph courtesy of Tor Torkildson.*

Tor Torkildson

Keep on keeping on!

I Wander Because I Wonder

I.

I started climbing mountains in earnest when I was twenty-two. My first real exposure to the high country was a trek around Annapurna in the Himalayas, a journey that turned out to be ill fated and one I felt would never end. I had been sent to Nepal on a mystical quest by the Beat writer, Pierre Delattre, who was a mentor of mine, to "Find the Living Goddess Kumari." Later, while living in the Canadian Rockies and Alaska, mountains became my obsession. I should mention that I had strong Buddhist leanings and had made forays into Zen under the influence of Dainin Kitagiri Roshi and the poet Gary Snyder. One day my friend Pat Morrow mentioned, mischievously, that I should look into the Yamabushi mountain monks of Japan. This led me to Snyder's essay, *Blue Mountain Constantly Walking*, and it became my goal to find these mountain ascetics who practice walking meditation, own nothing, feel the entire universe is their temple, and treat the great mountain ranges as their worship halls. I soon learned that Gary Snyder was the first Westerner to become a novice Yamabushi (*sentachi*) and to be introduced to the mountain deities, Zao Gogen and Fudo Myo-O. Becoming a sentachi became my new quest.

It is a clear and crisp autumn day when I enter the wooden torii gate with a letter from Gary Snyder neatly folded in my pocket. An elderly monk in white robes sweeps the courtyard. The smell of incense and wild herb-flavored udon soup wafts around the courtyard and into my nose. The bulging eyes of a stone statue representing Fudo Myo-O scrutinize my approach. It is the first day of my training and initiation (*shugyo*) into the esoteric Shegendo sect of the Yamabushi. Pierre's parting words ring like the temple bells in my head.

"Swirl with the swirl and whirl with the whirl, and no bones shall break."

Despite studying Japanese for four years, I am not ready for the esoteric language I am about to experience. The language of these monks is a language clouded in mystery and sacred mountain realms beyond my grasp. I will try my best to follow along. I will intensely observe everything that goes on around me, and adapt. I remind myself that I have survived dive training in the military. Several priests wander across the courtyard with high peaked hats and an air of authority. A muscular monk approaches me and I hand him my approval from the head priest, Kokuji, authorizing my presence in the forthcoming shugo. Sternly, the monk leads me inside, and motions for me to strip my clothes off. I am given a pair of straw *waraji* sandals; a kind of knicker, a deer pelt under-kimono; a hemp cloth over-robe; a conch shell in a net bag to wear over my shoulder; and a small black lacquered cap to wear over my forehead. Steadily, the other new initiates arrive, looking as afraid and bewildered as I feel.

I am the only *gaajin* (foreigner) in the group. In a smug way I am happy about this, yet also a little nervous, what with the language gap and cultural dissimilarities. There will be no sleep for me this first night, with my amped nerves, and the frog-like croaks of those sleeping besides me on the tatami-covered floor.

I am disoriented in the morning as the croaks are replaced by the sound of mantras and morning shuffles. Monks rise early. A conch shell blows the command to wake up and get dressed. Observing my fellow initiates, I learn what the commands mean. There will be no food or sleep for the next five days. I am fit and eager. My brain screams, "Bring it on, bring it all on, I want this badly!"

Inside the temple, the priest, Sho-Daisendatsu, performs a ritual to transfer our souls into the Oi for protection. We chant the Heart Sutra, and the horagai conch is blown to let the mountain spirits know we are on our way to the realm of the dead. The priest waves a long pole with white strips of paper at the top. One last blow of the conch, and we are off. I finger my *nenju* rosary nervously. Walking through the town of Haguro-machi in our white Yamabushi uniforms, as the townspeople look on in silent reverence, I am transported back to boot camp in the Navy. The geognosis of the Yamabushi gives them a special status in society and immunity from natural, and not so natural, threats from the mountains. Under my breath I hum a marching cadence and feel happy. I am so far away from everything and everyone. The cryptomeria forest around the mountain smells ancient and mysterious.

"Wa!" Inside the gate to the mountain realm, our group begins to run up the mountain's 2,446 stone steps. I feel wild and free, and the spirits are calling me forward. "Wa!" I scream, over and over, as I run up the mountain into the unknown. "Wa!" We pass a weather-beaten, five-story, 600-year-old, plain wooden pagoda. Stone lanterns flank the path. Halfway up the mountain, panting and out of breath, we stop at a small tea house for a drink of water. There will only be water from here on. "Wa!"

We stay constantly on the move, climbing, wading through streams, chanting in caves, and meditating under waterfalls at sunrise. There is only water. Day one is manageable, days two and three are hellish, and finally the bliss arrives on day four. I mean real, hot-damn-this-feels-good bliss. Who'd have thought that starving oneself could lead to altered states of euphoria? Day and night we move through the sacred landscape of Dewa Sanzan, with the Haguro, Gassan, and Yudano-san mountains our temple playground. Often we walk and climb vine-covered mountains for twelve straight hours before stopping for a rest. There is no sleep, only water. We build huge goma fires deep in the forest, practice complex hand mudras, and chant epic mantras. I begin to feel lost and found all at once. Initiates drop like flies, often simply wandering away, awash in the fairytale thought of a bath and hot meal down in the village. With their exit, I grow stronger, and wonder how far I can push this deprivation thing. On day four I begin to smell food miles away and see the landscape around me in a microspore kind of way.

I know that the Yamabushi come from the Shegendo sect, which is a combination of Buddhism, Shinto, Taoism, and mysticism. They were the monks of Japanese lore: warriors, mountain ascetics with supernatural powers like the folkloric character Tengu in Japanese drama. In a way, the Yamabushi are liminal beings who live between both worlds and have access to special knowledge, to which normal humans cannot be privy. They are folk magicians, divinatory messengers, and the overseers of demonic exorcism.

On day four, my warrior spirit begins to show itself and the forced marches become pleasurable and anticipated. On the morning of day five, we sit under a remote waterfall, the water hitting our heads dead center, while the sun slowly makes its appearance. With my newfound night vision, the change from night to day becomes meaningless. I am held suspended over a cliff by my ankles. Then I am offered a red umeboshi salted plum. It will be the first food I have eaten in five days, and I hesitate before stuffing it into my mouth. "Wa!" My brain explodes with the taste and I nearly fall to the ground. I am led to a small wooden building, along with the eleven other remaining initiates, to sleep. It is over, or so I think.

I feel deeply sick when the conch horn blows the command to wake up and get dressed. I have no watch, nor any idea how long I have slept. We are served a bowl of miso soup and two rice-ball onigiri. I feel beyond hungry and am convinced I could eat a tatami mat if it were served to me. We spend the entire day chanting mantras; I occasionally fall asleep and get wacked by the muscular monk who had initially given me my uniform. The toes I froze on Annapurna begin to cause me excruciating pain. I want to cry. At sunset we begin a round of full prostrations and there seems to be no end in sight. I quickly become drenched in my own sweat and the muscular monk seems to be purposely looming over me with his bamboo stick. I am sure he wants to torture me for some previous crime committed against him by a foreigner. My "Wa" becomes "Mu."

We are allowed to go outside to draw water. I wash my face and drink deeply. I look around at the other initiates and notice their weariness and their dog-eared determination. I realize we are down to the core group. The conch horn blows and we quickly return to the small wooden building. The windows are being shuttered. Several monks bring charcoal barbeques into the room: something isn't right. Hadn't I read somewhere about a "smoking out"? Or a *Nam-Ban* session involving chili peppers? I go into survival mode and cover my face with my kimono sleeve, creating an air pocket in which to breathe, as I would do if I were in an avalanche. The Ninjas arrive, dressed in black. Chili peppers are thrown into the coals and a great cloud of smoke rises and expands across the room; the Ninjas depart quickly and lock us in. I take a deep breath and go inward to wait it out. I hear horrific screams around me. Initiates are trying to escape and pounding on the doors. I drift into a dive memory; I am underwater and looking at tropical fish. Time becomes distorted and I seem to be swimming.

Fresh air assaults my face and my exposed hands. The ritual is over and the room looks like a war zone full of casualties. Many of the initiates are gagging and seem traumatized. I walk outside and look up at the stars, wondering what the next test will be. A large fire is built in the woods and I am convinced we will be made to walk across hot coals. Fortunately, this isn't the case: we are simply taught how to properly build a ceremonial goma fire and jump through it. This is the beginning of our re-birth and entry back into the living realm. Yes, the more advanced Yamabushi can walk on fire. I feel that I am permanently in an altered state of being. At sunrise we sit under a waterfall, chanting the Heart Sutra.

For lunch we are served our first proper meal, with sake, and are allowed to rest afterward. The comfort seems odd. Is this a trick? Sure enough, just as I am dozing off into a deep sleep, the conch horn blows. Once assembled, we are told that we will be having a Tengu sumo wrestling tournament, and that the villagers are invited to come watch. What next?

I step out into the sand ring, wearing my *muwashi* loincloth, feeling like I am in a Fellini film. There is a group of local villagers watching. I hear women gasp when they see my tattoos. To them it is a sign that I belong to the Yakuza, the Japanese mafia, which of course I do not. What the other initiates and monks don't know is that I was a state wrestling champion.

I lose one match out of ten and find myself in the championship round with the same man I had previously lost to. I have been told he has a black belt in judo. In the middle of the ring, we crouch nose to nose, waiting for the referee to drop the fan that signals the beginning of the match. One of us needs to throw the other outside of the circle. When our eyes meet I begin to growl and bare my teeth; it is my animal spirit rising up. For a split second I see fear in his eyes. The match is over in a flash and my opponent has no idea what hit him. He lies in a heap outside the ring and I am the Yamabushi sumo champion of Dewa Sanzen. The highest priests must now wash my body in a sacred stream and the initiates must each drink a cup of sake with me in my honor. I am quickly drunk and find myself witnessing an exorcism.

A middle-aged woman lying on the ground is surrounded by several of the priests from our group. I attempt to quietly hide behind a tree and watch (something tells me they know I am watching and want me to). I am drunk with sake and with the surrealism of the scene. There is a ring of candles around the woman's body and I notice another woman dressed in black holding the possessed woman's head in her hands. I wonder if she is a blind *Miko*—the women who help remove evil spirits during exorcisms. Five priests are making complicated finger and hand positions and chanting a haunting mantra. Suddenly, there seems to be a transfer of spirit between the two women, like a power surge. They both jerk about wildly and moan. I almost piss myself and quickly stagger away and back to our remote lodging, feeling half mad. Had I seen a fox, those malignant evil spirits, in Japanese mythology? I feel so weak and alienated: I want to go home and forget this ever happened. I admit to myself that I have been spiritual shopping; but I am not cut out for this soul-twisting upheaval. Again, the five-year old boy who still dwells within of me wants to cry, and be hugged.

During the second week, our initiation enters a new phase in which ceremony and ritual are transmitted to us while we move up streams and mountains, into remote forested valleys, and into the caves, where we often sleep.

Ritual for the Yamabushi is based on the needs of the parishioners and can include fortune telling, divination, prayers, incantations, spells, and the creation of charms. We pay reverence to former Yamabushi, through their skeleton bones, often left in the back recesses of the places where we sleep. I find this eerie and frightening in an innocent way. Monks often spend months alone in these remote caves, eating their mudras and drinking the mantras.

I grow tired of listening to the Japanese language, and of the competitive atmosphere that seems to be developing amongst the initiates. I feel the resentment because of my sumo victory, and the benefits I have received as a result. I am very close to abandoning the Yamabushi journey and simply wandering across Japan alone, like an old-world Komuso mendicant monk, seeking my own Way, like the monk Ikkyu, "Crazy Cloud."

One day, we complete the entire Dewa Sanzen circuit of the three mountains: Mount Haguro, Mount Gassan, and Mount Yudono. I enjoy being up high in the wide open spaces, breathing in the fresh air, and feeling the sacredness of my surroundings. Hikers back off the path, gawking when I pass. It is one thing to see a Yamabushi, yet another to see a foreigner dressed in the traditional outfit of the mountain mystic. I feel like I have gone from a death-like existence and come back to life during this initiation with the Yamabushi.

In a final ceremony, I must come face to face with the head Yamabushi priest for a final interview.

"What you have learned, seen, experienced, is not to be shared with the outside world," He says. "Ring the bell and leave."

"Wa!" I cry, and run down the mountain as a Yamabushi.

Following my shugyo initiation, I go on a week-long sake binge and fall back into the profane world from which I came. I am not ready for enlightenment yet. Or, as the travel writer Tim Cahill once said, "I'll pass on the enlightenment." For now.

Mount Haguro, Japan. *Photograph courtesy of Tor Torkildson.*

II

I am invited to circumambulate Mount Fuji along the ancient Ochudo route with Pat Morrow, Yuichiro Miura, and a team of vulcanists. We have special permission that allows our team to cross the dangerous lava flow regions. This is the first time I will meet, 'The Man Who Skied Down Everest', and who will go on to become the oldest man to climb Mount Everest at age 80. Yuichiro is built like, "a brick shithouse," as my grandfather Tork used to say. He is solid, low to the ground, and thick. I find it initially hard to read his face and I am slightly intimidated by his fame.

"I have been told that you are a Yamabushi. I have never met a foreign Yamabushi!" He says, smiling, and I sense he will befriend me before long.

"My family comes from the samurai class and fought alongside the Yamabushi. This Ochudo route we are on is over a thousand years old, and is very sacred for the Japanese people," he continues.

Circumambulating mountains, or Kora, the opening of a mountain, is a sacred and ancient tradition amongst Buddhists. In modern times, very few people are given this rare opportunity on Fuji. The Yamabushi were formally the gatekeepers to the mountain, and their burial sites are scattered around and within the mountain's caves.

Mount Fuji is a product of the subduction zone that straddles Japan, with the Pacific Plate to the north and the Philippine Plate to the south, subducting underneath the Eurasian Plate. There have been 16 eruptions since 781 A.D. My mind drifts back to the time as a young sailor when I rushed to the summit after months at sea. Determined to witness the sunrise from the peak, I had spent the night huddled, wrapped in my Navy woolen blanket. I nearly froze to death.

The weather is wicked and stormy when we start our trek around Fuji. Our group has waited in a bus for the weather to break. Finally, Miura declares it is time to go. I try to stay close to him and engage him in conversation. He has a strong and determined gait. I have heard that he maintains a special diet, much like a wild animal, which facilitates his great strength despite his advanced age. On a snack break, he tells us that his father skied down Mount Blanc when he was ninety-nine, and that he is going to top that feat by climbing Mount Everest. He asks me about the small green frog that I carry around with me in the mountains.

"This is Kairu. We Yamabushi can turn people into frogs if they disrespect a sacred mountain like Fuji," I say. This brings a great belly laugh from him.

"You are a very funny Yamabushi!" He says.

I delight in the dramatic rock formations that seem to give Fuji a "mystical splendor." We have to climb many ladders and use cables to navigate our way through the large flow regions. The vulcanists take samples and photographs as we go. Miura keeps the pace steady. I daydream about the era when the Yamabushi were the guardians of this mountain and often did long fasts in the caves, high up on the slopes. Today, there are only a handful of Yamabushi left, real ones that is, who spend long periods of time deep in the mountain landscapes.

The idea of disappearing into the mountains does hold a certain appeal for me. Pat Morrow, the first person to climb the Seven Summits, moves across the mountain with his camera like a lithe gazelle. I feel humbled to be on this sacred mountain with two of the greatest climbers on earth. The journey around Fuji ends with heaping bowls of udon, sashimi, cold Sapporo beer, and a round of speeches. Then we are told that the World Trade Center has been attacked.

III

The marathon monks of Mt Hiei do not play around when it comes to enlightenment. When a Tendai monk embarks on the *Kaihogyo*, (an ascetic practice that involves circling of the mountain), there is no turning back: the monk will either complete the ordeal and become enlightened, (*a Living Buddha*), or he will fail and commit suicide. When I heard about the marathon monks, I knew that I had to meet them or maybe even join them.

It was the kind of pact I like: sort of like the saying "If you are not living on the edge, you're taking up space" that used to float around the extreme sports world. After experiencing the Yamabushi initiation and circumambulating Mount Fuji along the Ochudo route, I am ready. I set my sights on Kyoto and the Enryaku-ji temple on the slopes of Mt Hiei. In Kyoto, I visit with the American poet, Cid Corman, who is the translator of Basho, the Japanese Edo period poet. Cid shares one of Basho's poems with me:

"*toshi kurena/ kasa kite waraji/ hakinagara-* another year is gone/a traveler's shade on my head/straw sandals on my feet."

I have walked much of the wandering route that Basho wrote about in his book, *Narrow Road to the Deep North*, and admire this poet deeply. Cid has been in Kyoto a very long time, and I enjoy his story of how he ended up living in Japan.

"I had been living in Europe, on a Fulbright scholarship, and hanging out with the poet Samuel Beckett, when I decided to return home the long way via India and Japan on a tramp steamer. When we docked in Japan, I went ashore and instantly realized that this was where I was meant to live my life." I had experienced something similar on my first trip to Japan and speculated that we had both lived in Japan during previous lives. There have been moments on this journey with the Yamabushi when I felt that eerie feeling of a past life, or a heavy déjà vu, creeping in. When I left Cid, his parting words to me were, "In this life you have to be brave, very brave."

After visiting the Enryaku-ji temple complex, contemplating Dogen's time on Mount Hiei and his return from China, I chant a few mantras in the inner sanctuaries before heading to the sub-temple in the woods where the Dai Ajari "Living Buddha" lives. My world smells of pine syrup, incense, and mystery. A young, fresh-faced monk greets me with a deep bow. Strange, since I am no longer in my robes, but in jeans and Western attire.

"I would like to see the Dai Ajari. I am coming from the Dewa Sanzen and have just completed my initiation shugyo with the Yamabushi," I boldly state. I sense how presumptuous and foolhardy I must sound to the monk.

"Please follow me," he says. Again, the young monk bows deeply, and leads me to a simple, eight-mat tatami room. There is a single vase with a flower in it, a picture on the wall of a monk I do not recognize, and seated cross-legged in the middle of the room is the Dai Ajari, with his long-toothed smile, translucent skin, thick eyebrows and vibrant eyes. There is a hole in the tatami in front of him with a teapot in it.

"Please have a seat here in front of me," he says. "You must be weary from the long journey you have been on? Let me serve you a cup of tea." With delicate hands, he takes the teapot and pours a dash of warm water into a square wooden box that smells like cedar. He places the tea pot back in the hole with calculated gestures.

"You must carefully whisk the fine matcha powdered green tea," he says. He takes a small brush, which looks like the type men use when they shave with a straight-edge razor, and swirls the tea around. The Dai Ajari is calm and precise in his movements. He places the wooden box in front of me and smiles. Again, I am amazed by the length of his front teeth, and try to remember the tea lessons I learned from the classic book, *The Way of Tea*.

I take the box and raise it to my lips. The smell is rich and earthy. I hold the tea cup with both hands, bow slightly, and take a sip, bow, and smile towards the Dai Ajari. I repeat this four times while rotating the box clockwise in my hands. The small room has a wabi sabi rustic feel to it.

"Why did you want to train with the Yamabushi? This seems very odd for a foreigner," he says, with radiant eyes. I am trying to stay calm and not lose my composure, because I am sitting alone with a *Living Buddha*.

"I tried Zen for many years and found sitting difficult," I tell him. "A climbing friend told me about the Yamabushi, how they climb in the mountains, and live deep in nature. It sounded perfect to me, so I came to Japan to see for myself." I struggle to express myself in Japanese.

"There are many paths up a mountain," he says. A monk enters the room and I am told it was time to leave. In parting, I bow deeply and bring my hands to my forehead as a sign of respect. The Dai Ajari simply smiles, with his long teeth and bushy eyebrows. Walking away along the mountain pathway, I feel the calm of my encounter with the Dai Ajari settling into my chest. It has been a strange, long journey.

IV

It is 1:30 a.m., and I am waiting in the dark for a monk who has recently embarked on the thousand-day marathon around Mount Hiei, the kaihogyo. The harvest moon illuminates segments of the forest with soft beams of light, and the atmosphere is otherworldly. I think about the kami spirits that might be lurking around me. I inhale the smell of thick moss and dead leaves. I am startled when the marathon monk approaches; he is like a fast-moving white apparition. In Buddhism, white is the color of death. The monk wears it to remind himself that his journey will take him to the limits of life itself and possibly beyond. This monk has set out to walk one thousand marathons around this mountain, which is a mandala, and to practice self-reflection intently amid the undefiled stones, trees, streams and vegetation. He wants to lose himself in the great body of the Supreme Buddha. I want to join him in the beyond.

"To live each day as if it were your entire life," I whisper to my inner self.

When the monk passes me, a chill runs up my spine. His stride is fast and has a certain unique rhythm to it. He is steady, eyes focused 100 feet ahead. I notice that his head is level, shoulders relaxed, back straight, and his nose and navel are aligned. He reminds me of the Lung-gom-pa runners of Tibet. The marathon monk wears hemp sandals, a long straw hat that seems like a balance, and he carries a tall staff that slides easily through his fingers. He is a well-oiled machine and I feel like he doesn't even notice my appearance. I am a ghost to him and he is a ghost to me: we are both hungry ghosts, yet he has embarked and I have not. I step out behind him and quickly find myself nearly running to keep up. After twenty minutes I give up and sit down to recover my breath and sulk. I feel as if I know the path, have it charted out, yet I just can't let myself fully embark on the journey. I moan in angst and ask the kami spirits for help.

The next morning, I am mentally prepared to follow the marathon monk around the mountain. I have a belly full of carbs, eight hours of sleep under my belt, and a flaming ego. It is soupy wet with fog, and the path is blocked with rope-thick spiderwebs. The monk appears, as if he were swimming through the wetness of the forest. I hear the tapping of his staff against the ground as he approaches and my heart races. I remind myself to calm down and remember that I am not running the 100-yard dash.

As if levitating, the white apparition floats by and leaves me standing dumbfounded. Was I dreaming that the monk had passed by? I begin to run down the path until I catch up to him: he is bowing in front of a stone statue of Fudo-Myo-o, one of his many ceremonial stops along the Way. With my chest heaving, I slow my pace and walk past the monk, who surprisingly, doesn't seem to mind my presence. Either that, or he has no idea that I am there. I wonder if he is in some altered reality. I have read that within seventy days of walking the *kaihogyo*, the monks develop a remarkable awareness of life and special powers of perception; they can hear incense ashes falling from distant temples and smell miso soup simmering in Kyoto.

After completing the 700th day of the marathon, the monk-gyoja faces his most difficult feat. He will have to survive nine days without food, water, sleep, rest, or light (sight would prove to be the most difficult of the senses to go without). This period is called the doiri. Several weeks prior to this ordeal, the monks begin to restrict their food intake. When the doiri begins they start to chant mantras over and over. There are attendant monks who rotate duty to keep the *gyoja* awake and to help him take his one trip a day to a well to wash out his mouth without drinking. It is said that they absorb the moisture from rain and dew into their skin for nourishment. The doira is meant to help the gyoja come face to face with death. By day five they will show many symptoms of being dead and they will experience a genuine feeling of transparency: their body is now the complete realm of good, bad, and neutral.

At the end of the running, the monk has become "at one with the mountain," flying along a path that is free of obstruction. The joy of the practice has been discovered and all things are made new each day. The plants, the sky and stars, the stones and the trees have become the monk's trusted companions. He can use the clouds to predict weather, the direction of the wind, and the smell of the air; he knows when the birds will begin to sing; and he takes absolute pleasure in the sunrises and the moonsets, poised in the center of creation. Yet, the practice has just begun.

The *doiri* becomes the turning-away point for my ambitions to become a Dai Ajari or a *Living Buddha*. I tell myself that there is nothing wrong with being an average guy who occasionally dabbles in the extreme, without having to kill myself for enlightenment. It has been reported that the *doiri* was once ten days long, but almost all of the monks died, so it was reduced to nine days. It was too dangerous to conduct in the summer because the monk's bodies rotted internally from overheating and lack of water. I decide that it is time to leave Mount Hiei and resume my life in Canada. It is not easy to be a holy man on this mountaintop. Since 1885, there have been forty-six monks who have completed the marathon, and gained the status *of Daigyoman Ajari*

"Saintly Master of the Highest Practice." I will not be one of them.

Along the Way I have learned much from my experiences with the Yamabushi, the Ochudo Route on Mount Fuji, my time with the *Living Buddha*, and walking with the marathon monks of Mount Hiei. I have learned that whatever you do with your walking, you only cheat yourself by pushing, pressing, and competing. There are no standards and no possible victories except the joy you are living while dancing your walk. I am truly dancing and celebrating life when I walk. My spirit is not separate from my body any more than the water is separate from the stream. Wa! I am whirling and swirling along my Way.

Questions and Answers

1. What compels you to walk?

I wander to wonder. Walking for me is a meditative process and one I do daily: I began walking with my grandmother when I was young, walked around Europe and Canada with my father later on, and I have never stopped walking. What could be better than walking a ridgeline in the mountains, through an old-growth forest or along a deserted white sand beach? Naturally, I walk for exercise and to keep my dog Seppe happy and fit. For me, the greatest benefit of walking is the ability it gives me to meditate on the landscape around me and to get in tune with my environment. To admire the flowers, listen to the birds sing, smell the fresh stream, and feel the earth under my feet are simple joys for me. I wander to wonder, and to feel my inner joy.

2. Do you experience instances while you are walking when your mind in somewhere off the trail and on its own journey?

Walking and writing go hand in hand for me: as I walk I compose and muse. Once I have developed my storyline for a book or story that I am writing, my mind begins to conceptualize the scenes, as if working from a screenplay. Suddenly, the light will shift, a bird will fly by, or my dog will jerk me back to the setting of the actual walk. So walking is a creative process for me. At other times I walk to work through the problem of the day, or simply to feel the landscape around me in a meditative way.

3. How do you manage to stay physically and emotionally healthy during long and arduous journeys?

Normally I do some sort of exercise on a daily basis before my journeys. There are rainy days when I like to go to the gym and spend an hour on the elliptical, yet most days I enjoy long walks with my wife Siffy and my dog Seppe. We are a walking family! If I am going on an expedition-like journey, I up the ante in the exercise department, as well as prepare myself mentally. I really like to challenge myself and train for mental toughness. For instance, one time while I was living in the Aleutian Islands, I decided to climb Mount Ballyhoo for thirty straight days. I started this project on January 1st, in the middle of the winter. Each morning I would wake up and quickly pull the shades back to check on the weather; 90 percent of the time it was horrific, with gusting winds and wet snow. On days like that, it is easy to roll back into a warm bed, but if you stick to your plan, a certain resolve and toughness is developed that will help you later on when the going gets truly tough. Another time, while preparing for a climbing trip into the Selkirk Mountains with the legendary guide, Reudi Beglinger, I decided to wake each morning at 3 a.m. in the dark and run 10 kilometers for a month. A few times I had to run when I was drunk: I often fell over geese along the Bow River, yet I never thought of quitting. I am a firm believer in enjoying a bottle of red wine every day—for the heart—with a chaser of water.

4. Please share a high and a low period that you experienced during your walkabouts.

There is no doubt that I have experienced many low points in my walkabouts around the world. I have frozen my toes in a blizzard, crossing the Thorong La Pass near Annapurna; suffered life-threatening amoebic dysentery in Gangtok; malaria in Sumatra; been thrown into a jail in Mali; and suffered a terrifying car jacking on the outskirts of Nairobi. Yet, if I had to choose one incident that seemed to be the lowest point in my travels, it would have to be in the Amazon rainforest. I am Norwegian; I grew up in northern Minnesota; and I love winter. Enough said.

I had started my journey in the Bolivian town of Rurrenabaque, along the Beni River, with a Quechan Indian as my guide. We traveled light and fast, walking through the canopy jungle and across the Madidi National Park. When possible, we built rafts to float the rivers. My objective was to reach the Amazon. It was extremely difficult for me to travel in the heat of the jungle: my sweat was like honey for every living insect and stinging assailant.

After a week of slogging through the thick canopy jungle paranoia set in, and I became convinced that my partner was out to kill me, or abandon me right there in an environment where I could not survive. I hung on as best I could, considering my emotional and mental state of being. One day we discovered a utopian-like village from the Stone-Age. The children hunted birds with sling shots and stones, villagers lived in thatched huts and wore orchids in their hair, nudity was the norm. On our second night in the village, I ingested an herbal concoction with the chief and suffered through a hellish nightmare, filled with black jaguars and frightening aeronautical feats, for twelve hours.

Rattled to my core, I helped my partner build a raft and we set sail to find the Mamore River and the Amazon. To this day, I am not sure what I was inflicted with, yet I often think it was a bad case of heat stroke as my ankles, joints, and lips swelled to three times their normal size. There was no help for this deep in the jungle. We survived on monkey meat cooked over the fire, giant ant eaters, speared fish, and wild turkey-looking creatures. As we floated slowly down the river I began to unravel. Then the hallucinations set in and my world became one big kaleidoscope: time became meaningless and worthless. I seem to have lost a week of my life and have no recollection of returning to Rurrenabaque, regaining my health, or finding reality again. A week was simply lost.

In my forty years of travel there have been so many high points that it is very hard to single one out. Often my mind drifts back to the times I followed the caribou migration across the tundra in the Yukon, or walked along a high dune in the Sahara, or hiked up to a sacred temple in Japan, or up the slopes of Mount Etna in Sicily. I have been very fortunate to be able to travel throughout the world, and often feel like I am just getting started. There is one moment in time that stands out, though. After reuniting with my wife Siffy after twenty-five years apart, we embarked on a series of adventures around the world to celebrate our love. Soon after reuniting, we ventured into the Tsum Valley in Nepal on a quest to find our own paradise. During our long and fantastic trek up the valley, we finally climbed the final ascent to the Mu Gompa monastery. Surrounded by the soaring peaks of the Himalayas, a stone's throw away from Tibet, we entered a Tibetan sacred world, a beyul, or Shangri-La if you will. There, in burgundy robes, the young initiates and wizened old monks greeted us with warmth and wisdom. In Mu Gompa I felt like I was shedding an old skin and embracing the infinite horizon of my life's journey. I knew at that moment that I was truly living the life I imagined as a young boy when I dreamt of travels to exotic lands, love, and the sense that I too belonged in the universe.

5. Have you experienced an important Encounter that somehow changed the direction of your journey?

In 2005 I wrote a book entitled, *Encounters with Remarkable People and Extreme Landscapes*. This book was a celebration of a philosophy that assumes that a single encounter can change the direction of one's entire life. I believe that we have to be aware and ready for those encounters. We must listen, watch, and be open to all possibilities despite our innate and debilitating prejudices. We have to be prepared for the encounter! I have had many such encounters over the years.

When I was thirteen I went to the public library and noticed a book on the shelf with a bright orange rising sun on the cover. It was called *On the Road*. I read the book that night and hit the road the next morning, hell-bent on hitchhiking to Mexico. That book had lit a fire within me that told me I was meant to travel and to experience the world.

During my second year at the University of Minnesota, I was befriended by the writer/artist, Pierre Delattre. Pierre taught me to see the extraordinary in the ordinary and to believe in the magical and mystical. He gave me the confidence to embark on the journey I had dreamed of with joy and celebration, to swirl and whirl my way through life.

Years later, after finishing college, I traveled around the world and eventually reached Nepal and the Himalayas. Seeing these majestic mountains for the first time enflamed within me a lifelong passion for mountain landscapes and the natural world.

Photograph by Siffy Torkildson.

Biography

Peripatetic traveler, Rob "Tor" Torkildson, is a lifelong seeker and explorer who has worked and lived around the world for the last thirty years. Torkildson has tramped through the Amazon, over the Himalayas, and across the Sahara in his quest to experience sacred landscapes in more than 120 countries. He has worked as a diver, a commercial fisherman, a ship's navigator, a customs and immigration expert, a speaker for the World Explorers Bureau, a writer and publisher, a fixer in Africa, and as a vintner. Torkildson has published three travel memoirs, a novella, and articles in such magazines as the *Kyoto Journal*, *Beat Scene*, *Ripcord Adventure Journal*, *Canadian Mountain Journal*, and *Travelers Tales*. Torkildson walks because he wonders, and despite having a university education, believes his true education has been "On the Road."

"Swirl with the swirl and whirl with the whirl and no bones shall break."

Parade in Mahalevona, Madagascar. *Photograph by Siffy Torkildson.*

Siffy Torkildson

Wandering re-establishes the original harmony that once existed between humans and the universe.
~Anatole France.

A Night time *Tonga Tongotra*

Daylight is passing into the nightscape that I so love. I feel the coolness of the rainforest's transition from the balmy day to the resounding sounds of the night. Towering rosewood and ebony trees, over fifty varieties of endemic palm, occasional coffee bushes, dangling vines, and the lush green world fade as daylight gives way to twilight. I inhale the scent of vanilla and cloves as we approach a small village. I am exhilarated to be in this tropical environment.

Frogs croak, birds call, and stars slowly begin to glitter, as my toes squish in the mud. I am trekking barefoot along the rice paddies on my way north to the border of Masoala National Park in Madagascar. Masoala holds over fifty percent of the island's biodiversity and two percent of the entire world's, including the endangered red-ruffed lemur, tomato frog, tenrec, fossa, serpent eagle, and boa, as well as many varieties of chameleons and butterflies.

Two Malagasy park employees, three local porters, and an American environmental scientist accompany me. We have hiked for several hours and will settle in Fizon, staying with villagers and helping with a three-day tree nursery training workshop. Cyclone Huda decimated the forest in 2000, and illegal logging of endangered rosewood, as well as *tavy* (slash and burn) had already contributed to deforestation.

As the landscape darkens, the researcher gets out her flashlight so she can see the trail. I walk back further, so the beam doesn't ruin my night vision, as the silhouette of a traveler's palm leads the way. I have been an avid night walker since I was young.

During trips to the north woods of Minnesota, and spring break trips to Florida as a child, my parents would take my family on long walks together. My younger siblings became tired, hungry or bored, while I longed to keep going. Once I was old enough, I walked alone, or with my parents, and have been walking ever since.

As a teenager, I went raccoon hunting with my father. My dad would ask a farmer's permission to hunt on his land. We would arrive at dusk, and then my dad would let the hounds out to tree the raccoons. We tramped through corn fields and forests, listening for the dogs' bays. The stars shone brightly over the fields, and we did not use flashlights until we reached a raccoon that had been treed. We often stopped to look up at the Milky Way. Walking in the dark, lying on the ground beside a cornfield and looking at the sky enhanced my budding interest in astronomy and star gazing.

As I walk through the rice paddies, I wonder why we have become afraid of darkness. The Milky Way is no longer visible in cities, where a majority of people live, and it somehow feels wrong to me that we have come to rely on flashlights to find our way in the dark. Many of the places I knew as a child are now lit up and the night sky is washed out. We are losing our universal night sky heritage that inspired all cultures to think about our place in the universe and dream about time and space.

When I look up at the Milky Way and the darkness in remote Madagascar, the stars seem so near that I feel as if I could embrace them. I'm brought closer to the infinite, and a sense of awe. I am merely a speck in this universe. The light pollution spreading around the world makes us lose touch with this universal marvel. Not only are we losing this sense of reverence that has fueled art and the sciences through the ages, but it has also been shown by scientists that bright lights cause cancer in humans, and confuse the internal clocks of migrating birds and animals.

I am sure that the Malagasy must have their own constellations, and myths in regard to the ancestors, but my Malagasy language skills are not advanced enough to ask about them. I assume that the elephant bird (a giant ostrich-like bird, 10 meters tall) which became extinct hundreds of years ago, must be in the sky, as well as a lemur, endemic to Madagascar. Many Malagasy still practice ancestral worship, which is thought to be a hold-over from the migration of the first humans to Madagascar, from Indonesia and Malaysia, around 600 AD. An important ritual is the "turning of the bones" ceremony (*famadihana*), when they periodically open tombs and re-wrap the bones in fresh *lambas* (cloth).

I point out Scorpio and the Southern Cross to my Malagasy companions. I attempt to tell them about the Greek constellation myths. "Orion, the esteemed hunter, was a great hero, but his ego undid him. He bragged about how he was going to kill all the animals on earth. Gaia, the earth goddess, did not take kindly to this idea. She sent a scorpion to kill him. Zeus, king of the gods, then put Orion on the opposite side of the heavens from Scorpio so they wouldn't fight for eternity."

One Western constellation I am sure they can relate to is the chameleon. Madagascar has over half of the world's species of chameleons, on an island the size of California. The Malagasy usually see them before foreigners do, and many people are afraid of them, despite the fact they move very slowly. Chameleons are associated with bad luck, since their eyes can look in different directions at the same time—one looks forward into the future, and one looks backward into the past. Their ability to change colors adds to their mystery.

When I show the Malagasy the stars through my binoculars, which they call *maso-lavtra* (faraway eyes) they exclaim, "Wow! So many stars!" That is how I feel,—seeing the stars with my unaided eye on this island, far away from bright lights.

The Malagasy don't use flashlights. They walk at night and their eyes adjust to the darkness; but in this region they don't have electricity, which is detrimental to night vision. When coming from a bright environment, it takes twenty minutes for one's eyes to adapt to the dark, and as dusk approaches, our eyes adjust to the dimming light.

Roads for vehicles have not yet penetrated this remote, rugged mountain area, and people think nothing of traveling by foot, wearing flip-flops or going barefoot for several days in order to visit relatives, work, or shop. The women carry things on top of their heads, while the men bear loads across their shoulders. They go for miles like this.

Malagasy travelers stop for the night and locals come outside after dark to socialize and amble up and down the village streets: they recognize each other and are not afraid of the dark. A common pick-up line is, "Do you want to go for a *tonga tongatra* (walk) with me?"

When I first moved to Madagascar, I wore hiking boots, or Tevas. I soon learned, by watching other Westerners, and by experience, that it is grueling to walk wearing boots. During the rainy season my boots would get sucked into the mud, and with the damp climate, blisters and other foot issues did not heal within the confines of my boots. My Tevas were also swallowed by mud, and it was a challenge to pull my feet out of the many deep, muddy puddles. I learned from the villagers that the best shoes to wear were flip-flops. Not only are they easy to walk in, but when I had to walk across mud, they were easy to take off and carry, as the Malagasy did. I wore my flip-flops in the villages to avoid getting the sand fleas that lay eggs around toe-nails. My neighbors helped me inspect my feet and take out any egg sacs. If left there, the sacs cause great pain and can lead to infection and even the loss of toenails.

As my group walks after dark, a few fireflies blink over the rice paddies. I look up at the southern stars and the familiar northern constellations, all "upside down." Beneath the sparkling sky, the dark forest of majestic rosewood, traveler palms, ferns, and other endemic tropical vegetation stands out even in the dark. Boulders along the stream become numerous, and the rapids cascade in the dark.

We arrive at our destination—a village of palm-leaf huts—where we eat a dinner of rice and fish, play dominoes, and practice the Malagasy language with the curious village children. We sleep in a local family's hut. I dream of a mouse lemur I had seen once during another night trek, staring at me with his big moon-yellow eyes.

> "The sun has barely left its bath.
> And again streams sea water
> From the gates of heaven—
> Until washing away the very moon
> In its fountains."
>
> ~John-Joseph Rabearivelo
> (famous Malagasy poet)

Questions and Answers

1. What compels you to walk?

Curiosity, relaxation, time to think, exercise, and being in nature compel me to walk. I like to see places up-close, on a small scale. Driving, or even riding on a bicycle, one misses so much. When walking, I can stop and check out a new plant, or look at the view, or sit in silence and experience the moment. I am not rushed. Even repeating the same route over and over, I often see something different on each outing. Walking calms me and clears my head. When I have had difficult times in my life, or when I am trying to make a big decision, walking helps me to relax and to analyze my problems and possibilities. Scientific studies have shown that it is good for your health to be in nature and to walk. As Richard Louv wrote in *Last Child in the Woods,* "The woods were my Ritalin, Nature calmed me, focused me, and yet excited my senses." Even large cities offer walking trails. When I lived in Minneapolis and in Las Vegas, I had my favorite trails where I admired plants and wildlife, from an oak tree I stopped to hug, to three-foot-long snapping turtles migrating across the route, to a bald eagle, and mallards in abundance in Minneapolis. Coyotes, road-runners, hares, and the scent of creosote bushes after a rainstorm in Las Vegas filled my walks on the wash trails.

2. Do you experience instances while you are walking when your mind is somewhere off the trail and on its own journey?

Having attempted to meditate with the Quakers, in Kwan Um Korean Zen, and Qigong, I have learned about the "monkey mind" and how to see my thoughts, recognize them, and let them pass. Although I have studied this, I still have a hard time with it. I think about problems to solve, things that are not important, the past, the future: yet I strive to live in the moment and notice things as I walk. I fade in and out of the present. I sometimes chant a mantra, such as *Om Mani Padme Hum*, to help me focus, especially if I am on a difficult slog, or the mantra *Kwan Seum Bosal* for friends and family in need of prayer.

3. How do you manage to stay physically and emotionally healthy during long and arduous journeys?

I try to stay positive and not let negative thoughts drag me down: I watch myself and bring myself back to positive thoughts if I start to go to a dark place. I observe the observer. I eat plenty of vegetables, and I always drink a lot of water. For the past fifteen years, I have started every day with a minimum of ten minutes of Spring Forest Qigong meditation. It is a Chinese healing art used to help oneself as well as others. Since I have practiced qigong, I rarely get head colds or coughs, which I was once prone to. I have also developed a stretching routine taken mostly from my former martial arts school, American Kung Fu, that I do most days.

4. Please share a high and a low period that you experienced during your walkabouts.

I have had many high points, often on solo backpack trips, from the frog that croaked in front of me while I meditated in the upper peninsula of Michigan, to the out-of-place birch forest in the dry, remote Toiyabe mountains of Nevada, to the coyotes howling in the Badlands of South Dakota, and the northern lights and timber wolves calling in northern Minnesota.

Other high points include taking my father on his first backpacking trip when he was 71 years old; and with both of my parents, the first time camping in the bush for my mother, while canoeing in the Boundary Water Canoe Area of Minnesota a couple of years later. Our first year canoeing it rained the entire time. I had chosen the longest portages possible, and we mostly carried our canoe on the muddy, wet trails. On these trips they always smiled and laughed: nothing deterred them. It was a great bonding experience.

But my trek to the Tsum Valley of Nepal, with a man I had recently reconnected with after 25 years apart (my husband Tor) was my highest point. We walked for over two weeks, slowly making our way from the tropical zone to the high Himalayan Mountains, with Mount Ganesh and Manaslu towering above the valleys. We stayed with villagers, and our guide taught us about the local culture, legends, and environment.

As for a low point: in Madagascar, I was racked with dysentery just as I arrived at the rainforest national park island, Nosy Manga Be. Despite being sick, I wanted to see the island. I didn't tell my local guide that I was ill, and I tried not to look as miserable as I felt. The warm tropical environment cheered me up, as did the chameleons, leaf-tailed gecko, blue coua bird, lemurs and other wildlife and plants, such as the pink mucuba flowers, that my smiling guide pointed out. At the beach, he showed me 400-year-old carvings in the rocks, created by Dutch pirates. I was bundled up in all my layers, despite the 90 degree Fahrenheit day. I lay in the sun on the beach warming up and felt better before walking on into the thick, moist forest.

5. Have you experienced an important Encounter that somehow changed the direction of your journey?

Yes. He was tall, good-looking and well-traveled, and he was my coworker in the supermarket at Glacier National Park during a summer I spent there between college semesters. He arrived mid-season to replace an employee who had left early. He was a wanderer with a bit of a bad-boy James Dean image. He was worldly, with a smooth voice, and he was full of adventure stories, including some about his latest travels—in the Himalayan mountains of Nepal. I was enthralled. One day that summer, we went hiking together. We borrowed a car from a friend and headed to the trailhead of Otokomi Lake, a twenty-two mile round-trip hike. We walked in silence, me with a daypack and a heart full of enthusiasm, he with a Nepalese bag strapped across one shoulder and wearing a jean jacket. At the lake, surrounded by steep mountains with snow patches still left over from winter, we ate our lunch. "Let's try to reach the top of that ridge!" I exclaimed. We walked highly tuned to our environment, as we were in grizzly country. We both yearned to keep climbing, yet we had to turn around, as I had to work the evening shift. We went our separate ways at the end of the summer, and we didn't see each other for 25 years. I googled him one day, discovered he had written a book called *Encounters with Remarkable People and Extreme Landscapes*, and I emailed him out of the blue. He responded right away, and three years later we were married. This walking encounter in Glacier National Park had never left my psyche, but I never imagined I would be married to a man I briefly hiked with 30 years ago, and that one day I would be planning to walk around the world with him.

"What is life, if always in the same deadly routine?"
~Annie Smith Peck, explorer, and author of
A Search for the Apex of South American

"It is above all by the imagination that we achieve perception and compassion and hope."
~Ursula K. LeGuin.

Siffy viewing a total eclipse of the sun with solar-filtered binoculars. *Photograph by Tor Torkildson.*

Biography

Siffy (Caroline) Torkildson is a geographer, cartographer, life-long star gazer, author, and book designer for Sacred World Explorations. She has served in the U.S. Peace Corps in Madagascar, worked at two science museums, a Canadian travel map company, as a researcher for the U.S. Forest Service and the U.S. Environmental Protection Agency, and has taught an introduction to the history of women explorers at Southern Oregon College, as well as astronomy at the Eisenhower Observatory in Minnesota. She has published a travel guide-book and a travel memoir, and is working on a book about the adventurer, Annie Smith Peck. She has published in *Ripcord Adventure Journal* and has won a *Traveler's Tales* Solas Award, and is a speaker for the World Explorers Bureau. Torkildson has B.A. and M.A. degrees in geography from Humboldt State University in California, as well as a M.S. in geographic information science from St. Mary's University of Minnesota. In her twenties she discovered backpacking in the mountains of California and the Pacific Northwest, and in her thirties she ventured out on solo multi-day wilderness trips in the Western and Midwestern United States. In her forties she started trekking overseas, from Nepal to Morocco.

Photograph by Dhawa Gyanjen Tusmba.

Dhawa Gyanjen Tsumba

Why would you not want to walk in life?

This essay was transcribed by Tor and Siffy Torkildson, based on a conversation with Dhawa Gyanjen Tsumba and Phunjo Lama.

The Avalanche

I was leading a trek into Upper Tsum Valley near Prangkarpo, Nepal, with a French couple, Françoise and Pierre Fay-Chaterlard, when the world started sliding and crashing around us. We were experiencing the Great Earthquake of 2015. Suddenly, my clients' lives were in danger, as was my own. Rocks, mud, and trees came crashing down the mountain around us. Time seemed to stop, and my life passed before me. The French woman began to cry uncontrollably. What was I to do? For a split second, I thought of running away to save my life; I thought about my children, and my wife Phunjo who was currently climbing Mount Everest. What about my friends, family, and the community that depended on me? No! What about my responsibility to my clients?

There were loud and thunderous noises all around us. The world kept sliding beneath our feet. As a Buddhist, isn't saving another life the best karma one can obtain? The woman was crying and slumped over a rock. But…my family, my life? The French man began to cry. It was a desperate situation, and I needed to react, one way or another.

I ran to the woman and lifted her over my shoulder, then dashed for shelter under a rock overhang. The couple were crying as rocks and dirt kept falling past us. I am a man of the mountains, trained in avalanche and earthquake safety, and I know that an aftershock is likely to come soon. My instincts told me to climb as high as possible. I felt inner strength growing inside me, a life force, the will to live.

"Follow me!" I called out to Pierre. I carried his wife as he followed me straight up the mountain. Rocks were dropping and bouncing beside us while trees toppled above our heads.

In seconds, fueled by adrenaline, we had climbed hundreds of meters. Suddenly, we were on the top of the mountain, and nothing could fall on us. A great feeling of relief and love surrounded me. We had survived.

The first village we encountered after our near escape was Chokang. It was shocking to see many of my old friends wailing as we approached; the villagers' homes and walls were all destroyed. I comforted the villagers as best I could and told them I would seek help for them. When we finally reached my village, Burji, I found my house was still standing beneath Milarepa's cave. Twenty-six trekkers from nine different nations were stranded with a Nepalese guide and porters. I realized that my valley had suffered greatly, and the rebuilding would take a long time and much effort. The real journey began as I eventually walked out of the devastated Tsum Valley to seek help from the outside world.

Questions and Answers

1. What compels you to walk?

We have no choice; we have to walk to get to school, to buy supplies, or for work. We walk many miles every day just to survive. Also, we must walk if we want to see the world! Hauling wood and taking care of our yaks keeps us very healthy and makes us feel good and satisfied with life. Walking is spiritual and a way to communicate with the natural world around us. My mother walked to meditate. Phunjo, my wife, climbs mountains to set an example for the young girls in Tsum Valley and Nepal. She thinks that it is better to show the girls by doing, instead of just talking. Less talk, more action. She is walking for freedom and the equality of women. Why not walk?

2. Do you experience instances while you are walking when your mind is somewhere off the trail and on its own journey?

Phunjo and I try to stay in the present; this is the most important thing. I try to show love and compassion at all times and to all people and sentient beings. Also, I try not to make the same mistakes twice, so I often think about that while walking.

3. How do you manage to stay physically and emotionally healthy during long and arduous journeys?

We are social animals and we need to move. Walking keeps us healthy. Phunjo and I eat healthy organic food and fresh water. When we have problems we must share them with others to get relief from the head and heart. Being a lonely person is not good for our health. Sharing and listening are very important.

4. Please share a high and a low period that you experienced during your walkabouts.

The best part of walking for me is connecting with my trekking clients as we move along the path and high into the mountains. My clients bring the world to me and teach me many things. I also teach them about our life, spirituality, and deep respect for the natural world. We exchange knowledge and eventually become like a family.

The worst situation was what I described in the story I've just told you. I had never had an accident in 15 years of guiding and that time was very close. I ended up helping the couple, and we survived. I am glad I wasn't selfish in the end.

5. Have you experienced an important Encounter that somehow changed the direction of your journey?

My special encounters were with my two fathers and my mother. My one father taught me to have kindness for all animals. My second father taught me how to interact with others and how to be a social person. My mother instilled in me love and compassion.

Dhawa in Nepal and Phunjo on the summit of Denali. *Photographs courtesy of Dhawa Gyanjen Tsumba.*

Biography

Dhawa Gyanjen Tsumba and Phunjo Lama are from the sacred (beyul) Tsum Valley, Nepal. Dhawa is a mountain trekking guide, lodge owner, relief organizer, and photographer. His wife, Phunjo, is the first female long liner (helicopter) aerial rescuer in Nepal and recently summited Mount Denali, Alaska, and Cho Oyo (8,188 meters) Nepal solo and with no supplemental oxygen. Phunjo has dedicated her life to inspiring and helping the young women of Nepal.

Photographs by Dhawa Gyanjen Tsumba.

Photographs by Dhawa Gyanjen Tsumba.

Photographs by Dhawa Gyanjen Tsumba.

Photograph by Dhawa Gyanjen Tsumba.

Dhawa and musician. *Photograph by Tor Torkildson.*

Dhawa and Phunjo.
Photographs courtesy of Dhawa Gyanjen Tsumba.

"As you begin to Walk on the Way. The Way appears."
~Rumi

Angela Maxwell

To Cross the River Woman

I sat defeated and disappointed on the edge of a protruding rock, facing a mighty skeleton of trees and boulders that was once a bridge; a bridge that was my link to continuing across the central steppes of Mongolia. This bridge was essential to cross a sixty-foot-wide river. The cold wind curled around my neck and ankles as I sat there, looking down over the strong current dancing around fallen logs.

When I first outlined my route through Mongolia, I was excited to follow horse tracks and corrugated dirt roads through the dense mountains. As the sun melted the snow and evaporated the puddles, I thought it must get easier from here on out, since nothing could be more difficult than pulling one hundred pounds on two bicycle wheels through snow and ice. But there I was, pulling a hundred pounds through sand.

What appears as a road on a map of Mongolia, in reality is a series of sand paths that may or may not be heading in the same direction. There can be up to ten different paths within a few feet of each other, where eight of them will join back together while two may verge off to a settlement.

At the top of the mountain ridge, a nomadic woman cocooned in a purple traditional Mongolian robe and a yellow headscarf, which flickered gently in the breeze, stood steadily still with a staff in hand amongst her flock of goats. As I panted, warm tufts of vapor from the exertion to get up the ridge, a shape took form on her face. Her smile was a warm light in the cold.

I slowly made my way toward her and noticed her hand was stretched out in my direction. Her eyes spoke to me with no words. I placed my palm in hers, and her warm fingers firmly grabbed mine. She began rubbing my fingers as if starting a fire. It felt harsh and jarring at first, but her kindness eased my clenched and cold body. Then her finger pointed in the direction of her ger (a Mongolian yurt). I saw smoke bursting from the top, and the thought of warming myself by the stove brought euphoria to my mind and body.

Inside her home, she began boiling water in a large iron bowl. This fit perfectly into the top of the stove. Then she placed assorted biscuits and a bowl of yak yogurt in front of me. I was pleasantly surprised to find it all very tasty and nourishing. Then she poured us both a cup of herbal tea, infused with yak milk. We sat in the warm silence on the floor next to the stove. I warmed my hands near the wood flames and occasionally we smiled at each other. Even if we could speak the same language, I felt that we would have been women of few words together, sharing kindness and recognition through our presence.

I walked with her out to the barn where she pointed at a small wooden stool for me to carry. She lifted the heavy log that served as the gate, which led to a round yak enclosure, and closed the gate behind us. The woman pointed to a calf that was nursing from its mother and then to another enclosure that was small but empty. I had only a small handful of experiences on farms but my guess was that she needed to put the calf in the enclosure to keep it from feeding. She patted the wooden gate to the empty enclosure and I held it open as I watched her use her hips to shove the calf aside and then through the gate.

She took the stool I had carried and placed it next to the mother yak. Then she pointed for me to sit. She kneeled down, pushed the long yak hair aside and showed me how to milk the mother. It took several tries for me to get the rhythm, and it was oddly comforting as she proceeded to lean against the wood posts and nod at me when she heard the strong bursts of milk hitting the tin bucket. Back at her ger, the woman poured the warm milk into a plastic bottle and handed it to me.

I could tell I only had three hours of sunlight left, so I packed the milk, offered my gratitude and stepped outside and headed toward my cart. Calmly, but with enthusiasm, she shook her head and crossed her arms in an X shape in front of her body. I knew this meant NO but I was confused at what this related to. She pointed in the downhill direction I was heading and kept shaking her head.

"But I must walk. I'm sorry I don't understand. Is there danger?" I mouthed my concern in English even though I knew she didn't understand my words.

She sighed, shook her head and patted my shoulder as she gave up on our charades.

I smiled through my confusion and walked down the mountain toward the tree line, and the water. My belly was warm and my heart full of magic.

It felt so magical to have spent the afternoon with a beautiful and strong elderly woman who had appeared as if she were waiting for me. I wondered if she was real, or if my imagination and longing for feminine interaction had conjured such a dream-like experience. I wondered, if I went back, would there be anything there at all on that mountaintop?

I caught a glimpse of the stone and wood that lay half-buried by the riverbank. I then understood her unspoken words; no bridge. I sat momentarily in disbelief. But that soon turned to curiosity and determination. There must be a way to cross. Watching the river dive, twirl and twist, I sat on the edge of the bridge's corpse and listened. I listened with my eyes and ears. I sat until my nose was numb. The sun was setting, and the freezing wind was catching speed. I decided to set up camp. A warm meal would refresh my body and mind.

I woke before sunrise and made a cup of coffee. I took my spot amongst the ruins again and watched the sun wake the hills and warm the birds. I would try to cross the river on foot.

For a little soul-confidence, I played Elle King's "Ain't Gonna Drown," a few times before I packed up camp. I placed my most important things in the three waterproof bags. I looked in both directions to find the slimmest width possible to cross. About a half kilometer south was a slender section with a sandy island in the middle. This island could serve as a halfway point.

The challenge of crossing the river included a strong current, unconfirmed depths, freezing temperatures and my own lack of experience. But even if I crossed successfully the first time, I'd have to do it four more times.

My cart would have to be folded, tied and carried overhead along with my gear in separate bags. I wasn't sure this would work but I had to give it a try. It was either walk a week south along the river to the next possible bridge, or cross it here and now.

After a few deep breaths, some procrastination, and a couple more cups of coffee, I began stripping. The wind licked my skin as I stood in my underwear and bra. I needed all my clothes dry, and would layer up as quickly as possible once I got to the other side. Although I had no experience with hypothermia, I knew it was a possibility, as was drowning.

I grabbed the smallest and lightest river bag, faced the current sideways and slowly crept in. There were mostly small rocks under my feet, making it difficult to gain a good grip. The water was cruelly frigid and I let out a loud howl followed by a maniacal laugh. I thought it was a risky idea from my perch but with my flesh dancing in the body of the river, I was coming to terms with just how dangerous this was.

As I continued my grapevine into the river's heart, the water crawled mid-thigh in a seductive current. I focused on keeping my knees bent and every step meant finding a new balance point. Steady, steady, I repeated like a mantra. I could see the sandy island in a sensual closeness; perhaps another twenty steps and I'd land my body on the solid form.

My right foot led the way and on my next step I felt the ground sharply plummet down. The realization came after I stepped and found no foothold. I fumbled forwards, face-planting into the icy water. My body followed and I gripped my bag as the current carried me downstream.

The sound in my ears, like the ocean in a storm, captivated my senses and it was as if there was no thought or reaction. I was frozen and terrified. I was only aware enough to know that I had to grab something. I was floating toward the logs that had fallen from the bridge into the water. I didn't have to try to swim to them; I was being catapulted right at them. A new fear hit me; I could be crushed at this speed.

Throughout my journey I have found that every day there is a little miracle. A perfection of timing that reminds me that I am not alone. I cannot tell for sure but I believe I had time for a smile to cross my face as I saw that my body was being carried towards a log pile that branched out from the riverbank. It was a dark mass that looked as if its arms were reaching out to catch me.

I bent my knees into my chest, reached out with my right arm and quickly grabbed hold of a thick branch. I threw my bag on top and began climbing my way up, using both arms and legs.

I grabbed my bag and cuddled it like a child. I laid in a fetus position for several minutes, listening to the pounding in my ears and chest. I opened my eyes and stared across at the other side of the river. I would not be setting foot in that valley. The cold of my body slowly came to my consciousness. I got dressed and walked upriver to my gear.

I believe in something more purposeful and powerful than luck, but it's easy to say I was lucky to have landed on the same side as where I started and that I was lucky to leave the river unharmed.

Water has an inherent ferocity and kindness; it demands to be respected, for although it nourishes life, it can also take it away from those who underestimate its power. When I look back on the experience, I am aware that I could have easily become a memory: lost bones in the middle of Mongolia.

The day before I crossed the river, a woman had embraced me and invited me into her home with kindness and generosity. The day I tried to cross the river, it saw me safely but roughly to shore, reminding me that Mother Nature cannot be shaped or conquered. I packed my belongings and humbled heart and began my walk south toward the next bridge.

The Furry side of Things

I remember every face and personality I've encountered on this journey. The places I've slept are harder to remember; the most beautiful and the most frightening become the easiest to recall. For example, in northern Turkey, the night I heard a woman's scream cut off by the sound of a gunshot. I remember the cadmium-red rust on the tin where I pitched my tent behind a gas-bottle storage unit. I remember the ferns. I remember waking before the sun and tripping over a rotting pine log as I attempted to leave as quickly as possible.

Or the day I stopped for a toasted sandwich, shocked at the price of white bread and two slices of ham and was told about a secret garden just two kilometers up the road. Behind a large hill was a field of poppies so full and fantastical that I lay down like Dorothy in Oz and fell asleep for over an hour. I awoke to a sunset that bled like watercolors. In the morning, I picked blueberries and mixed them with creamer to make a rustic smoothie.

In Georgia, I remember many camp spots. But the pups that would enter my life so effortlessly and leave too quickly saturate most of my memories. They were all so different. No dog was the same in color or personality. Yet, the one similarity they all possessed was that they were abandoned and starving for food and attention.

Before beginning my walk in Georgia, I made a deal with myself: I would not feed a dog. I would not! At least not immediately.

After walking across Mongolia with Oogi, nurturing the friendship and trust between us, only to have to leave him there, I didn't think I could do that to another dog, or to myself. The heartbreak of leaving Oogi behind in Mongolia was more difficult than anything I had encountered on this journey so far, more than the sandstorms, heat stroke, dehydration, or being physically attacked. The deepest wound was, and still is, walking away from Oogi as he ate his favorite meal, canned sardines in tomato sauce. A nomadic family was going to raise him on open fields and he would have sheep he could help muster. I walked away a salty-wet mess.

I couldn't do that again. To prevent a dog from following me, my plan of action was to eliminate the main cause for furry followers. But like most heartbreaks, there's more than one. And we survive. And for the sake of love itself, we endure it all over again.

Tamar, whom I named after a 12th century Queen of Georgia, was full grown, had a pure white mane, napped and matted on every curve of her body, with large black eyes. She came bolting out of an old railroad shelter with offense dripping from her tongue. This was the first dog I had encountered that I thought might attack. I avoided her eyes, but kept a gaze. I continued walking forward. She stepped aside but would not cease her bark for almost a kilometer. Thinking boredom would set in, and she'd head back to her shelter, I carried on. But so did she. She stayed several paces behind me all day and watched me, patiently and curiously, as I pitched my tent behind a corn field, slipped on my dress, and cooked my noodles.

She watched through the tall grass, keeping her distance but with a direct gaze on me. Before zipping the door of my tent, and a last gaze to meet her eyes, I told her, "Good night. You were a great walking companion. But please go home." Later, I realized that most canines in central Asia don't have a home. I fell asleep, hoping she'd be there in the morning.

As I sat up, scratching my head and stretching into a morning yawn, I saw tufts of white hair poking through the bottom of the vestibule.

"Good Morning."

No movement. I carefully unzipped the door, reminiscing over the previous day's engagement of sharp teeth and vocal aggression. She didn't move. I made a cup of coffee and began eating my bread. Holding true to my agreement, I still didn't offer her any food. She sat up in an erect perch with soft eyes.

As I began walking for the day, I watched her move from a few paces behind me to a few paces in front of me. She led, as if she knew where I was headed, all the way to the border of Turkey. I fed and cuddled with her, and pulled her dreadlocked hair out with my fingers to cool her, and held her back from attacking every passing vehicle and human.

In her time with me, she bit the ankle of a young boy, lunged at an elderly man, fought with a dog twice her size (and lost the battle as he pinned her and bit her nose), and never, ever, let me out of her sight. She paced the windows of the store as I perused the shelves for my instant noodles, and canned sardines for her.

She wasn't the only dog. There were up to five of us walking together. Pepper, a four-week old, rode in the shade of Athena (my cart), between my camping pot and sleeping mattress, yelped instead of barked, and the yelp made her whole body tremble in an attempt to make herself known.

I found her in a cow paddock, in the bright afternoon sun, hovering over her sibling, who had been severely injured and was slowly bleeding to death. It is common for female dogs to be killed or abandoned in Georgia. The owners don't want more dogs to feed, and neutering is practically non-existent. So, keep the males and kill the females—a dishearteningly common approach throughout history.

Then Splinter joined the gang for a few days. She looked like a small pup, peering fearfully at me from behind tall blades of grass. As I shrunk down to size, kneeling on the ground and holding my hand out, with her whole body clinging to the ground like spider-man scaling a high-rise, she nudged toward me, all bones and thin skin; another abandoned female. She reminded me of the rat from Teenage Mutant Ninja Turtles I dearly loved as a youth, so I gave her the name, Splinter. She was a few years old, or at least had endured so much heat and famine that she looked older than she was.

Chupa barked at me as I paralleled a river. It was beginning to rain and I stopped to put on my parka. He made himself a home in the drainage under the road. Maybe he was born there, perhaps with others, and mom had left no more than a month ago. In the drainage was a decaying corpse, another sibling that didn't make it. With little to none of mom's milk, he looked like he had a diet of grasshoppers and plastic. I sat down under a birch tree a few feet away from him.

A steady hand and patience invited him into my lap for a snooze as we waited for the downpour to subside. When I stood to keep walking, he tried to keep up, but his little paws simply couldn't equal my large human steps. I fashioned my scarf into a baby-carrier and placed him next to my chest. I carried him like that for several days until he was lured into a furry gang that were professional beggars at a tourist "spot."

All of the dogs were called to different opportunities beyond the walking tribe. Pepper befriended a woman at the back door of her cabin. Splinter was fed a large loaf of bread at a petrol station where a trash can would hopefully give him more than he had in his previous life in the bush. But Tamar wouldn't stop walking, even when her paws were burnt and the rocks had cut them. She paced herself for over 150 kilometers at my side.

And it was with Tamar that I would face that heartbreak again. Turkey didn't allow any dogs from Georgia to enter the country without a passport, full vaccination and accompanying a citizen. If it were even attempted, the dog would be detained and most likely euthanized. With no shelters or funding, homeless dogs are shot. There is no money for a humane needle-cocktail.

There was hope though: a minute chance that she would get randomly picked up by the city and tested to become a safe stray. But they only perform these tests every six months. Tamar would have to be lucky to be chosen. Or lucky not to attack a human who might kill her or call the authorities, who would kill her.

I had stuck to my agreement: I didn't feed any of them—immediately. The initial withholding of food, a day or several kilometers down the road, was enough for me to learn that no matter how hungry they were, it was the attention and love that they craved. A gentle pat on the head or scratch at the tail was just as alluring, if not more so, than a piece of bread. I will never be able to withhold love and affection.

I am doomed to heartbreak, to those wild abandoned beasts that are just as homeless as I am; who long for company as I do, and will sacrifice security for the adventure of following their heart.

I took Tamar to the ocean, coffee in one hand and canned sardines in the other for her. It was a new and beautiful location but a dreadful emotional landscape.

I opened the sardines, for a moment seeing Oogi's eager eyes as Tamar shared the same expression of excitement. I don't doubt an animal's ability to sense emotional distress and even if they were able to sense I was about to leave them, they could never comprehend that I would only ever do it because I thought I was saving their lives. They would never be able to understand that I would forever feel guilt and sorrow, constantly searching for another way that they could be with me here now.

I set the sardines down and when her snout was anxiously devouring the depths of the can, I walked away. No. I ran away. I ran fast so she couldn't trace my smell and so I could keep myself from walking back to her. I didn't. But she found me in my dreams where I like to think we can still walk together.

Two weeks with a Bushman

"If you're determined to get heat and sun stroke, do you mind not adding dehydration to it? It makes my job more difficult."

"I'm drinking plenty of water, thank you!" I replied with a little sass in my voice.

"Well, if you start seeing stars, you know the whistle. Then sit down in the shade and I'll be to you soon."

The day I met B I learned that when you think you're alone in the desert, you're probably not. I had just put my headphones in and began singing along to a Cranberries song when I noticed two men walking out of the bush toward me. My heart leapt at the same time my hand leapt to my walking stick. They were both shirtless, barefoot and had a black dog in tow. They were most interested in Athena, my cart, and my solar panel.

"Are you the woman walking?" one asked me with a friendly smile.

"Yes, well, I'm walking." I replied.

"I heard about you a little south of here. Was interested in your rig set up. Looks nice."

They both seemed genuinely kind and the dog, named Taz, nestled herself in the shade of Athena. They were heading up north; one on a bike and the other in his car. They offered to share a camp for the night a few kilometers up the road. I was hesitant to agree to go off into the bush with two men that I'd only spent ten minutes with but it felt safe and I began drooling at the thought of lamb chops and steamed veggies. We decided that they would choose the camp, set up and cook for us. That night I ate myself stuffed, drank red wine and slept next to the fire that B kept going throughout the night.

B traveled by foot and bicycle. He carried very little with him and the only time I saw him wear anything on his feet was when he was pedaling. He rolled and smoked a cigarette every twenty minutes and enjoyed white wine with water once the fire was lit and the food was cooking. He stood several inches over six feet; his skin was dark and weathered, perhaps making him look older than he was. He had many traits similar to the Aborigines, such as the wide nose and dark skin color, but he could easily pass as a sunburnt German. He didn't ask many questions and preferred not to be asked many.

B offered to show me a few things about the bush lifestyle before he continued to go north. I felt that he could see how little I really knew about living on the road, with my poor diet of yogurt bars and muesli. He kindly gave me two weeks of support and bush experience without busting my confidence bubble.

Once B found our camp for the night, he placed an orange flag under a stone on the ground to notify me of his location. I would give a whistle in three tones so he knew I was entering camp. He rarely chose a place that had a path or trail. I often had to pull Athena over dead trees, spinifex, sand and puddles.

The first night I arrived at camp, I was a bit apprehensive about how we would work together. B had seen me coming and waited for me at the entrance of the trail, staying somewhat camouflaged behind a tree. He put his hand up as if to stop me. He pointed at his eyes with two fingers and then north and south, the direction of the road. He was trying to tell me to watch for cars and wait until there was no one on the road before entering camp. Once it was silent from passing vehicles, I ran into the bush toward B. He grabbed Athena's handles from me and with wide and steady strides he pulled her quickly behind him as if she were no heavier than an empty wheelbarrow. I had to run to keep up as I attempted to push her from behind.

He had a fire lit and spaghetti noodles boiling.

"I've put up my tent for you so you can rest under the mesh to avoid the evening mozzies. I'll get dinner ready."

With gleaming joy that someone was going to take care of the necessities for the night, I settled into the tent for a sunset meditation.

He began heading back toward the road.

"Where are you going?" I asked.

"To cover our tracks. I'll show you that tomorrow. You rest for now."

This was the beginning of learning to move unseen.

Questions and Answers

1. What compels you to walk?

When I committed myself to walking solo around the planet, I didn't know why. To walk as I do didn't come from a love of walking but rather a devotion to following my heart.

I am most interested in discovering greater depths within myself, learning to listen with more than my ears and open to greater possibilities and miracles.

For me, to walk is a challenge. The elements can be quite cruel and unforgiving and escalating up a mountainside with forty kilos is far from a holiday. But it's rewarding and I learn more about myself by the way I handle the difficulties.

I walk to learn. Walking is the most compelling thing to me at this moment in my life.

2. Do you experience instances while you are walking when your mind is somewhere off the trail and on its own journey?

My walk is mostly an emotional landscape that I explore through my body's movement. It would feel out of integrity for me not to notice what my mind wanders into and through, particularly when I feel afraid or worried. I walk with the intention of becoming more astute to the workings of my mind and heart. It's a greater challenge than pushing the body beyond its comfortable limits. Physical pain is little compared to the emotional journey.

I've been asked what I think about or do when I'm bored. I don't experience boredom although I do experience bouts of loneliness and doubt, the same as I did back in the comforts of my home and career. Walking and watching my mind, without judgment, easily keeps me from boredom and sometimes I choose to simply enjoy where my mind goes.

And I find that humor brings the light back into my mind and electrifies my heart. I find myself singing classic Christmas songs or talking aloud in a strong Southern (American) accent, because it makes me giggle, and laughter carries me further than ambition.

3. How do you manage to stay physically and emotionally healthy during long and arduous journeys?

Walking twenty to thirty kilometers in a day keeps my body in good shape but going too fast, without breaks, easily wears down my body, and in turn, affects my mood. I've learned to take as many breaks as I desire, which allows me to feel more deeply connected with my surroundings. Though I must admit, I move quickly through towns or villages, as I am most uncomfortable walking through them.

When I'm tired and before I start walking in the morning, I dance. It opens my heart and helps me embrace the unknown I'm about to explore. This is when I dream.

What has supported me most and keeps me walking is the willingness to feel everything. It's easy to allow the joy and excitement but quite difficult to feel the emotions that are uncomfortable and painful. I often have moments of doubt, fear, grief, sadness, and loneliness. And I also experience joy, anticipation, excitement, acceptance, and love. At the end of the day, I measure my greatest accomplishments by my ability to be with my thoughts and subsequent emotions; it's never about how far I walked.

4. Please share a high and a low period that you experienced during your walkabouts.

The very beginning of my walk was a transition from grief to freedom. Australia was my first continent and I was excited about the solitude and terrified of the terrain. Venomous predators and scathing heat awaited me. The heat lived up to my expectations. I was pushing up to 40 kilometers a day. What was I walking so fast for?

I realized I was trying to get home from across the planet. If I walked faster maybe five years would become four. I was missing what I had left behind: my friends, my family and my career. It had felt good to let go of all my belongings when I was preparing for the walk. But I couldn't prepare for the grief I would feel in the Outback. I found myself crying often as I mourned all that I thought I had been and the fear that surrounded my future. What would I do for a living after years of walking?

The desert slowly and painfully stripped me of thoughts of the future. Grief became less constant and I began to hear the birds that I hadn't noticed before.

I became enamored by the wildlife and grew an affinity for the smallest insects. Stopping for tea and crackers in the shade of the afternoon and watching a colony of ants was my greatest pleasure. I became comfortable with the dirt in my fingernails and smell of not showering for weeks on end. The sound of life around me was my leading light, guiding me more full-hearted through my walk, stripping away my doubt and fear of tomorrow.

I was hairy, stinky, and filthy—and I never felt more beautiful. By the time I finished walking through Australia, I felt like I had become a woman.

5. Have you experienced an important Encounter that somehow changed the direction of your journey?

I wanted to find out just how strong I could stand in the face of fear but I still ultimately hoped I wouldn't experience anything frightening. I wasn't naïve to the dangers of walking alone, as a female, and I was well aware that it was likely I'd finish my walk with some bruises. I took a self-defense course but had little practice and absolutely no real-life experiences to prepare me for an attack.

So, when at two a.m. a nomad in Mongolia silently approached my tent and fought his way in, I was stunned, terrified and caught off guard. I had become complacent and illusions of safety in the golden sunsets left me anticipating little in the way of harm. My nightly routine had become lazy. I experienced a woman's worst fear. But as terrifying as it was to experience, and perhaps for people to hear about, it was the night that changed my relationship to the walk.

That night, my naïveté died. I learned a few things about myself. One is that I could and would fight when faced with danger. And that I'm not as strong as the female superheroes I fantasized about being, but strong enough to endure what life hands me.

The morning after the attack, I reached a village and rented a room from a family with two young boys. I spent three days recovering my body and nourishing my heart. Sometimes I closed myself in the room for hours at a time. Sometimes I helped the mother make handmade pasta noodles. On the morning of the fourth day I packed my gear and kept walking west. The important thing for me is that my direction and my walk didn't change, but rather my conviction and dedication to my walk strengthened. To keep walking despite my fear of the encounter changed me. I had found courage within me that I had not known before.

Photograph courtesy of Angela Maxwell.

Biography

I walk as a free woman who chose a crazy experiment over a secure job in a world where many women still can't choose their husband or education. I walk with them in my thoughts. And the little that people give to me, I give to them. I left my growing business in Oregon to pursue my calling to walk. It is an experiment in living on less. I walk into a web of the unknown and slowly watch the world around me shape itself into being. To walk the earth, for me, is to practice being deeply connected to the subtlety of every moment and how it changes and forms itself. This walk is like a marriage. When things get tough, I'm not going to quit or choose something more comfortable and beautiful. I may reach the end of my walk and still wonder what this walk is about.

"Not all those who wander are lost."
~J.R.R. Tolkien

David Downie

Paris to the Pyrenees
a skeptic pilgrim walks the way of Saint James

Paris Prelude

We sealed our bargain in the shadow of the Tour Saint-Jacques, the flamboyant Gothic tower on the rue de Rivoli half a mile from where my wife Alison and I live in central Paris. The tower is all that remains of the celebrated medieval church and hostelry of Saint James the Greater from which pilgrims in their thousands for over a thousand years began walking south following the main European branch of The Way of Saint James—"The Way," for short—from Paris to the Pyrenees. That was where we were headed.

A few days before Easter, we strapped on our pedometers, booted up, and marched south from the tower through crowds of commuters and tourists. Crossing the Île de la Cité, we stopped for a moment of quiet reflection at Notre-Dame cathedral. Then we headed down rue Saint-Jacques, poking our heads into churches, former pilgrims' hostels, and the Paris residence of the abbots of Cluny—now Paris's museum of the Middle Ages where the enigmatic *Lady and the Unicorn* tapestries hang.

The French call The Way of Saint James *le Chemin de Saint Jacques de Compostelle* while the Spanish call it *El Camino de Santiago de Compostela*. Either way, this pilgrims' highway was built on top of an ancient Roman road that linked northern Europe via Paris to the heartland of Gaul and then continued south to Spain.

Straight and true like most Roman roads, today's rue Saint-Jacques still mounts past the Pantheon, then follows the edge of the Reservoir de la Vanne to the sprawling Cité Universitaire campus. It changes names four times. Beyond the university greenbelt on the pot-holed rue Henri-Vincent, my talking pedometer informed us we had walked 3.26 miles and burned 234 calories. Soon after this, we reached the point where The Way of Saint James dead-ends. It's no longer Paris's glorious roadway to Spain but rather an off-ramp from the Boulevard Périphérique beltway a six-lane moat isolating Paris.

As we pondered the snarled cement colossus, it seemed unlikely many pilgrims would flock to the Tour Saint-Jacques again. Questers no longer set out from Paris, we realized, a city of 12 million ringed by industry, housing projects, expressways, freeways, and railways that are lethal to even the fleetest of foot. Today's pilgrims nod at the Saint-Jacques tower and visit Notre-Dame for a symbolic bend of the knee. They then board buses or trains to other points along "The Way"—smaller, more welcoming locales such as Chartres, Tours, and Poitiers, or Arles, Le Puy-en-Velay and Vézelay. After a sleepless night of anxious excitement, that's exactly what we did, hopping on the first train to Vézelay the very next morning at dawn.

THE WALKABOUT CHRONICLES

Part One
Caesar's Ghost
Across le Morvan from Vézelay to Autun

Saints Alive

The storied medieval pilgrimage site of Vézelay stretched lengthwise across a hogback Burgundian ridge like a patient on a psychiatrist's couch. At the head of the hill was the Romanesque repository of Mary Magdalene's relics. Our hotel stood near the former fairgrounds at the saint's feet. The simile seemed imperfect. I had heard much about the site's purported psycho-therapeutic powers, though no psychiatrist's couch I've seen is ringed by tall, crumbling walls, studded with belfries and surrounded by Pinot Noir vineyards and cow-flecked pastures.

As a seriously overweight freethinker with wrecked knees, a crazed individual proposing to walk 750 miles on pilgrimage routes, perhaps my vision of Vezélay was impaired by a skeptical outlook, and I was the one who needed a therapist.

A natty innkeeper and a sculpted wooden effigy of Saint James greeted us at the Hôtel du Lion d'Or. She wore a tailored winter-weight pants suit. Saint Jacques wore his signature upturned floppy hat. It looked startlingly like the khaki-colored cotton sunhat the unrepentant optimist Alison had bought at a sports emporium in Paris. A ski cap would've been more appropriate.

I hated to disappoint James or the solicitous hotel manager, but Compostela by whatever name wasn't our goal. The Spanish section of the trail—from Roncesvalles Abbey in the Pyrenees Mountains to Santiago—is mobbed by hundreds of thousands of pilgrims each year. Their main preoccupation is to find food and a place to sleep each night, as we'd seen with our own eyes. Our goal was different. We wanted to cross France, not Spain, following age-old hiking trails, and do so unmolested by cars and other pilgrims, making the pilgrimage our own maverick way.

The truth is we weren't really religious pilgrims. At least I wasn't, and I could only speak for myself. Outwardly, the irrepressible desire I felt to hike across France had little to do with spirituality, a profitable concept whose meaning has never been clear to me. After twenty years of living and working in France, I simply felt the need to make my own mental map of the country by walking across it step by measured step and thereby possess it physically, intimately, something I'd failed to do through a car's windshield. I also needed to reinvent myself from the bottom up, restore something I'd lost, discover things I'd never tried to find, make an inner as well as an outer journey, and ask the big questions again, the What's-it-all-about-Alfie ones I'd stopped asking once out of adolescence. Among those fundamentals was, did I want to stay alive, or did I prefer to explode like an over-inflated balloon?

A quarter century of high living as a travel and food writer had demanded its pound of flesh. Many pounds, actually. I had become a hedonist and glutton. The cookbooks I'd written, the recipes I'd tested, the buttery croissants and fluffy mousses I'd savored in every imaginable locale, from bakery to multiple-starred restaurant, had buried me in radial tires, like the Michelin Man. I had also consumed gallons of wine, Calvados, Cognac, and even Inspector Maigret's *Vieille Prune*, a lethal eau de vie distilled from plums. Though I'd often tried to repress or control my gluttonous urges, change without crisis had not occurred.

Then one fine day, while eating my way through southern Burgundy, I'd keeled over and awakened to be told I was, in essence, a walking foie gras. I'd become a life-sized, green-hued liver, an organ afflicted by something called "steatosis." A second French doctor leaned over my hospital bed and nodded with undisguised disgust. He explained that steatosis means "marbled with fatty veins and pocked with fatty globules." I also had viral hepatitis, probably from food poisoning. I was, in short, experiencing liver failure.

Not that this was the first serious health crisis I'd faced in my nearly fifty-year existence—and ignored. A decade earlier, I'd been visited by sudden-onset optic neuropathy. It had gutted my vision, leaving me blind in one eye, my addled brain permanently dazzled by twinkling, spinning lights. But this tap on the shoulder with an angelic feather had not saved me. On the contrary. It had driven me to eat and drink even more, to forget my misery.

Still in Burgundy, trying to recover from liver disease, I vowed to change my life, seriously, this time. Really. Really. First I'd stop drinking and lose those saddlebags of fat that made me look like a pack mule. Second, I'd stay off computer screens long enough to see if my kaleidoscope vision improved. Third, I'd jump-start my jalopy and then slowly trickle-charge my batteries, and, who knows, perhaps bring a lilt back to my stride. Irreverent irony was my worst enemy. I was exhausted by flippancy and the forced cleverness of corporate magazine writing. Crossing France on foot, starting in Vézelay, was something I'd always dreamed of doing anyway, in part because Burgundy was so green and gorgeous, in part because of its historical associations with Rome and the ancient world, a lifelong obsession of mine. It seemed as good a place as any in which to force myself toward a new and improved lifestyle. I calculated that, if traversing Burgundy didn't kill me, I'd find some way to keep inching south until I'd crested the Pyrenees into Spain. Clearly, the best trails were the old Roman roads and pilgrim routes, where you could walk for miles without encountering a car. The only hitch as far as I could see was religion.

As a skeptic born and raised by skeptics in 1960s-70s San Francisco, a survivor both of the Haight-Ashbury and Berkeley's Telegraph Avenue, I felt queasy at the prospect of becoming an official pilgrim, with a pilgrim's *Crédenciel*—a handsome, foldout passport issued and stamped by the Catholic church. The Crédenciel entitled you, among other things, to sleep in pilgrims' hostels along the way, for the price of a donation, but I couldn't face asking for one. I hadn't escaped the gurus and drug culture of California to wind up a Catholic in France; that was reason enough to devise my own unofficial pilgrimage, a journey into the past, to focus on the present, and, if I was lucky, to read the future.

Practically speaking, I planned to follow the 2,000-year-old Via Agrippa and pre-Roman, Gallic footpaths, routes predating Christianity, safe in the knowledge that, unbeknownst to most pilgrims, they underlie The Way of Saint James just as surely as Paganism underlies Roman Catholicism. I'd take the roads less traveled, the longer secondary routes from Vézelay via the ancient Gallic stronghold of Bibracte, then onwards to Autun, Cluny, and Le Puy-en-Velay. Julius Caesar and the Gallic chieftain

Vercingétorix had battled along this route. Charlemagne had ridden down it for the epic Pyrenees battle against the Moors recounted in *The Song of Roland*. Cluny had been the second Rome, with the biggest abbey church in Christendom, and, despite the Internet and cellular telephony, all roads, at least metaphorically, still lead to Rome. Forget Santiago de Compostela, I told myself; if I could make it across France, nothing could stop me from one day hiking across the Alps into Italy and down the boot to Rome.

So here I was, a prematurely hobbled, sardonic miscreant, an admirer of Caesar who had long hoped the Vatican would be toppled by earthquakes, about to keep my solemn promise to myself and begin a cross-country quest in the company of Saint James. Originally my plan hadn't included Alison, a professional photographer with a busy schedule and a considerably less troubled psyche. But she'd insisted on accompanying me, possibly because she herself had a host of family-related issues to think through, and was also an avowed walk-aholic. Mostly, I knew, Alison wanted to come along because she feared I'd die of exhaustion, be murdered, or go back to gorging myself en route. My opposite number, she was afflicted not only by quiet optimism, altruism, and wisdom, but also by chronic slimness. She'd never put on weight even though she'd eaten as much as I had for decades, earning a living by turning roast ducklings and strawberry tarts into lovely still-life photos. Her athletic physique hid one minor flaw: an elegant, S-shaped backbone, the result, she claimed, of the wooden grade-school chairs of her youth. Two cameras, one hundred rolls of film, and a gross of digital photo chips was all she would carry in her small knapsack. I would play not only Don Quixote to her Sancho Panza, I would also be her pack-donkey.

Cockles and Muscles

The most appealing sign on Vézelay's steep, slippery, cobbled main street showed a familiar seashell and belonged to a *crêperie*. It was called Auberge de la Coquille—the scallop. A mouthwatering scent of melting butter, sugar, crêpes, and hot coffee blew toward us on the wintry wind. I studied the sign, hesitating. Would I ever be able to resist the temptations of gluttony and lead a normal life? There was scope for serious doubt. I was already feeling faint from hunger. We'd left Paris on a pre-dawn train. Stiffening my resolve, I hiked on, comforting myself with thoughts not of food but of history.

As any pilgrim knows, especially if he's read up on the subject, the French call scallops *coquilles saint-jacques*—shells of Saint James. The scallop shell symbolizes this enigmatic individual. But the scallop is also the generic sign of questers of all kinds, which is why I've always loved it. Never mind that before the pilgrimage route was built, the scallop, cockle, and conch denoted Venus, born of virginal sea-foam, immortalized in Botticelli's painting and countless myths. These shells had been signs of the divine—of fertility and love—for centuries before James joined forces with Jesus.

I felt inside the wet, clammy right-hand pocket of my windbreaker. Though an appealing shade of red and despite the manufacturer's claims, the garment was clearly not waterproof. There I'd placed the misshapen shell I'd found years ago on Utah Beach, in Normandy, when we'd been on another kind of pilgrimage, to see the Normandy landing beaches on the fiftieth anniversary of D-Day, in 1994. Using raindrops to polish the shell, I thought fondly of my father, and Alison's, both recently deceased, both World War Two vets of the best, most skeptical kind. I kept at it, stroking the cockleshell, and soon enough we were out of range of Auberge de la Coquille's dangerously caloric scents.

"I've found the technique," I said proudly to Alison. "It's my first epiphany!"

Starry Skies and Compost Heaps

Despite our zealous desire to reach the basilica a quarter mile away atop the hill, the spring storm grew stronger, forcing us to seek shelter. In a cozy café we had several rounds of coffee and watched the rain turn to hail. I felt dazed and panicked. I'd pored over books and encyclopedias before leaving Paris. But somehow I hadn't been able to focus my mind on the actual reality of the journey ahead, or the cast of characters. All those unfamiliar names, dates, and places, and the thought of walking for nearly three months across rural France, without access to Google, now filled me with something akin to terror. I took out the concise biography of Saint James that I'd photocopied and, squinting, read aloud to Alison. This was a novelty. She's the one who usually reads aloud to me.

Alison sipped her coffee and agreed that it was easy enough to see how Iago—pronounced Yago—became the northwestern-Spanish equivalent of the Latin name Jacobus—pronounced Yakoboos. So Sant'Iago changing to "Santiago" was a logical step.

The origin of the winning name "Compostela" was less clear. *Campus stellæ* meant "field of the star" and sounded euphonic, ringing like a Catholic retrofit to explain something unsavory. The story goes that a Spanish shepherd saw unusual blazing stars pointing to a mound. Hidden by vegetation stood the ruined tomb of the saint, which the shepherd soon ensured was discovered by persons more noteworthy than he.

This was certainly more uplifting a tale than the other, possibly more credible origin-myth for Santiago de Compostela and the real reason for the spot's unusual-sounding name. According to modern archeologists, the tomb of two Roman patricians named Athanasius and Theodore, discovered somewhat inconveniently under the main altar of the Cathedral of Saint James, their names sculpted on it, seems to confirm the existence of an ancient Roman villa beneath the holy shrine. The rational explanation for the name is simple enough: the villa had become a cemetery or dumping ground—a *compost* heap—and the word "compost" had evolved into Compostela. I folded the photocopy and felt warm inside, encouraged by the thought that a humble compost heap had become a site of miracles, the source of hope and inspiration, misguided or not, for millions of fellow questers.

Boning Up

Possibly because I spent several formative years in the mid-1960s living in Rome, and was dragged by my mother into hundreds of places of worship there, as an adult I've actively stayed out of churches. It was with trepidation that I now approached the basilica of Mary Magdalene, a UNESCO World Heritage Site. Perched high on Vézelay's hill, it attracts about a million visitors each year. The façade is not handsome, despite the best efforts of architect Eugène Viollet-le-Duc, the 1800s over-restorer of France's monuments. He rebuilt the basilica as we see it today, rescuing a ruin while trying and perhaps not entirely failing to preserve its magic.

Tradition has it that the Saturday before Easter is a mournful day, anticipating Sunday's rising of Christ. Consequently there were no tapers to light, no flowers on the altar, and no singing. But we, the visitors shuffling down the soaring nave, made our untidy presence felt. Were pilgrims also allowed to be tourists, I wondered. And vice versa: Could tourists be true pilgrims?

We let the crowds thin before climbing down a steep staircase into the dark, damp crypt. I stumbled on the uneven stone floor. Behind bars in a niche was Mary Magdalene's reliquary, an ornate neo-Gothic arc of gilded silver borne aloft by angels and holy men. In the early 1000s, Alison reminded me, the abbot of Vézelay discovered the remains of Mary Magdalene somewhere inside the monastery, or so the story goes. What were they doing in Vézelay? To query their provenance was to doubt the miraculous nature of the discovery. And doubting raised the uncomfortable, associated question of how a saint had been made of a wild young woman of alleged loose virtue, a long-haired temptress who had dried Jesus's feet with her hair and might be on stage or in a padded cell were she alive today.

"Relax," Alison whispered, taking my hand. "You're trembling."

"I'm cold," I said. But the origin of my nervousness had little to do with the temperature.

I closed my eyes, allowing the presence of Mary's relics to bestir feelings of spirituality. More tourists crowded around, some with flashing cameras. I tried to meditate, beginning with progressive relaxation, but that didn't help either. I changed tack, and thought again of history. With Mary Magdalene's bones in its crypt, Vézelay had soared in status, becoming not merely a stopover on The Way of Saint James but the starting point and, for many, the goal of pilgrimages. Here we were, at Ground Zero, by the saint's bones.

Mary Magdalene's reliquary niche was designed to hold an entire skeleton. But I knew from my readings that there'd been a minor hiccup: the Vatican had de-authenticated the relics in 1295, and Mary's tomb had vanished. Happily some of the bones stayed behind and were placed in containers. We were in the presence of the largest portion of the relics. *Pop, ping, zing* went the flashes and camera lenses. Cell phones rang. A guided tour group tramped in. Feeling like a spy in the house of love, I was swept away by disbelief.

Another reliquary is on the ground floor, in the church's right transept. As we headed for the cloisters, we stopped to look at it. Crowned by a gaudy modern sculpture, the reliquary had been vandalized. A pocket-sized niche stood empty, a wire grate bent back. The miniature effigy of Mary Magdalene had been stolen by souvenir hunters in the early 2000s, the relics too.

"Are you sure you don't want to get a pilgrim's passport?" I asked Alison, feeling a twinge of guilt. She was a lapsed Catholic and, I reasoned, might want spiritual insurance while walking. "Just because I refuse to submit doesn't mean you shouldn't have one." But she firmly shook her head.

We found an unoccupied bench on the tree-lined road called Promenade des Fossés paralleling Vézelay's oval ramparts and enjoyed our first picnic as pilgrims, albeit unofficial pilgrims. Alison had picked up the local newspaper. It carried the Easter address by Archbishop Yves Patenôtre of nearby Sens-Auxerre. He noted that our lives overflow with unanswered questions regarding mortality and the loss of loved ones. The big question was why did humans have to die? Even Jesus had asked God why he had to die. However, according to the archbishop, the good news was, Jesus and God were still among us, in the streets—alive. The joy of Easter, alas, would always be mixed with the gravity of the human condition: finitude. Mortality. But, for people of faith, with the balm of hope that they too, in some way, would rise again as Christ did.

Lingering over my apple, I contemplated the apparent infinity of the scenery, and felt the irreverence drain out of me. Skeptic or believer, there was much to chew on in the archbishop's words.

I chewed on the words as we walked down a rocky path into the Valley of Asquins. Edging a thicket stood a tall wooden cross. We slid down to it, mindful that here, in the year 1146, the militant abbot Bernard of Clairvaux, not yet a mystic or saint, had harangued an assembly of thousands, from King Louis VII down, calling for a second Crusade to free Jerusalem from the Infidel—thereby restoring trade and Christian control of the Near East and Mediterranean. Petroleum and terrorism were not yet on the agenda. I squinted, imagining the sleepy valley alive with knights in shining armor, foot-soldiers, mercenaries, farmers, and priests. The assembled dignitaries could not fit into the basilica of Mary Magdalene. Anticipating the overflow, the abbot had erected a country chapel. It still stands and is named La Cordelle.

I was glad that the rain and wind had swept away other visitors. After the crowds at the basilica, we were alone at last, inside the chapel's mossy walled compound. The beauty of La Cordelle lies in its simplicity: un-faced gray stone walls and a floor of beaten earth. There was no noise from outside. Eyes shut, I felt the pleasant weariness that comes from rising before dawn, riding a train for several hours while seated backwards, walking for several more hours, talking to pious strangers, and wrestling with the ghosts of adolescent existentialism. I'd probably thought more and deeper about the human condition in the last six hours than I had in the last ten years. It had been quite a day. Perhaps "spirituality" was no more than an altered physical and mental state attainable by sleep deprivation or the fatigue of labor, prayer, or pilgrimage? Often, in my experience, it was the least likely candidates who had spoken the loudest about their spirituality and possession of religious feelings. Was I joining the choir?

What I really needed was another cup of coffee. Everyone knew that sleep deprivation was the favorite weapon of the medieval monastic orders, and plenty of contemporary sects, the kind that brainwashed adepts. I banished the thought and felt strangely elated. Birds chirped. Rain pattered. The silence was not silent—it hummed. We hadn't even begun to hike down to Spain. But I felt I'd crossed a threshold. Maybe the walking would not be necessary after all. Maybe we could call the whole thing off and go back to Paris after Easter.

Sacred Fires

The real challenge in getting to the 10 p.m. Easter Eve ceremony at the basilica was not the rain, wind, or cold. It was overcoming the desire for sleep that dogged us after dinner. We admired Vézelay's lichen-frosted, floodlit old houses as we marched. Other diners teetered along full of good wine. Bells rang out. The night was full of other sounds, including the roar of a motorcycle engine. Around the parking lot facing the basilica rode an adolescent boy, his tricked-out, four-wheeled Quad motorbike scattering pilgrims and other worshippers.

Darkness has its advantages. The basilica's homely façade had undergone a transformation. Illuminated by spotlights, it hovered and glowed, an amber-colored hologram against the indigo sky. I thought for a minute about my confused state of mind and realized I was wrestling holograms of my mind's own making.

Inside the enclosed porch, the darkness teemed. I could barely see. A woman handed me two wax tapers with white paper hoods. A choir of voices emanated from the basilica's nave. A figure in robes appeared, his face lit by a flickering taper. He positioned himself beneath the central tympanum, stooped, and lit a fire.

As if fed by gasoline, the fire exploded into a blaze. It cast the priest's shadow upward, across the tympanum where Christ reigned. A dog-headed man and the figure of Saint James glared down at us. With flames leaping and shadows prancing around him, the priest spoke. I could not make out what he was saying. I grappled with slippery emotions, my mind jumbled with thoughts of the primal fire, the eternal flame, and the campfires of my childhood. The priest tipped his taper and lit the candles of the men and women standing nearest. They lit others' candles. One by one, the twinkling points of light illuminated arms, necks, and faces, a throbbing canvas. And then a bell tinkled.

Unable to speak from the emotion, I pressed Alison's hand. As I lit her candle, her face leapt out of the darkness. I caught my breath as the basilica's giant doors yawned open. The faithful broke into song, their faces painted by childlike grins made strange in the dancing candlelight. I felt myself slipping into an intoxicating oneness with my fellow human beings, the torch bearers, the happy, the saved, the faithful.

But as the assembly filed from the porch into the nave, and the spotlights came up to enchanting harpsichord music, the stagecraft overwhelmed the authenticity. My cheeks burned with shame. I'd been hoodwinked. I'd hoodwinked myself. Shuffling forward, my candle before me, I felt like a walk-on in a cultish theater performance. The bone-china spell had broken. Toto had dragged open the curtains, revealing the Wizard of Vézelay. The words of an aged, atheist friend spoken years before welled up from memory. "If I had to do it again, I'd be a Catholic," she'd said with a wicked smile, "for the pageantry, the ritual, the marvelous hocus-pocus."

It was marvelous. With incense, bonfire, and candles burning, we took seats in the artfully lit nave—Plato's cave transmogrified by the Brothers and Sisters of Jerusalem, keepers of this extraordinary temple. I sneezed and felt at once foolish and guilty, a spy in the house of love all over again.

The Easter Eve sound-and-light extravaganza segued into the days of Creation. But my teeth chattered from the cold and my backside went numb at the thought of a French version of Intelligent Design. As the fourth day of Creation dawned, I rose silently from my seat and stole out of the basilica. The harpsichord's notes played up my spine, and the candles became voices roaring with skeptical fury.

Back outside in the parking lot, I watched the acne-scarred adolescent buck his Quad onto its back wheels, making it rear up like a horse as he rode around. I wondered how I could explain to Alison that I was not cut out to be a pilgrim after all. I'd been insane to think otherwise.

Easter with Astérix

Dawn's surly light discovered us already at the breakfast table, our packs ready by the door. The sun's first rays had barely begun to tickle the town as we settled up and strode out. I'd had a change of heart in the night. Today was another day. I would hike. I would do it my way…

Exerpt Copyright © 2013 by David Downie, *Paris to the Pyrenees: a Skeptic Pilgrim Walks the Way of Saint James* First Pegasus Books edition April 2013 ISBN: 978-1-60598-432-2 Reprinted by permission of the author.

Questions and Answers

1. What compels you to walk?

That's the great mystery, isn't it? As one elderly priest I met at Conques Abbey about halfway between Paris and the Pyrenees told me, sometimes you know before you start, sometimes you discover five years after you've done your pilgrimage, sometimes you never know. It doesn't matter. What unites all walkers whether spiritual, religious or skeptical pilgrims is the irrepressible need to go. I must do this. In my case I'm still not 100 percent sure but think it is some kind of ancestral need of all humans to explore, wander, stray off the beaten path.

2. Do you experience instances while you are walking when your mind is somewhere off the trail and on its own journey?

Definitely, my mind journeys all the time, whether I'm walking or not, but especially when I'm walking. The startling thing about pilgrimages is, you spend considerable amounts of time just walking, being physical, weeks or months or even years, and the "mind off the trail" phenomenon becomes the norm—at least for me. It is a great liberation, a release. In any case I've always done my best writing while walking. When I was researching my book A PASSION FOR PARIS about the Romantic period in Paris I discovered that Gerard de Nerval, Victor Hugo, and Honore de Balzac—among others—were also walker-writers, experiencing their best insights as they strolled or marched across Paris. That made me feel great, as if, for the first time, I belonged to some kind of brotherhood of walker-writers.

3. How do you manage to stay physically and emotionally healthy during long and arduous journeys?

It's a work in progress! When I get up I do about 45 minutes of stretching and muscle building based on Yoga and Daruma Taiso—the traditional Japanese exercise routine all school children do (or did, at least, in Okinawa). I did martial arts for decades, was a runner, skier and scuba diver, and while I am now in advanced middle age and not in perfect shape I do my best everyday. It has to be a habit, something regular. Oh, and I also walk about 2 hours every day, rain or shine.

4. Please share a high and a low period that you experienced during your walkabouts.

The low point was definitely in the Southwest of France in some place whose name I cannot now remember, it had been raining for a week and the mud was so thick and clinging that you literally could not walk forward, you just kept slipping back. My wife and I got stuck on a hillside in this mud. It was a vision of Hell, a kind of nightmare. We later learned that this mud is famous in France and is called "boue amoureuse"— love mud, because it is so sticky and clings... The high point was a few days from the Pyrenees in Basque Country, when I was very tired and on a kind of permanent runner's high, and saw a flock of woodcocks swirling overhead, and had some kind of vision of the rightness of everything, the lack of a beginning or an end and therefore a complete change in the Western view of time, birth, the origins of the species, of the planet, or the universes and galaxies. It only lasted a few moments. I hope one day I experience that vision again. It was sublime in the truest sense of the word.

5. Have you experienced an important Encounter that somehow changed the direction of your journey?

I think it may have been that monk—the priest—at Conques Abbey. For most of my life I have been militantly secular, atheistic and anticlerical, and while I in no way became a religious convert on my journey, I think I learned important lessons of tolerance, and came away with a mind and heart more open than when I left. That changed the feel of my journey in big ways.

Biography

Best-selling author and private tour guide David Downie has been based in Paris for three decades and spends part of each year in Burgundy and Italy. His most recent book, *a Passion for Paris: Romanticism and Romance in the City of Light* is published by St. Martin's Press in April, 2015. Please visit David's Blog and Books pages for his latest posts and updates on book tours and events.

Donkey and camel caravan plows through aftermath of summer snow storm in search of Tibetan antelope birthing grounds with biologist George Schaller, near the end of a 30 day trek through the Kunlun Mountain Range, China. Photograph by Pat Morrow.

Baiba and Pat Morrow

Travel is fatal to prejudice, bigotry, and narrow-mindedness.
~Mark Twain

Footsteps In The Clouds..........A Journey into Sikkim

Story by Baiba and Pat Morrow

In the early morning of April 24, 1998 Pat and I fell in line with the locals strolling around Observatory Hill in the old colonial tea town of Darjeeling. Elderly Buddhists spun their prayer wheels in dizzying rotations. Mantras hung in the air like the mist. As everyone in Darjeeling knows, "the hill" offers one of the best panoramic views of the Himalaya in all of India. We hoped to catch sight of Kangchenjunga – the third highest mountain in the world and the most sacred of all the fourteen 8000-meter-high peaks.

As we rounded the hill's north end the clouds gently parted. The devout instinctively turned and bowed their heads, hands clasped in prayer. Kangchenjunga, their sacred guardian, commanded everyone's attention like some ancient giant Buddha. I, too, felt compelled to offer my prayers – or something – in reverence. Overawed, all I could muster was a hushed, "wow!"

While today Mt. Everest, the darling of the mountain world, monopolizes the imagination of Hollywood film executives and aspiring motivational speakers alike, it was Kangchenjunga that was the most famous of all Himalayan peaks in the last century. (Until 1849 it was thought to be the highest mountain in the world.) Its glistening, snowy summit straddles the border of Nepal. The Indian state of Sikkim was a familiar sight to the British gentry who flocked to this popular hill to escape the heat of the plains during the days of the Raj.

British colonials weren't the only ones to come here. An eclectic roster of European mountaineers, explorers, mystics, artists, and social misfits passed through the bustling tea town on their way to the unexplored Sikkim Himalaya and beyond, into the forbidden, mysterious enclave of Tibet.

On September 5, 1899 Italian mountain photographer Vittorio Sella and the seasoned English climber Douglas Freshfield set out on horseback along with four other Europeans from this ridge-top town. The team was intent on circumnavigating the huge massif, 74 kilometers away, that so dominates the northern skyline from Darjeeling.

The expedition took seven grueling weeks; the adventurers returned, well weathered yet triumphant as the first westerners to circumnavigate a big Himalayan peak. The subsequent combination of Sella's hallmark photographs and Freshfield's skilled narrative made Round Kangchenjunga an instant classic in Himalayan annals. A century later, the book inspired us to make a similar journey.

As we set about planning our own trip, we knew that a true circumnavigation à la Freshfield was no longer possible. India, China and Pakistan now jostle for dominance like bullies in a schoolyard; they guard their borders with distrust and hostility. Until only recently, Sikkim (not much bigger in size than Prince Edward Island yet strategic because of its low mountain passes into Chinese-occupied Tibet) remained virtually off-limits in its northern region to both foreign and domestic travellers.

Not wanting to cause an international border incident (and not relishing the thought of being shot at by the trigger-happy Indo-Tibetan Border Police like a Tibetan mountaineer friend from Darjeeling nearly was), we divided our circle of Kangchenjunga into two journeys. The first leg took us into Sikkim's restricted northern area in the spring of 1998. Besides exploring the northeastern side of the mountain we included the additional challenge of climbing one of Kangchenjunga's satellite peaks, 6887-meter Siniolchu. Six months later we would complete the 30 day long second half of the circumambulation with a trek in Nepal.

Now, on our first morning in Darjeeling, I gazed longingly at the holy mountain of Kangchenjunga (roughly translated from the Tibetan as the Five Treasuries of Snow). In its shadow lay a "Land of Mystic Splendour" where deep mountains, mysticism and ancient Buddhist beliefs titillate the traveller's dreams of a Shangri-La. Then the fog rolled in like waves of an incoming tide. The heavenly vision disappeared but its impact lingered.

The following day our group of eight North Americans plus five Sherpas from Darjeeling crammed into a small bus piled high with gear. Paul Kallmes, the expedition co-leader from Massachusetts, headed the team roster. Three mountaineers from Colorado – Ali Palmer, Kit Katzenbach (who would marry to become Kit Leslauriers, first woman to ski from the summit of Everest) and Ace Kvale, an old friend from European Alps skiing days) – rounded out the climbing team.

Six hours later our bus laboured up Sikkim's National Highway 31A to Gangtok, the region's hilltop capital. A snarl of trucks, jeeps and mini-vans used as taxis jammed the steep, narrow road. Four-to-five-storied buildings clung to a hillside so precipitous that rooftops touched entranceways. Dozens more concrete structures grew from the mounds of sand and gravel that lay haphazardly in an obstacle course on the already crowded streets.

"Gridlock in Gangtok," grumbled Pat in open disgust. He slammed the window shut as black, choking clouds of diesel exhaust gushed over our vehicle.

The urban sprawl of this city of 50,000 people should not have surprised us. Quaint mountain towns throughout the world, including Aspen, Zermatt and even our own Canmore, on the edge of Banff National Park, have fallen prey to industrialized tourism. In the last ten years the central Indian government has sacrificed Gangtok's charms to the onslaught of raw commercialism. Huge financial losses caused by the ongoing civil war in the once-idyllic tourist mecca of Kashmir, by the border of Pakistan, must now be made up for in Sikkim.

We found tranquility at the Mintokling Hotel, located far above the hustle and bustle. In a garden amidst graceful bamboo trees and blooming cosmos flowers we sipped lukewarm beers and admired the snowy brow of Kangchenjunga. To the east,

Siniolchu poked above the wooded ridge – a reminder of our goal.

"Well, folks," ventured Ace. "I believe we have an expedition on our hands." We clinked our glasses in a rallying toast and rehashed our trials and tribulations up til now. The permit wrangling with the Indian Mountaineering Foundation (IMF), a sort of mountain-guarding administration attached to the Ministry of Home Affairs, had been harder than saddling a wild yak.

When we arrived in New Delhi on April 20th, we realized that little had been done to process the permit, even though we had sent in our application forms and paid the exorbitant US$10,000 permit fee (for the privilege of accessing and climbing Mt. Siniolchu) three months before. In the end we wasted nearly a week languishing in no less than eight government offices before we could continue beyond Gangtok. The IMF seemed to have an unwritten rule of fitness for foreigners: if you can endure the bureaucracy, than you can survive the rigours of any climb.

"All Freshfield needed a hundred years ago was a letter from the King of Sikkim," Paul joked.

"Long live the king!" piped in Kit with enthusiasm.

"Sadly," interjected Pat. "The king is no more."

Chogyal Palden Thondup Namgyal, Sikkim's last king, died of cancer in near-obscurity in New York City in 1982. When the British Raj withdrew from India in 1947 Sikkim began to lose its political footing. In short order it became a Protectorate of India under a special treaty. By 1975, the Buddhist kingdom buckled under pressure and became India's 22nd state. This was the end of a 340-year-old dynasty.

With a fistful of government documents and Inner Line Permits to allow passage through Sikkim's numerous army installations we set out by jeep for our trailhead at Lachen, 150 kilometers away. As we rumbled up the narrow confines of the Lachen Valley in the late afternoon, a vibrant double rainbow spanned the overgrown ridges to the east like a welcoming banner. A good omen, I hoped. By darkness, we were in Lachen.

Morning found this remote hamlet in northern Sikkim immersed in traditional Buddhist ritual. As the sun crept into the valley with the stealth of a stalking snow leopard delicate curls of juniper smoke from hanging braziers purified the mountain air. High above the village's tight cluster of 50 houses stood the Lachen gompa, or monastery. Yellow paint brightened the wood around its pagoda-style roof and windows. Prayer flags, the omnipresent icons of Buddhist country swayed gently in the breeze from tall bamboo poles like strands of seaweed bending in the ocean current. Their purpose was simple: to send prayers off to the heavens for the benefit of all sentient beings.

In preparation for leaving we rearranged our equipment and food in the government compound opposite our guesthouse. A gaggle of ragtag kids pressed up against the high, barbed-wire fence around the enclosure to watch. Their curiosity gave us the impression that foreigners rarely came here. Yet nearly a hundred years ago Sikkim, known to the British as the "Switzerland of Asia," found many Europeans exploring its mountains. Just about any climber involved in the early attempts on Everest, Kangchenjunga or a host of lesser peaks passed to or fro through Lachen.

Nima Norbu, our Sherpa sirdar (a sort of expedition foreman), commandeered the

40-or-so porters we needed to carry our gear to base camp, a four day walk away.

On April 28th, we strode out of town, thrilled to be on the trail and leaving this last outpost of civilization. After six kilometers we headed west. Steep granitic ridges, seeping with moisture and overgrown with moss, shored up the gateway to the narrow Zemu Valley. The twisted branches of rhododendrons made any pretense of deviating off the path impossible. At some point further along we entered Kangchenjunga National Park, Sikkim's largest ecological reserve.

By the fourth afternoon we reached our base camp at 4,570 meters. It was located in the narrow trough of vegetation beside the 30-kilometer-long Zemu Glacier. The Sherpas had already established a kitchen by a low rock wall left by a previous expedition. As a welcoming gesture Pasang, our cook, presented us with cups of sweet milk tea and biscuits. I glanced around with delight.

In spite of all the surrounding rock, ice and snow there was an unlikely rich network of life here. Low-bush willows sprouted soft furry buds; dwarf rhododendrons held tiny blossoms in tight clusters of colourful promise. Stunted juniper carpeted the dun-coloured hillsides where dozens of bharal (Himalayan blue sheep) grazed. Soon choughs, a cousin of the raven with bright yellow beaks and red feet, discovered that our camp made a perfect scavenging zone. Their calls – halfway between a caw and a whistle – pierced the crystalline air like sharp arrows.

This camp was to be my home for the next two weeks. I had decided long before that I would not join Pat and the other four – Paul, Ace, Kit and Ali – on the climb. Now seeing Siniolchu on the other side of the glacier confirmed the wisdom of my decision.

Graced with the pyramidal form of Europe's Matterhorn or Peru's Alpamayo, Siniolchu pierced the sky at 6887 meters. With its hanging glaciers and two crumbling ice fields, the symmetrical spear of snow and ice looked formidable and dangerous, just as it did in Sella's photographs.

Pat saw it differently. "I can now see why Freshfield described it as 'the most superb triumph of mountain architecture'." Almost completely unknown outside of Sikkim, the peak has been climbed only five times.

I knew Pat longed to be on a big mountain again where living in the extraordinary world between earth and sky offered precious opportunities for clarity of thought. My incurable mountain-loving husband now pulled out binoculars and intently studied the climbing route.

In the other direction, less than 20 kilometers away at the head of the Zemu Glacier, Kangchenjunga squatted on its powerful haunches like a broad-shouldered sumo wrestler. An alpine battalion of stalwart guards surrounded it: the Twins, Nepal Peak and Tent Peak, all named by Freshfield a century ago.

Soon the fog charged up the valley like a racehorse sprinting for the finish line. The air moved so fast that I could feel it brushing against my cheek. The sweltering heat of Delhi now seemed like a distant memory.

By 7 p.m. we had all retreated to our tents. From the silence I heard Pasang exude one final prayer: Om mani padme hum. Hail to the Jewel in the Lotus. The petition came out with the ease of an exhaled breath and evaporated into the darkness. I hoped it would help Pat in the days to come.

Pat's Diary:

May 5: From the very beginning I sensed that Siniolchu was grossly out of shape. The heavy, isothermal snow on its lower glacier was the first sign that much trouble lay ahead. It forced me and my four team mates to wallow and grovel upward, making each day feel like a summit day. To our chagrin, Paul's thermometer shot past 30 degrees Celsius in the direct sun. Nevertheless, our resolve to climb remained strong. We had, after all, come half way around the world to explore the challenges of this peak.

We left Camp 1 in the darkness. It was 4:30 a.m. I felt in top shape. I was psyched and focused.

Being the grizzled "stair master" – the one with the most experience at slogging up big mountains – I felt obliged to break trail and negotiate most of the way through the first icefall. The others followed, roped together, with heavier loads. We followed a circuitous line that zigged and zagged up a series of snow ramps, weaving amongst a forest of seracs (ice towers).

To my bewilderment we came across a set of tracks, possibly those of a fox, that had wandered through here a day or two before. "What had this animal been looking for?" I wondered. Probably something more tangible and tasty than we were after.

We left our loads at a high point and made it back to Camp 1 just past noon. A huge slushy avalanche originating from 1,000 meters above had covered our tracks with truckloads of snow. Somewhat shaken by the magnitude of the debris, Ali spoke her mind. "Maybe we should think about beginning our days earlier – a lot earlier – when cooler temperatures will help stabilize the slopes."

Taking this unsavoury but necessary step would turn our climb into a nocturnal one. But we knew that this was the only solution. We unanimously decided to reinvent our meal times and catch our deepest sleep early in the evening, between seven and midnight. In my 21 years of expedition climbing, the conditions were looking among the worst I had seen on any mountain.

May 6: My alarm sounded with a depressing thudding noise. It was 12 a.m. Groggy, I glanced out and saw the heavy fog muffling the starlight. Light snow fell with a hissing sound on our tent. The air was moist – a prime avalanche warning. We decided to call it a rest day. I read my book all day.

May 7: We headed out into the jet-black abyss, following yesterday's tracks by the narrow light of our headlamps, to cache supplies higher up. The work was hard but mindless. The darkness cradled inner thoughts.

Back at Camp 1 the sky cleared and I hopped out of the solarium-like tent nude. I couldn't resist splashing slushy snow all over my body. The impromptu bath made my skin tingle and considerably lifted my spirits.

"We're gonna climb this bastard!" I yelled to Paul who remained motionless inside the tent.

"Right," he hollered back, "and let's make short work of it!" Paul, who had been feeling sick since our arrival at Camp 1, was acclimatizing poorly. The tent was quickly becoming his prison and the mountain his nemesis.

May 8: I was getting used to the routine now. Up at midnight and off by 2 a.m. We moved our tents higher up to the site of our Camp 2, a spot relatively protected from avalanche danger. As the midday fog rolled in we resumed our customary horizontal position on the suppurating mountain. I read my book.

May 9: We made this another rest-and-acclimatization day. Keen to scope a route through the upper icefall to our next and final camp Ali and I went for an hour's stroll with binoculars in hand. From what we could see there were only two choices of ascent: to skirt the icefall on the right side by ascending a vertical ice trough threatened by rotten seracs; or take a zigzag approach in the middle on steep ice ramps beneath rotten seracs almost twice as high as those in the lower icefall. Neither route looked very appealing. We returned to camp. I read some more.

May 10: Paul who was now suffering from sleep apnea stayed at camp. The rest of us shouldered heavy loads and headed into the darkness. In the limbo of pre-dawn, it was hard to find the route to the foot of the icefall that Ali and I had picked out the previous day. Daylight came to our rescue just as we reached an ascending snow ramp. A gompa-sized serac loomed above us. Kit went first. With an ice axe in each hand and crampons on her feet, she kicked her way up a three-meter-high vertical wall. Then Ace tackled the final 25-meter section across an exposed drop-off.

By now the sun had burned through the clammy fog and the mercury began to soar. The intensifying heat and collapsing snow urged us to face a difficult decision: go on or retreat.

As a last resort, Ali and I struck off to look for a passage through the final section of the icefall. We stepped gingerly over a decaying snow bridge that spanned a dark-throated crevasse and came up against two other parallel crevasses. We could see our goal, the top of the glacier, a tantalizing 20 meters above us. But I did not like the look of it at all. It meant climbing a rotten honeycombed ice wall. We returned to where Ace and Kit waited and reported our findings.

With our energy ebbing quickly we traced our steps downward, frequently plunging into snow above our knees. Back at camp, snow began to fall.

May 11: Yesterday's squall developed into a full-fledged storm.

The whoosh and boom of avalanches charging down Siniolchu's north face kept me on edge. For nearly an hour at midday, when the sun was near its zenith above the clouds, an avalanche crashed down the mountain every five minutes.

In mid-afternoon, as I lay dozing, a deafening thunderclap echoed throughout the mountain arena. Electricity charged the air. Ace's hair stood on end when he went outside to clear snow from the tent walls. Whenever the white-hot fog fitfully parted, the mountain glared down at us, haughty. Night came. The full moon rose unnoticed somewhere above the gloom.

May 12: Feeling thoroughly chastened by the savagery of the weather, we held an impromptu meeting in our tents. Uncertainty and danger faced us all around. In the end it was obvious. We decided to play it safe and retreat. Beneath Siniolchu's charm and beauty lay a hard message that needed to be listened to.

Our thoughts now turned to salvaging the trip. Although thwarted by the mountain, I was still hungry to see more than just the inside of a storm-bound tent. We discussed plans to return to base camp, rest a day, and then head up to the end of the Zemu Valley for three days. We figured we had just enough time to reach Nepal Gap on the border with Nepal before the porters were scheduled to come and pick up our gear at base camp. This would complete our first half-circle around Kangchenjunga.

Baiba was both surprised, and relieved to greet us as we staggered toward her and the cups of tea proffered by our Sherpa base camp team. Nima, our sirdar and an Everest summiteer, comforted us with, "Mind should be clear when climbing. If too many other things to worry about, then not clear. Then no good." We were glad to get back to terra firma.

May 17: With a waning moon lighting our way Ace, Ali, Kit and I left our camp on the Nepal Gap Glacier at 3 a.m. We walked slowly but steadily for 10 kilometers and eventually gained the 1000 meters over fourth class mixed climbing to the top of the pass.

I stood perched on the narrow band of rock and ice at 6000 meters – teetering on the edge of Nepal and Sikkim. I could see the northern base camp of Kangchenjunga that Baiba and I and a new team of friends would arrive at in six months time, and relished the thought of launching out on a new adventure.

To the south Siniolchu, a slender dancer frozen in a pirouette, teased me in the full sunlight of day. I knew that I would chew hard on the disappointment of not reaching its summit. But at this moment that didn't matter. There would be other opportunities and other mountains.

Adapted from Pat and Baiba's book *Footsteps In The Clouds – Kangchenjunga a Century Later*, published by Raincoast Books.

Questions and Answers

1. What compels you to walk?

Pat:
Walking played second fiddle to climbing and ski touring until I trekked all the way from the outskirts of Kathmandu to climb Mount Everest with the first Canadian team, in 1982. Until then I had fixated on the climb but on the way in I discovered the friendly hill tribes, and eventually the Sherpas. This sparked a desire to walk more widely through the Himalaya and the other mountain ranges in anticipation of meeting and spending time with my fellow mountain folk. I continued climbing and skiing of course, but more and more the "expeditions" Baiba and I launched out on were geared toward garnering "tribal wisdom in the modern world".

2. Do you experience instances while you are walking when your mind in somewhere off the trail and on its own journey?

Baiba: All the time.

3. How do you manage to stay physically and emotionally healthy during long and arduous journeys?

Pat:
During a seven month overland journey wherein we hiked, biked and trucked around the Himalaya range, about midway through the journey we realize that we began to suffer from a combination of homesickness and mental "road rash". The remedy was to find a comfy but simple hotel (we had been camping for much of the time) and veg out for a couple of days. As the journey wore on, we started to take a day or two off every couple of weeks.

4. Please share a high and a low period that you experienced during your walkabouts.

Baiba:
There are highs and lows on every walkabout so I randomly picked a trek into Dolpa district of western Nepal the year it opened in 1989. We were with old friend Stephen Bezruchka with whom Pat had been on a couple of climbing expeditions. He had written the first trekking guide to Nepal and spent his first two years in Nepal working as a Peace Corps worker at the Tibetan refugee camp in Dhorpatan, so we were warmly received by his friends when we got there. We had brought Mathiessen's seminal book "The Snow Leopard" and traced his and Schaller's day to day travails as we went. (they had chosen to hike at the height of the monsoon in order to arrive in time for the rutting season of the bharal, central to Schaller's biological study to determine whether it is in the goat or sheep family).

The highlight of the trip came about a kilometer to Ringmo, the tiny village by Phoksumdo Lake where we had planned to rest for a few days.

Long before we saw the yak caravan, the delicate strain of its bells drifted to us on the crystalline air. A boisterous procession of a family and their beasts, groaning under 80-kilogram sacks of rice, rounded the corner. Powdery dust kicked up by the shuffling yaks and their hybrid dzo cousins stuck to the animals' tongues, which lolled almost to the ground.

"Tapai kaha jane?" I asked them in my pidgin Nepali. "Where are you going?"

"Hami Ringmo jane! Come with us."

The herders' festive shouts, whistles and laughter beckoned us down from our mountainside perch, up near the sky, where we had been resting, munching nuts.

After sixteen days on the trail, our bodies honed from the rigours of walking in this perpendicular world, we had finally reached the region of Dolpo, a forgotten corner of the Nepal Himalaya. It was a familiar landscape for Rocky Mountain residents like us but here the land beat with a Buddhist heart.

The magnetism of the yak driver's wife drew me to her and we ended up walking together. Her broad cheerful face belied the hardships of life on one of the highest inhabited plateaus in the world.

Impulsively she grabbed me and we skipped down the trail holding hands and laughing at the spontaneity of a friendship that asked no questions and made no demands. The world was perfect that moment, that day. I wanted nothing more than to simply be there.

The downside of the trip came the very next day on the shores of Phoksumdo Lake where we were forced to turn back because in those early years Inner Dolpa was still closed to foreigners. I'll never forget setting out with Pat at a brisk pace to see how far we could get before the Nepali police stationed at the lake came running after us. It took about an hour before we were turned back, but we got just far enough to get a stunning view along the trail cut right out of the cliff face framed by the azure water of the lake below. One of my favourite moments in Eric Valli's magnificent film, "Himalaya", was shot on this precipitous trail, showing a yak caravan carrying traditional goods like salt and cheese from the Tibetan plateau to trade in the foothills for rice and sugar. Another high – getting to our end point at village of Jumla and listening to a Peace Corp worker's shortwave radio at the moment the Berlin Wall started to come down.

5. Have you experienced an important Encounter that somehow changed the direction of your journey?

Pat:

On many of our project journeys, while shooting a film, book or magazine piece, we have encountered "real" travelers who have cut loose from their home countries and been on the road for years, with no sponsors and thus no sponsorship obligations. They get along by mooching and working their way around the world. Not many of them are walkers per se but even so they've done their share of walking. What it boils down to is the longer you are immersed in the journey the deeper the experience. At the end of many of our self-imposed time limits of, say, month-long treks, we find that just when the experience is starting to sink in, regrettably it's time to return to the "important" time-based world we had left behind.

Biography

From the cloud brushing wonders of the Himalaya to the mysterious jungles of Irian Jaya to the mountain wilderness of their backyard Purcell Mountains in southeastern British Columbia, Canada, Pat and Baiba Morrow's careers have defined adventure journalism for 35 years. As a climber Pat forged challenging new routes, while his natural curiosity and keen storytelling sense took him not only to the top of the world as a member of Canada's first Mount Everest expedition in 1982, but also to become the first to climb the highest mountain on each continent (Carstensz Pyramid version of the Seven Summits).

As photographers, writers and filmmakers, Pat and his wife Baiba have trekked through some of the most remote and exotic destinations on the planet.

But far beyond capturing captivating images of landscapes, flora and fauna, their books, magazine articles and films embrace the people of each of those places, honouring their unique customs, histories and cultures.

They have spent over 1000 days hiking, biking and climbing their way through the Himalayan range, and an equal number in other ranges of the world.

Selected walks: for Pat, to the base of 20 high altitude peaks around the world as a prelude to attempt to climb them.

30 day ridgewalk, traversing the Japan Alps from the Sea of Japan to the Pacific Ocean.

80 day trek from Annapurna to Everest, ascending an amount of elevation equivalent to climbing Everest five times from sea level.

60 day circumhike of Kangchenjunga and an attempt on the lovely 7000 m peak, Siniolchu in Sikkim.

3 day kora around Mt Kailash, the holiest mountain in Asia.

Thirty day ridgewalk traverse of the Japan Alps, from Sea of Japan to Mt Fuji-san and the Pacific Ocean 1995. *Photograph by Pat Morrow.*

Pat doing a Mary Poppins in Ladakh. *Photograph courtesy of Pat Morrow.*

Thamserku Peak seen from the entrance to Gokyo Valley, Khumbu, Nepal, at the end of an 80 day trek. *Photograph by Pat Morrow.*

Nearing the north base camp on the Nepal side of Kangchenjunga – since the mountain straddles the border with Sikkim, we had to split the seven week trek in two. *Photograph by Pat Morrow.*

Phang Lhabsol monastic dances celebrates the unifying forces of the five summits of Mt Kanchenjunga, Rumtek Monastery, Kagyupa order, near Gangtok, Sikkim, India. 1998. *Photograph by Pat Morrow.*

Even though our first attempt to get to Carstensz Pyramid in Irian Jaya was thwarted due to political complications, we spent a highly rewarding month in the Baliem Valley with the Dani people. *Photograph by Pat Morrow.*

"If you want something bad enough,
make it the most important thing in your life."
~Tony Mangan

Tony Mangan

Start with your dream, not your circumstances.
Starting with your circumstances leads to excuses not to live your dream.

The Irishman Who Ran Around the World

"What do you want!" barked the owner of another trading post.

"An ice cream," I replied as I browsed the camping gear.

"I thought you wanted ice cream? What are you doing over there? Ice creams are over here!"

I selected a chocolate ice cream cone and moved a box off a chair to sit down. A picture of Geronimo, the legendary Indian chief, hung on a wall, which had the caption, "Homeland Security Fighting Terrorism Since 1492." Just then, a young Navajo man in his twenties came in for some beer.

"Hey Mickey, how is your day going?" the young man asked the store keeper.

"So what are you up to? That's a nice and fancy GPS you got around your neck and is that a compass too?"

"Yes, I have to stake my plot up around the back!"

"But you can't do that, it is private property!" said Mickey.

"Listen, I am Navajo and it's all mine I can take which plot I like."

The government gives every Native American one plot of free land for a 99-year lease. Mickey turned his attention back to me. I was still eating my ice cream, but the wrapper fell onto my lap.

"When you finish with that wrapper throw it in the trash can!"

I felt as if I was a young boy again, being schooled.

I told Mickey, "You know, I nearly didn't stop here but almost kept going."

"I know, I saw you stopping on the road, and I pitied you. That's why I let you sit down, not like that Aussie nutter that stopped this morning on his bicycle with his guitar slung on his back. I hate tourists; all they do is come in here to gawk! They ask the price of twenty things, never buy anything and ask if they can use the restroom even though I got a No Rest Room sign. That's why I put those railroad ties in the parking lot—to keep them out! All they ever do is pull up here and throw their trash in the can, shit around the side of my store, and suck cock!"

Just then a tourist drove up and took a photo of the trading post.

"Look, some more cock suckers!" He shook his fist at the window. "Go away, we are closed!" he roared.

"But you must lose a lot of business acting like that Mickey?" I asked.

"The number of times I depend on a sale from one of them is about once a year. My real business is with the Navajo. Even with all their problems, they are good for me. You know, they got 60% unemployment on the reservation, and you know as well as I do if you want to get a job you will always get one. I have been working since I was eight years old and I will be working until the day I die. They come in here and ask me to slide them a six pack with all the money they get from the government and casinos. They get an allowance from the government and free medical and everything they need, and if a casino is built on the reservation, each family gets five grand a month."

"That sounds like a lot. Can I quote you on my blog?"

"You can say whatever you want, and you can go in there and do it now on my computer...I am from Brooklyn... You ever heard of Brooklyn? Well in Brooklyn you've got to be tough. Out here it's still the wild west. If I call the cops, they won't be here for an hour, so I gotta take care of things myself."

He showed me a Browning pistol in an old brown holster under his jacket.

"I also got a shotgun under the counter."

He continued, "A while ago, a tourist came in and asked me what this place is called. The Reservation! Lady, you are almost on it. Then she asked me if she needed a reservation for the reservation! So I told her to get out of my store and to go back to California. Then she told me I was the rudest shopkeeper she had ever met. I told her she had forgotten all of the ass-lickin' shopkeepers, but she will never forget me! Ha! Ha! That's for sure!"

I stood up to leave, and Mickey invited me to spend the night in his home, a 40-foot trailer.

Although it sounded entertaining, I declined, as I wanted to keep running.

Just as I was opening the door, he shouted, "Nuts!"

I was a bit confused and then he said... "Do you want a bag of peanuts? Take them off the shelf—they are great for protein."

Mickey followed me outside and warned me about the motorists and the people in Flagstaff. While preparing my gear to continue my run, I cranked up my iPod and turned on my external speakers that are attached to Nirvana, my cart.

"What cocksuckin' music are you listening to, Pink Floyd? Wish You Were Here? I have been trying to sell this damn place for three years now!" Then he called me back.

"Here is $10 for you. I don't want you going down the road calling me a rude bastard! Remember, run like hell in Flagstaff; it sucks and they are all cocksuckers!"

"You really do like Pink Floyd. Don't you Michael?" I laughed, and then I ran down the road to the National Forest and rolled out my sleeping bag behind a hedge. It can be difficult to find camping places in most of America as most fields are surrounded by barbed wire. I wondered if it could be for liability reasons.

Extract from *The Irishman Who Ran Around the World, Part 1: All of the Americas*.
Reprinted by permission of the author

Questions and Answers

1. What compels you to walk?

I am new to journey walking, but it's the same as when I was on my world run and before that on my world cycle trip. I love meeting people on their 'home turf.' I have always enjoyed stopping for a chat or a cup of tea; all these methods of transport make this happen. There is something about crossing a country from border to border, or a continent from coast to coast, that is rewarding. I love nature, and when you travel by foot you can't help but come across it—snakes and all. And bird and animal sounds; I wish I knew what species they were.

2. Do you experience instances while you are walking when your mind is somewhere off the trail and on its own journey?

We spend so much time on our feet, that it is difficult to stay focused 100%. When I ran through India, it was very difficult for me. I was always harassed; and drivers of cars, trucks and motorcycles constantly cut in front of me. It was 'jump or die.' It was so bad that I carried a stick to smack the motorcyclists out of my way. There was one occasion when a motorcyclist shadowed me at high speeds on the road's shoulder. I ran through many of the troubled states where there are so many social issues. India has left a scar on me; if I was examined by a psychologist I am sure I would be diagnosed with post-traumatic stress. I find it difficult to fight the trauma of India off, as I keep going there in my mind when I wake up in the morning on the road. India haunts me.

3. How do you manage to stay physically and emotionally healthy during long and arduous journeys?

Physically, I am pretty much a wreck! I am just plodding along. I have serious muscle wastage on my left leg, perhaps the measurement around that thigh is about 10% less than on my right thigh. Obviously, my right leg is much stronger than my left. When I finished my world run, it was in a bad way. I did some weight and physio exercises for a year, but it hasn't improved. Emotionally, I try to keep my mind off any negativity. I try to turn those thoughts into something loving; it's a lot easier on the mind, and a great feel-good factor. I also practice on keeping my mind as sharp as possible by working on my memory. I sometimes have a problem remembering the name of a city that I have spent two weeks walking to. Yet, I have mastered a memory technique that has helped me to remember a list of twenty items, in sequence, backwards or any numbered item at random. Sometimes, I make up a new list, and I need about ten seconds to memorize each item.

4. Please share a high and a low period that you experienced during your walkabouts.

The low point on my world run was on the day I crossed from Bolivia to Argentina. I received a message from home that my mother had been diagnosed with bladder cancer. She would not let me stop or shorten my world run. Mom had a prognosis of two years and I had more than that still to run. My dream had become her dream and she told me that had I stopped, she would have been heartbroken. A year-and-a-half later, when I was running through India, I was worried that she might die. That added to my already nightmare experience there. If my mother was going to die before I got home, I didn't want it to be in India.

The high point was that my mom lived to cross the finish line with me. I believe we kept each other going. She lived for another five months after my run, before eventually dying of liver cancer.

Other highs include when I crossed the Colorado state line. I had lived there for many years. It has always been a special place for me and part of my dream was very much alive with me when I lived there, so it was a sort of homecoming. I also remember one particular night while running in the Australian Outback. Most of the time I didn't listen to music, but one night I was listening to Handel's Messiah. I was at one with myself and the world. I wish I could have framed that moment in time.

5. Have you experienced an important Encounter that somehow changed the direction of your journey?

No. Other than my mother's illness as already mentioned.

Photograph by Ilya Uzhegov.

Biography

For over twenty years I have had a fascination with walking. In 1979, I had cycled around the world after being inspired by an Irish woman who cycled to India. Years later, my real dream in life was born; it was to run around the world. I stepped up in distance from running ten-Ks and marathons to ultra-running (multi-day events). Back then I couldn't see how I could logistically run the world; it seemed easier to slip on a backpack and walk, instead of run, out the door. For several years, I was flip-flopping from a run to a Plan B walk, and then back to a run. In 1998, I was living in Colorado, USA and returned to Ireland to set out to walk around the world. I was just four days from my planned start when I decided to pull the plug. I would somehow find a way to run around the world. However, after my competitive career took off, I decided to delay my global journey until I retired from competition. In 2010, I decided it was time, and four years later I completed it, having run across five continents, in 41 countries and ran exactly 50,000 kilometers. After that, I wrote two books. Part 1 and Part 2 of *The Irishman Who Ran Around the World*. However, I still haven't found a publisher. That kept me occupied for a year; after which I was twiddling my thumbs and wondering what to do. I was missing the road, so I decided to live my old Plan B dream. That's where I am at now.

John Francis

Who we need to be is who we are.

Living on the Road: Up in Smoke

The transition to life on foot, though voluntary, is not easy, and not everyone is happy with my decision. Already I have lost my job as the manager of a struggling avant-garde music group, Spectrum of Sight and Sound. My job is to book and promote concerts throughout the Bay Area, and chase the elusive recording contract. Relegating myself to foot and phone, I find that I am not effective. I am not surprised when I am let go.

Still, I try to do those things I've been doing before I stopped riding in cars. When I am invited to play in an impromptu volleyball game in Point Reyes Station I make the four-mile, one-hour trek while everyone else makes the five-minute drive. The game is nearly over by the time I get there. Going to the movie theater or meeting friends in San Rafael, twenty-five miles away, is even more problematic. I have to leave the day before.

I have been walking for only two months when the first big test of my new lifestyle arises. I can see it coming as I walk down First Valley and over one of the little wood bridges that cross the creek. When I arrive at the firehouse the large doors are open and I can see the shiny red La France fire truck that is the heart and soul of the Inverness Volunteer Fire Department. I have been a member of the fire department for nearly six months. Dick Gravison, the fire chief, is polishing a chrome fixture on the side of the big truck. He sees my reflection in the chrome and looks up and motions me over.

His stooped shoulders, leathery neck, and bald head, give him the appearance of a human turtle, old and wise. His moves are slow and deliberate. His voice is gravelly.

"Hi John. Thanks for coming down."

"It's not a problem, Dick. What's on your mind?" I ask, but I already know the answer. It is the same thing that has been on my mind since I started walking everywhere. How do I fit in to a sixty-mile-per-hour world while I am traveling at three?

"Well, people are saying that they've been seeing you doing a lot of walking between here and Point Reyes Station and that you're not riding in cars anymore." He smiles and chuckles to himself as he looks over the rim of his wire tortoise-shell glasses, then moves to another chrome fixture that is the pressure gauge for the water pump.

I think back to the road. It is not unusual to see someone walking along the road between Inverness and Point Reyes Station, nor is it unusual to be offered a ride from a passing motorist. Most of the people traveling this stretch of road during the weekdays are local residents. Beyond Inverness the road ends at the beaches and the Point Reyes lighthouse, a favorite spot for tourists.

I walk at almost any time, no matter the weather. Frequently I'm offered rides. I always refuse them. Most of the time this is the end of any discussion, and I continue on my way.

But sometimes the occupants of the cars want more—some explanation other than my simple desire to walk. Then I would talk about the oil spills and air pollution that I do not want to be a part of. It is the only explanation I can give, besides being able to enjoy where I live for the first time. It is, despite their blank expressions, what they seem to want to hear. Some nod their heads slightly while others voice their agreement, telling me how they wish they had the time to walk. Many of these very same people had helped with the bird rescue and cleanup during the San Francisco spill. There is often an uncomfortable silence before they drive off, leaving me to my thoughts.

In his autobiography, Malcolm X, when commenting on his conversion from atheism to Islam, wrote that the hardest and greatest thing for any human being to do is to accept that which is already within and around him.

There is no question in my mind that walking is in me to do. Besides, over two thirds of the world's people still get around on their own power. Birds are born with wings, I was born with feet. I can remember spending summers walking on Uncle Luke and Aunt Sadie's farm along the Chesapeake Bay. There was no electricity or running water. Water was drawn from the well. There were no cars. Once we stepped off the train, we walked the sandy roads and trails, and tended the oyster beds by sail.

I remember the horse-drawn wagons of the Amish in the countryside of my native Pennsylvania. We passed them slowly on our Sunday drives. I would wave excitedly but they usually did not look and never waved back. My father told me that they didn't believe in driving cars. In my youth I wondered why. For me, two decades later, walking is a personal solution to my own and to some of society's ills—reaching back in search of something lost and striking out in the hope of finding something new. Whether I can survive on foot, physically or emotionally, in an automotive culture as the Amish do, is another matter, and after word of why I am walking gets around, a few people stop me on the road to argue the point.

I am surprised at the arguments that my giving up driving and riding in cars has caused in the community. Even though many people talk about wanting not to ride in cars because of the oil spill, everyone still does. The response to my decision is harsh and immediate. Once I am nearly assaulted for refusing a ride with someone. "What am I, not good enough for you to ride with me?"

In some instances I am told, "The reason you're doing this is just to make the rest of us feel bad." Granted, there is some truth to this. I naively expected at least part of the community to park their cars and pickups and like the Pied Piper, walk off with me into an environmental utopia. This does not happen. However, the chief criticism the community has is put in the words of a close friend. "John," she says. "You are just crazy. One person walking is not going to make any difference in reducing air pollution or oil spills. In fact, it's just going to mean more gasoline for everyone else."

The comment gives me pause. Maybe I am crazy. How can one person make a difference?

One day just outside town such a person stops me. He is a familiar, mustached face I had yet to attach to a name. The gravel crunches beneath the tires of his car as he pulls onto the shoulder of the road. Rolling down the window, he smiles and asks if I want a ride. I thank him but say I want to walk.

"Why don't you want a ride?" he asks. His eyes narrow. The smile disappears from his face and I can tell he wants more than just the usual.

"I like to walk." But he doesn't wait for my answer.

"I heard about you," he snickers. His eyes narrow. "You don't want to ride because you think you're better than me. Isn't that right?"

I shake my head and try to explain about the oil spills and automotive pollution, but that makes little difference.

"Oh yeah, well, I like birds too. Are you trying to make me feel bad? He shouts.

I find myself standing beside the road yelling at this man who is yelling at me while trying to make a point. I can soon see that nothing I say short of accepting his offer of a ride to town will make any difference. He tells me he looks at my decision not to ride in cars as a personal attack. While this is a very revealing point of view, I do not like the direction this yelling match is going in and I'm more than relieved when Lance walks up and defuses the situation by making some enthusiastic remarks of his own about living in a free country.

I leave them there still talking and continue on to Point Reyes Station. My head is full, replaying real and imagined conversations, attempting to prove to myself that I am right. I do not like the anger I feel; it eats into my gut. I realize now that I have taken a stand that challenges a way of life, a way of seeing things. It is no wonder that people challenge me. I am challenging myself. I feel frustrated because though it is clear to me, I am unable to articulate beyond the simple phrase why I walk. Even more difficult for me to understand is the burgeoning feeling of something spiritual and sacred in the ordinary act of walking. I start to feel that each step taken is part of an invisible journey, for which there is no map and few road signs. I am not sure I am prepared, and the discomfort both frightens and excites me.

A few evenings later I stop at a phone booth and dial my parents' home in Philadelphia. My mother answers and we speak for a while about relatives and things. I casually mention that I have stopped riding in cars and how happy it makes me to walk. She laughs a wry laugh and asks me how I am going to get home to visit. The question has occurred to me. I do not have an answer.

"Well, that's very nice, Johnny," she says. "But when a person is really happy they don't have to tell people about it. It just shows."

I ask her what she thinks about me not driving. She says she thinks it is fine and then adds, more for herself than for me, "Don't worry, you'll be riding in cars again. This is only a phase you're going through."

The next day I find myself crying beside the road. Each time a car passes I feel as if the world is passing me by, and I am getting left behind. It occurs to me, as it often does, that only my stubbornness is keeping me on foot and I should start riding in cars again. It has been about two months since I began walking and I am getting tired of it. Sometimes I feel as if I am dying. Parts of me are.

Dick is still talking. Still polishing little bits of chrome.

"So if you aren't riding in automobiles, does that include fire trucks?" He stops polishing and looks me full in the face. The expectant expression tells me that he is hoping that I have written some caveat into my new lifestyle. "It's not like you're using a car for your own pleasure. When you're in the fire truck you'll be looking to help someone. Really, you'll be helping the whole community."

"No, Dick, it's all motorized vehicles, that includes the fire truck."

"That's too bad."

"I do know all the trails, I bet I can get to the fire before the La France."

"That may be true in some cases, but the idea of you running alongside the fire truck to get to a fire up on the Mesa might disturb some people."

"Yeah, you might be right about that."

"I know," he says. There is a twinkle in his watery blue eyes. "You can be the dispatcher. We need someone here at the fire station to operate the radio. That can be you. It's the perfect solution. Now just don't stop talking." We both laugh.

One morning Jean and I are finishing our breakfast. When we get to the last cup of coffee she stops twisting the ends of some strands of hair and reaches across the table. She gently runs her fingers down the side of my neck. I grit my teeth to keep from wincing.

"How long have they been there?"

I know she is talking about the swollen lymph glands on my neck, but I ask the question just the same. "What?"

She points. "Those lumps growing out of your neck, that's what."

"Oh that. I don't know, maybe about a month. They don't hurt though." The fact is they do hurt, and I am worried about them. When they first started out as a cluster of raisin-sized growths on my neck where it meets the shoulder I tried to ignore them. Now they were the grape-sized and impossible to disregard.

"You have to promise to walk over to Point Reyes Station and see the doctor. I'll walk over there with you."

I do not feel ill but I make the appointment. The next day I make the four-mile walk to Point Reyes Station to see my doctor. The doctor expresses even more alarm, and speaks guardedly about cancer, Hodgkin's disease. He suggests that the glands be removed as soon as possible. I am just as concerned but settle for a biopsy. It is a simple operation done with a local anesthetic, but it will have to be done in Petaluma, twenty-five miles away.

That evening on the phone I tell my mother about what the doctor said and she dismisses it by saying, "I wouldn't worry about it, cancer is not in our family history."

I decide to continue walking even if I am sick. If death is inevitable, I reason, then I might as well die living what I believe, no matter how naive. Anything else, I think, is giving myself up to sickness.

The Point Reyes–Petaluma road makes its way through some of the most rural landscape in the county. There are only two large hills to climb, and if I leave in the early morning I can reach Petaluma in a day, register at a motel close to the surgeon's office, spend the night, and make my appointment in the morning.

It is hot as I make my way up the last hill. All day turkey buzzards circle overhead and made me think of the dead and dying hidden among the summer-gold hills. I hurry past a fallen deer—a road kill. The putrid smell of its rotting flesh rises from sweet grass and makes me nauseous. I am growing tired, and my feet are starting to hurt. At the top of the hill I can see an old black oak offering shade at the side of the road. I tell myself, "That is where I will stop and rest. I will have a cigarette and sip on the water in my daypack."

Once beneath the tree I remove my shoes and lean back against the rough trunk and light up. The vultures still circle in the summer thermals—dark thoughts in a blue sky. Their lazy circles remind me why I am climbing the hill and why Petaluma is stretching out before me in the distance, and I think, "What if I do have cancer?" For the first time fear of dying seizes me.

I look away from the silhouettes in the sky and extract the pack of cigarettes from my pocket. Blue-gray curls of smoke are already wafting in the air when the absurdity of my actions strikes me. I wonder how I can in all honesty care about pollution caused by cars, or be so concerned about the health of the environment, when I do this to myself?

Then I realize that walking is not enough. Perhaps it is a beginning, but now I see that I am going to have to change not just on the outside but on the inside too, in more ways than I can now imagine. I think that maybe I have already begun this inner change. It seems that all change begins unseen or at least unnoticed in the journey that we call life. I shake my head as I read the familiar warning on the package label, cough a laugh and give up smoking then and there.

I walk the rest of the way into Petaluma and arrive in time for my surgery. The following week I am back in Point Reyes Station and I find out the lymph nodes are not malignant. But on that hill outside of Petaluma, I vowed to live my life as if they were—to learn to balance on the edge between awe and taking life for granted.

My vow gives me a new understanding of Kurosawa's film Ikiru. It is about a bureaucrat who, upon finding out he has cancer and only a year to live, realizes that he has not really been living. He leaves his job and spurns his family to search for what he has been missing, which he mistakenly believes he finds in the affections of a young girl. Only when he is rebuffed and at the bottom of his depression does he discover that life for him is helping the residents of a poor district overcome the monumental obstacles they encounter when they attempt to build a park for their children. In one scene a writer who befriends Mr. Watanabe, our hero, shortly after he finds out about his illness, says, "How interesting it is that men seldom find the true value of life until they are faced with death."

The film makes an interesting comment about how undergoing a personal crisis can instigate an unusual and often altruistic action. In other instances researchers in social work have noted that successful survivors often "engage in some secret service to others" that gives them "a sense that something constructive is coming out of the horrible circumstance." These people are said to look with great commitment for every opportunity to do something helpful, no matter how small. The people who really do well when undergoing a personal disaster are those who look at the problem as an opportunity for change and not as a threat.

I receive a letter from a friend, who with his family has given up the use of automobiles for "walking-in-place" when the death of his father becomes imminent. I write back and ask him what bearing the death of his father has on his decision. In his reply he says:

"Since a teenager I've felt the call to walk around the world. A couple of years ago I decided to start walking-in place . . . When I returned from the New Mexico fire tower work this past summer—to Saint Louis and my dying father—I knew it is time . . . and what better time to begin than on the arrival of Hiroshima Day—with its around-the-world connotations . . . and also better to begin with my father still alive . . . as a continuity with him and by way of including his life force in this work of mine."

At first glance I think the death of my neighbor, Jerry, has this effect on me, and the realization of my own mortality is reinforcement. The context of my walking expands into the realm of service.

Not long after Jerry's death there was some talk in the community about establishing a bay watch. Tomales Bay is only about a mile across at its widest point, and on a clear day people on either side can see any boat that might be in trouble. Still, it had taken almost an hour before anyone responded to the capsizing of the Tanners' boat. I joined a group of Inverness residents and took a course in seamanship the Coast Guard Auxiliary gives.

We had hoped to establish a coordinated search-and-rescue unit on Tomales Bay. However, the residents of the bay are an independent lot. There is resistance to conforming with the uniforms and regulations associated with a Coast Guard Auxiliary unit, so we work with another ad hoc association known as the West Marin Advisory Group, whose goal is to come up with a West Marin disaster plan. A fire that destroyed the town's historic hotel earlier in the year brought the group in Marshall together.

The first objective of both groups is to make a house-to-house canvas in each area to locate buildings, water supplies, liquid propane gas tanks, and main electric circuit breakers. The location of these things will be relevant during any disaster. Under the heading of "Search and Rescue" the plan is to have people who live on the water report any emergency. An emergency number will be furnished and arrangements with Synanon, a drug rehabilitation facility, are in the process of being made so that they will dispatch a rescue boat tied up at their marina. I become the "walking coordinator and liaison" between the Inverness and Marshall sides of the bay. It is a good way for me to meet most of the people who live on the bay. It is a good way to introduce people to other aspects of my walking.

It's a fourteen-mile walk around the bay from Inverness to Marshall: four miles to Point Reyes Station and then ten miles north on Highway One. I had made the drive often to spend Saturday night drinking and dancing at the Marshall Tavern that adjoins the hotel. After a few drinks the fourteen-mile trip back home can be deadly. It has claimed the lives of several friends. I have been lucky.

I still make the trip, but now on foot. It is a pleasant walk along the two-lane highway lined with cypress and pungent eucalyptus trees. The road rises, dips, twists, and turns along the eastern shore as it passes the occasional house, amid small herds of dairy and beef cattle behind barbed wire fences. Bright orange poppies crowd the shoulders of the road as it skirts a cluster of rustic fishing cottages and vacation homes. On weekends, especially in the summer, traffic is heavy and tiresome. When the tide is low I take the old railroad right-of-way close to the water. The tracks have long since been removed. Only the roadbed and the skeletons of the trestles that once crossed streams and mudflats remain. Sometimes, just a few yards from the highway, I feel like I'm in another world. Like sailing on the bay it is accessible solitude—a wilderness beside the road.

One stormy day I find myself rowing on a stormy Tomales Bay; having shunned motorized transportation I often spend many hours on the bay rowing a small dory or sailing our little Blue Jay. The tide has changed and a south wind forces me to land this particular day on the shore of the Tomales Bay Oyster Company, which sits across the water from Inverness. I make my way over a barbed wire fence and along the beach to the house set back beneath some cypress and knock.

Gordon Sanford opens the door. He is a rotund man, perhaps a bit overweight, who smiles from behind steamy glasses.

"We're closed," he says, removing his frames and wiping them across the front of his shirt.

"I know you're closed," I answer. "I just rowed up on your beach and I'm wondering if I can use your phone to call home. They might be worried with this storm coming up the way it does."

He looks surprised, peering past me into the gloom, then invites me in and shows me to the telephone.

"You been out rowing in this weather?" he asks.

I nod yes, and make my call. On the other end of the phone I have hardly been missed.

Gordon introduces me to his wife Ruth and insists that I stay for tea and something to eat. The conversation turns to oyster farming and I talk about spending my early summers in Virginia with my aunt, uncle, and cousin without electricity by the Chesapeake Bay, with hand-drawn water from a well and harvesting oysters from a small inlet. I haven't thought about that in such a long while, it is as if I am hearing it for the first time. For a moment I am a kid again, feeling the mud of the Chesapeake between my toes and chasing fiddler crabs down into their holes.

It turns out that they once lived on the Chesapeake, too. I am offered employment on the spot, and for the next several months I work there, harvesting and culling oyster. I learn about acquiring the seed, planting, rack construction, predation control, health standards for public consumption, and the importance of water quality, which after the oil spill in San Francisco Bay has special meaning for me. But even Gordon thinks it is odd when I refuse to use the motor launch to inspect the oyster beds. I row or pole instead. Then one day, straining against a flooding tide, I have to acquiesce. Gordon comes smiling and tows me in.

We sit on the worn gray wooden bench in the sun in front of a concrete work shack and talk. I learn that Gordon is a retired physicist.

"Heart problems forced me to look for a less stressful occupation," he says, as he lights a cigarette, inhales deeply, and coughs.

Immediately I see his chain smoking in a different light.

"Oyster farming seemed a natural."

We talk a little about that for a while and then he bring's up my walking.

"You know, I really admire you for standing up for what you believe," he says. "But do you really think it's going to change anything?"

I hunch my shoulders and say, barely audibly, "Probably not."

A flock of seagulls rises on the wind from a mound of sun-bleached shells and hovers in the sky, screaming.

"Take oil, for instance," he says. "When we run out of that we'll just find something else."

Anticipating what the something else is, I tell him that I do not think nuclear energy is a good idea. It isn't safe. But so no nuclear accidents have occurred and Gordon is ready with all the figures that make my simple statement sound ignorant and uninformed.

"Besides," he continues, "you're talking fission. The new technology will be fusion. Pure and clean unlimited energy."

For the next few minutes he tries to explain. I try to understand, and for a while I live in his world where technology will save us. "It's just around the corner," he assures me. I have never met a physicist before, and I like Gordon a lot. When he talks about the Chesapeake he reminds me of home. Perhaps what he says is true. I don't know, and in a way it doesn't matter. I like the way I move over the land and water. I know I will continue just the same. For in the walking I discover a thread that runs through time, beyond the need of personal protest, connecting me to that life with Aunt Sadie and Uncle Luke on the Chesapeake Bay. I never use the motor launch again.

Excerpt from *Planetwalker: 22 Years of Walking. 17 Years of Silence*. Reprinted by permission of the author.

Questions and Answers

These answers were transcribed by Tor and Siffy Torkildson, based on a conversation with John Francis.

1. What compels you to walk?

I gave up motorized vehicles and started walking when an oil spill made me realize I was contributing to the oil pollution problem. Walking helps to clear my head and deal with everyday problems. For me, it's a way of life, but even though people call me the 'Planetwalker,' I don't have the corner on walking. Through walking, we pass through different environments and situations. I was able to address an environmental problem. I think walking helps us learn to be who we are as individuals and human beings on the planet and in society. Formal education is important, but also the informal learning that comes from years walking is just as important. Walking helps us find out who we need to be. I think this is something important for schools to teach young people.

2. Do you experience instances while you are walking when your mind is somewhere off the trail and on its own journey?

As Thomas Merton wrote, we are on a physical and an inner-journey. My mind was often in an altered state, especially when I walked in silence. So many of us are time driven. I like just to stop and be. Life will gather around you as you are there. I look for opportunities not to rush, to spend time with people, help them; go to school. Walking makes you even more present (hyper-present).

3. How do you manage to stay physically and emotionally healthy during long and arduous journeys?

Music and painting are very important, as is doing community service—not necessarily through an organization, but it could be helping someone build a house. Helping people is important. Listening is important.

4. Please share a high and a low period that you experienced during your walkabouts.

Soon after I started walking, two men with guns confronted me. One man pointed his gun at me and said, "We don't like your type here." I immediately thought hey, this is the end, and I was sad and afraid. But then something happened; I realized the person with the gun was familiar, and I realized this familiarity was death. Death, I thought, had to be familiar because death was a part of life; of course it's death. I could die this very moment. I told myself not to be afraid. Besides this being the end of my life, I was unhappy because I hadn't done my daily watercolor for the day. Surprisingly I was able to walk away. I was shaken and thought of giving up walking but realized that death would find me, no matter if I gave up out of fear or not. I was motivated to keep walking across the United States and eventually the length of South American. I guess this is both low and high, like being tired, cold, and wet after climbing a high pass, and seeing where you've been, and all that is before you all at once.

5. Have you experienced an important Encounter that somehow changed the direction of your journey?

Right here right now is my favorite place. Everything and everyone is an encounter. You can't have the outer journey without the inner journey. In this state of being, everyone has a message and something that is important. I am here to listen, in total awareness.

Photograph courtesy of John Francis.

Biography

John Francis was in his twenties when a 1971 oil spill in San Francisco Bay jarred his comfortable life. Even as he joined the volunteers who scrubbed the beaches and fought to save birds and sea creatures poisoned by petroleum, he felt the need to make a deeper, more personal commitment. As an affirmation of his responsibility to our planet, he chose to stop using motorized vehicles and began walking wherever he went. His decision was greeted with surprise, disbelief, and even mockery—but it was only the start of a much deeper transformation. A few months later he took a vow of silence that would last seventeen years.

During that time, he founded Planetwalk a non-profit environmental awareness organization, received a B.S. degree from Southern Oregon State College, a Masters degree in Environmental Studies from the University of Montana-Missoula, and a PhD in Land Resources from the Gaylord Nelson Institute for Environmental Studies at the University of Wisconsin-Madison. Ending his silence, John served as project manager for the United States Coast Guard Oil Pollution Act Staff of 1990, in Washington, DC, where he assisted in writing oil spill regulations. For this work, he received the U.S. Department of Transportation's Public Service Commendation.

In 1991, for his work in raising environmental consciousness, John Francis known the world over as the Planetwalker, was appointed the United Nations Environment Program's Goodwill Ambassador to the World's Grassroots Communities.

Over the years, John Francis has walked across the United States, walked and sailed through the Caribbean, Venezuela, Brazil, Bolivia, Argentina, and Chile. He recently began a walk studying organic agriculture and sustainable development in Cuba, and is developing Planetlines, an environmental education curriculum based on the walking pilgrimage for high school, college and civic organizations. In 2005, he published *Planetwalker: How to Change Your World One Step at a Time*. In 2009, the National Geographic Society republished it as *Planetwalker: 22 Years of Walking, 17 Years of Silence*.

Since John Francis began using motorized vehicles to return to and from his walking pilgrimage he speaks and consult with a variety of audiences around the world, including redefining environment for the travel and tourism industry, introducing the role of ethical advisor for civilian/military humanitarian operations, and encouraging diversity and inclusiveness within traditional conservation and environmental organizations.

On Earth Day 2005, he began a walk retracing his route back across the United States, looking for differences in the landscape and the conversations. His goal is to redefine the environmental problems we face into an inclusive concept, and to form partnerships among Native and non-Native people, cultures, businesses and organizations across America that might traditionally feel they do not share the objectives and values of environment and conservation. His thesis is that if we as human beings are an integral part of the environment, then how we treat each other and ourselves directly and indirectly effect the physical environment. His most recent walk was in China, Planetwalk Hangzhou: 2014.

Cherifa, Ariane, Hassana, and Ahoudan, with Soriya and Arouna on Zorro the donkey, on a walk in their Niamey neighborhood.
Photograph courtesy of Ariane Kirtley.

Ariane Alzhara Kirtley

It is no use walking anywhere to preach, unless our walking is our preaching.
~Saint Francis of Assisi

We are proud to present two chapters that highlight a multi-generational walkabout history. Contributors Michael and Aubine Kirtley are the parents of fellow contributor Ariane Kirtley, whom they took trekking throughout the Sahara beginning when she was a year old. Ariane is now doing the same with her three young children.

Aristotle of Africa

"Ariane, you are a péripatéticienne!" jokingly declared my friend Issouf. I had just declined his offer for a ride to go pick up my son Soriya at school. It was a thirty-minute walk away. "No thanks, it's too close," I responded. "Plus, I need to walk to think, and I need to think right now."

"Péripatéticienne?" groaned my husband, Denis, with a half-grin. "I didn't know my wife was a lady of the night!" In fact, the etymology of the word—peripatetic in English—comes from "street walker" in ancient Greek, ergo the confusion. In modern times péripatéticienne has become a euphemistic French term for a prostitute, but it originally came into vogue to describe the legendary Athenian philosopher Aristotle, whose greatest thoughts came to him while walking together with his student disciples.

This is the usage the erudite Issouf was referring to: since I need to walk to think, and am often with my disciple-like children in tow, I am indeed a modern-day péripatéticienne. "Aristotle of Africa," I mused. Why not? I held my head high. While I cannot claim greatness as a philosopher, I walk to think every day, hours at a time. And I often use my walks to teach lessons to my children.

"It's scorching right now." Issouf insisted, not fully understanding how I'd rather walk outside at noon in 40°C than ride inside an air-conditioned car. I yearned for my thinking time, and was also looking forward to greeting the friends whom I encountered on the way:

The group of old beggar-women who sit every day on the same street corner on my pathway to school. They giggle every time I try to chat with them in Hausa. (I made sure to bring extra change for them.) The house watchman who calls me "Ma chérie" when I'm alone, and "Madame" when I'm with my husband Denis. The Tuareg shopkeeper Fati. Ever since I visited her after she narrowly escaped death when a drunk driver ran into her boutique, she always gives me cookies for my children.

I also cherish the pungent smells of noontime, when the women of every household—the squatters and the landladies—prepare their various cooking sauces. I like guessing which sauce is being prepared behind the concession walls. This one must be maffé peanut sauce. That one, I'm sure it's a beef and vegetable sauce. And this one, such a rich aroma, tomato and onion sauce announcing my favorite dish, niébé (cowpeas) with rice!

I was living in Niamey, the capital of the Republic of Niger, one of the world's poorest nations. Many describe the city as "uninteresting, dusty, and boring," or "the armpit of Africa." Others, like one of my American friends, fear the city. "Aren't you scared of the terrorism?" she asked me. "Me, I never go walking in the streets where people can see me. If I go out in my car, I dress in a boubou, and sit between two Nigeriens, so that I won't be noticed."

My friend's concerns are understandable. The threat of terrorism is all around: Al-Qaeda to the northwest in Mali, Boko-Haram to the south in Nigeria, ISIS to the northeast in Libya. Niamey itself was struck by terrorism in 2011, when a commando out of Mali invaded the heart of the city, ending in the death of two Frenchmen. This heinous act hit particularly close to home when I found out that one of the two dead hostages had planned on marrying my friend Kiki the following day.

I am therefore not oblivious to reality. However, contrary to my friend who never goes out alone, I am not frightened of Niamey. In fact, I find the city utterly fascinating and welcoming.

Whenever I come across men who appear to be radicalized (their long beards, sometimes dyed red, give them away), they clearly try to avoid me—the western woman, very "haram". I wave at them and share a cheerful greeting, like any polite Nigerien would do: "How's your health? How's your wife? How are your children? How's your work? How are your animals?" They are left with no other choice but to salute me similarly in return. I feel rewarded to use my walks to connect with them as a fellow human being, rather than as a strange scared white woman skulking down the street. Perhaps I have helped for a fleeting moment to promote the chances of friendship between our two clashing worlds.

Niamey is my home. So without fear I walk her streets. Shunned by many other Westerners, her dusty roads and back alleyways have become my personal garden of hidden treasures. She is also my muse. I spend my days discovering her patterns, meeting her inhabitants, and inhaling her fragrances. These daily walks have inspired my short stories and led to unforgettable friendships.

Denis and our three children, Fassely (8), Soriya (4), and Indima (1), join me on my walks as frequently as they can—on my back, by my side or on their donkey. Mari and Cherifa, my sons' best friends, join us too, often carrying Indima on their back. I keep a diary for my children to read when they grow older. Thus I include them on my walks even when they can't join me.

Following are excerpts from my walking diaries:

January 8, 2016 – Niamey's Brown Men

My Sweet Princess Indima,
We just came across a homeless man. The homeless in Niamey are completely brown,

that's how I recognize them as homeless. Their clothes are brown, their skin is brown, and their hair is brown. Brown, because they are all covered with dirt; they blend right in with the sand and weathered concession walls of Niamey. I call them "Niamey's brown men."

The brown man that we passed by today was dressed in military garb, covered by a dusty brown trench coat. He had clearly been digging through trash, and was busy sticking his finds inside his coat. He looked nine months pregnant! We greeted him and he glanced dazedly at the ground.

Homelessness in Niger is rare. Typically, no matter how poor you are, even if you are a beggar, you are not homeless. You have a family to go back to. You are taken care of and fed, and have someone to love you.

Most homeless people here are foreigners. They have come from other places in Africa and somehow have found their way to Niamey… like the man I met years back while driving to Agadez. He was walking along the long stretch of road between Doutchi and Dosso. He waved at me to stop, and so I did. He asked for water and food, and I gave him a little. I would have given him a ride too, but he was heading in the opposite direction, to Niamey. He had been walking months from distant Cameroon, and was planning on walking months more, all the way to France. He was homeless but not unhappy. He had a plan.

I wonder how Niamey's brown men have landed here. What is their story? Do they have a plan, or are they simply wanderers—like me? Am I so different from them?

April 3, 2016 – A Crocodile in our Backyard

My Beautiful Bunny Soriya,
What an adventure, tugging Zorro from one block to another, with five kids in tow: you, Fassely, Mari, Cherifa, and Arouna, the donkey-keeper's son.

Your donkey simply did not want to budge today. Granted, this morning was so hot that our dear Zorro would have clearly preferred munching on hay and compost at home.

Egged on by Arouna, Fassely and the girls went around "borrowing" fresh mango leaves that protruded over the concession walls, in order to entice Zorro to keep walking. This ploy only worked for a while. A small crowd of boys and girls gathered around us, offering advice or twig switches to motivate our recalcitrant donkey. Two of them climbed on Zorro's back, while you tugged on his rope. They teasingly placed your Superman baseball cap on Zorro's head. The sight of a three-year-old white boy pulling two teenage Nigeriens on a donkey was hilarious!

Zorro shifted a few steps forward, and then became immobile again. I was flustered by the ruckus of all the children, and our walk was going nowhere. I'm clearly a faster walker than he!

I told everyone to be quiet; I had to speak with this donkey. "Zorro, I'm not going to let anyone unleash their switches on you anymore," I whispered into one of his long ears while caressing his coarse muzzle. "You are our friend. We'd love for you to walk with us, and I'd be most grateful if you'd come along easily. But if you really don't want to walk today, I'll take you home."

I was so deep in conversation that I failed to notice a young woman walk by; on her head she carried a large metal bowl filled with freshly-ground millet. "Clang!" fell the bowl, spilling the millet into the sand. Unhappy cries followed. The woman, flabbergasted to see you holding the rope and me speaking with the donkey, had lost her balance. I looked up just in time to witness her tearful distress, as she labored frenziedly to scoop up the top layer of grain, its sweet scent permeating the street. Men and women from all sides chuckled—though some felt badly for the woman, I'm sure. Millet is so expensive, and quite possibly 20 kilos of it lay on the ground. I was tempted to let Zorro eat the remainder. One guy snapped a photo of us with his phone.

Over the past month, we have become the neighborhood "live series". People stop their taxis just to take a photo or shoot a video of us with Zorro. I am told that we have become stars on Nigerien social media, and I have been approached by folk from distant parts of Niamey who know me as "the donkey woman", thanks to Facebook. I had no clue we'd be so popular and unique when I bought Zorro for you last month. I haven't even posted photos on social media myself, hoping to keep our presence in Niger off the potential terrorist "radar." Boy do I have a strange notion of how to stay off the danger grid!

I stood up, taking the rope from your little hand. After asking one of the boys to jump off the donkey, I placed you up there in his stead. With everyone observing our next moves, I secretly prayed that Zorro would heed my request. Please don't make me lose face in front of all these people. I gently tugged on his rope. Drum roll, please… he moved. He walked. He even walked swiftly. A real donkey trot! I held my head up proudly.

From then on, any time he slowed down, I'd stop and whisper gentle words in his ear, all the while caressing his ears or muzzle. Soriya, your mommy has become "the donkey whisperer". Post that on Facebook, Nigeriens!

It wasn't even 10 AM, yet temperatures were already close to 40° Celcius. At this point, we had been walking for over two hours. You were thirsty, I was thirsty. Arouna, the girls and Fassely were thirsty. The half-dozen kids following us were also thirsty. I considered purchasing Pure Water, the small plastic water bags sold at every street corner. But a quick glance at a lonely tree standing nearby, disfigured by multiple plastic bags flapping in the wind, reminded me that buying disposable water bags was not the right solution to our dilemma. Non-biodegradable plastic bags are the plague of African landscape!

I did notice the water-filled clay jugs that often sit in front of homesteads. One of the many beautiful Muslim customs is to have water always available in this way for thirsty passers-by. Despite their inviting look, I stopped us from taking water there, knowing it might be contaminated by dirty hands.

You didn't understand why you couldn't drink from the jugs: "Mommy, I'm thiiirrrrrssssssty!!!"

As I looked down on your gorgeous whiny face, and glanced toward Fassely and our thirsty friends, my mind wandered back to 2005, when I had walked for months among Tuareg and Fulani children of the Azawak. Children, whose entire daily chore was a desperate search for water. For days at a time, I had awakened with them before the break of dawn, watched them prepare their donkeys with loads of empty jerry-cans and traditional gourds made of sheep skin, and then walked by their side for more than 25 km, often until noon or later, to very deep open wells. There, we would wait hours, while several donkeys laboriously pulled liters of thick, muddy water seemingly from the bowels of the Earth, sometimes over 120 meters below the surface.

It was excruciating to observe the gaunt donkeys, as they tripped and wobbled while hauling their heavy loads up from such depths. Once we had filled our jerry-cans and gourds, we would painstakingly load the donkeys with the precious liquid, and trudge the 25 km back home, in up to 45° heat. We'd arrive back at camp before the setting sun, welcomed by eager mothers and younger siblings.

The water we brought home was very murky; the quantity, sorely insufficient. Nonetheless, the families were joyous, just to make it one more day through their thirst and hunger.

Now that, my child, was thirst! This painful memory of the people that Daddy and I have now devoted our lives to, to bring them clean and abundant water, reassured me about you. No, neither you nor I would die of thirst today. Our adventure continued.

Near noontime we headed home. You were hungry and Zorro was stalling more and more often. My whispering magic was definitely wearing off. On the way, we stopped by a trash dump to watch boys fishing with mosquito nets. Rain water had seeped into the deepest part of the dump, creating a small garbage-filled pond. Yuck! Catfish apparently lived at the bottom, and the brave (or crazy) boys dove deep into the black waters to retrieve their catch. One of the boys ran over to us, proudly showing off a poor flailing fish. You, of course, wanted it for dinner. Fassely wanted to join the boys fishing. I whispered in Zorro's ear to take us home.

As we arrived at the small mosque between the first and second laterite roads, near my favorite back alley, Arouna proclaimed, "There are crocodiles behind that wall over there."

"Yeah, whatever" was my dismissive reply, walking on. "Mommy, mommy, I want to see the crocodiles!" you yelped, while hitting poor Zorro with your stick, and trying to slide off his back all at once. "Stop hitting Zorro, and stop trying to get down. Arouna's just joking, aren't you Arouna?" I looked over to the 12-year-old boy, pleading with my eyes for him to shut up. "No I'm not," he declared. "You wanna go see them?" I gave in. We attached Zorro and followed Arouna around the public water fountain that stood behind the mosque. I noticed a low adobe wall, covered with wire fencing and rubbish.

"Come look!" Arouna ordered. Peering through the thick fencing, and into a garbage heap, there I spied two fully-grown Niger River crocodiles. "What in the world?!" I asked myself.

"Let me see, let me see," you screamed. I picked you up so you could see for yourself. Yes, right there, only a few hundred meters from our house, lay two gigantic crocs, with only torn fencing and a very short wall between them and us. "This is dangerous!" I exclaimed. "Anyone can stick their hand right in. Fassely, please be careful!" He was getting too close. I felt sorry for the poor creatures that lived there amidst plastic bags, empty insecticide cans, and other nondescript trash.

"Yep," Arouna said soberly, "the other day a kid stuck his hand in there and got it bitten right off before a man pulled him out." He continued, with a straight face: "...and behind that wall lives a hippo!" I didn't know what to believe anymore. I do know that I'm going to find out why we have crocodiles in our neighborhood!

January 7, 2015 – The Banana Gift

My Salamander Hunter Fassely,
Today you began school at Alliance Bobiel Primary School. As the only Caucasian student, you are nervous. You have been feeling so color conscious that, yesterday, you smeared your hands and arms black with face paint. I hugged you tenderly, explaining that as a child growing up in West Africa, I too did not always enjoy being the only white kid around (with uncle Tercelin, of course). Other children would touch me and caress my blonde hair. I just wanted to blend in.

As if aware of our earlier conversation, while we later went on a walk to buy fruit near the Orange phone store, several neighborhood kids ran up to us, trying to touch you and Soriya. Protectively, I got a little upset with them, and asked them to leave you alone. They stopped touching you, but kept following us. We laughed and joked around with them. Some things don't change, even after 30 years.

Together with your newfound friends, you and Soriya climbed up onto a large fallen tree, and yelled at the top of your voices "I am the king of Niamey!" We all felt very free and powerful and jubilant.

Of course, you also ran up and down the ubiquitous piles of sand. Playing on these mounds is always a favorite activity of yours, even though you aren't supposed to. Masons create these piles outside of concession walls, ready to use on location when they make bricks or create mortar for building construction. They neatly pile up the great big heaps of sand, and often surround them with bricks so that their clean sand won't mix with the dirty brown street sand. But you and Soriya shamelessly clamber up, leaving the door open for several other children to run up and down with you, joyfully cackling as you jump and slide. The masons or sand guards inevitably chase you away, and we race away with our newfound sand-climber friends.

Today, as we passed by a beautiful white mound of sand, typically your favorite, I was surprised you didn't jump onto it. "I don't want to dirty it with my black paint," you respectfully explained.

We walked past several men brewing tea at their fadas (hang-out spots for men and teenage boys). They brew the green tea in tiny kettles over small coal furnaces, often mixing it with mint. The sugary bouquet of the beverage is irresistible. You walked over to a young man pouring a cup, and asked for a sip. He laughed, and answered in singsong French, "not this one, my boy, it's the first round and the tea is much too strong. Do you want to wait for the third round?"

Tradition has it to make three rounds of tea, each sweeter and lighter than its predecessor. The third round is your favorite, as it was mine growing up. We are both particularly fond of the froth that forms as the tea is poured. We thanked the man and chatted a moment, but to your disappointment, I prodded you onward. We could not forget our fruit-buying mission!

"Clickshsh clickshsh clickshsh click!"

"What's that noise, mommy?" Soriya asked, ears perked. It was the clicking of scissors, his favorite "toy". Behind us walked a man, snapping his scissors to inform people behind concession walls that he would happily give them a manicure if they so wished. You asked him if he would cut your nails, and then we all laughed.

My precious Fassely, this is one thing I love about Niamey. Everywhere I walk, other walkers sell their goods and services: Sewing Machine Man, Fruit Juice Woman, and Camel Milk Boy. All going from house to house, followed closely by others selling fruits, wood, woven mats, cookies, tofu…, and the shoe repair guy. There is even a man who goes door to door to pick up your unwanted recyclable items. In fact, we would almost never have to leave our home, thanks to these walking merchants.

After many long detours, we at last reached Mali Bero road, where our fruit vendor has his stand. Imagine our disappointment when we discovered that he had closed for afternoon prayer. Too hungry to wait, we headed over to buy our fruit at the stand across the street.

While buying fruit, a little boy handed me a black plastic bag containing something I had not ordered. "What is this?" I asked. Before he could respond, the bag moved. You and I peered inside, and there, lying at the bottom of the bag wiggled a baby hedgehog. "Oh mommy, can we keep it, can we keep it?" you begged. Soriya demanded to get off my back to see our newfound friend. Then he pleaded, in his sweet little voice, repeating your request, "can we keep it, can we keep it?" "Where is the mother?" I asked the little boy. "Dead," he responded. We had no choice but to take the wriggly animal home.

Both Soriya and you couldn't wait to get home and show Daddy our new pet. After crossing back over Mali Bero, we ran into a dwarf boy missing an arm. I gave him a banana. You asked me why so many people here have deformities. That led us into a conversation about health care inequities. As if on cue, we passed by a man missing a leg, walking through the sand with crutches. I greeted him with a "fofo" and walked on. You afterward asked: "He didn't have a leg. Why didn't you give him a banana?" I did a double take, and thought about your question. I suppose I gave to the first beggar because he was a child. But you were right. I was being inconsistent. Thank you my darling sons for the fantastic walk—now we have to figure out how to care of our hedgehog!

January 25, 2014 – The Deaf Lady

My Prince Fassely,
A deaf lady sits near your school at lunchtime. I see her every day as I walk there to pick you up. She has a shy daughter who is around Soriya's age, and a baby on her back. I think she is also blind in one eye, and her face is scarred. She's quite pretty in a unique sort of way. She's young. She always smiles, and in return, I give her a little change.

While on one of my daily walks to the Total gas station to buy yogurts the other day, I remember very distinctly thinking about her. I wondered what her life was like. How does she live the rest of the day, when she isn't begging? Where is the father of her children? What does the little girl do for fun? Where do they live? What do they eat?

Just as I turned the corner off of the big laterite road, near the borehole drilling company, there she was with her children. I'd never seen her in that area before. It's at least a half hour walk away from your school, so the encounter did not seem like a coincidence. I smiled at her. She smiled back. I was disappointed because I had no change to give her. I tried to explain in Hausa that I planned on coming back with change, but then I remembered. She is deaf.

I went ahead and bought my yogurts at Total, and made sure to get change, just in case I saw her again. I went around the block and there she was, at yet another unexpected spot. I handed her the little change I had. I smiled, this time feeling better, and enjoyed my half hour walk home.

It's kind of silly, really. Why should that make me feel good? I know that the change I gave wouldn't take her that far. But I gave her enough for a meal, for her and her children. I'm pretty sure that's how she handles life, one meal at a time. She does not have the luxury to think about the future. So maybe if I can help her make it from one meal to the next, then for her, a few pennies are significant.

This is how life is for so many here in Niger. Never forget this reality. We have the luxury to think and worry about your future, our future. Many here can hardly think about the next day.

February 4, 2014 – The Warty Cow

My sweet Soriya,
We love buying little millet pancakes from our friend Hadiza, to eat for breakfast. Her friend Zeinabou sits next to her, frying up tofu, which I often buy for our lunch. Their stands are far from the house, but clearly popular and worth the forty-minute walk and the ten-minute wait in line. Mostly, you love peering into Hadiza's concession, to watch her animals as you munch on pancakes. She has a small hut with chickens running freely; tied to a post are a cow and a sheep. These animals are a fascinating sight. The diminutive dark brown cow is covered with warts and blisters. This sickly-looking creature spends its day licking its friend, the sheep, clean. The sheep just sits there, adoring the attention. The two animals look and act quite simply in love.

March 8, 2014 – Ibrahim and the Garbage Diggers

My darling Fass,
I spent several mornings these past few weeks walking through the various garbage dumps in our neighborhood. I am fascinated by what many consider to be places of abject filth—to avoid at all costs. Ok, I am careful where I step, because I know all too well the foul things that lie there.

I have come to understand that I should not wander through the dumps during the earliest hours of the morning, quite simply out of respect for those who use the garbage heaps as their latrines. You see, my dear boy, we are lucky to have not one, but three bathrooms in our house. Many of our neighbors are squatters, and do not even have a pit latrine where they live. So, they hide as best they can amidst the rubbish of the dumps, to relieve themselves. I've found myself eye-to-eye all too often these days with a child, or even worse a grown man, literally taking a dump behind a pile of junk.

I've recently changed my early morning itinerary to the gardens, and visit the heaps after the garbage diggers have arrived. They spend most of their day rummaging through the trash, ferreting out reusable stuff. Also scrounging around are vagabond cows, goats, and dogs looking for a bite to eat. The goats butt heads over cardboard and plastic bags to munch on.

I feel kinship with these treasure hunters of squalor, for I worked many years at the recycling department at Yale. I'll admit without shame that my colleagues and I often engaged in "dumpster diving", pulling out all sorts of recyclable riches. I found some of my best furniture and clothing this way. And although our boss CJ did not condone our freely digging through garbage, out of fear that we might get pricked by a needle, or hurt by broken glass, we loved playing trash detectives!

Therefore, being a retired garbage digger myself, I have the utmost respect for these practitioners of the pits—though I do feel ambivalent about how this all happens here in Niamey. You see, the vast majority of "recyclers" are children. They dig through heaps of muck looking for reusable glass, metal and plastic, which they sell for a few centimes each. They wear nothing to protect themselves from broken glass or abandoned needles. They repeatedly touch feces left fresh from the morning. And none of them, I'm sure of it, wash their hands with soap when they are finished (they'd probably need bleach!). Most have no running water, much less soap, waiting for them at home. And of course, these boys and girls don't go to school, since they spend all day in the dumps.

So, while I respect the art of recycling, I'm definitely not happy that these children have been forced into this abominable chore, without a chance for an education, or access to basic safety.

Fassely, I would never in a million years let you work under such conditions. We are fortunate that I have the luxury to make that choice.

When I walk through the dumps, I smile at the children. I speak with those who understand French. Sometimes I bring them dates or sugar cane that I've bought on my way to visit them. In one section of the dump near the gardens, some of the older boys have set up makeshift tents out of cloth and rods they have uncovered in the trash.

When Daddy and I walked through this section of the dump earlier today, we saw one young man resting in an abandoned infant car seat. He called out to us in broken French, "Hey, are you guys married?" When we answered, "yes" with a smile, he responded, "that's very nice," and then resumed rocking on his improvised throne.

Later in the afternoon, I went back to the same section of the dumps. The young man had not budged from the car seat. I went over to him, this time addressing him in Hausa, "Ina Wuni. Sannu da Aiki" (Good afternoon, welcome to your work). He quietly leaned back, and held out his hand. I could tell from his face that something was wrong. I inspected his hand. It had a large bloated wound, oozing with pus. With all due respect, it was disgusting.

"What happened?" I asked. One of his trash-digger friends walked through a pile of plastic bottles, shuffling his way toward us. "He cut himself yesterday on some broken glass," he explained. "He hasn't been able to work all day today." Of course not, how could he? He was feverish. I asked him his name. "Ibrahim", he whispered, clearly in great pain.

I did not bother asking if he had washed his wound with soap, or treated it with Betadine. I knew the answer to those questions already. "Get up, Ibrahim, you are coming with me to the pharmacy," I commanded. His friend Saidou helped him up. He could not stand by himself. So, together with Saidou, we carried Ibrahim to a pharmacy owned by my friend Doctor Ferdinand. Just as Ferdinand was bandaging Ibrahim's hand, whoosh, to our horror, the boy fell to the ground. He just fainted, right then and there. Saidou explained to us that Ibrahim and he hadn't eaten a single thing all day. We propped Ibrahim's feet up and bought him a bottle of coke— doctor's orders—to get sugar into his blood and him back on his feet.

After a while Ibrahim started feeling better. I bought him antibiotics and bandages, and gave the boys money for food and for the taxi ride back home. I promised to visit them in a few days. Spending time with Saidou and Ibrahim brought the reality home to me of how atrocious the conditions are at the dump. Doctor Ferdinand and I spoke this evening about creating an association to teach the diggers about basic hygiene, and to buy gloves and soap, alcohol and bandages, and other items to help treat their wounds, and to improve their conditions ever so slightly.

At bedtime I narrated my encounter with Ibrahim to you. But the story was different; it took on a fantasy life of its own. In it a genie appeared to the boy while he was passed out in the car seat, urging him to continue digging in the dump. While digging, Ibrahim uncovered a healing flower that cured his hand, and healed anyone else around him who was sick. How miraculous it would be if such a medicinal flower existed, so that Ibrahim could travel all over Niger, to heal the injured and the sick!

March 12, 2016 – Shelled by Stones

My Sweet Indima,
Occasionally, while walking in various parts of Africa, children have thrown stones at me.

The first time that I remember that happening was as a child, while walking with your uncle Tercelin through a beach town in Senegal. I so enjoyed walking barefoot in the sand, hand in hand with my brother, through the meandering streets. Out of nowhere stones came flying from all directions. Tercelin grabbed me, and we scrambled back to the house of Moustapha, a friend of my parents. Before finding refuge behind the concession walls, we looked back for only a moment to see several teenage boys laughing at us, more rocks in hand.

This memory came flooding back to me today, as I walked through our neighborhood in Niamey, with you sleeping on my back. It was midday, and I chose only shady streets, to shield you from the sweltering sun. While you were contentedly lost in sleep, I was just as contentedly lost in thought, and hadn't noticed a group of young children spying on us. If I had, I would have greeted them in Djerma, one of the local languages. A rock suddenly whizzed by my face, brutally jarring me out of my daydreams. Another hit my foot.

It took me a moment to realize what had happened. I didn't even want to believe it. Everyone knows us in our neighborhood. I'm that "white woman who walks everywhere", or "the donkey lady". Who would want to hurt us? But then a third stone hit my arm. Normally, I would have walked away. Or I might have more calmly tried to talk to the stone thrower. However, realizing how close the rock had come to hitting you, my motherly instinct locked in. I reeled around and ran after the little punk, who screamed in horror and ran away. I chased him down the street, yelling "You almost hit my baby!!! How dare you throw stones at my baby!!!"

He ran faster than I did, and found refuge behind the skirts of a woman who had come into the street, curious about the commotion. She protectively shielded the boy, while I yelled at him in French. Calmly she reassured me, while staring balefully at the boy, that he would no longer throw rocks at anyone. My heart was pounding as though I had just run a marathon. Finally calming down on the way home, I wished I had been wise enough to approach the child peacefully, and to explore what motivated him, especially since I was carrying a baby on my back. I'll try to act out of wisdom in the future, my beautiful child.

February 21, 2016 – Election Day, "Un Coup KAO!"

My Little Monkey Soriya,
Today is Election Day. Neighbors warned me not to leave our concession; riots could easily break out and the streets might become dangerous. Especially for Westerners. But you know me, a day without a walk simply isn't imaginable. I did decide to head out early, rationalizing that riots wouldn't break out until later in the day, if at all. So at 5:30 this morning, I wrapped my scarf around my head, grabbed an apple and my voice recorder, and stepped out into the mostly empty streets, before any activity might begin.

Dawn is my favorite time of day, which inevitably begins with the crowing of roosters. Wherever I am in the world, I always associate the rooster's crow with Niger, and with "home".

In the early morning, hues of golden light splash over the otherwise monotonous brown. The sandy ground and concession walls fuse so perfectly in this light that I almost forget I'm in a city.

I truly enjoy being outside even before the Nigeriens. I pass by the street sleepers, usually young men with nowhere else to slumber. This chilly morning, most of them were wrapped tightly in blankets from head to foot, cocoon-like, with their blankets covering even their faces.

These young men are not necessarily homeless. Many have come from afar, looking for work in the city. They clean cars and houses during the day, or windshields at red lights. Some guard boutiques that have been left open during the night. Others are Talibey boys that are sent into the city by their parents to study with Islamic holy men called marabouts. These boys spend their day begging for food and money for their marabout, and retain only a tiny bit of food for themselves. Daddy and I are always sad to see them panhandling. They would be so much better off going to school. Then again, so would all the street kids.

When we pass by the Talibey, you ask me where their mommies and daddies are, confused at how their parents could leave them in such horrendous conditions. One day, my son, you will better understand the consequences of extreme poverty in this world. You certainly are exposed to it here on a daily basis.

One thing that struck me is that, overnight, the colorful posters and banners that had adorned Niamey like a gigantic birthday present these past months have all come down. I felt a little sad... not because of anything having to do with the election, but because it's been fascinating to watch the people of Niamey decorate their city like a little girl when she plays princess. Niamey has been particularly cheerful and pretty, in an odd sort of way. All the streets have been bedecked with pink, blue, white, yellow, and green and orange banners. Posters of presidential candidates plastered all the buildings. Even cars were painted or postered in colors representing the various candidates.

Most popular of course, was the bright pink for President Mahamadou Issoufou, competing with the orange and green for his main challenger Hama Amadou. Signs declaring "Un Coup KAO!" ("Win by a knock-out!") show off Issoufou's faith in his own victory.

The irony is that Hama Amadou is currently imprisoned for allegedly having illegally adopted babies from Nigeria. This is why everyone fears riots today. He's the people's candidate, and the poor are angered that he was not released to represent himself during the electoral process.

But, back to the colorful sights... we've quite enjoyed, while out with Zorro, watching pickup trucks full of dancers ride by, swaying and singing for Amadou or Issoufou, speakers blaring political slogans.

Niamey has been particularly musical during this time, as partisan stands have cropped up on street sides, booming propaganda music for their favorite candidate. You like breaking out in little jigs, joining the ever-present electoral party. What will we do without all the fanfare?

As usual, men woke up for the prayer call at 6AM, trudging zombie-like to their mosque to pray. Today it seems that they are out in greater numbers than usual—perhaps to pray for the success of their preferred contender?

The women, as always, began sweeping the streets around 6:30. It's a fascinating sight: women across Niamey wake up, and one of the first things they do is sweep the sand in front of their concession or home wall. It's not even their sand; it's public sand. But they feel so proud to keep the front of their homes pristine, that they all take ownership, creating a beautiful ballet of sisters simultaneously dancing with traditional hand brooms made of straw, backs bent over, arms swinging in unison, sand flying through the air.

Everything in Niamey still felt normal around 7AM, when the markets began opening to sell fruits and vegetables, eggs and meat. Women set up their cooking stands. I was greeted, as usual, with friendly "fofos" and "sanus", particularly from children who had been sent to purchase the morning meal. A little boy followed me for a while, pushing a wheel with a stick. Another boy sat silently beneath a tree, holding up a sling shot to shoot down a bird. If you and Fassely had been with me, you would have run and played with the wheel-pushing boy, or asked to borrow the older boy's slingshot. But you both were still fast asleep.

The atmosphere felt expectant, filled with an unusual sense of anticipation.

I entered a wealthier neighborhood, and felt slightly ill at ease. The nouveau-riche competitively build outlandish "chateaus", each taller than the next, contrasting like overgrown mushrooms next to squatter huts and tents. These monstrosities look so misplaced in my village, where adobe one-story cottages traditionally adorn the landscape.

A little after 8AM, fancily-dressed fast-walking men and women appeared, with obvious purpose, showing the first sign that the election process had begun. I hastened over to a school near our house, to watch the voting begin. While I eagerly awaited the first voters to show up, a man in military garb greeted me and kindly suggested it would be better if I went home.

I reluctantly followed his suggestion, and took one of my favorite pathways—the alley behind the school that infuses with nauseating smells of garbage and urine, where you obsessively observed a dead chick rot away over the space of a few weeks last year. I can't explain my fondness for this alleyway, other than it is calm and almost always empty.

This afternoon, we were so tired of being cooped up in the house that Daddy and I decided to go walking with the three of you, to pay a visit to Zorro. We figured that, since the election results wouldn't actually come in today, any danger of rioting would arise later in the week. Strangely, Niamey had become a ghost town, with only stray goats and dogs—and we five—heeding no warning.

Once at Zorro's home, you and Fassely played with Arouna and his siblings. You chased Arouna's brother, Abdoulrazac, in and out of their squatter huts, while Fassely kicked around a soccer ball with Arouna. They were pleased to finally have company on this very boring Election Day. Daddy and I visited with Abdoulkarim, our donkey keeper, and some of his friends.

To make conversation, I commented, "Whew, we're lucky that things didn't get violent today!" One of the men whipped around angrily. "It's the fault of you white people if there is danger," he raged. "It's your fault that people are angry at Issoufou. It all started when he declared 'Je suis Charlie' next to your president!"

This man's eruption brought back unresolved feelings from a walk we had taken during the whole Charlie Hebdo period… feelings of sadness at all the confusion, which had led to mayhem at the time all over Niger.

January 17, 2015 – Charlie or not Charlie?

My lovely Fassely,
It's been a crazy and even scary time in Niamey these past few days. Just ten days ago, monstrous violence hit France when Al-Qaeda terrorists stormed the Charlie Hebdo Magazine headquarters in downtown Paris, killing a dozen people. In solidarity with France, President Issoufou stood publicly alongside President Hollande during the "I Am Charlie" commemoration at La Place de la République.

Issoufou's gesture of unity did not go over well in Niger, particularly when Charlie

Hebdo came out with a new cartoon perceived as blaspheming the Prophet Muhammed. Instead of understanding that the stance taken by Issoufou was against terrorism, many Nigeriens interpreted his action as condoning Charlie Hebdo cartoons of the Prophet.

For the first time in my long memory of Niger, large numbers of Nigeriens became hostile towards whites and Christians. In retaliation, roaming mobs burned down many buildings that symbolized Christianity or Western culture, all across Niger—churches, bars and restaurants. I was particularly saddened and alarmed to find out that they had torched the Gondwana Hotel just down our street.

These riots still did not stop us from walking around Niamey. No, we are unstoppable, and will not allow hatred to change our ways! This evening, as we walked with Daddy and Soriya, a young man screamed at us, "Go home you French. We don't want to have anything to do with you here!" Then several young men crowded around him, chanting "Yeah!" every time he hurled out an insult. The situation was very ugly, and could have gotten out of control.

Pregnant with your sister, with Soriya on my back and you by my side, I suddenly feared for our safety for the very first time in Niger. I felt like an outcast in our beloved neighborhood. But as we hurried home to get you kiddoes to safety, I regretted having felt scared. I should have used our family walkabout to talk to this young man. His response towards us was born of ignorance and confusion.

Instead of running away, I could have invited him to walk with us, to meet you, Daddy and Soriya. I would have explained that I too did not want to blaspheme the Prophet, and that we should walk hand in hand in peace. He might have seen us as individuals with a common goal, not as random white folk scorning his beliefs.

So to me, the low point of this unfortunate walking adventure was not in being shunned by this man's hateful outburst; no, it was that I failed to grasp the opportunity to offer a hand of friendship during such a critical time in Niger's history. My son, may you be wiser than I, and always use such incidences to build bridges of unity rather than to cower in fear and indirectly tolerate misunderstanding.

April 20, 2016 – The Green vs The Brown

My Darlings,
We have been back in France for only a few days, and it always takes me a while to adjust. I'm on a walk in the plains of our Loire Valley right now, with Indima on my back, and I can't help but feel sad. I keep thinking about Niamey, the sand, and my walks, and just saying hello to people. The kids playing. The smells. The caustic smells. The nice smells. The smiles. The laughter. The sand. The brown. Our donkey. Our friends…

I miss taking Mari and Cherifa everywhere with us, and watching you play together. I cannot imagine a deeper, more sincere friendship among children. I miss Halimata and Ibrahim, and their utter devotion toward us. I miss our walks with Arouna and his brothers and sisters. And Zorro of course. I desperately miss Fati, my soul sister—who despite extraordinary personal tragedy still approaches life with a smile, and through her sweet nature teaches me about forgiveness.

Why do I need Africa? There's nothing easy there, for anyone. But there is something that's miraculous at the same time. Something about….no, I can't explain it. I can't explain it… there's nothing tangible. There are a million things that are tangible, and nothing tangible at the same time…

Why do I love walking from one block to another? Why do I love walking in the sand? It's not like I miss the pristine desert sand of the Sahara. No, I miss the brown dirt.

I miss seeing people hard at work, and people living outside all the time. There's life. There's just life all the time. There's reality. No hidden life. You see the good and the bad. You see it all. It's right there. It's in your face.

Maybe it's the simplicity that I miss. Maybe it's the minimalism of going to the boutique next door and buying an egg for 50 centimes. On the other hand, there's nothing "organic" in Niamey. There's nothing of good quality—it's all substandard imports. Everything I refuse when I'm here in France. But yet, there in Niamey, I love it. I miss it. And I want it.

Here in France everything is so green and beautiful. Just so beautiful. The beauty that you don't find in Niamey except sometimes near the river…

And yet, something here is incomplete. There's no brown here. It's the brown, the dirt that I want, covering my feet as I trudge through the sand. I resent the grass. I resent the green and the blossoming spring flowers.

Maybe I will get used to being back in France, and I'll feel a little less incomplete. I wish I didn't feel this way. I wish I didn't have this need. I wish I were not a girl of Africa.

I know I'm not African. I'm white. I'm blonde. I don't speak the languages very well. I don't fully understand the culture. And yet I'm not French—because I'm African. I'm not American because I'm French and African. I'm nothing.

And yet, I am African, because I long for Africa. I long for the air, the smells, the sounds, the people, and the walking. I don't long to sweat profusely under a 45° sun. Yet, I do long for that too. I long for the difficulty. I hate the power outages, I hate the malaria, and I hate the poverty. Here in France, we have everything. Yet I feel empty. I am a child of Africa.

And, of course, I am also a péripatéticienne. Always, walking keeps me steady.

What will you be, my wee ones?

Questions and Answers

1. What compels you to walk?

Born into "God's family of walkers," as Henry David Thoreau baptized it, I walk as much as I can: all day long, all the time, and everywhere. God has given me no other choice than to be a walker. In fact, I joke that I am a reincarnation of Thoreau, given how eloquently he expresses my own feelings about my walking compulsions in his essay called "Walking".

I walk to think.

It is not that I think better while walking, but rather that I need to walk in order to think. My brain, in essence, is connected to my legs! I have been this way as long as I can remember. As a middle-schooler in Bardstown, Kentucky, I often worked on projects in groups with my classmates, who were usually happy to have me on their team because I offered creative ideas. Several of them realized that my best ideas always came to me after a trip to the bathroom. After a while, they urged me to go on frequent bathroom trips. In fact, I just needed to walk to think. The bathroom being the only legitimate excuse I could use to leave the classroom, I ended up taking an exaggeratedly high number of bathroom breaks! Even today, as the founder of the international NGO *Amman Imman: Water is Life*, I carry out much of my work while I walk. Thankfully, my team understands that this is how I operate and think; hence, a majority of our team meetings take place while we go walking. Even our partners know that when they are on a phone call with me, it will likely be while I'm out walking. They've learned to put up with the background noise and to appreciate this eccentricity.

I walk to be creative. I walk to connect.

Walking is the crucible of my writing experience. Not only are my short stories written while I walk (dictated into my voice recorder), but they are almost entirely inspired by the people I meet and the things I see, smell, hear and experience when I'm walking. I therefore also walk to discover, to learn, to encounter, and to share. In this way walking grounds me deeply to the world's human and natural treasures.

I walk to survive.

By this I don't mean to survive as in "survival of the fittest", but rather "to stay healthy in spirit." Walking is my "word", since it describes not only what I do much of the time, but also my frame of mind and my existence. Walking is therefore, quite literally, my solace and key to sanity. I walk to fulfill one of my basic necessities, as vital to me as eating and sleeping. I walk to exist; without my walking, I feel I would cease to be. In this way, I commiserate with Thoreau when he writes, "I think that I cannot preserve my health and spirits unless I spend four hours a day at least—and it is commonly more than that—sauntering… absolutely free."

Walking is my road to spirituality.

When I walk, my mind releases itself of burden and anxiety, thereby opening the door to profound meditation and prayer. Unhindered by obligations and stress, I spend my walks communing with my God; my God of peace, of love, of compassion for mankind and nature alike. Together we talk, we laugh, we cry; we become one. I spend my walks not only praying for myself and those I love, but also for solidarity among all humans, and for an increased global consciousness regarding the preservation of the earth's resources. I pray for the children across the world who are born into poverty and war, so that doors of opportunity, hope and peace open to them. I thank my God every day for the many wondrous opportunities I have been bestowed, and for allowing me to share my life with the world's most amazing human beings, my three children. I meditate to grow in strength, patience and wisdom. Sometimes, I get angry with my God, railing about the mess the world is in. Walking helps to sooth such agitation. Close to God, when I walk I feel more complete.

I walk to stay true to my ecological essence.

An essential component of my spirituality is my moral obligation to have a minimal impact on the earth's precious resources, both on a personal and a global scale. As much as possible, I strive in everything I do to be a positive example—a vector for social and environmental awareness. On a more practical level, unnecessary motorized forms of transportation seem like such a waste: environmentally, energetically, and spiritually. Walking opens up a door to the world in a way that is respectful of our planet and humankind.

2. Do you experience instances while you are walking when your mind is somewhere off the trail and on its own journey?

Walking is a journey for my mind. I rarely walk to walk. I walk to think, to pray, to be inspired, and to encounter the world. More challenging to me is keeping my mind on the trail and in the present! I have made some of my most inspiring encounters when I stay focused on my surroundings. But my mind then wanders, while I assimilate and digest the encounter. When I walk, I therefore experience moments when my mind is in the present, embracing my current environment. At other times, my walk is a pathway into unforeseen journeys of thought. At these times, the setting of my walk doesn't matter. All that matters is that I am walking with an open heart and mind.

3. How do you manage to stay physically and emotionally healthy during long and arduous journeys?

Pacing and reflection, along with moments dedicated to rest, help keep me healthy. The more arduous a walk is, the more I use it to meditate and pray. Embracing the walk as a spiritual venture turns scorching heat, bone-chilling cold, drenching rain, hordes of infuriating insects, and debilitating fatigue into a healing tool. For me, it is the NOT walking that challenges my health! On the contrary, walking—no matter how long or arduous it is—keeps me feeling alive and healthy.

The more pertinent question to me, rather, is how do I manage to stay healthy when I am not able to walk? The truth be told, I don't manage very well!

One of my hardest periods was during the last three months of pregnancy with my first-born, Fassely. Six months pregnant, I climbed for a couple of hours up the snow-covered hills of our French back-country through a blizzard, to an appointment with my midwife. "Ariane, I can't believe you walked here," she chided me. "It puts too much pressure on your cervix. Let's have a look!"

During the consultation, she determined that my cervix had dilated to the point that in order to not lose my baby, I had to be bedridden until childbirth. In the wink of an eye, I went from hour-long daily hikes to permanent bed-rest! How was I going to survive three months with no walking—except to the bathroom? At first I became very depressed, but I learned to cope. I meditated, prayed, and read Thoreau to imagine myself on walks. Turning toward spirituality kept me from going crazy.

4. Please share a high and a low period that you experienced during your walkabouts.

Low point: One of my lowest moments happened in 2005. After years of nostalgic yearning, I made my way back to Tofatat, a fabled natural chateau made of huge piled-up stones, hidden deep within Niger's Bagzan mountain range, tallest in the Aïr. I had ventured to this secretive pilgrimage site as a five-year-old with my family, and had been dreaming of my return ever since.

Together with a couple of friends and our guide Ahoudan, I marched for several days across the boulder-strewn valleys of the Aïr Massif, and scaled the Bagzan escarpment up to its sandy plateau. After another day of laborious walking, we arrived at the sacred boulders of Tofatat. Drained of energy and severely dehydrated by a month-long bout with amoebic dysentery, I simply could not climb any more. I lay down in the shade and watched, jealously and longingly, with half-open eyes, as my friends clambered up and disappeared into the passageway to Tofatat's hidden spring, high in the rocks. They evacuated me the following morning. To this day, with the ever-increasing risk of terrorism, I do not know if one day I will return to Tofatat.

See the next essay by my parents Michael and Aubine Kirtley, about discovering Tofatat the first time in the 1970s. They were also accompanied by Ahoudan, the "gatekeeper" of Tofatat's secrecy.

High point: In 2011, my husband Denis and I were hired to design a nomad-appropriate development program for the BaAka pygmies of the western Central African Republic. Although they are often treated as no better than animals by surrounding populations, the pygmies are in fact fascinating experts of the African rain forest. The times we spent walking with them, observing their tremendous knowledge of their sylvan world, was both humbling and other-worldly. The adventures I shared with them rank among my fondest memories. We even chose to name our daughter Indima, which means "the forest" in the BaAka language. Following is a journal entry that I wrote to our eldest son, recounting an unforgettable walk among our BaAka friends:

May 19, 2011

My Dearest Fassely,
We have just finished marching for more than four hours through the rain forest. Now I am resting in a forest clearing. You would have been impressed; it was cleared in a matter of minutes by powerful pygmies, furiously wielding machetes. Behind me sit

two newly-constructed "bee-hive" huts, the typical style of forest dwellings for pygmies. Teenage boys are swinging on a liana to which they attached a branch that serves as a swing. I tried it a minute ago, and my head is still spinning!

We began our trek this morning, departing from the pygmy village Lidjumbo at the break of dawn. The rising sun quickly gave way to rain. It's funny, the pygmies live in the rain forest, but they despise the rain. They created umbrellas from colossal fronds, along with hilarious pointed hats, while we trudged through the muddy forest. There is nothing calm or meditative about walking with pygmies. They chatter ceaselessly, as if engaged in a noise-making competition. Sometimes their gossiping gives way to the women's polyphonic singing, which is entrancing. They half dance and half walk, with their baskets attached to their foreheads and their babies in cloth swings on their sides.

Before pausing to enjoy lunch, we hunted with the men and women. They stretched out nets tied one to the other in a 60 meter long half-circle across the forest undergrowth. True to their constant cacophony, they clapped and yelled to frighten animals on the perimeter into their nets. They cheered when a mother and baby duiker ran toward their trap. One of the hunters jumped on the baby duiker and swiftly snapped its neck. The mother bolted and narrowly escaped. Secretly relieved, I laughed when one of the men yelled angrily "my meat ran away!"

After the hunt, we resumed our walk. One of the men caught a tiny bird from a low-hanging pouch-like nest. He broke its neck and threw it in his basket, looking forward to cooking it for lunch. "What a waste. It's not big enough to provide two bites!" I secretly thought. The elderly man "carrier of fire", responsible for transporting hot cinders, spotted a massive snail. He grabbed it and later cooked it (I kept the shell for you). As we walked, the same man periodically bent down to explore dead tree stumps, hoping to catch a slumbering creature there.

As the men set up camp, we walked to a nearby stream with the women. They built a dam with mud, rotting twigs and other varieties of debris. Held back by the dam, the pooling water yielded plentiful fish, shrimp and crabs. You would have loved chasing these creatures! Back at camp, the catch was smoked and then cooked with Koko vine leaf that the women collected while we walked.

After lunch we hiked for several more hours, deeper into the jungle, past fast-flowing streams and stagnant leech-filled pools of muck. Daddy, who had worn sandals instead of boots, fought off the blood-thirsty leeches. Near the stagnant ponds the pygmies grew silent for a moment, on the alert when pant-hooting chimpanzees leapt frenziedly from tree branch to tree branch up ahead.

Our walk resumed. Along the way men and women gathered edible delicacies. I tasted a small red fruit that they eat like candy. To me it was terribly bitter, so I secretly spit out the flesh along with the small black pith. We also picked paillou, a forest nut which, when cracked open, has a heart-shaped core. They pound the nut into a rich black peanut butter-like paste and mix it with Koko leaves. It's delicious; this mixture is among my favorite dishes in Africa.

In the evening we sat in the moonlight listening to the women singing and the men drumming. Out of nowhere, forest spirits abruptly appeared and danced in the clearing! The first looked like a giant porcupine, and another, like a duiker. If there hadn't been a full moon, the spirits would have glowed, covered with the magical phosphorescent dust that coats the leaves on the forest floor—a miraculous sight that I witnessed for a second while walking back to my tent.

The next morning we hunted for honey with the men. After a couple of hours walking, some men suddenly yelled that they had discovered a honey tree. A canopy of precious tiny white flowers on the forest floor alerted them to honey 50 meters above, high in a tree. Our friend Dimanche nimbly scrambled up the tree, while men on the ground prepared woven liana-and-leaf baskets to collect the honey, and a smoke-out tool to frighten the bees away, rigged from burning dry leaves. Sometime later, Dimanche sent the baskets back down, filled with glorious honey combs dripping with golden goo.

Daddy and I gorged ourselves on the succulent sweet stuff. The sugar rush made me euphoric; I felt very tipsy during the trek back to base camp! I saved some of the sweeter light golden variety for you, my son.

5. Have you experienced an important Encounter that somehow changed the direction of your journey?

In 1998, during my sophomore year at Yale University, I spent a semester researching chimpanzees in western Uganda, inside the Kibale National Forest. One day, while walking from one research station to the other, I had an encounter with elephants that changed my life's journey forever.

That day I departed on foot from Kanyawara, the park's main research camp, at 10:30 AM. I was excited to be making the four-hour hike alone back to my base camp, Ngogo, deep in the forest. In fact, I had just turned down an offer for a guide to accompany me.

Along the way I stopped several times to photograph blue and red colobus monkeys playing in the trees, and dung beetles pulling their heavy loads along the path. At around 1:30 PM, I noticed fresh elephant dung on the trail. Suddenly I heard loud stomping noises nearby, followed by angry trumpeting.

I started walking as silently and as fast as possible, praying that the elephants would not smell me. It is always dangerous to run into a herd of elephants on a jungle path, particularly a mother with her calf.

The trail ahead split into two directions. I chose to take the path leading away from the sound of the elephants. In panic mode, I failed to notice when the trail faded away, leaving only an overlapping network of small animal tracks to follow, each eventually dying off. By the time I realized I should turn back, it was too late. I was lost! The main trail was nowhere to be found. Every direction I turned looked the same. Because of the thickness of the jungle, there were no isolated trees that I could climb to orientate myself, no landmarks, no hills… nothing but dense green.

Luckily, I had my trusty Coleman hiking compass hanging on a cord around my neck; my father had given it to me just before I left for Uganda. Also around my neck was a whistle; I later learned that it probably would have scared the elephants away.

Unluckily, I had little water.

I chose to go east, hoping to stumble onto the trail system that surrounded my base camp. Not yet overly worried, I sat on a fallen log and enjoyed the few biscuits and dried fruit I had brought with me. Gulping down most of my remaining water, I reassured myself, "strength for the way forward!"

After many more hours of battling through tangled vines and lianas, struggling over fallen trees twice my size, sinking knee-deep in swamps, and trudging through impenetrable grasslands, my hope dissipated. I was terrified. I cried out for help, knowing all the while that no one but forest denizens would hear my screams.

Night approached. Thirst kept me walking east, despite my growing exhaustion. Before sundown, I came upon a fast-flowing stream. As tempted as I was to drink, I decided that thirst was a safer choice than risking a sure and immediate case of severe diarrhea. So I walked on, deeply regretting my choice hours later.

Near 9 PM the batteries in my flashlight died. At wit's end, I lay down on the ground in the pitch dark forest, covering myself with my emergency blanket. I twisted and turned, anxious and afraid. Tortured by thirst, I laid out my blanket in an attempt to collect dew. I licked at the humidity, but found little comfort in the few droplets that clung there.

After several hours of torment and fantasizing about water, I got up and pushed forward, making my way thanks to the scattered moonlight that filtered down through the trees. I tried eating leaves, but most were much too dry. I needed to pee. I couldn't deal with the idea of wasting this precious liquid, so I urinated into cupped hands, and tried sipping. I spat out the salty stuff, feeling even more dehydrated than before.

Eventually I came to the grasslands that bordered the forest, and tried my luck eating tall elephant grass. Its juicy bitter insides rejuvenated my hope. I continued marching falteringly for several hours, all the while chewing on grass. Unexpectedly, out of nowhere, I heard the stomping of large animals. I cowered low in the grass, again fearing being crushed by a herd of elephants. But this stomping was accompanied by men's voices.

I had been lost without any provisions for around 16 hours; I don't know how much longer I could have survived—before thirst, exhaustion, and despair got the best of me. I giddily rushed towards the sound of voices.

A trio of lanky men were herding cattle along a small forest trail. Hardly believing my eyes, I ran up to them, begging for water. They offered me none.

Exasperated, I tried asking them to steer me in the direction of a familiar town, but they did not speak a word of English and I did not understand Rotoro, their native tongue. They laughed at me. What was a "muzungu" (white) woman doing in the forest in the middle of the night? Through hand gestures and a few recognizable words, I deciphered that they were on their way to Fort Portal. I knew that Kanyanshu, the tourist center of the park, lay in the direction of Fort Portal. So I walked along beside them. My mind started wandering; after all I'd been through and with my overwhelming thirst, this walk seemed interminable.

Suddenly one of the men gesticulated strangely at me. I thought he wanted food. I tried gesturing back that I wanted water. Realizing I had misunderstood, he pulled out a condom, waving it smugly in the dimming moonlight. Terrorized thoughts raced madly through my mind; was I going to be raped on this forlorn forest trail? Then, when I least expected it, God sent me a sign—a great big white sign on the side of the road, with a black arrow and "Kanyanshu" written in bold black letters underneath!

Somehow drawing upon reserve strength I didn't know I had, I ran away from the men faster than I ever had run before, to seek safety at the tourist center. Once at Kanyanshu, careful to make little noise in case I had been followed, I looked for traces of water and people. There were trails entering the forest, but I feared getting lost again if I ventured there. Finally I came upon several isolated adobe buildings. I knocked on the doors but no one answered. I walked around camp, but found no sign of people. I was terrified and desperately thirsty.

To my relief, I uncovered an abandoned jerry can which seemed to contain water, and swigged down the brown liquid inside. Thirst partially quenched, I sought shelter in one of the buildings. Once again I covered myself with my dependable emergency blanket, and rested for a few hours.

Around 7 in the morning, I was brutally awakened by men screaming outside my building. I gingerly opened the door. To my horror, three assault rifles were pointed at my head! I yelled "don't shoot, don't shoot!" and fell to the ground, bawling. Fortunately, the guns were being held by park rangers; the one closest to me slowly lowered his gun, and the two others followed suit.

The rangers later informed me that if I hadn't emerged at that very moment, they had planned on shooting through the door. They had heard me roaming around camp during the night, and had thought I was a thief or a rebel. Just the day before, while I was lost in the jungle, rebels in Bwindi National Park, less than 100 km away, had captured and killed eight English-speaking tourists. The rangers' nerves were understandably very jittery.

Things quickly turned jubilant. I became their local celebrity: the first white woman to make it out of the jungle, alone and alive! They informed me that others, including some Ugandans, had not been so lucky.

Before leaving for Uganda, I had been an ardent conservationist; I idealistically wanted to defend animals and forest at all cost. While working in Kibale, and especially after my brush with death, I changed the course of my budding career. I came to realize that sustainable conservation can only be achieved when the needs of both humans and nature are met. We are symbiotic in our shared destinies.

My encounter with elephants thus indirectly led me to my current environmentally-conscious work among minority populations in Africa, where I help them in their daily struggle to survive sustainably in their harsh environments. Although getting lost in Uganda was terrifying, I cannot imagine a more traumatic experience than waking up day-after-day wondering if my children were going to have enough water to survive; this is the plight of the people I serve.

ARIANE ALZHARA KIRTLEY

Biography

I am Ariane Alzhara Kirtley. Ariane, the woman in Greek mythology who led Theseus to safety. Alzhara, Arabic for a rare, ephemeral flower of the Sahara, renowned for its beauty. Kirtley, "over those hills" in Old Gaelic.

My destiny has been forged around the meanings of my name. Like the Alzhara flower I blossomed in the wondrous wastelands of the Sahara, where I also nourished my passion for helping others to safety. All the while, my inner compass steers me "over those hills" and beyond, propelled by an irresistible compulsion to walk, seeking new worlds of adventure, discovery, and meaning.

At six months old, I crossed the Sahara Desert for the first time, lying in a baby basket secured to the back seat of my parents' Land Cruiser. From those earliest moments forward, I enjoyed the most unconventional lifestyle imaginable, thanks to my parents Aubine and Michael Kirtley, photo-journalists for *National Geographic* and *GEO* magazines at the time. My older brother Tercelin and I were "home schooled" while floating down the Niger River, trekking in African rain forests, and camping throughout the vast reaches of the Sahel. My fondest memories are of playing with my "best friend" Julia, a baby gorilla in Gambia's Abuko Nature Reserve.

Soon after graduating from Yale University with a B.A. in Anthropology and a Master's in International Public Health, I returned to the Sahara in 2005 as a Fulbright scholar. I spent several months walking alongside Tuareg herders in Niger's Azawak Valley. There I witnessed children dying from dehydration: young boys and girls who walked up to 30 kilometers a day in searing 45° heat—not for pleasure, but out of desperation to find water. In 2006 I turned this walkabout into the international NGO *Amman Imman: Water is Life*, to address the needs of minorities in Africa, beginning with constructing deep borehole wells for Niger's nomads.

To foster cross-continental and cultural friendships, *Amman Imman* holds annual "Walks for Water" together with thousands of children around the world. These walks of solidarity remind Western schoolchildren of the plight of their brethren in the Sahel, and are a vector for nurturing understanding and solidarity through global consciousness.

A confirmed walking addict, I have trekked through the jungles of the Central African Republic with the BaAka Pygmies, chased chimpanzees in the Ugandan rainforest, scaled peaks in Appalachia and the Alps, and have become Niger's "walking Donkey Whisperer". I am a walking storywriter, not only gathering ideas from my encounters while walking, but also my stories as I walk, dictating them into my pocket recorder.

I am also the mother of three children: Fassely (8), Soriya (4), and Indima (1). Similarly to how my parents raised me, my husband Denis Gontero and I travel the globe with our children in tow, to accomplish our international development work. The world is their classroom, and like the Greek philosopher Aristotle with his disciples, I turn our walks into their roving schoolbook. I keep journals for my children, telling them about our walking adventures. My walking essay in this book is a collection of journal entries written to them about my long walks—often accompanied by them—in the streets of Niamey, Niger.

Ariane Kirtley on camelback at 5 years old, while traveling through the Ayr Mountains, Niger. *Photograph by Michael Kirtley.*

Ariane Kirtley printing photos for children in the village of Kijigari, Niger. *Photograph courtesy of Ariane Kirtley.*

Ahoudan the guide and Michael Kirtley tending to fire, during Kirtley's second trip to Tofatat, in Niger. *Photograph by Michael Kirtley.*

Ariane Kirtley with her friends Mariama and Ouma, Niamey, Niger.
Photograph courtesy of Ariane Kirtley.

Michael Kirtley and his dog La Nuit, sipping from seasonal wash in Ayr Mountains, Niger. *Photograph by Aubine Kirtley.*

The rocky citadel known as Tofatat, viewed from one kilometer away, deep in the Ayr Mountains, Niger. *Photograph by Michael Kirtley.*

Ayr Mountain landscape in Niger. *Water color by Aubine Kirtley.*

Michael Kirtley atop sand dune in the Ayr Mountains, Niger.
Photograph by Aubine Kirtley.

*"Go confidently in the direction of your dreams!
Live the life you've imagined."*
~Thoreau

Michael and Aubine Kirtley

What makes the desert beautiful is that somewhere it hides a well.
~Antoine de Saint-Exupéry, *The Little Prince*

An Invitation to Tofatat

Story by Michael and Aubine Kirtley

1. In the shadow of the Bagzan

Ahoudan, a sinewy man with a shy smile and a melodious voice, was packing our food and bedding into two large ornate camel bags. This morning he was testy: "I shouldn't take you to Tofatat," he stated emphatically in impeccable French. "It may bring me bad luck and my camel might die. There are plenty of other interesting places to visit in the Bagzan." He carefully slung one of the heavy bags across the back of his camel. "I've never taken an anassara (white person) there before, and I've never heard of anyone else doing so. It is a place where marabout elders go to pray; it is not for ordinary people." He then knelt down on a mat lying on the smooth sand to carefully wrap "boule" in a cloth. He took enough of this traditional nomadic breakfast cereal—made of pounded millet, dates, and chookoo (dried goat cheese)—to last the duration of our impending journey.

Our guide was noticeably unsettled by his offer to lead my wife Aubine and me to this sacred destination inside the Bagzan—a vast mesa rising to over 2000 meters in the Ayr Mountain Range of northern Niger. We had hired him a week before, and were about to ascend the rugged 350-meter escarpment into a land where few outsiders had ever ventured. Even before departing on our walkabout from his hometown of Tabelot, Ahoudan had procrastinated, while consulting with his marabout (holy man in Sufi Islam) on the most auspicious moment to escort us. He had stocked up on special talismans, hoping to assure good fortune for the trek.

"Then why did you propose taking us there in the first place?" I inquired, somewhat annoyed, sitting down beside him on the mat. My question made him reflective. "After these past days we've spent together, I feel we are kindred spirits," he finally responded, a sparkle in his eyes. "So our kinship prompts me to want to share my secret place with you."

Was his response genuine, or was he filibustering for a pay raise? Not knowing what to believe, I smiled and told him to do what he thought was best. He carefully rearranged his black tagelmust (head scarf of Tuareg men), pulling it up over his mouth. Without another word of complaint, he stood up and organized the "boule" inside the remaining camel bag. Our two Labradors, Smokey and La Nuit, sensed that the game was now on, and bounded jubilantly around us.

***

This scene took place four decades ago, in the spring of 1976. Throughout most of the 70s and 80s, Aubine was my spouse, my adventurous companion, and my journalistic partner. During that time, we wrote extensively about our journeys throughout the Ayr and its neighboring Ténéré sand sea. But this is the first time we have published anything about Tofatat, one of the Sahara's most mysterious retreats for prayerful solitude.

Up to now, we were reticent about revealing the location of this spiritual nexus, in part because some of its sacredness is due to its other-worldly isolation, and partly out of a belief in synchronicity—if you are allowed to go there, then it is thanks to cosmic destiny. You don't seek or stumble onto Tofatat; it finds you. It is by invitation only. And it is accessible only to Walkers.

2. An unexpected pregnancy

"Monsieur and Madame, you are going to have a baby. Congratulations!"

Our initial reaction to the doctor's announcement was cognitive dissonance, a mixture of joy and denial. We had recently driven across the Sahara to settle for a while in Niamey, the dusty capital of Niger. It was January; we planned to go trekking soon in the highlands of the Ayr. Aubine had written in her journal, just the day before: "There are places, as there are people, that one longs for, passionately waits for, and that are explored at the risk of one's life. From the banks of the Niger River in Niamey, I dream of such a place—the mysterious island made of sand and stones that they call the Ayr." Fiefdom of the lordly Tuareg nomads, the Ayr was our spiritual Eldorado.

How would the doctor's news affect our planning? Blithely we decided that *it wouldn't change anything in our lives*. So we continued to prepare for our expedition as if the "baby news" were a blip on the radar screen. Almost three months later, at the beginning of the hottest season in the Sahel, we drove to Agadez, legendary Saharan crossroads and lively gateway to the Ayr. By then Aubine's condition had become worrisome; she was vomiting every day and the heat was bloating her legs. A nurse we visited there told her that our expedition was risky: "It's too hot, your condition is too unpredictable, and you'll be unable to reach out for emergency help," she insisted.

Aubine remained upbeat and unwavering: "We want to explore the Ayr because we believe our lives as a family will be enhanced in beautiful ways," she responded. "Besides, my condition will be better off in the coolness of the mountains."

3. Finding our guide

Our drive up the Barghot kori (seasonal wash) into the southern Ayr was a romp through a magical landscape of volcanic hills, sand dunes, acacias, and wind-polished rock. Smokey and La Nuit got a good workout loping next to our Land Cruiser, from time to time sprinting off after an ostrich or a goat. The occasional shepherds heartily greeted us, "Tabaykos! Tabaykos!" If we learned nothing else of Tamajek, the Tuareg language, at least we had gotten the greeting down pat.

We arrived in Tabelot, an idyllic adobe village in a garden-dotted oasis valley to the east of the Bagzan, which emerged in the distance. It seemed like the entire population came out to meet us. Extending my hand, I greeted everyone with a hearty "Tabaykos!" Curiously, everyone laughed and pointed at our dogs. It felt like a big celebration for our arrival!

I inquired as to where I could find a reliable guide for our ramble into the Bagzan. All signs pointed to an "Enad" named Ahoudan, highly respected for being a silversmith and stone carver. Enad is the singular of Inadan, the artisan caste whose crafts beautify an otherwise austere setting for the nomadic Tuareg.

As we drove up to Ahoudan's homestead, children, chickens, and goats scurried away. From within came a loud burst of rock music. Hearing our vehicle, the craftsman had pumped up his cassette player nearly to distortion levels. His foreign visitors must know he is "with it."

"Tabaykos!" I greeted him warmly. He bent over laughing, keeping his hand over his mouth. "Why are you calling me a dog?" he asked, barely containing his merriment, as if I were the only one not in on a big joke. It turned out that the shepherds in the Barghot kori simply had been shouting their amazement at seeing two dogs running after our Land Cruiser—I was glad everyone saw the humor in my misunderstanding!

Not displeased to have an audience, Ahoudan brewed the customary three cups of tea for us, and prepared for the day's work at the forge. While we were laying out our request about trekking to the Bagzan, his comely young wife Hayatan floated in like a butterfly and sat down with us. She exuded charm and strength. We learned that our new friend split his time between his homes in Tabelot and a town 40 km away called Abardokh; he had a wife in both places. I asked him if his wives were ever jealous of one another. Hayatan giggled when Ahoudan translated for her. "She thinks your question is hilarious," he said. "She asked me how she could be jealous of her sister."

After some time pondering our request to use his services, Ahoudan responded, "I know of no Westerners who have ever been atop the Bagzan, but I will take you there, God-willing." We set Sunday as our departure date, three days hence. During that time we regularly visited him and his family, observing his intricate work and learning more about his caste. The next morning he gave a delicate silver Cross of Agadez to Aubine. This is the most popular of the thirty "crosses" created by the Inadan to represent the largest cities of Niger. It has been compared to the Egyptian ankh, a symbol of life.

Ahoudan told us that the Inadan were the stewards of most artistic expression in Tuareg society. The men fashion silver jewelry, camel saddles, stone jewelry and implements, and wooden utensils. The women are elaborate hair stylists, make and play the tendi drum, make leather pouches and bags, and weave the palm-frond mats that are used in building their homes. "Mountain guide" was not a typical pastime for an Enad.

4. The walk finally begins

Ahoudan postponed our trek for a week, because Sunday and the next four days turned out to be "inauspicious" for traveling, according to his marabout. It is impossible to make a Tuareg leave from his home on a day when his marabout forbids it. If you insist a little, the cameleer will tell you a story about a friend who was robbed, or whose camel died, for taking such a risk.

This wasn't the last time our guide would bring us to wit's end. However, as is often the case when you keep your heart open to the vagaries of African planning, the wait paid off, because it allowed the three of us to stoke our budding friendship. On the third day of our forced patience, Ahoudan offered us an uncommon gesture of confidence. "I have decided," he announced, 'not only to take you into the Bagzan, but also to invite you to my secret asylum there. The place is called 'Tofatat'. No stranger, not even our noblemen, has ever been there. It is the most sacred spot in the Ayr."

"What is Tofatat?" I asked, my curiosity piqued. "In Tamajek, Tofatat means 'the most beautiful'," he explained. "It is where nature has created a perfect harmony of stones. A dying marabout elder told me where to look for it, when I was one of his students. It took me a long time to find. Only two or three holy men go there each year, always alone, for peaceful prayer. For the locals, its existence is a fairy-tale; they have no idea where it is."

Suddenly hushed by the magnitude of what he was proposing, though not fully comprehending, Aubine and I told him that we would be honored to visit his hallowed sanctuary.

The evening before our departure, Ahoudan's brother invited us to eat at his home. Our host served us one of the best-prepared meals I have had in the Ayr: millet with green leaf sauce, bread baked in sand, and sweet date-encrusted "boule". He apologized that he hadn't been able to slaughter a goat for us. I reassured him that we thoroughly enjoyed his wife's cooking, and that it was not unusual to eat meatless meals in the West. "That's impossible!" he exclaimed incredulously. "Why would any rich man intentionally go without meat?!" I realized he would not understand any explanation I might give, so I responded, "the white man's ways are often baffling."

Finally the propitious day arrived; Ahoudan showed up tugging a scrawny white camel for our baggage. He told us its name was Awinyaray. "It means 'white with red spots'," he explained. "It is a little camel that didn't grow up very much because his mom wasn't very big." As we were to learn, things were never simple between Ahoudan and his camel!

After packing the camel we began our day-long hike toward the foothills of the Bagzan. Like a massive gray turtle shell, the vertiginous granite cliffs of the plateau loomed above the valley ahead. On several occasions, we stopped to fill our canteens at garden wells. Camels, hitched to ropes, pulled out overflowing buckets that tipped into hand-made irrigation trenches, supplying onions, lettuce, and tomatoes along the water's path. Doves were cooing, water was gurgling and a munificent cool humidity seemed to rise up from the ground. This lushness contrasted drastically with the otherwise arid landscape. The distant foothills looked forebodingly like gigantic dark piles of rubble.

Near noon, Ahoudan spent nearly half an hour at one such garden well, chatting with a tall light-skinned man he called his cousin. As we waited, sipping boule mixed with camel milk, we observed the two men laughing uproariously. Aubine, already worn down by the heat and the walking, lay under a date palm to rest. As we resumed our hike, I asked Ahoudan about his encounter. "Ah, yes," grinned our guide, "he is of the noble caste, the Imajaran. It is our tradition to joke with them, and to ask them for favors. He complained that he was like a goat and I was a jackal trying to eat him!"

Throughout the Tuareg world, Ahoudan explained, the Inadan live as a subordinate caste side by side with their nomadic overlords. Noblemen and craftsmen viewed each other suspiciously, but carried on a joking banter between the castes. In this rare symbiotic relationship, the Inadan—in return for services—expected and received gifts and various indulgences from the Tuareg nobles and vassals. "At times, if they insult us, we destroy their encampments; but usually we just tease them, and they wonder what we're up to," he added with a knowing smile.

Aubine stumbled; she was clearly faltering. Ahoudan pushed her to mount Awinyaray, telling her she'd have plenty of time to test her legs on the ascent. With misgivings weighing on my mind, I tried to enjoy myself, throwing sticks for the dogs to chase; their gleeful antics kept me distracted from my preoccupations.

I was relieved when Ahoudan proposed to bed down at a large sandy clearing in the otherwise pebblestrewn foothills. After dinner we admired the pink-and-amber glow of sunset, while sipping on Ahoudan's always-syrupy tea. I wished I felt elated that tomorrow we'd be setting off into exciting, seldom-explored country, but I was apprehensive about Aubine's resilience. We all were feeling a little glum. And then suddenly, out of nowhere, five young men raced by us on their camels—right hands waving wildly, left hands loosely clasping their reins. Clad in the proud flowing robes of noblemen, they whooped and shrieked piercing war cries—they looked like an apparition straight off a movie set! As they disappeared into a cloud of reddish dust, Ahoudan laughed. And then we all laughed. "You have become popular my friends," our guide declared. "Our boys wanted you to know you are welcome into our land.

Our journey immediately felt "right" again—the Sahara will always offer great surprises when least expected! Before we bedded down for the night, Ahoudan gave Aubine a little Agadez Cross he had carved for her out of soapstone; he threaded it onto a string that he then attached around her neck. "I will make a new cross for you every morning, so that each day may be blessed!" he told her encouragingly.

5. Ascent into the Bagzan

From the foothills the plateau looked almost unscalable without mountaineering equipment. In fact, Ahoudan told us that few people who lived in the valley ever attempted the grueling trek through the narrow canyons that mount steeply to the top. Aubine was pale and losing weight. I could not imagine that she could make the climb, in her condition. I decided we might as well call things off, and told her so.

"If that poor little camel can make it to the top, with heavy bags on its back, then I can make it," she responded resolutely. And that was that. Although I admired her courage, I couldn't help but think the fever had gotten to her brain. However, I understood what she meant about our pack animal; its legs didn't look thick enough to hold its own weight.

Soon after sunrise we began the day-long ascent. The sun bore down heavily; there was no shade in this parched and rocky landscape. For a short while, Aubine sat on top Awinyaray; but soon the trail steepened, and the animal stumbled as it hunted for footholds on the slippery stones. So she dismounted, and we walked together. As much as possible, I steadied her body with my hand, as did Ahoudan. She assured us that she was ok, but I was not convinced. She had hardly eaten and looked frail. Our dogs, on the other hand, were in their element; they seemed overjoyed and raced back and forth across our trail, pausing occasionally to take a sip from the spring water that bubbled up here and there.

Ahoudan trod slowly, but with much assurance. I enjoyed walking at his side and asking him about the places and people we would encounter on top. He told me the story of Saidou the Old, the first inhabitant of the Bagzan. Saidou came out of Zinder in the south, wearing only animal skins. During the day he hunted with his bow and arrow and traps; at night he slept in the trees to avoid being eaten by the lions and hyenas that lived on the plateau.

In an especially narrow passage we encountered a little boy trying to coax his baby camel to stand up. The animal had fallen down with its baggage, and there was no room for it to find footing enough to arise. Maneuvering around him posed a problem for our camel, but after unloading it Ahoudan and I were able to pull off the trick by gingerly stepping over the fallen animal. Our guide gently scolded the boy for overloading his beast, and then proceeded to help get the forlorn creature back on its feet.

Aubine offered the boy some water, but he mistakenly understood that it was she who wanted some—so he ran to his water bag and filled her canteen. When he returned, Ahoudan traded him a tin of sardines against a few squares of chookoo.

Nearing the top of the canyon trail, we encountered a small oasis with a few palm trees, the only ones we would see in the Bagzan. The air felt refreshingly cooler, and I suggested that we halt in the meager shade to give Aubine a rest.

6. Zigzagging through the Bagzan

After a few more hours of tripping and sliding, we finally clambered to the top of the plateau, where the land flattened into a startling panorama of sand and broken rock, created by immense volcanic forces. The wind flowed like a river across the trail, kicking up a stream of sandy particles that whipped gently around our feet. "The boulders are like lizards," Aubine declared, suddenly revived by the cooler temperatures. "They face the sun every day, always weary but ever patient. I have the impression that they, like me, are tired, full of cracks, and bloated." Her fever seemed to engender bizarre musings: "Maybe there are so many split and broken rocks," she ventured, "because that's how rocks give birth. Like cell division." Several veins in her legs had burst and spread out over her skin. Her pregnant belly was beginning to show.

At Aoukadédé, the first village we encountered, a group of women gathered around Aubine, looking somewhat astonished but curious. They walked beside her and engaged in animated discussion, gesturing at Aubine's hair—which was so long it reached her waist. One of the women approached and asked if she could touch the hair. Of course Aubine gave permission, and within minutes all the other women followed suit. "I feel a strong affinity with these guileless women in their Garden of Eden," she told me. "I am honored to walk with them, and happy that my long hair interests them!" We rested for a day outside the village, to allow her to recover from the climb.

After leaving Aoukadédé, we walked for hours up sandy koris snaking between the volcanic hills that gently rose around us as we made our way northward. Desiccated at this time of year, the koris awaited the late summer rains that would rush through them in violent torrents, replenishing the water table and nourishing the sparse vegetation that punctuated the sere environment. Ahoudan dug into the koris to refill our gourds with water. The first time he did this, I did not understand what he was doing. He knelt down in the dry kori, and dug. In only a few moments, transparent, cool water formed a puddle from which we sipped. The water had a cleaner taste than I had remembered ever enjoying. This was yet another desert secret that Ahoudan shared with us—as long as a kori was nearby, it would always provide the water we needed.

Everywhere we walked, the landscape was littered with boulders—thousands of them, in the strangest of formations. Unlike elsewhere in the Ayr, there are neither sand dunes nor ostriches in the Bagzan. But we saw other birds and gazelles and monkeys just about everywhere, along with tracks of the elusive desert mountain sheep called mouflon. And, even if we didn't see them, we were constantly aware that jackals surrounded us, due to their nightly wailing.

The only greenery was near the villages, thanks to gardens irrigated from deep wells—where sand-coated children led gaunt camels and donkeys through the squeaky, repetitive ritual of pulling up water-filled buckets via ropes and wooden pulleys. The gardens here reminded Aubine and me of those in the High Atlas of Morocco—perhaps this is fitting, since they were both built by descendants from the same Berber culture. The limited crops—tomatoes, potatoes, and onions—were cultivated mainly to sustain the needs of the population.

Gliding along the surface of this great plateau were young shepherd girls, soundlessly driving their herds of goats. Sometimes they hid behind the stones and looked out at us, furtively spying on intruders inside their territory. Every once in a while we came across their belongings, left at the foot of a boulder. Curious, I asked Ahoudan, "What do the girls have in their hands?" I had noticed that they were always busy at work. "They spend their days weaving dyed fronds into mats. The day that they will get married, they will use these mats to build their family huts."

"These shepherd girls," he continued, "are also the keepers of our medicine. There is one medicine that cures all ailments. It is made with 27 plants, all which can only be found in the Bagzan. Only these girls know which plants to pick to make this special treatment."

Most people here lived as they might have lived 2000 years ago. In silence, peace, poverty, and purity. A kind of purity that was so naïve that it made me afraid. Exploring this parcel of virgin earth where people lived independently and sufficient to themselves, but without the bare minimum, I feared that their hardships may one day lead to their being duped by outsiders.

Some of the young people gave me hope that my fear was misplaced. They had visited the world outside the Bagzan, but they hadn't been sullied by it. They spoke French passably, and had a great sense of humor and kindness. For now they seemed to accept their lot, loyal to the rigors of their existence and their traditions, faithful to their legacy as farmers. Since they didn't use insecticides, without knowing it they had suddenly become modern in a world seeking "organic" solutions. Behind for centuries, the Bagzan were now ahead! In the future, I told myself, perhaps they'll see the arrival of outsiders who will want to learn from them.

In the Inadan quarter of the large village called Amerig, the old women worked on crafting dyed goat skin into intricately-woven camel bags, rich in color but sober compared to the ones from lower elevations. Strewn about the village, chiseled stones littered the ground—the fruit of work done over many years by craftsmen. That night we learned something astonishing from Ahoudan: "The anassara think we are Tuareg, but we are not," he told us. "We don't have the same roots, we have a separate language, and we don't look the same." Over the next few days I asked him much more about this declaration, and later I talked to others about it. Nobody in the Ayr contradicted him.

The next evening, as Aubine and I bedded down, Ahoudan stood meditatively next to Awinyaray for a very long time. He was looking towards the hills to the East. "That way is Tofatat," he stated solemnly. "We will go there tomorrow."

7. The Tao of Tofatat

From far away I spotted our destination, dominating a valley encircled at a respectful distance by small hills—Tofatat was a rocky desert queen on her sandy dais. Our footsteps quickened, keeping time with our racing heartbeats. La Nuit sensed our new fervor and barked incessantly. As we got nearer, no one spoke; even our Labradors seemed entranced. Arriving at its base, we just looked up in amazement, and understood why Ahoudan had been so proud to bring us here.

Much of the Bagzan is like a holy fountain that spewed huge stones into the air. When they fell back to the Earth, they cascaded atop one another, dotting the landscape with rock castles. The most extraordinary of these is Tofatat. A surreal monument towering 50 meters high, it is the inadvertent Stonehenge of the Sahara.

Tofatat is a natural paradox. It is a game of rock Jenga that got too tall, crashed to the ground, and in a one-in-a-million stroke of good fortune, created balance out of imbalance. It is a craggy citadel whose many chambers all break the ground rules of engineering, as if it were designed by celestial architects on hallucinogens. Palaces of giant stone mushrooms, mysteriously posed on top of one another, bigger ones frequently on top of smaller ones. Truncated pyramids, boulders ripped asunder. A few isolated rounded stones, polished by the wind. All of these together formed a perfect congruence derived from mayhem.

I now grasped why Ahoudan had never attempted to describe what we would find at his secret sanctuary. You can't describe Tofatat, any better than you can describe "love"; you experience it, you say what it is about, you write poetry about it, but its essence is lost in translation. Although Tofatat is made of lifeless stone, it is the most life-giving natural phenomenon I have ever experienced.

Tofatat is the beauty in bedlam, the yin in the yang, and the ephemeral in the eternal. Its very existence is proof that great art may come from randomness. It is a metaphor for humanity, maddening in its discordance while at the same time vibrant in its diversity. And here we were, specks of human and animal dust, basking in its unclaimed majesty. Transfixed like the stones themselves, we huddled together—an American, a European, an African, two bastard dogs and a bony camel—sensing that we had now arrived at our cosmic apotheosis. In communion with this ageless pile of weathered stones, I felt a oneness with everything that has ever existed or will ever exist.

Amidst our reverie we set up camp. Aubine was sitting, perched on top a broken stone, lost in contemplation. Our dogs crouched in the sand and gazed up at her, seemingly mesmerized by her stillness. I asked Ahoudan to go on a walk with me around our newfound playground. For the most part we didn't talk. I looked in awe at all the variations of form, all the nooks and crannies to explore—they seemed endless! To me, the place felt alive.

It took us almost an hour to circumambulate Tofatat. During that time night fell swiftly and the stars came out. The constellations seemed brighter and closer to me than ever before. The silken spiral of the Milky Way spun just meters above our heads, and the great boulders rising above us seemed to pulsate with a kind of mystical moonlit vibration. Under such intoxicating influences, universal mysteries felt more solvable, and peace seemed to be the natural order of the Earth.

"Ahoudan, would you mind if Aubine and I stayed here alone for a couple of days?" I asked. "I think it is important that we explore this place with the eyes of a newborn." My friend said that he totally understood, promising he would leave in the morning.

When we arrived back at camp, we found Aubine sitting in the same spot. She looked down at us, her face radiating a smile filled with tenderness and love. "I have made peace with everyone who has ever hurt me," she declared. "I have no more pain in my heart."

Although neither Ahoudan nor I understood the specifics, we understood nonetheless. At Tofatat you turn your madness into sanity, and your personal wars into peace offerings. Aubine's words reminded me of an ancient oriental saying: "When arrows hit me, they turn to flowers, and I feel compassion for my enemy." I think Tofatat is the embodiment of the Taoist principles of unified existence, where chaos is the loving sister of serenity, and light is the blood brother of darkness.

8. Alone at Tofatat

Ahoudan left early in the morning, promising to return two days hence. It seemed strange watching Awinyaray and him become dots on the horizon; for more than a week he had been our anchor and steadfast companion. But for now, we would let Tofatat be our guide.

The next thing Aubine and I did was to climb high into the boulders, through indescribably twisted passageways where we repeatedly had to help one another. At the summit of Tofatat we discovered a natural marvel whose existence still baffles me to this day: there was a small limpid pond surrounded by an earthen sward where a few flowering acacias and tender shoots of grass grew. In our travels we had occasionally chanced upon pools of water in rocky Saharan environments—called "gueltas" in Arabic, they were usually fed by rain but sometimes by springs. However, we never before had encountered such an anomaly at the highest spot in a citadel of stones, especially during the dry season! Because of the vegetation we decided that our guelta must be fed by an underground source; but where could spring water come from, here at Tofatat; and how did it rise to this level?

Aubine and I were enthralled at finding this unexpected Shangri-La. We danced and hugged each other, and splashed rapturously in the water. Grateful that the life growing inside Aubine could experience our euphoria, we felt more blessed than ever by Creation. Together with our child-to-be, our growing "family" became like a vessel for the energy flowing from the boulders, the guelta, the trees, and the deep blue sky.

The remainder of our two-day hiatus was a time of love, renewal, and learning more about Tofatat. Aubine and I explored the various spaces and lookouts of our new home; I baptized one room "the star portal", because its pinnacles formed a circular window peering heavenward. On several facades we discovered rock paintings—giraffes, zebu cows, and strange-looking humanoids. These attested to an era, not that long ago, when the Sahara was a lush pastureland, easily traversed by wandering herdsmen. Aubine added to this artistic legacy; she spent much of her time painting, memorializing Tofatat in water colors.

At the foot of Tofatat there were two shanties made out of branches—the refuges of marabout elders who came for solitary meditation. Inside them were delicately-crafted leather-bound books that contained holy writings in Arabic. Several meters away there were circular stone ruins, attesting to another kind of habitation that was used in the dim past.

Together Aubine and I practiced listening to Tofatat. We could divine the wind's tender flirtation whispering through the stones, and understood why the coarse rocks grew smoother under its timeless caress. I took to lying down on flat boulders and closing my eyes; I heard sounds I had never heard before, and sensed the presence of things I could not name. Sometimes La Nuit and Smokey lay silently next to me, seemingly on their own mystical journeys.

During our interlude alone at Tofatat, Aubine was reinvigorated; the problems related to her pregnancy seemed to have greatly dissipated. She and I renewed our commitment to maintain our freewheeling lifestyle after the birth of our child. When the third day arrived, we regretted that we had not given ourselves more time alone at Tofatat. Then again, we would not be unhappy to welcome our friend Ahoudan back to our lofty lair.

9. Ahoudan reveals his plight

On the morning Ahoudan was supposed to fetch us at Tofatat, he was a no-show. Same thing all afternoon, and we became a little restless. Near sunset we spied a golden cloud of dust approaching us in the distance. It was he, talking in a hoarse but soothing voice to Awinyaray, who grunted emphatically in response.

"I lost my camel," he explained. "Every evening he comes back to eat straw, and last night for the first time he didn't come. So, I went out searching for him, and I looked all night long. Finally I had some good luck; I found him on the other side of Bagzan N'Amass."

"How did you find him?" I asked laconically. "By following his tracks," he responded. "I always recognize them because I tie his two front legs together. But the batteries in my flashlight went dead. In the dark I got his tracks confused with those of another camel. I'm really tired."

That evening he was especially attentive to Awinyaray, who remained strangely immobile in front of a tree, tail between its legs, tears in its eyes. For Ahoudan, there was no doubt the camel was getting sick: "If I leave him like this, he will just kneel down and not get up. He will refuse to eat, and get skinnier." I thought our guide was going to have a sentimental breakdown.

The next morning we left our mystical haven. Aubine and I made one last climb to the guelta and prayed for the endurance of our couple. We resolved to persevere with our venturesome lifestyle and to share it with our future family. We would bring our children with us, wherever we would journey. And we vowed to one day return to Tofatat with the child growing inside Aubine.

Our plan had been to roam around the volcanic remnants south of Idoukal-N-Taghès, the highest peak in the Ayr. But Ahoudan appeared to have been traumatized by the experience of chasing down his camel during the night. He steadily complained that the uneven lava flow would injure his pack animal. "We don't stop enough to let him graze," he lamented.

"Why are you so concerned about this camel?" I asked peevishly. "I'm sure he'll be just fine!" Ahoudan stolidly plodded on, and I wondered if he might quit on the spot. Finally he spoke, abashedly: "Before the drought I owned nine camels. I always loaned them out to friends, to go travelling. When they returned from a trip, I fattened my camels in green pastureland. With the dryness and browning of grass, my camels died off, one by one. I could not find enough work in the mountains. The nobles had no silver and no money to hire me, no goats to exchange. I was reduced to begging in Agadez for any work I could find. Now this one camel is all I have left."

From this story we understood that our mate was basically broke, ruined by the lack of rain, holding on to what he could. Of course I knew that during the punishing Sahel drought of 1968-73, the people of the Ayr were hard hit. But it hadn't dawned on me that camelback guides might have only *one* camel. It was my turn to feel ashamed, and from that moment our relationship ripened. Today, he is a treasured friend.

10. Down from the Bagzan and out into the world

Following our dustup with Ahoudan, the rest of our Bagzan trek evolved exquisitely; the land was as pristine as it was consistently surprising. Aubine, miraculously refreshed by our stay at Tofatat, was almost her old self; she especially enjoyed playing with the children in the villages. The three of us held long discussions around the campfire, where Ahoudan regaled us with tall tales of the mountains and the constellations; in turn, we answered his myriad questions about life in the outside world. We learned much about the ways of the Tuareg and the Inadan, and couldn't stop thinking back to the transformative power of Ahoudan's secret sanctuary. Happily in one sense, all special things must come to an end, or we'd not be able to remember them as special!

At sundown we camped just beyond Aoukadédé, near the entrance of the canyon descending from the plateau. Faraway we heard a weird chorus of braying donkeys. Down the trail an unknown creature was rustling. Soon thereafter, jackals added their jarring cacophony to the ethereal setting. Out of the dark a large animal suddenly ran into our camp, made strange sounds and knocked over one of the tents. The Labradors bayed wildly. I was momentarily spooked.

What is that?" I asked, alarmed. "Oh, it's just a lion," Ahoudan nonchalantly replied. "There are a few of them left in the canyon." He took out his flashlight and lit up the rear end of the fleeing animal. Under any other circumstance I would have seen it was simply the rump of a donkey, but that night I was the ass. Trusting Ahoudan as I did, and unnerved by the howling jackals, I believed him.

What should we do?" I asked him, concerned for our safety. Ahoudan looked at Aubine, lay down on the ground, and doubled up in uncontrollable laughter. Aubine too burst out laughing. "Michael, take my joke as a sign of my appreciation," declared Ahoudan between his guffaws. "I have adopted you as my cousin!"

The descent out of the Bagzan was torture, especially for Ahoudan's little white camel. With its heavy load it could hardly squeeze through the craggy passageways, where the jagged outcroppings dug into its sides, and the stones and thorns were much greater threats to its padded hooves than when climbing. It couldn't easily navigate the almost vertical gullies, and sometimes needed to jump across them, risking a broken leg. At every step it took, Ahoudan's stoic expression betrayed his dread that tragedy might strike—for once his concern seemed legitimate. Aubine told me she suffered more for the animal than for herself, even though the climb down was the most treacherous that she had ever faced. In order to not overtax her, we stopped frequently to rest.

We breathed a sigh of relief when the land leveled out and we headed into the valley; our dogs, sensing the way, scampered ahead jubilantly. By that time Aubine's legs were swollen to twice their normal size, and she was limping badly; she was elated to be able to ride Awinyaray again. Upon our arrival late that night in Tabelot, we drank the traditional three cups of tea with Ahoudan and Hayatan, who also offered us a bowl of fresh dates and ministered to Aubine. While savoring the third cup's frothy, sweet aroma, Aubine and I discussed a plan we had hatched thanks to our walkabout in the Bagzan: we would find a way to tell the world about the Inadan. Their intricate culture, little known outside the Sahara, had piqued our curiosity.

When we returned to Niamey, and then to Paris, it soon dawned on us that no one we met fully understood the unique heritage of the Tuareg craftsmen. Even specialists at Niger's National Museum and at France's National Scientific Research Center (CNRS) scoffed at the notion that the Inadan were of separate ethnicity from the Tuareg—a trait that is fully acknowledged today.

Who are the Inadan? A teacher in Tabelot told us that Tuareg legend describes them as "older than memory, proud as the crow, and mischievous as the wind." Some scholars say they descend from Nubians, or that their roots are among Middle Eastern blacksmiths. Adding to the riddle is their secret language called *tenet* and their darker complexion—which sets them apart from the often honey-skinned Tuareg nobles, who are descendants of the Berbers of North Africa. But no one really knows the full story.

Our son Tercelin Layr Kirtley was born in September. Shortly thereafter, Aubine and I began giving conferences on the Inadan in France and America. Three years later, in August 1979 and after another trip back to the Ayr, we published our first article for *National Geographic*, entitled "Artisans of the Sahara". The story was largely inspired by what we had learned from Ahoudan during our first trek into the Bagzan. Four years after that, Aubine and I kept our vow made at Tofatat—we returned there with our two children, Tercelin and his sister Ariane, in 1983.

11. Today

It is July 2016; I am in central France. For the first time in a decade, I just spoke with Ahoudan; he was on his cell phone, in the Ayr. He informed me that the government recently chiseled out a road to the top of the Bagzan plateau. "There are many motorcyclists, and the farmers grow different kinds of vegetables," he said, expressing delight that the people there could have a better life. I couldn't help but feel wistful about the lost sense of timelessness in a world driven by the belief in constant "progress", and in a land threatened by the expanding tentacles of extremism. I only hope the inhabitants of the Bagzan do feel happier, now that they have motorbikes, cell phones, and more reliable access to food—now that they have joined modernity, with its noise and consumerism and stresses.

Ahoudan told me some other good news: he confirmed that Tofatat is still only visited by holy men on spiritual retreat. Forty years after he first took Aubine and me there, he asserts he is still the lone guide who knows how to find the place, which is not indicated on any map of the Bagzan that I have studied.

If you ever find yourself in the Ayr and someone invites you to visit Tofatat, it will be because you are in the right place at the right time; it will not happen by accident. Don't hesitate. Go! You will not be disappointed.

Questions and Answers

Answers by Michael Kirtley

1. What compels you to walk?

I walk for a variety of reasons: to exercise, for fellowship, to resolve problems, to escape into a dream-world, and to reach those extraordinary spots in the world that are otherwise inaccessible. In these places I find deep connections to the spirit of the Earth. Anyone who has hiked through tropical forests, in high mountains, deep into the desert, or inside walking-only fantasylands like Arches National Park, will know what I mean.

I also love walking because it is one of the few physical activities that I can do on the spur of the moment, without advance planning or equipment.

There is something quite special about sharing a long walk with a friend or loved one. Doing so offers a closeness that I don't believe can be equaled by other forms of outdoor activity. Contrary to biking, driving, or travelling together on the backs of animals, walking creates an intimate bubble which belongs uniquely to the two companions, where they are independent of the need to control anything other than their bodies and direction.

It's as if the very act of moving together, outside of those things that define us daily, strips away our dependency on these reference points, allowing us to foster a new kind of relationship, based on simplicity and a lack of inhibition.

When I am walking, I often feel more like the kind of person I want to be. I no longer need to interact with a multitude of distracting people, news, and circumstances. In this sense, walking is like a vacation. I think this feeling must have something to do with the proximity of my feet to the ground; I feel rooted to the Earth and to her timelessness.

2. Do you experience instances while you are walking when your mind is somewhere off the trail and on its own journey?

Especially when walking alone, I often feel a little intoxicated. Seemingly slipping into another dimension, I frequently forget where I am; my physical surroundings become a ghostly tapestry that I intuitively know is there, but has little influence on what is going on inside my mind. I enter a zone where time is no longer linear.

Occasionally this sensation has even been shared with a companion. Many years ago, when I was 20, I visited Marrakech, Morocco for the first time. I started walking from the new city to the Medina, together with my erstwhile travelling sidekick Reid Autry. It was around a 4 km tramp, along a wide boulevard lined with palm trees, luxuriant gardens, and striking edifices. After arriving sometime later at the renowned Jemaa-el-Fna square, with its loud, colorful, and pungent bombardment of the senses, it was as if I had awakened from a trance. Reid and I looked at each other quizzically; neither one of us had any recollection of the walk we had just made! In this magical land, had we been teleported from one end of the city to the other, on some invisible flying carpet?

I could recount dozens of such dissociative moments, when walking became an inner, seemingly purposeless journey, similar to dreaming. There is no other form of travel where I have experienced such out-of-body moments so readily or so often. After many of these episodes, I have felt compelled to ask myself questions about the meaning of reality, especially of my own reality.

3. How do you manage to stay physically and emotionally healthy during long and arduous journeys?

As are many of us in this book, I am called a dreamer of impossible dreams. My most powerful and life-affirming moments have come about thanks to my optimism in the face of seemingly hopeless odds, where happy outcomes seemed unpredictable and fortuitous. Confidence in myself, therefore, is essential to tackling the punishing day-to-day of long journeys.

For me, by far the most important concern is physical health; if we are healthy in body, we are predisposed to staying emotionally healthy, and are readier to face unknown risks. To maintain physical health, my watchword is "prevention"; it's obviously preferable not to get sick if it can be avoided, and to know how to treat oneself if ill or injured. This means keeping vaccinations up to date and getting good first-aid training before setting out. In my opinion, it also means taking a robust multivitamin every day, drinking lots of water, having an adequate medical supply, and making sure to get comfortable sleep.

Sadly, the internet has created a virtual threat to our mental well-being while on a walkabout. Although it has undeniably brought great opportunities for solitary adventurers, it also has given rise to social media "barking dogs". These are people who feel their role in life is to tell us where we're going wrong, and who over time can sap our spirits. I try to tune them out, confident that the star I'm following is bright. This is not always easy.

Thankfully, my mental health during long journeys usually depends on three personality traits: my ability to laugh at myself, my refusal to dwell on the past, and my unshakable faith in the goodness of humanity. Whenever I get too downhearted I just look up into the sky and scream. That helps me laugh, because I always am startled by my scream. Then I wear a smile, even if no one else is around. A sustained smile on the outside is like a shot of endorphins into the brain.

4. Please share a high and a low period that you experienced during your walkabouts.

<u>Low point:</u>
"Zaragoza"

Throughout my three-year "thumbabout" as a single-minded go-anywhere hitchhiker, I often heard the refrain, "When you hitchhike, you should do a lot of walking; it will help you get a ride." Frankly, this admonition made little sense to me; I always would stick out my thumb wherever my last ride dropped me off, and just wait there—on an open road, outside a gas station, or in the heart of a city. Therefore I have never experienced what for others seemed to be integral to the art: walking long ways to find the "right" spot, or just to alleviate the tedium of standing beside the road.

Except for once, when I was 20, while crossing Aragon.

It was the summer of 1970. During those years Spain was a total bust for hitchhikers; I invariably would wait for several hours to get picked up. I had been forewarned by other hitchhikers: under the dictatorship of Generalissimo Francisco Franco cars were just beginning to become a common household belonging, and Spaniards were overly protective of them.

My last ride had dropped me a little before noon in "la ciudad central" of Zaragoza, an inland city 270 km northeast of Madrid. After trying to hitchhike for an hour with no success, I felt frustrated and decided to test the "walking theory": I started ambling to find the road to Valencia, my next destination. Due to my limited Spanish, asking directions of bystanders was an exasperating experience. So I followed the road signs marked "todas direcciones".

After another couple of hours and much confusion, I finally found myself on the right road. Continuing to walk, but with my thumb out, I eventually felt dejected. I had just arrived in Europe from America ten days before, and was planning on hitching across Africa. If I was having so much trouble now, what would things be like later? To shake off my negativity, and while softly cursing the drivers who whizzed by, I kept on walking into the baked prairie ahead of me. Little by little I started picturing myself as a reborn Don Quixote, striking off for chivalric quests in La Mancha!

Full of such reverie, I tramped around 15 km away from the city, until it unexpectedly started to rain. Up ahead was an abandoned farmhouse. I went inside, laid down my sleeping material on the upper floor, and quickly dozed off, confident I had conquered enough windmills for the day.

Sometime later, I woke with my heart pounding. In the pitch darkness, "things" were crawling over my sleeping bag. One of these creatures halted right above my chest. I poked at it and it jumped. And then I jumped! Quickly shedding my sleeping bag, I turned on my flashlight. Its beam created a ghoulish festival of tiny dancing lights—the sparkle of little eyes. Rats surrounded me, dozens of them, everywhere! Startled by my sudden movement, the rodents drew back against the walls, but did not run away.

I hastily gathered my belongings into a bundle and scuttled out into the rainy night, kicking away a group of these vermin that had gathered on the steps up to my room. Around a half-kilometer up the road, I could spy the light of a hacienda, and I dashed towards it. Despite the late hour, I banged on the front door. No one answered, so I retreated under an adjacent carport, and once again laid down my sleeping material—by now, soaking wet.

I had been asleep for around an hour, when bright lights and the loud honking of a car horn suddenly jarred me awake again. I sat up; from what I could tell, I was lucky the driver saw me on the ground before pulling inside the carport and running me over. He gunned the engine and kept on honking, rudely bidding me to get out of the way. Then he stepped out of the car and started screaming at me.

I was too exhausted to care about any of his antics. Besides, I couldn't understand his hot-headed verbiage, so I just stared at him blankly. Disgustedly he turned off his car. His young wife got out of the passenger side, and looked at me, just shaking her head. Together they walked into their home. They didn't bother me during the rest of the night.

In the early morning the woman brought me some breakfast, but didn't invite me in. Weary from my surreal and soggy ordeal, I soon made my way out to the road, where I stuck out my thumb. I waited at that spot, all too happy to soak up the warming rays of the morning sun. Three hours later, a Frenchman picked me up.

I had learned my lesson. From that point forward I disregarded those people who maintained that hitchhiking was supposed to include lots of walking. On the other hand, my hypnagogic saunter into the Spanish steppe marked the beginning of my adult love of long walks, and of my desire to include walking as an integral part of my travels. Thereafter, whenever I reached my final destination, I always took a two-to-three hour walkabout to better understand my new environment, and would seek out longer treks when they were possible. I just made sure to separate walking from hitchhiking—two very distinct disciplines!

<u>High point:</u>

"Chegaga"

During a weeklong desert walkabout with my Moroccan friend Abbass Sbai, successive miracles of nature occurred. Abbass, as witty a man as I have ever met, is from a semi-nomadic Sahrawi tribe in Mhamid-el-Ghizlane, an oasis settlement in southern Morocco. It is thanks to Abbass—now a doctor and occasional tour guide—that I initially fell in love with the Sahara Desert. We met in Mhamid during my first trip to Africa, in 1970; I have visited him many times since then.

Abbass, who is my age, walked everywhere—through palm groves, sand seas, and rocky flatlands. With his lithe and confidant bounding through the nearby dunes and gullies, he reminded me of a gazelle. One day he decided to race a bus which was lumbering along on a dirt road, and won!

Together Abbass and I decided to tramp out to the Chegaga sand sea, around 50 km away. Even today, it is one of the hidden jewels of southern Morocco, much less visited than the more accessible Erg Chebbi, several hundred kilometers to the northeast. But it is bigger, wilder, and just as mesmerizing.

Along the trail we passed by several black Bedouin tents, dotting the flat sandy landscape like large angular stones. Contrary to what I had noticed elsewhere in Morocco, the nomad children watched us from outside their abodes, but didn't rush up to join us.

"The Bedouin here are very discreet," Abbass explained. "Even when they come into town, they seem like ghosts."

A few Bedu children joined us around the campfire that evening. They appeared unannounced out of the dark, and stayed in the shadows, seated at a respectable distance. They whispered among themselves, occasionally breaking out in soft, bell-like laughter. Abbass brought them water. I wondered how they could live in this barren landscape.

These boys returned the next evening near sunset. All of a sudden they became uncharacteristically noisy, as if something had shaken them from their quiet nature. I looked in their direction; they were all staring at the sky. Following their gaze, I saw why they were awestruck: like gossamer sentinels, dozens of strangely-elongated white clouds had lined up across the blue-and-golden sky in a perfect V-formation that pointed towards the setting sun. Then, lemming-like, the clouds all followed the dying orb over the horizon, disappearing with it into the embers of dusk. The starry night sky emerged in their wake.

All of us were dumbfounded. The Bedu boys darted their eyes at one another, as if they were spooked. Abbass and I sat wordlessly by our campfire; both of us realized we might never see such a display ever again.

The next morning the wind picked up, as we were entering Chegaga. In the otherwise crystalline air, funnel clouds filled with sand particles danced over the dunes, wraithlike performers for our arrival. Otherwise, Chegaga was empty.

There is nothing quite like the joy of hiking into a sand sea. There, life clings by the flimsiest of signs—a single blade of grass, the curvy track of a sidewinder, and the eyes of a fennec at night. The absence of life heightens the significance of living; when I enter such wondrous surroundings, I burst out into song, joyful to be alive.

That evening another oddity occurred at sunset: contrary to the singular directionality of the sky the day before, the heavens were ablaze 360° in the round—as if the sun were being drawn through a dizzying chariot race, making fiery panoramic spirals encircling us. It was as confusing as it was dazzling; how conditioned we are by the everyday occurrence of the Earth's rotation!

Since that time, I have witnessed a full sky sunset only once again, in Big Bend National Park.

The following morning Abbass and I got up before dawn and tramped to the top of the highest dune in Chegaga. Just after the sun arose, something very strange took place: as if playing a frantic game of catch, a few wispy black clouds rolled in over the dunes, chasing one another—they could not have been more than 20 meters above the ground. Under the clouds it was raining, while just above them there was a rainbow!

Just as fast as they had appeared in front of us, the rain clouds skated away, leaving a clear blue sky behind.

I turned to my friend and asked, "Abbass, what's going on? Have you ever seen anything like what's happened over the past couple of days?"

For once Abbass was tongue-tied. All he could do was shake his head and whisper, "No, I haven't. But it's wonderful to be here!"

Often I have said that what keeps me coming back to the Sahara is the intimacy with the land and its people. But it is likewise true that only in deserts have I experienced such random displays of natural magic. So I also go back to witness the supreme performance by the greatest magician of them all, the Earth. I know she always has a nifty surprise in store for me there.

5. Have you experienced an important Encounter that somehow changed the direction of your journey?

"Fatima"

For almost the entire time I have traveled to North Africa, the land border between Morocco and Algeria has been problematic, due to various political differences between the two nations. The first time I crossed this border, in the late summer of 1970, was life changing for me.

I had arrived in Morocco only a few weeks before, planning to hitchhike from Casablanca to Botswana via the Nile River. At that time, driving into Algeria from Oujda, the easternmost city of Morocco, was prohibited. However, one could walk from the Moroccan border post to its Algerian counterpart, though few travelers braved this five-mile no-man's-land in the blistering heatwave that summer. I had of course hiked five miles many times before; therefore, filled with the hubris of youth, I ventured forth around noon into the mountainous desert. I figured the trip would take me no more than a couple of hours.

As my route snaked gently into the mountains, I began to feel a little woozy. At first I ascribed this to the implacable sun, but in fact, I must have picked up some form of food poisoning. By the end of the first hour I was experiencing explosive bouts of diarrhea and vomiting.

At that point, around halfway to the Algerian outpost, I was literally spewing my guts out in both directions, getting weaker by the second. I was too feverish to think about anything other than finding a cooler place to be sick, but the road was as treeless as it was empty of life. I had no choice but to drag myself forward.

Around fifty meters further along, I rounded a bend between two hills, and noticed a ramshackle barn that stood a hundred meters off the road. Doubled over with pain, I crawled there and collapsed into the piss-smelling hay inside. Although I dimly realized that no one on the road would notice me in this secluded refuge, at least I had found some shade!

Too miserable to even sip from my canteen, I just lay there. I was in great distress throughout the afternoon. I didn't know if anyone had gone by on the road, but I did understand that I might die if things didn't improve. I was panicked, but could do nothing about it. The only thing I could think about was wanting to call my mother.

Suddenly from outside the barn I heard the bleating of sheep, accompanied by the soft patter of hooves. Entering out of the bright light in the doorway, a shadowy figure approached and knelt down beside me—it was an attractive young woman dressed in humble peasant robes. An old scarf loosely covered her dark blond hair. Her blue eyes showed deep concern.

She smiled caringly and touched my face, all the while chattering away in a melodious language I couldn't identify. Her comforting presence felt to me like an apparition of the Virgin Mary. She motioned for me to wait, and went outside. I think she was chasing away her sheep. Everything went silent again, and I passed out.

The next thing I knew it was morning. I woke up and saw the same woman, sitting in the hay beside me—I could tell from the fresh smell that she had changed it overnight. She was singing to me, while softly caressing my hair. Every so often she would swab my face with a cool wet cloth. Seeing that I was awake, she forced me to take a sip from my canteen. I still felt very ill and could not swallow. This made her unhappy; she tried to cajole me with a stream of serious-sounding words. Then she gave up, her speech once again comingled with laughter.

Over the next day and night, this cherubic shepherdess never left my side, except to build a little fire, where she made tea. She coaxed me into taking periodic sips. We could not communicate verbally, though we did exchange names. Hers was Fatima.

The following day I began feeling better. Fatima forced me to drink syrupy green tea and to eat a kind of gruel made from barley. Again, all day long she lingered by my side, nursing me back to health. The next morning I was strong enough to stand up and walk. At that point my only thoughts were of escaping from this bizarre limbo before the day got too hot.

Fatima disapprovingly shook her head when she saw me gathering my things together. Accepting that I was resolved to leave, she stepped outside and softly called out to her sheep, who ran up and gathered around us. Together with her small herd we took up the direction towards Algeria. She carried my backpack; whenever I stumbled, she steadied me.

After another hour or so, we spotted the border post up ahead. As suddenly as she had appeared, Fatima called together her sheep and left, looking back at me over her shoulder with a radiant smile. She and her flock slowly melded into the mountainside.

I wish Fatima had given me time to thank her properly; I am convinced that she had just saved my life.

Thanks to her merciful intervention, I began to imagine my journey differently. Before this episode my ideas of Africa had been informed mainly by adventure books and movies. I had seen the "everyday people" as a colorful, folksy backdrop of a fascinating continent to cross. After my encounter with Fatima, I never saw them this way again; they had become a flesh-and-blood reality—full of complexity and surprises.

My "African adventure" evolved. No longer was the grand exploit of traversing the continent such an imperative; meeting Fatima helped shape my lifelong commitment to understanding and communicating about the extraordinary people of Africa. Over the ensuing years, I have learned so much from them. Like Fatima, they have given me considerably more than I could ever hope to give them in return.

Michael and Aubine Kirtley with the Sultan of Agadez, Niger.
Photograph by Michael Kirtley.

Biography

Michael Kirtley's biography.

I was raised in Bardstown, Kentucky, a small town well-adapted to children who sought to go tramping. By the age of twelve, I had roamed the hills and valleys several miles in the round. I always walked barefoot.

At the age of 19, I left MIT and headed out to discover the world. Over the next four years I amassed more than 200,000 kilometers hitchhiking, including two trips across the Sahara Desert. My "thumbabout" imprinted a freedom-loving, child-like attitude onto my future adult memory. During this period I went on numerous long treks in Morocco and Algeria.

Soon thereafter I met my future wife Aubine, an art historian who loved Africa and adventure as much as I. After a short-lived stint as Saharan guides, we fashioned ourselves into international photojournalists. Our first article, in *National Geographic*, was the product of highland tramps we made in the Ayr Mountains of the southern

Sahara—which we evoke in our essay, "An Invitation to Tofatat". In the ensuing years we produced many feature stories for *Nat Geo* and other major magazines, and also did exclusive interviews of many heads of state, including Muammar Kaddafi and Nelson Mandela.

Aubine and I went on many more foot journeys together, most memorably in the Taï rainforest of Ivory Coast. Everywhere we went, we would take our son Tercelin and our daughter Ariane with us, "home schooling" them wherever we decided to camp. As you will discover from reading Ariane's insightful essay "Aristotle of Africa", she followed in our adventuresome footsteps.

In the past couple of decades I have expanded my rambles into Europe, Mexico, and Central Africa. Moreover, I've gone on unforgettable tramps in Yellowstone, White Sands, Rocky Mountains, Arches, Big Bend, Death Valley, and the Bisti Badlands.

Walking has been a central component of major initiatives I have created. In the late 1980's I founded The Peace Caravan, an international effort to raise the image of Africa by accomplishing the first West-to-East non-vehicular crossing of the Sahara. Unfortunately the expedition was cut short by the Gulf War. After the tragic events of 9-11-2001, I founded The Friendship Caravan, a worldwide call to walk across America together in favor of inter-cultural understanding. Although our program was ultimately restricted to the East Coast, we attracted a global media audience of more than 8 million.

"May your trail be crooked,
Winding, lonesome, dangerous
Leading to the most
Amazing view."
~Edward Abbey

Photograph courtesy of Candace Rose Rardon.

Candace Rose Rardon

For truly we are all angels temporarily hiding as humans.
~Brian L. Weiss

Two Angels in Anatolia

When I decided to walk the Evliya Çelebi Way, a 220-mile trail across northwest Turkey, named after the 17th-century Ottoman traveler whose pilgrimage to Mecca it follows, I didn't exactly stop and consider whether doing so as a woman on my own would be safe.

I did question if my decision not to purchase a pricey GPS in Istanbul beforehand was foolhardy—the authors of the only guidebook to the route had deemed the item "essential," after all—but for the most part, there was little that gave me pause before embarking on the journey. Not the fact that my backpack tipped the scales at nearly half my own body weight; nor the fact that sleeping alone in a tent along a mountainous path might prove more frightening than fun; nor the fact that I spoke no Turkish and would be passing through remote villages where my chances of coming across anyone who spoke English were incredibly slim. In fact, my only real concern on the day I left Istanbul had been finding an appropriate pair of waterproof trousers to wear on the trail.

For the first three weeks, however, my time trekking through Anatolia was a brilliant success. I befriended farmers and shepherds, was invited to sleep in local families' homes, listened to the call to prayer ring out across the olive groves and tomato fields, reveled in ruins over 2,000 years old, picked up dozens of new words in Turkish, and every day, grew a tiny bit closer to the route's final destination of Simav. And yes, the waterproof pants had held up remarkably well against all manner of rain, wind, mud, stream crossings, bushwhacking, forest navigating, and encounters with curious goats.

One Sunday morning, my twentieth day on the Evliya Çelebi Way and just two days from Simav, I arrived in the village of Gürlek. There wasn't much to distinguish it from the scores of villages I had already passed through. A small sign at the entrance to the town read *Hoş Geldiniz*—one of the first phrases I'd learned, Turkish for "welcome"; all the narrow dusty streets led to a silver-domed mosque with two minarets, the sapphire tiles on their pinnacles gleaming in the bright sunlight; and when I came to the village *kahve*, or teahouse, I was quickly ushered inside by several gray-haired men for a steaming cup of *çay*.

Like the countless other villagers I'd met during the trek, they laughed away any attempt to leave a lira or two in the saucer of my tulip-shaped teacup.

By the time I left Gürlek, my belly was warm from tea and my heart from yet another gesture of kindness from strangers. I had heard stories about Turkish hospitality before arriving in the country, but it had been altogether different—and profoundly humbling—to experience it for myself, time after time. So caught up was I in my reverie, reflecting over the generosity I had been shown on my journey thus far, that it took me longer than it should have to notice two young men following me out of the village.

They seemed to be in their early 20s, and I recognized one of them from the *kahve*. He had offered to accompany me over a mountain, claiming it was a shorter way than the stabilized road I planned to take, but I'd declined. Apparently he hadn't accepted my answer. No matter how fast I walked, they held my pace. This went on for fifteen minutes, until I turned around and thought I might as well confront them head-on. I planted both feet in the ground, Superwoman-style, and held my walking stick as though it were more than just a long branch I'd found on day eight and carried with me ever since.

"What do you want?" I asked, hoping I looked far more formidable than I felt. "Why are you following me?"

Sly grins broke out across their faces. "We go to our fields."

I couldn't argue with this, but still I was shaken. I passed a small farmhouse and saw an older couple sitting outside. We waved hello to each other, and though I contemplated stopping and waiting for the guys to pass, I kept going. Minutes later, a car pulled up and lowered its window. It was the same couple, offering me a ride to the next village of Üçbaş, some two hours away on foot. This wasn't the first time I had been taken as an unsuccessful hitchhiker. People were constantly slowing down beside me, and I was forever having to tell them that I was *gezmeye gitmek*, or taking a walk. A very long walk, you might say.

I didn't know if this couple was merely being kind, or if they had seen the guys on my trail and taken it upon themselves to convey me safely to Üçbaş. As we talked, I watched the pair come into view and turn down a side road between fields. I watched them until they crouched to the ground and disappeared out of sight. I thanked the couple, explained that if at all possible, I wanted to walk every mile to Simav, and continued on the path. A little voice inside me asked if I was being stubborn or just stupid.

After a few minutes, I glanced behind me and saw the men cutting across the field, once again heading in my direction. That's when my annoyance turned to fear.

It isn't something I experience often in my day-to-day existence as a writer and artist, sitting at my desk or sketching on-location. But here there was no mistaking it— the pulse-quickening, blood-thickening instinctual feeling of fear, pumping a steady surge of adrenaline into every cell in my body. I could feel it at the tips of my fingers, coursing through my veins, making every hair stand on its unwashed end. The last time I'd felt fear so physically was at the edge of the Nevis Highware Platform in New Zealand, as I was about to throw myself off the country's highest bungy jump. But there had been a safety cord around my ankles then, and despite official warnings and waivers, I had every reason to believe I would be just fine.

There was no such assurance on the road out of Gürlek. Again I had thrown myself off the edge of a safe life into the unknown, and for three weeks, by the grace of God or chance or some uncanny combination of the two, I had stayed out of harm's way. The villagers I met never failed to warn me of the dangers I faced—of dogs and bears, wolves and wild pigs, and those they called "bad people." The first question they always asked was *korku*? Was I afraid? Every time, I blithely assured them I was not, that I had met nothing but good people, but deep inside me that same voice spoke— was I trusting or just naïve?

I couldn't help but think that maybe my luck had at last run out. Had the limits of my innocent faith in the world and its ability to take care of me been stretched too far? I was alone on a deserted road in rural Turkey, I hadn't checked in with my family for days, and I didn't even know if the road I'd taken was the one I needed to be on. Behind me were two guys whose intentions for following me were anything but clear. Did they have their eyes set on the expensive camera swinging from my neck? Perhaps the wallet one guy had seen me take out of my backpack in the *kahve*? Or was their objective much darker? As a woman who usually travels alone, I am all too used to conjuring up a hundred worst-case scenarios in my mind.

I didn't want to let the guys know I was worried, so I forced myself to keep my gaze fixed straight ahead. I walked as fast as I could until it would be considered running. I came to a stretch in the road where it partially bent back on itself, and when I crossed a short bridge that was sheltered by oak trees, I cast a quick glance behind me through the branches.

Not only were the guys still there, now they were the ones running.

And so I did what I'd done a few other times on the path when things were getting desperate. I stopped walking, looked up at the big blue dome of a sky stretching out above me, and said three words: "Please help me."

What I had hoped would materialize was another car—preferably one aiming for Üçbaş—but what I couldn't have known to pray for were two middle-aged men suddenly emerging from the forest, walking sticks clicking in time with their stride, ambling towards my path as though this were a perfectly normal place to be on a Sunday morning stroll.

"*Merhaba!*" I called out to them. Hello!

I waited for them to reach the road, and was relieved when they said I was heading in the right direction. We said goodbye and went our separate ways—me to Üçbaş, they to Gürlek. I felt some of the stress begin to fall away, knowing there was now a buffer between the two guys and me. I was even wondering what the guys might say if they encountered the men when I heard a loud voice booming from above.

I looked towards the top of the bluff and saw it was the same two men. I didn't understand what they were saying, but again, I stood there while they made their way down the road. And when they got to where I was, they carried on walking with me as though we hadn't just parted five minutes earlier. I didn't get it. Had they, like the couple from before, come across the guys and realized I might need help? Or had they simply discussed the situation between themselves—this blond-haired, fair-skinned female foreigner walking on her own—and decided she could use some company to the next town?

They walked with me for an hour, and as we walked, I got to know them. Their names were Ismail and Murat, and from what I could tell, they had been friends since they were kids. Ismail was 62 with salt-and-pepper hair and a matching mustache. Murat was five years younger and several inches shorter. They were each dressed in the standard male villager's outfit—button-down collared shirt, pressed pants (or jeans, in Ismail's case), and a blazer with patches on the elbows. Although they both grew up in Gürlek, Ismail said he now lived in the seaside city of İzmir, and was back for two weeks seeing family and friends.

Walking with Ismail and Murat, I'd never felt safer on the trail. In an instant, the pendulum of my fear had swung to the other side. I could relax and finally notice how beautiful the countryside around us was. The open rolling hills, which before had seemed almost too open, too quiet, were once again inspiring, their slopes a pastoral patchwork of autumn's glory. The two men laughed a lot, and I imagined it to be the laugh of old friends ribbing each other. They introduced me to a few shepherds we passed, and every so often, Murat would stop and dig around in the soil along the road with his walking stick. I didn't know what he was looking for until at one point, he kicked away dirt from what appeared to be a round white stone, reached down, and wrenched from the ground the largest mushroom I had ever seen. He carried it with him proudly, his walking stick in one hand and the mushroom held high in the other. It took Ismail 45 minutes to remember he had a plastic grocery bag in the front pocket of his blazer, which he then ceremoniously fluffed open and gave to Murat to transport his prize in.

Soon after Üçbaş came into sight on the horizon, we arrived at a junction. I would go right, the men would go left and return to Gürlek. I wanted to hug them, but settled for modest handshakes. With each man, I placed both my hands on his and tried to communicate—through osmosis if not by words—just how much I appreciated their company, just how much of a gift and a godsend it had been. I'm not sure they understood, for when they walked away, I only saw them shake their heads and mutter, "*Maşallah, maşallah.*"

God has willed it. God has willed it.

I will always wonder why Ismail and Murat turned around that morning, why they decided to go two hours out of their way to walk with me. I will always wonder what would have happened if they hadn't.

One of the things I've learned in my wanderings is that travel demands a certain amount of trust from us. This trust may sometimes seem naïve, but if we were to let our fear of fear have its way, we would never set off on a trip—indeed, we might never leave our homes. For as soon as we step out the door, off the edge, and open ourselves to the world, we also open ourselves to the possibility that things may not always be safe.

But I have found the rewards the world offers us are almost always worth the risk. As they were on that Sunday morning in Anatolia, when two angels walked with me on the Evliya Çelebi Way.

This extract is adapted from *An Innocent Abroad*, © Lonely Planet 2014. RRP: $15.99. www.lonelyplanet.com

Questions and Answers

> *The walking of which I speak has nothing in it akin to taking exercise... but is itself the enterprise and adventure of the day.*
> ~Henry David Thoreau

1. What compels you to walk?

I'm compelled to walk by a desire to move through a place more deliberately and with greater attention, especially in cultures that are unfamiliar to me. For me, every step is a chance to study a new world—and to slowly find my place in it.

2. Do you experience instances while you are walking when your mind is somewhere off the trail and on its own journey?

Absolutely—and in fact, I would say that staying present mentally in my physical journey is one of the greatest challenges I face on long walks. I often begin a walk when I'm in a place of transition in my life, so the questions and possibilities surrounding each transition are ever-present in my mind.

3. How do you manage to stay physically and emotionally healthy during long and arduous journeys?

Physically, the greatest health challenge on a long walk is making sure I get enough sleep when I'm not walking—as it can be tempting to stay up late writing notes from the day, talking with the people I've connected with in that place, etc.

In terms of my emotional health, something I've struggled with on all three of my long walks are feelings of isolation. When you're deeply immersed in a journey, it can feel as though you've lost touch with your own community back home. What helped me stay emotionally balanced on my longest walk was taking a day off about once a week—to talk with my family, send a few emails, and regain a sense of connection.

4. Please share a high and a low period that you experienced during your walkabouts.

My highest and lowest moments from a journey happened on the same afternoon of the same walk—a 22-day, 350 km trek across northwest Turkey called the Evliya Çelebi Way.

For some reason, I didn't question my decision to complete the trek alone, with no map and only a compass to help me follow the directions in the route's guidebook. Getting lost swiftly became as much a part of my daily routine on the trail as did saying hello to the farmers I would pass, or searching for somewhere to sleep each night.

But on my second-to-last day on the trail, I became more disoriented than ever in a certain stretch of thick forest—as I wrote in my notes, it was the "most lost" that I had been yet. I fell out of sync with the guidebook's directions, so that eventually, all I could do was point my compass northwest and keep walking—whether it was walking on an actual path or pushing through dense sections of trees and brush.

I could tell then, even while I was still very much in the heart of the forest, that what I was experiencing was a perfect analogy for other less literal journeys in life—that sometimes all we can do when we're on a path that gives no guarantee of where it's taking us, is walk.

When I finally emerged from the forest into a quiet valley at sunset, I stumbled across a small home. My only hope was to pitch my tent behind the house for shelter, but what awaited me there was much a much richer blessing. As soon as I walked up to the house, the family welcomed me inside, shared their dinner with me—not to mention stories about their life—and made a bed for me to sleep on. As the house didn't have running water or electricity, it was lit only by a small kerosene lamp.

Between the cozy, one-room house, the lamp's warm glow, the delicious, simple meal, and the family's extraordinary kindness, the night felt almost like a dream. I'll never forget this particular day of walking in Turkey—for the way it brought me to my lowest moment yet on the trail, and how I then went from being the "most lost" to "found" and at home with the family. There is nothing quite like finding connection where you least expect it.

5. Have you experienced an important Encounter that somehow changed the direction of your journey?

The encounters each journey holds are always my favorite element of a trek—whether it's meeting fellow pilgrims and hospitaleros along the Camino de Santiago in Spain; Buddhist monks and priests on the 88-Temple Pilgrimage around the Japanese island of Shodoshima; or farmers and shepherds in rural Turkey, as I walked the Evliya Çelebi Way.

When I think about it now, it isn't that these encounters necessarily changed the direction of my journey—as I normally follow a predetermined route—but for me, every encounter and meaningful conversation confirms the direction I'm going in…both on the physical trail, and in my larger journey through life. The kindness and generosity I've experienced on each trek always remind me that the path I'm on is one worth walking.

Biography

Candace Rose Rardon is a writer and artist whose stories and sketches have appeared on numerous sites, including BBC Travel, AOL Travel, World Hum, Gadling, and National Geographic's Intelligent Travel blog. A serendipitous invitation to move to London after her college graduation sparked a six-year love affair with the world—one that has taken her from a black pearl farm in the South Pacific, to a 2,000-mile rickshaw run across India, to a remote village of nomadic sea gypsies in Thailand. Originally from the state of Virginia, Candace has also lived in England, New Zealand, and on a rural island in Canada.

After walking part of the Camino de Santiago in Spain and the 88-Temple Pilgrimage on Shodoshima Island in Japan, she then set out on her own to complete the Evliya Çelebi Way across northwest Turkey—a 22-day, 350 km trek following in the footsteps of a 17th-century Ottoman traveler and writer. According to the trail's founders, Candace was the first person they knew to have walked the route from end to end.

"You simply have to put one foot in front of the other and keep going. Put blinders on and plough right ahead."
~George Lucas.

Robb Saunders

If you put your mind to it, you can accomplish anything.
~Doctor Emmett Brown, from the film 'Back to the Future.'

A Date with Tomakomai

Stop being such a fatty! Stop eating unhealthy western fast food all the time, you big lump! You are in the ancient civilization of Japan, a country that was already rich in history before your own was even founded! The whole purpose of going on this damn solo walking trek for three months was to experience a new land, new culture and new people, but here you are, sitting inside McDonalds eating a large Big Mac meal again! Waving at the Japanese as they stop by the window of your booth to take selfies with the hairy bearded man eating plastic looking fast food. There's a sushi bar right next door, but no, you had to have another Big Mac, why? Because you are too scared to step out of your tiny little comfort zone, idiot.

***

"Running late Robb," said my manager.

"Yeah sorry, the train was delayed." I replied.

He knew I was lying but I honestly didn't care. Being only twenty minutes late I wouldn't have done anything productive during that time anyway.

I should have attempted some form of enthusiasm; the guys could see my depleted manner of late. As I was their team leader, it wasn't a very good way to lead by example, which has always been my philosophy. I was feeling more empty and unfulfilled than ever in my career. I'm heading in a trajectory where in a few years I could be the chief engineer of a major hotel, but I cringe every time I think about it.

"It is better to be at the bottom of a ladder you want to climb than halfway up the one you don't." A quote from the BBC's 'The Office' was beginning to resonate with me entirely, and I realized I needed to find something new to aspire to, I needed a change.

***

I never truly understood distances until I started walking. Never appreciating how easy it was to drive a car or even ride a bicycle ten kilometres without thinking about it, but believe me, traveling that distance on foot, you most certainly feel every kilometre, every metre, every step.

For perspective, I guess it's like waiting for a large pot of water to boil. The first minute under the heat, you have ample time to think about other things.

"Do I need to get the meat ready? Have I chosen enough vegetables?"

Then once everything else is prepared, you return to the pot, assured it would be boiling over. It hasn't, but any second now the bubbles will flow...they don't...you stare at the still water intently, hoping that maybe your Jedi abilities have kicked in and you can boil it with your mind, but alas, it sits there motionless and still, taunting you with its stillness...your positivity begins to diminish.

"What the hell is taking it so long?"

You double check the flame is on and aren't silently suffocating yourself. Another ten minutes ticks over, and by the time it is finally ready, you've raided the junk food stash and wonder why you even bothered cooking in the first place.

Once the meal is finished, having achieved your goal, the frustration during cooking subsides and you are left happy with the aftertaste of a delicious dinner.

With walking, the first few kilometres are fine, you feel determined and energized. Five kilometres in, you feel like you must have walked eight, and when you do reach eight you feel the people who created this measurement of distance are imbeciles because you most certainly have already walked ten. Another hour or two ticks over and by the time you actually reach ten you can't understand why you didn't just rent a bloody car!

All the same, at the end of day, after all that physical exertion, I would get up the next morning and have no memory of my boiling frustration and assure myself that it was an outstanding walk. So I'd put my gear back on and do it all over again.

***

Sitting at my desk, I received an email from my manager asking to see him in his office, which was less than two metres away from me. I turned villainously in my swivel chair and asked him what he needed. He said nothing and gestured with his hands for me to come in. I reluctantly got up, walked two steps into his office and asked him again what I could help with.

"Please take a seat."

I sat down, folding my hands together on my knees.

"What's up?" I asked, trying not to sound annoyed.

Quoting phrases he learnt from a generic business management handbook about work ethic and integrity, he began to explain that I needed to be seen more after 5:00 p.m. by the hotel's upper management. Apparently, he and other department heads felt I was not putting in 100%. My manager explained that I should stay after my allotted paid work hours to prove to them I am committed to my work.

"There's no need for me to stay for up to three hours unpaid. My work is done at the end of every day. I'd be sitting around doing nothing most of the time for no money just so the heads might see me and be impressed. It's pointless."

I hadn't told my boss that I was in the process of selling my house so I could escape this sort of ridiculous time-wasting nonsense.

"Regardless, we feel you should be more involved in the culture of the hotel," he said with gritted teeth.

"Fine," I said, knowing when my house sold I'd be gone, leaving a Robb-shaped hole in the wall of the office, never to be seen again.

***

In Japan's top island of Hokkaido, I was sitting on the sidewalk outside a convenience store, using their free Wi-Fi. I was on Google Maps researching a route to Hokadate, but at the rate I was walking (far slower than anticipated); I wouldn't make it to Tokyo in time. I was due to meet my father, stepmother and younger sister in five weeks' time. My father and I were scheduled to climb Mount Fuji during that week, so I was absolutely not going to be late for that.

Instead of heading for Hokadate, I decided to walk to Tomakomai and board a ferry to Sendai, a city on Japan's largest island of Honshu. Tomakomai was eighty kilometers away, and for an unknown reason, perhaps due to my considerably slow pace, I set a goal of pushing to arrive there 48 hours later. Consistently, I had managed only twenty or less kilometres a day, so the next two days were going to be long treks.

"I can walk that far."

***

How did I end up in Japan anyway? Originally, I planned to trek from Beijing to Shanghai. Pouring over maps and details consumed my thoughts every day. I filled a folder with names of hotels and destinations I would be going to, wrote itinerary and equipment lists over and over, just to keep my motivation in the sweet spot of high activity.

Everything was organized. Once the house was sold, I would have the money to buy my gear, so all that was left was a Chinese visa.

Heading into the Chinese Consulate in Melbourne, I handed over my folder full of documents, maps and my precious passport.

"What this is?" The stern woman at the counter asked in broken English.

"My documents. I'm not sure what the process is. I'm walking from Beijing to Shanghai, you see."

"How long you go?"

"Three months."

"No, only one month. One month." She said while sliding my folder back unopened.

"Is there anything I need to do in order to stay longer?" I asked in desperation.

"You stay with person? Family? Friend? They write letter of residency?" she asked, tapping on the folder.

"Um, no, I don't know anyone in China."

"One month. Next." she said, waving forward the next person in line.

I stepped out of the consulate in a daze and walked for an hour to clear my head. I called my brother-in-law for some advice. After discussing some options, he had an idea.

"What about Japan?"

***

The first day was going well. It was a great day of walking, despite the lack of sleep the night before. Checking into a hotel the previous afternoon, I couldn't sleep after I was woken in the middle of the night by an intruder trying to break into my room. I needed some energy to keep going. I stopped at a small convenience store to stock up on non-perishable delicacies such as chocolate and potato chips, as well as sandwiches to get me through the day, and most likely the night.

It was a long walk, but the weather was cooperative. The sun was shining with the right amount of ultraviolet rays my pale skin could handle without transforming my face into the shade of a crisp ripe tomato, and the breeze was cool enough to keep me from sweating like a hydrant. Since traveling from Sapporo, I could feel the difference in the climate as I ventured further south. Japan was slowly leaving the winter months, and walking became more like a wardrobe change at a fashion show. I removed my large waterproof fleece jacket when the sun peeked through the clouds, to then again putting it on once the clouds returned, with the wind and rain not far behind.

The scenery changed quite a bit since the first day, starting in a micro-metropolis full of apartment buildings and shopping centres, to morphing into rural and coastal terrain an hour later. Since day one, I had forced myself to use the GPS, considering how much it cost, but I found it utterly useless. I now decided not to use my maps or GPS. Instead, I followed the route of the train tracks, which careered directly to Tomakomai. All I needed was to keep the tracks nearby, and I'd arrive at Tomakomai in no time.

There was a stone wall between the train tracks and the beach. Walking along the beach proved difficult with the combination of the soft sand and my heavy pack. The opposite side of the wall next to the tracks was covered in tough prickly flora that I would most likely become stuck in and ruin the only pair of pants I had. The tracks were not an option. If my own experience and the film 'Stand by Me' had taught me anything, it's to never risk walking along train tracks, especially if you are slow and uncoordinated. To the high stone wall I went.

Hoisting myself onto the wall was more complicated than anticipated. My plan was to ninja jump up, skip along the wall until it came to an end, whereby I would do an awesome forward somersault back to the ground again, but with my heavy twenty plus kilogram pack it didn't eventuate as awesomely. I thought about taking my pack off, and slinging it up first, but from the last few attempts of getting the pack back on from the ground, I would surely topple. It was so awkward and heavy that the risk of falling off during the maneuver was too high to take my chances. If anyone saw me trying to get up that bloody thing they would have fallen themselves due to hysterics.

I found a piece of wood. It was thin and appeared to be just at the brink of rotting away from years in the damp sea air, but it would have to do. I rested the wood on the earth between a gap of thorny shrubs and leaned it on the top. The incline was steep, so to test its durability I pressed my weight on it.

"Yeah that'll work."

As I started walking up it instantly warped, and the sound of the rotting wood slowly cracking under me was worrying.

"Almost there…"

***

I accepted another night shift again. All I seemed to do was cover for shift workers who were sick until further notice, or who had quit months ago and had yet to be replaced. The department manager wouldn't help cover shifts with me, so I was the only shift engineer. Outside of work, my adventure planning had rebooted since I was now going to walk from Sapporo to Osaka, Japan, instead of in China.

I felt fitter and more capable every week, as I continued to walk to and from work to prepare for my journey. Unbeknown to me, the universe had something else planned, which was a devastating setback; my Red Wedding moment…well OK, not that dramatic.

The hotel where I worked had a contract with a local hospital for new mothers. They were able to stay in the hotel for a few nights to relax with their newborns while a midwife looked after them both. Each time there was an arrival, we needed to move a desk out of the room to make space for them.

It was a heavy, awkward desk, built out of thick glass, supposedly made of safety glass, but from my previous glass breaking experiences it was always a good idea to be careful unless you like large obsidian-looking shards lodged in your body. The desk legs were made out of weak, round pieces of timber connected by one bolt.

I was moving a desk back in to the room after a mother had checked out. After making some adjustments to repair the desk, I moved it onto a trolley to transport it. The trolley tilted and the desk began to fall to the hard concrete floor. Instinctively I went to catch it, and in the process jerked my back. It hurt so much I couldn't dare move again without receiving a swell of pain pulsing in my lower back. The desk eventually dropped but the glass didn't break, which annoyed me. I was keeled over like an elderly man who had lost his walker. I grabbed my phone and called the manager on duty for help.

"I'll call you back," she answered, promptly hanging up before I could say anything.

I tried to call my department colleague, hoping that he hadn't left work yet.

"Hello Mr. Robb," he answered in his cheerful Sri Lankan accent.

"Hey sorry have you left yet?"

"Not yet, what do you need?"

"Umm, I've hurt my back moving one of those desks."

"I knew this would happen, did I tell you this would happen, where are you? I come over."

"In the store room, cheers mate."

"I will come, I on the way."

Waiting for assistance felt like forever but in reality it was less than ten minutes before the store room door opened. My colleague arrived and tried to move me, but the pain was excruciating. The duty manager walked in with a wheelchair a few moments later, horrified that she had hung up on me. After apologizing profusely, she helped me into the wheelchair. I was wheeled to the front of the hotel and into our chauffeur car to be transported to hospital. Once checked in, I was placed onto a flatbed covered in sterile paper with no pillow. I couldn't sit up. It felt like a block of concrete had been placed on my chest while the Hulk was punching me in the spine. My walkabout journey was over before it had even begun.

***

Lying on my back after not making it atop the stone wall I panicked thinking of my back injury incident, and my laptop. Fortunately I was fine. For space and weight concerns I opted not to place my laptop in a protective case, and let it sit cozily in between my unused clothes. I opened my pack and pulled it out, it was ok. If it wasn't for my big fleece jacket that I removed earlier, it more than likely would have succumbed to the laws of gravity.

Readjusting and heaving my pack back on, I returned to the task at hand. With the decayed wood in pieces on the ground, my next option was to try and roll myself up onto the wall, like a seal getting onto a rock after eating its weight in fish, nothing like the ninja flip I had in mind. With my hands holding the edge of the wall, I slowly lifted myself up, flopped onto the shelf stomach first, and rolled forward using my head as a counterweight; however, the pack added more velocity than I could contain. Having underestimated the motion, it caused a great thud, smacking my chin in the process. I shrugged the pain to the back of my mind. Still only half on and gradually rolling back off the wall like Humpty Dumpty, I pivoted my body and hoisted myself onto my knees, perched on top like Spider-Man's not so cool cousin. The top of the wall wasn't wide enough to allow much sideways movement. If I had been fit enough and didn't have a gut from countless hours watching Doctor Who, I would have made it up on the wall with no fuss at all. I finally maneuvered my way to a standing position. I looked around to see if anyone witnessed my feat of spectacular incompetence, but I was in the clear.

"Victory!" I said out of breath, arms raised as high as I could muster without losing my balance.

After walking along the stone wall for forty-five minutes, it became level with a sand dune. I didn't get my chance to somersault off it, but nonetheless it was very convenient. I was back to walking along the beach. The yellow coloured sand was easier on the feet and more solid than a few kilometres back.

An elderly fisherman appeared in the distance next to an old wooden rowboat, wearing large electric blue gumboots keeping his legs dry from the tide. His tattered white bucket hat looked as ancient as he was. The long frayed strands of material around the brim fluttered in the breeze. I would love to know what epic adventures that sun bleached headwear had been on with him. Throwing his line way out into the still serene ocean, he didn't notice me. I decided not to stop but made certain to cement this moment into my mind.

Walking closer, I peered into the boat and saw a thatched bucket with two bouncing fish inside. I've never caught a fish before. You would assume, growing up in a country surrounded by water that I would have caught a fish. That's not to say I haven't gone fishing. I found it devastatingly boring and could not justify the time spent sitting there waiting to catch a little fish, when I could be doing more constructive activities, like playing PlayStation or trolling people on the internet.

With the old man in my rear view, I heard the sound of a train approaching, still out of view. I headed toward the track to get a closer look.

Memories of my childhood came flooding back—skateboarding down to the local train tracks with friends to watch the massive diesel freight trains sounding their loud booming horns as they went by, while we stood as close as possible to feel the rush of bellowing air pushing us back from the high velocity locomotive. It was ridiculously stupid and dangerous. As we stood waiting at the tracks, having not seen one come by in a while, we agreed to walk on the tracks and venture under the motorway overpass. We rested our heads on the cold steel to guess when a train would arrive, daring to see who could lie face down the longest before succumbing to rational fear. One friend, Jim, decided to leave and began walking back home alone.

Ding Ding! A train was finally coming. Still standing on the tracks under the overpass, I and two others watched it head toward us. We studied it to figure out which track it was traveling on in order to shuffle ourselves over to the safety of the vacant track.

"Which side is it on?" Jim yelled, hands around his mouth to guide his words. He was already quite a distance away, almost out from under the overpass. He couldn't see the train as clearly so he was more concerned about which track he should be on.

We looked again closely.

"You're all good. It's on our side!" I shouted replied confidently.

He gave us a thumbs up and turned his back to the train and began walking again.

"Wait, hang on..." I said, confused.

The train must have gone through a changing point, or maybe we weren't looking close enough. Either way, the train was on the other side, Jim's side.

"Jim! Run!" we screamed.

He turned. Realizing a deadly metal rocket was about to consume him, he ran faster than I'd ever seen him move before.

"There's no way he'll make it out the way in time, why isn't he moving across to the other track?" My other friend Sam said in worried frustration.

He must have known before us that there was a train coming in the opposite direction, so he couldn't move to the other track. We had space to stand out of harm's way, so we were relatively safe, but Jim had nowhere to go.

The trains rushed by, bellowing their air horns louder and more frequently than usual, but the sensation of its air rushing by was no longer a good feeling. After the trains rolled past, we looked and surprisingly there he was, gripping the wall of the overpass for dear life, frozen in shock. We ran over to see him shaken up but reasonably fine considering the circumstances. He cursed at us for talking him in to coming in the first place. He had red marks on his face from the stray cling film wrapping sheets used to contain the pellets on the countless open carriages. We decided not to go back after that event.

Up on the bank toward the Japanese train tracks, I noticed a handmade ladder constructed from wooden sticks, tattered rope and what looked like strips of bamboo. I wanted to get close to the tracks before a train came by, so I decided to make my way up the ladder. It was long enough that the incline was not too steep, but close to the top I slipped and fell forward. My impeccable hand-eye coordination missed the rungs of the flimsy ladder's edge by an inch. I came crashing down stomach first. The feel of the cool breeze blowing against my belly that had popped its way out of my shirt and was squeezed in between the lower rungs of the ladder felt strangely jubilating. I gathered my composure and stepped off the ladder onto the grass atop the bank.

Fortunately, the fisherman hadn't noticed my embarrassing kerfuffle, I pressed on and headed for the railway tracks once more.

I could still hear the train making its way toward me. I was sure not to get too close to the tracks, since I didn't want to cause a commotion like my friends and I had years ago. I saw a path through shrubbery on the opposite side of the tracks. I was half way over the tracks heading for the path, when I decided to stop and wait for the train to come into view. When it was barreling toward me, I wizened up and kept moving, walking into the shrubbery. Hidden by the thick plant life, I turned and knelt down as the train sped by, feeling the wind gush toward me. It was a passenger train with two carriages. I waved hello when one passenger noticed me crouched beside the tracks. His hands pressed up against the window as he urged his friends to look. By the time his friends looked out I was nowhere to be seen, I was a ghost, a dark knight.

"I am Batman." I whispered as I disappeared.

***

You would think being off work for almost a month, every detail of my adventure would be planned to a tee. Alas, that wasn't the case. The majority of my planning was deciding what to watch on television. With my back injured, the bed and the couch were my main venues of relaxation. My house wasn't selling, which was a blessing in disguise—not having to worry about moving heavy furniture was especially comforting.

As my destination was now Japan, I didn't require a visit to their consulate before leaving Australia, as they grant tourists a three-month visa upon arrival. This was sufficient time to walk down the country. All that was required now was Wolverine's mutant healing abilities, and for my house to sell for a pretty penny.

***

As fantastic as it is walking down an entire country, the amazing scenery, the lifestyle and the kind people you meet, sometimes walking can be a pain in the arse!

The tiredness was something I could deal with. My back was sore but manageable. At this stage the weather was my enemy. The change from hot sun to cold wind and rain was getting to me. Having not yet worked out an easier routine (which I did a few weeks later), I was frequently removing my pack. I had to strip off the waterproof rain cover each time I wanted to open it up. I'd take off my jacket, and roll it up enough to squeeze it into my pack that I was forever wishing was bigger. It was tiresome.

When I'd bought the pack from an outdoor retailer back home, the salesperson told me that I shouldn't pull up the pack, but to put it on using the shoulder straps.

"How am I going to lift it up from the ground?" I asked.

She recommended squatting down to the ground, putting the pack on and standing up with it already on my shoulders. I'm not a typical adventurer that you see on the television or in films. I'm more like the guy on Gogglebox, eating Pringles and drinking Coke while watching programs about adventure on television. I could barely lift myself up from a squatting position, let alone with the weight of a small child on my back. I pretended to agree with the kind salesperson, but all the while I knew I would most certainly be pulling the shit out of those shoulder straps come walking day. There were a number of things I didn't test prior to going on my journey. When I say a number of things, I mean everything. I did test the durability of the walking poles, but flailing them around pretending to be a Jedi probably doesn't count though.

***

Walking back into work a month after injuring my back was both dispiriting and uplifting. I was back in the world of high end customer service, consumed with repair requests for overreacting guests, but I was also back to adventure training. I spent afternoons walking two hours home from work, as I slowly added more weight to my backpack. I listened to Japanese language audiobooks, which to be honest didn't help, and continued researching routes with the wonders of Google, and speaking to adventure experts.

Now all I needed was my real estate agency to get their act together and sell my financial prison of a home. It took six months, but I finally sold my house and turned in my resignation at work. On my last day, the employees in my department took me out for going away drinks. I was soon drinking alone with my manager. I finally got to know him for who he really was. I thanked him and walked home for the last time.

***

I didn't camp as much as I should have whilst in the land of the rising sun. I did some research prior to leaving about the social protocols of camping in residential areas of Japan. I would most likely be spending nights closer to apartment buildings and residential roads than lakes and forests, I wanted to make sure I wouldn't be breaking any laws, or worse, becoming one of those pompous westerners that feels like they can do as they please when traveling around foreign countries.

After walking close to forty kilometres from the town of Date, it was the end of the day and the sun was setting. The orange glow subsided behind the identical looking apartment buildings surrounding the streets I was walking down. There were signs that seemed to show a large park was in the vicinity. I found a McDonalds and stopped for dinner (yes I know, again). Using their Wi-Fi to look up Google Maps, I captured a screen shot of the route to the park. Finishing my large Big Mac Meal, I tried to ignore the stares I received from everyone in the restaurant while I struggled to put my pack on.

I found a park just after night fell. It didn't appear to be the one I was looking for, but it was small and out of the way, behind some bushes. This was the first night of camping and my tent was still in the package. Erecting my tent was a learning experience. I assumed it would be simple, like the dome tents I've used in the past. Due to the lack of light, apart from a head torch, it was pot luck trying to find the right pieces, but eventually I had it together. It was much smaller than it looked on the picture, not as sturdy either. I knew I must have done something wrong, but couldn't be bothered anymore. I just crawled in, dragged my gear inside and tried to get some sleep. It was snug, but every adjustment made for comfort tended to move everything else, which eventually needed readjusting again. I went into vampire mode and toughed it out. I would have preferred a coffin, because soon after an overhead street lamp turned on, bleeding through the thin canvas. Sleep eluded me…

Waking up the next day, I was feeling very lethargic, my legs and feet were stiff and aching. How the hell was I going to walk another forty kilometres! When I moved around in the tent, I noticed everything was wet. Hoping I hadn't somehow regressed to before I was toilet trained, I checked my lower regions. As I looked up at the canvas ceiling, a droplet of water hit my face. I concluded it was from the cold night outside, and the humidity in a sealed tent interacting with my body heat.

I heard laughter and playful yelling, so I unzipped my tent to look out. I realized I wasn't in a park, but it was a baseball field, and I was set up just outside the field of play while a pee wee game was setting up. The bushes hadn't hidden me as I had expected. I quickly climbed out of my tent, packed my damp minuscule tent away, and hastily threw my gear in my pack. I waved to the children as they stood in surprise watching the western beast in the wild, excited to see such a creature, but too cautious to get any closer.

I turned a corner and found a convenient store, so I stocked up on some much needed sustenance. I'm not a coffee drinker, but on this occasion I bought two 600 ml iced coffees in a can, along with two bottles of water. As it was iced coffee, I assumed it would contain milk, but it was straight black coffee and it tasted like the bitter tears of regret.

It was a frosty morning, fog was covering the road ahead, and the sidewalk was long and continuous for many hours. I could hear the trains going by somewhere to my left, hidden by beautiful tree-laden mountains.

Just before 11:00 a.m., I walked by a group of teenage boys playing baseball. I stopped to watch them and began thinking about my younger brother who would be close to their age. I realized how far away I was from everyone I knew. It was the first time loneliness took its hold of me, so I pushed on down the road, blasted the Beatles through my headphones and tried not to think about it.

An hour later, having walked twenty kilometres before lunch, I was beginning to feel a little drained. I had quite a sweat on, and my lips were cracked and dry. I figured it was due to the sun blazing down on me. On a stretch of road next to the coast, water slapping down on the sand, with no sign of civilization in any direction was when the trouble began. My stomach was tearing itself apart. Something was not agreeing with me, and whatever it was, it wanted out. I contemplated heading to the beach and relieving myself, but with no apparent hiding place it seemed likely I would be seen by a passerby. I did have toilet paper with me, but in the rush packing in the ball park, it was buried at the bottom of my pack. I vowed not to stop until I found a toilet. It was the only thing keeping me intact.

Half an hour later, a house appeared in the distance. I tried to keep my composure as I eased closer. It was an old single storey home on the coast side, made of salt-stained wood with a tin roof. There were large crates of ice sitting outside in an overturned fridge, and the front door was open. I realized it was a fish monger's building. I couldn't wait any longer so I walked toward the two men standing in the doorway, staring at me like they had witnessed an alien sighting. I smiled and bowed.

"Konichiwa!" I said as happily as I could.

The two men smiled and nodded in reply. One had the longest cigarette I have ever seen hanging from his mouth.

"Toilet?" I asked trying to enunciate as clearly as possible.

They both looked in confusion.

"Toilet?" I said again whilst gesturing toward my pants and motioning the universal male sign for peeing.

"Oh hai hai!" They laughed as they waved me inside.

I rushed in to the building, not noticing the height of the entrance until my pack hit the doorframe and catapulted me backward and onto my back. I laughed as I was lying down, trying to hide my stomach pain and stress as to what could have just broken in my pack. The two men helped me up and I threw my pack off and left it at their cashier desk. The man with the cigarette went into the back room while the other showed me to the toilet. Walking through the hallway, I slowly began to understand that it actually was a house; the living quarters were in the back, his family was sitting in the lounge room watching television. I waved as they all stood in amazement seeing me. I didn't speak, as pleasantries were out the window by that stage. The kind man opened the door to the toilet, and there it was, a frigging squat toilet!

How the hell was I going to maneuver myself to use this? I hadn't used one before, and this wasn't the ideal time for a first try. I removed my boots, my pants and my underwear. I placed them in a pile in the corner like I was throwing them into a laundry basket, and hung my jacket on the door hook. I was skipping around like a child playing hopscotch, trying to get all this done. I tried to squat, but my legs were shaking from all the walking. There was no time and nowhere to hang onto, so I just sat down on top of it. Safe to say, it was the worst restroom experience I've ever had.

Ten kilometres to Tomakomai, the light was visible at the end of the figurative tunnel. I expected to feel better after the fish mongers but in contrast I was feeling worse, I think as a result of malnutrition from eating junk food and McDonald's food for the past few days, my body was finally taking its vengeance out on me.

"Not long to go, dude, you can make it," I said in between tired breaths.

A small, locally run convenience store was nearby. Walking in, I picked up some cold water from the fridge, and on impulse bought some energy bars in the hopes they would give me Popeye spinach power. The smiling, thin, gray-haired man at the counter was happy to see me and began talking in Japanese while pointing to a bucket of sparkling mineral water he was promoting. I shook my head and smiled as money was exchanged for my water and power bars.

I sat outside next to the road to text my family on my progress.

"Sumimasen?"

I turned to see the old smiling man standing behind me with a bottle of the lime flavoured sparkling mineral water.

"No thanks." I shook my head once again.

He handed it to me, not taking no for an answer. Pulling some money from my pocket I handed it to him. He refused and continued to smile, as if he held the universe's secrets in his hands.

"Sun hot. You drink." He said before turning back into his store.

Finally walking into Tomakomai, I was taken aback by the infrastructure of a city I had never known existed a few days prior. I found a nice hotel and checked in, threw my pack down in my room and fell asleep instantly.

Eighty Kilometres in two days, whose idea was that?

It's had only been three weeks since the end of my adventure walking in Japan. Yes, I agree the walking wasn't as life affirming as I expected, no epiphanies. I didn't become one with the universe, but that's life—nothing turns out exactly the way you envision, and yet, I wouldn't have changed a thing, not one step.

Now it was for my grandest adventure. I landed at Tullamarine airport late the night before, and my girlfriend Dale and I agreed to meet the next day after she finished her final university exam. She didn't' know that I was already in her house (not in a creepy way); her roommate let me in. I bought the engagement ring before I left for Japan. The thud of her car door closing in the driveway brought butterflies to my stomach; I knelt down, opening the wooden ring box in the entrance hallway, the front door unlocked…

…she said yes!

Questions and Answers

1. What compels you to walk?

Why did I feel the urge to go on such a walk? The answer is something hard to pinpoint. Did I choose to walk down Japan because I wanted to test my metal? Was it to escape the mundane life of five days on two days off? Or was it simply an ancient primal feeling to walk in the footsteps of old? My answer changes on any given day depending on my emotions.

The seed that initially sprouted my quest for something adventurous, was watching the around the world motorcycle documentary, 'The Long Way Round' with Ewan McGregor and Charley Boorman. It resonated in me the urgency to aspire to something adventurous. Next thing I knew I was in Japan.

2. Do you experience instances while you are walking when your mind in somewhere off the trail and on its own journey?

During my journey there were many times I was not thinking about the road. I created stories in my mind, some that I wrote down later. One was a script for a situation comedy based on my comedic experiences working maintenance for the hotel industry.

Drifting off thinking ahead of myself happened on a number of occasions. I thought of where I would be tomorrow, or in a few weeks' time. I tried to focus on the task at hand, and live in the moment, but the thought of the future was too strong. At some point I would find myself talking to my GoPro camera; it was my 'Wilson' to Tom Hank's character, like in the film 'Cast Away.'

Wondering what life would be like upon returning home to Australia creeped in more than once a day, for I had an even bigger adventure awaiting me back home. A month before I left, I designed and purchased an engagement ring for my girlfriend. I was often adrift playing out scenarios of the future, how to pop the question, will she say yes, will it be a surprise for her, will she like the ring?

Most surprising to me was catching myself throughout the day not thinking anything at all. I was almost completely one with the environment around me, like falling into a meditative trance of the mind. Completely free from thought, like how the Dude feels when bowling. It was experiences like that which made it an amazing journey.

3. How do you manage to stay physically and emotionally healthy during long and arduous journeys?

I have never been one for physical activity. Granted, when I was a child, I spent my days riding my bike and skateboarding to the point where I had to call my mother to come and pick me up on the far reaches of town. The months before my journey I walked two hours home from work each day, but that was the extent of my training.

The physical aspect of staying healthy during my adventure was mainly the hours of walking from destination to destination.

Emotional health on the other hand was exercised by winding down after a long day of walking. After spending an hour writing in my journal, logging the day's events, I would pull out my laptop and watch a television show or movie. It was the best way to switch off.

4. Please share a high and a low period that you experienced during your walkabouts.

Throughout my journey there were a number of low periods that I wasn't expecting. The most significant low point wasn't physical. After spending a week in Tokyo with my father, step-mother, and younger sister, and climbing Mount Fuji, I had an equipment issue. I had two external hard drives that stored the past six weeks of traveling documentation, but my laptop stored most of my photographs and videos from the previous week. They appeared to be lost forever. My camera's memory was also full so there was no device to free up space in order to continue documenting my journey. I caught a train back to Tokyo and found an expat who could repair it. I was stuck in a town called Kamata, living in a capsule hotel for three weeks waiting for it to be repaired (why it had taken three weeks to repair I'll never know). The waiting and isolation took a toll on me mentally. It was a male only hotel, and only a small amount of people spoke English, and no one seemed to want anything to do with me. It was a depressing and lonely experience. A contributing factor was my diminishing finances; I was eating little and doing as little as possible to have enough to make it to Osaka.

5. Have you experienced an important Encounter that somehow changed the direction of your journey?

I think the most significant encounter I experienced during my journey was with myself and my own limitations. A few months before my adventure began I injured my back and was bed ridden for many weeks. My journey appeared to be over before it began. I spent time recovering and strengthening my back to be as ready as possible. The journey didn't do my back any favours either, by walking long distances with a pack the size of a small child every day. There were days when my back was in pain for most of the day, and I stopped short of my destination. This caused me to change my route in several sections, in order to make it to Tokyo on time to meet my father.

Photograph courtesy of Robb Saunders.

Biography

Robb Saunders spent the majority of his life being more of a couch potato adventurer than a world exploring trekker. It wasn't until the winter of 2013, while watching an unhealthy amount television, he discovered where his dreams were hiding. The couch potato turned adventurer, and the following year walked solo down Japan, from Sapporo to Osaka.

Mt Kailash. *Photograph by Edwin Bernbaum.*

Edwin Bernbaum

Still round the corner there may wait
A new road or a secret gate,
And though I oft have passed them by,
A day will come at last when I
Shall take the hidden paths that run
West of the Moon, East of the Sun.
~ J.R.R. Tolkien

The Prisoners

I stood on the ruins of a Nepalese fort, watching the setting sun dissolve into a yellow murk of dust and heat over the plains that I would have to return to the next day. Somewhere far behind me, toward Tibet, were the clean white peaks I had come to see but failed to glimpse for the clouds. Where was that world of clarity and freedom I was looking for high in the Himalayas?

A lone palm, out of place on this ridge high above the jungle, rattled desolately in the wind, one of its fronds dangling broken. Around it the walls of the fort, built by Gurkhas a century and a half earlier to repel a British invasion, lay moldering under grass and earth. Here and there across fallen stones, half-buried in dirt, canon barrels pointed blindly at the empty sky. Lost and forgotten, who ever came to walk –

"Namaste."

Two men were walking toward me, picking their way over the walls. One, the shorter, wore Nepali dress—white pants loose around the thighs and tight on the calves, a shirt hanging free from the waist, and a black topi or cap. He had a curved nose and slender face. The other, tall and strongly built with curly hair and broad cheeks, had on western slacks and shirt.

I returned their greeting and the shorter man asked in Nepali, "Where are you coming from?"

"From there, near Ramechap," I said, pointing in the direction of the Himalayas.

"And where are you going?"

"Down to the Terai." I did not bother to point toward the sickly haze that had now swallowed the sun over the plains.

"Tell me, please, where is your home?"

"In America. Where is yours?"

"Just below Sindhuli Garhi."

"And yours?" I asked the taller man.

He crossed his arms and smiled. "Far away from here."

His companion added, "He lives in Sindhuli Garhi now, in the jail."

He must be the jailor, I thought. I looked at the shorter man and asked, "What do you do here?"

"I'm a schoolmaster," he answered, straightening his shoulders.

"And you?"

The taller man shrugged. "Nothing."

"Nothing? What do you do in jail?"

"I am a kaidi."

I pulled my little green Nepali-English dictionary out of my pocket and looked up the word: the entry for kaidi read "prisoner." That must be wrong, I thought with a frown and searched for the word for warden or jailor but could not find it. I must have heard it wrong—perhaps the Nepali words for prisoner and jailor were very close. I turned back to the taller man. "What did you say you were?"

"A kaidi."

"Kaidi?"

"Yes."

"Don't you guard the jail?"

"No." He was smiling at my confusion.

The schoolmaster, who had been peering around my shoulder at the dictionary, said, "He stays in the jail."

"But then, what is he doing out here?"

"Oh, he can go out during the day."

"He's a kaidi and he can?"

"Yes, he's the mukhya of the prisoners."

I flipped through the dictionary to mukhya: it meant "chief or headman." I stared at the word in disbelief.

The Mukhya said, "I have to sleep in the jail at night."

"Yes, the warden lets him out during the day, but he must come back to be locked up at night—and it's time for him to be back now," the schoolmaster added.

The sun had set and the sky was grey with twilight. The Mukhya glanced at the darkness spreading from the walls and said, "Come with us to the village; we'll find you a place to stay tonight."

As we stumbled over stones in the gloom, the schoolmaster explained, "You see, the prisoners elect a chief, and then the warden is allowed to let him go free during the day."

"But why don't you . . . uh, leave?" I asked the Mukhya.

He shrugged. "I have friends and I like it here. Why should I want to escape? And where would I go?"

It seemed too absurdly reasonable to believe, and I remained unsure that I was understanding their Nepali, although they spoke it clearly enough.

The main street of Sindhuli Garhi, a path, meandered along the ridge crest between houses plastered with red and white dung. Women in phariyas, sheet dresses with red sashes wound about the waist, were climbing up from a spring below the village with jugs of water propped on their hips. Groups of small children wearing only shirts, their rear ends powdery with dust, were playing outside the houses. A couple of water buffalo, looking greasy and reptilian, lolled beside a teashop, where some porters in loincloths crouched puffing on a water pipe.

The Mukhya ducked into the teashop and spoke with a man tending the fire. After a few words the man followed him back out, and the Mukhya said, "Here, this man will take your pack to the policeman's house, where you will stay tonight."

Without waiting for thanks, he said goodbye and hurried off into the twilight. The schoolmaster pressed his hands together into a prayer-like gesture of farewell and followed him. I stood there wondering who they really were and how much I had really understood.

The man led me down a stone pathway across a rice terrace and into a house. We climbed a ladder to the second floor, and he put my pack on a bed—a table padded with a thin cotton mattress. "They will cook rice for you at the tea shop," he said and left.

I crossed the room, stepping over cracks between the floorboards, and looked out the window: it faced north toward the Himalayas but greyish black clouds obscured the view. I had hoped to glimpse the snow peaks at nightfall when the sky sometimes clears. But I could not even see the next range of hills. There's nothing, I thought, nothing.

There was nothing in the room either but the bed and darkening gloom. I looked over my pack to make sure everything was there and groped back down the ladder. Outside, men were smoking bidis, local cigarettes, and chatting, while inside women cooked dinner. A group of boys dashed past, laughing and shouting, and somewhere in the distance a baby began to cry.

I heard music coming from a large grey building. Drawn by the sound, I followed a path between two fences to a door with iron bars. It was the prison. I peered in: beyond another door a group of prisoners were singing and dancing in a courtyard. An emaciated man in a lungi, a sheet wrapped around his waist and hanging straight to his ankles, was playing a drum slung across his stomach and swaying from step to step. Several other prisoners were following him, singing a lively Nepali song, while the rest clapped in time to the beat. The drummer picked up the tempo and the dancers' feet darted faster, kicking up dust. The singing and clapping whirled up into a frenzy of shouting and smacking that suddenly ended in silence.

The warden, who had been in the courtyard watching the dance, slipped his hand through the bars of the inner door and opened it with a key dangling from his waist. After passing through and locking the door behind him, he saw me and said, "Ah, namaste, Sahib. Come watch from here."

I started to tell him I could just as easily watch from outside, but he simply opened the door and ushered me in. I hung back in the dark, not wanting to disturb the dance, which had begun again. The warden nudged me closer. He was a plump man with a tiny mustache. The keys to the prison hung on a large ring attached to his belt, as if they were house-keys that nobody would ever think of grabbing from him.

The Mukhya suddenly appeared out of the crowd and rushed over to the inner door. With a pleased smile he said, "You have come to visit us, come in!" He glanced at the warden, who added, "Yes, go ahead."

The warden unlocked the door, and before I could object, I found myself in the courtyard. The lock snapped shut behind me. Was I trapped? What if they refused to let me out? No one would know to find me here. I looked for the warden, but he had vanished into the darkness behind the door. I glanced nervously around the prison and noted with relief that I could easily jump onto the low roof running around the courtyard and scramble over it.

The warden reappeared, unlocked the door, and came in to join us with the keys hanging invitingly at his waist. There were no guards. Why didn't the prisoners mob him and open the door? In fact, why hadn't they already escaped over the roof? I looked around at their faces, messy with stubble, but their eyes disclosed not the slightest thought of escape. And yet among them were surely housebreakers, robbers, embezzlers, and murderers.

The Mukhya took me by the arm and said with a tone of pride, "Let me show you around our prison."

We walked to a doorway framing a black pit, which he ushered me into. "This is where we sleep." I could dimly make out benches littered with greasy blankets. A stench of sweat and stagnant air overwhelmed me, and I mumbled a nicety and hurried back out, breathing deeply to flush the foul air out of my lungs.

The prisoners, some in tatters, others in new clothes, followed us to the kitchen, the next stop on the tour. The cook, wiping his nose with a grimy hand, was stirring a pot of grayish rice. There was an aroma of rotting garbage. The Mukhya greeted him but did not bother to ask what was for dinner.

Once again we emerged into fresh air—the dirt courtyard was looking more and more like a garden. What if a man had to stay inside all the time? I thought with a shudder. The Mukhya pointed to another doorway and said, "Those are the women's quarters. They stay inside."

"Are they prisoners too?"

"Some of them. The rest are prisoners' wives."

The prisoners gathered around us and eagerly began to ask the questions usually asked on Nepali trails: "Where are you going? Where are you coming from?" I started to ask the same questions in return but suddenly realized that these people were neither coming nor going. I halted in awkward silence.

But they continued their questions. A stout man wearing sandals and a topi asked, "Where is your home?"

"America." I hesitated, eyeing him—he looked like a government official imprisoned for embezzling funds—and asked, "Where is yours?"

He pointed north toward the Himalayas and said, "In Tose, five days walk from here."

"Is that in the Himalayas?" I asked with sudden interest.

"They're farther north."

"Do you ever go up there, to Solu Khumbu near Mount Everest?"

He smiled. "No, I have no reason to go."

The other prisoners were watching us, listening intently to our conversation. The walls of the prison were tight and grey around them. I stopped in embarrassment.

The cook began to bang on a pot, and I hurriedly asked, "What do you eat here?"

"Rice, bad rice."

"Nothing else, no dal?"

He shook his head. "We never have any."

The sky was dark now, and I could no longer make out faces in the dusk. A fire burned fitfully in the kitchen, casting a glow into the courtyard and making me aware of the steamy smell of boiling rice.

"My food must be ready at the teashop," I said to the Mukhya.

"They'll keep it hot for you."

Glancing nervously at the bars of the inner door, I said, "I should go now."

At an order from the Mukhya, the prisoners dispersed, and he led me to the door. He pressed my hand and smiled at me. I felt a spasm of guilt at being free to leave, as though I were taking advantage of some unfair privilege, and mumbled goodbye. Then the warden unlocked the doors, and I left the prison, looking back to see the Mukhya wave in farewell.

Walking slowly up the path, I mused over the friendliness of the prisoners and their reluctance to escape. Was it more than reluctance? Were they, like the Mukhya, happy to be there? Didn't they realize that they were in prison and could escape whenever they wished? If I were in their position, I would be long gone. Or would I? Why had they been so friendly to me, treating me like one of them? Was I in some way like them—a prisoner who didn't really want to escape? I looked up with a sudden twinge of realization. Somewhere behind me the drumming began again, and a prisoner started to sing. I glanced back at the prison and beyond it toward the plains, spreading invisibly into the darkness.

After dinner I paused to sit on a wall between rice terraces. The sky had cleared and the air was hazy with moonlight, softening and rounding the distant ridges. There was a smell of night, cool and clean with a scent of fresh earth and mist. I sat there for a long time, no longer straining to glimpse the silver of a snow peak, just gazing at the ridges and valleys, feeling them dark and close. Then I went inside, unrolled my sleeping bag, and went quickly to sleep.

Published in *Search: Journey on the Inner Path* edited by Jean Sulzberger, 31-38. New York: Harper & Row, 1979. Reprinted by permission of the author.

Questions and Answers?

1. What compels you to walk?

The Tibetan word for a human being means literally "one who goes or walks." It's human nature to walk and walking is the best form of exercise and the best way to move through the landscape and experience and come to know the world around you. I walk because I enjoy the flow of walking and the feeling of being on a journey.

2. Do you experience instances while you are walking when your mind is somewhere off the trail and on its own journey?

Yes, quite frequently. In fact, I most enjoy walking on a high, level trail where you can get into a meditative state and let your mind merge with the space above, below, and around you.

3. How do you manage to stay physically and emotionally healthy during long and arduous journeys?

First, I make sure to treat water if needed and to avoid foods that make me sick. Then I pace myself and get into a rhythm that makes the miles flow easily by. It also helps to have good companions with whom I can talk and also spend times of silence together. Planning well—in terms of equipment, food, route, etc.—play important roles as well in avoiding anxiety and physical difficulties.

4. Please share a high and a low period that you experienced during your walkabouts.

High period: After many days of travel on an expedition over a series of mountain passes in search of the hidden valley of Khembalung in the Himalayas east of Everest, we reached the top of the last pass and looked across snowfields to the rim of a green valley that sank away into depths hidden from sight. Somewhere down there was the place that a Sherpa friend had told me about—a stretch of jungle with an invisible palace of a king at the secret center of Khembalung. A graceful ice peak soared directly over it, and all around snow mountains gleamed in the early morning sun. A line of cliffs around the head of the valley cut if off from the snowfields where we were standing. There seemed to be no way into it. We crossed over to the rim and peered down. There, far below us, lay a peaceful valley like none I had ever seen in the Himalayas. A slender river lined with white stones wound across a level floor cushioned with meadows and forest and sheltered by walls of rock. Two pointed snow peaks hung in a blue haze over the far end. I had never expected to find a place that so closely fit my dream of a hidden valley, and my heart began wildly beating.

Low period: On my first trek up into the Himalayas, alone during the monsoon, I encountered for the first time leeches. I looked down to see a trickle of blood flowing from my stomach where one of them had injected anti-coagulant. I shuddered with revulsion and went on. The trail I was on became confusing, and I yelled at a Nepali asking the way to the pass of Gosainkund. He pointed to the right—or so I thought. Following his directions, I took a path into a jungle and soon got lost in web of paths. The day was getting later and later, approaching nightfall, and I had no place to stay and no tent. What would happen if I had to spend the night out in the leech-infested jungle? Would I wind up drained dry of blood by morning? How did you survive with so many leeches all around you? I came to a meadow and looked down through the darkening mist to a large boulder. If only it were a house! The mist thinned and to my surprise and delight the boulder turned into a house. The people there took me in and directed me back to the main trail. So I didn't need to find out what happened to people forced to spend the night out with leeches.

5. Have you experienced an important Encounter that somehow changed the direction of your journey?

While trying to climb Annapurna South in the Himalayas, I got caught in an enormous ice and snow avalanche that marked a turning point in my life. I was completely convinced that I was going to die: as far as I knew, nobody survived an avalanche of that size and kind. I thought I would have nightmares afterwards but that night I had the best sleep I had had in weeks. Over the weeks that followed I thought more deeply about why I was climbing mountains and realized I was looking for unusual experiences, and getting caught in and surviving the avalanche was much more unusual than climbing an unclimbed peak. Where everything had seemed to go wrong before the avalanche—the culmination of a series of setbacks including leaving the Peace Corps in Nepal after being posted on the plains—everything changed and went right. I fell in with a fantastic Sherpa, who had made possible the first ascent of Everest; climbed the most difficult peak I had ever climbed; walked back to Kathmandu with the Rinpoche or Head Lama of Tengboche Monastery; learned from him about the Tibetan myth of Shambhala, about which I wrote my first book; and came up with a project to microfilm Tibetan texts at his monastery near the foot of Everest. And finally, the memory of the avalanche led to series of profound insights that changed the subsequent course of my life.

Photograph courtesy of Edwin Bernbaum.

Biography

My earliest memories are of snow-capped peaks of the Ecuadorean Andes where I lived between the ages of two and five. I was drawn to snow and mountains, and at the age of 11 I went with a school group in a yellow school bus camping across the US and talked my way into climbing the Grand Teton. When my family returned to Ecuador, I began climbing high peaks with an Ecuadorean mountaineering club. I continued climbing in college and went on an expedition to Mount St. Elias, the second highest peak in Alaska, on the Alaska-Yukon border. The expedition made the fourth ascent of the mountain, by a new route. I went with the Peace Corps to Nepal and did some climbs there, but became more interested in trekking with its greater freedom and broader range of experiences. I also became increasingly interested in what mountains mean to people in cultures around the world, and, after writing a book on Tibetan myths and legends of hidden valleys and going on an expedition to an unexplored area east of Everest where one of these valleys was said to be, I wrote *Sacred Mountains of the World*, which won the Commonwealth of California's gold medal for best work of non-fiction and was the basis for an exhibit at the Smithsonian Institution. Since then I've been working on projects having to do with integrating the cultural and spiritual significance of nature into the interpretation and management of protected areas around the world, including national parks in the US, such as Yosemite, Mount Rainier, and Hawai'I Volcanoes. I've also developed and led leadership development programs trekking in the Himalayas and the Alps.

"The highest art is the art of living an ordinary life in an extraordinary manner."
~Tibetan proverb

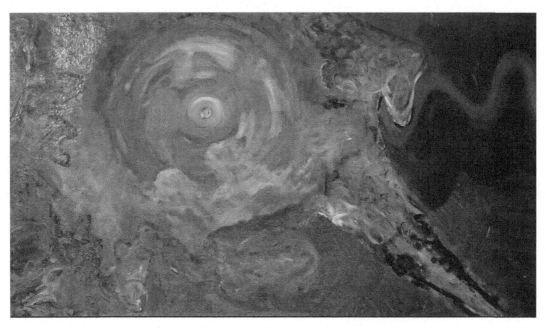

Painting by Moataz Bonser. *Courtesy of Mr. Ripon Sarkar, painting owner.*

Moataz Bonser

This essay was transcribed by Tor Torkildson, based on a conversation with Moataz Bonser.

Eye of the Sahara-Mauritania

I left my home in London for a two-week vacation to west Africa and was gone for months. I just kept walking, painting pictures for food and places to stay, and moving toward the Eye of the Sahara. There were times when I hitchhiked, or rode the old trains, but normally I simply walked and met the people.

One day, suffering from heat exhaustion, I walked from the town of Atar toward the ancient holy Sufi city of Chingutti. The city is the seventh most holy city of Islam, and home to the great Qur'anic library as well as a medieval manuscript library without peer in West Africa. It is where debates took place on the finer points of Islamic Law.

I was exhausted, yet felt like swirling as a Sufi Dervish. I was connecting on a deeper spiritual level like never before. My quest was not over yet, I felt drawn to Guelb-Richat, the Eye of the Sahara.

I walked and walked across the desolate landscape for 180 km until I reached Ouadane, where I collapsed in a heap in front of a small hut. When I came to, an old wizened man with skin like leather was looking down at me. For days the old man fed me and poured water into my mouth.

"I need to get to Gelb-Richat, man." I told him. He smiled and gave me more water. We managed to communicate using several languages and hand gestures.

"Why is your hand wrapped?" I asked him.

He slowly unraveled the cloth; his hand was deeply infected and oozing. I cleaned it as best as I could and he was very grateful.

In the morning I set out. The old man followed me.

"Stay together, sleep together; I take you to Gelb-Richat."

We walked and we walked, sleeping side by side, until we reached the Eye of the Sahara. As suddenly as he appeared, the old man vanished. He had been my holy guide to the great Richat structure. For days I walked around and around the rings, which are equidistant to the center, and remain a great mystery (it is believed to be a highly symmetrical and deeply eroded geologic dome that collapsed).

Months later, after returning home, I began to paint. It suddenly dawned on me that my journey to Gelb-Richat, and the hardships I suffered, had led me to my true calling…painting. It is now time for another walkabout.

Questions and Answers

1. What compels you to walk?

I walk to meet people and myself.

2. Do you experience instances while you are walking when your mind is somewhere off the trail and on its own journey?

I have great philosophical debates with myself all the time while walking. These debates often go on for days at a time.

3. How do you manage to stay physically and emotionally healthy during long and arduous journeys?

I go with no preparation.

4. Please share a high and a low period that you experienced during your walkabouts.

My high point was being saved by a goat in Saudi Arabia, and my low point was having my gall bladder burst high in the Himalaya.

5. Have you experienced an important Encounter that somehow changed the direction of your journey?

I am still waiting for my encounter with Idris the prophet.

Photograph courtesy of Moataz Bonser.

Biography

Moataz Bonser is an Egyptian/British artist and musician who travels, often by foot, to the far corners of our planet's most remote landscapes. He comes from a long line of Egyptian artists: including his grandmother, Nahed El Sadr; grandfather, Ramzi Mostafa (1926-2015); and great-grandfather, Said El Sadr; all are renowned artists. "I am simply trying to understand my emotions through the painting process that I found myself dropped into." He was last seen walking across Europe strumming his guitar.

"I am prepared to go anywhere,
provided it be forward."
~David Livingston

Levison Wood

Twenty years from now you will be more disappointed by the things you didn't do than by the ones you did do. So throw off the bowlines. Sail away from the safe harbor.
Catch the trade winds in your sails. Explore. Dream. Discover.
~Mark Twain

"It was a damp and soggy morning and the monastery of His Holiness the Dalai Lama was still shrouded in a low mist. The shrill squawk of macaques echoed through the thick air and the soporific chants of Buddhist mantras resounded across the courtyard. The heady aroma of saffron, juniper and cannabis wafted over the stupas and golden statues.

The monastery and residence of the Dalai Lama is in McLeod Ganj, a small town that clings to the rolling green foothills of the Himalayas in India. When he was forced to flee Tibet in 1959, India offered him refuge and the little settlement has been home to the Tibetan in exile ever since. Last time I was here, I'd missed the chance to catch a glimpse of the spiritual leader of Tibet, but on this journey—walking the length of the Himalayas, from Afghanistan to Bhutan—I was determined to seek an audience.

I waited on the terrace with my friend Ash, amid cross-legged devotees, while children scampered about beneath prayer flags and dogs strutted between the pilgrims. Next to us, a young monk made a call on his smartphone, his Nike trainers poking out from beneath his saffron robes. He informed us that photography was forbidden, chiefly because there were Tibetans here who'd sneaked over the mountains—travelling in disguise under the cover of darkness, desperate to meet their spiritual leader before making the perilous journey back to their occupied homeland.

So when we were hauled out of the crowd by a stern-looking armed security guard, I was convinced that our surreptitious photo taking had scuppered our chances. But, I was mistaken; we were ushered through pretty courtyards and soon found ourselves in the Dalai Lama's living room, assured that he would join us any minute.

I racked my brains for something to ask him. What does one say to the living incarnation of Buddha? Questions buzzed around my head. 'What's the meaning of life?' Too generic. 'How do we find happiness?' He'd tell me to read his book. 'Do you like walking?' Oh god, this was disastrous.

The door opened and in walked the Dalai Lama, without fuss or fanfare. He wobbled in a slightly ungainly manner, but not one that indicated frailty—more a vivacious enthusiasm to get about, in spite of his 80 years. His cheeky grin and creased eyes told of a lifetime of laughter. He grasped my hand and shook it, but he didn't let go.

"So, you're walking to Lhasa?" He had the voice of a 30-year-old; young and authoritative, with a clarity I could hardly believe. Before I could answer, and tell him that I was hoping to get to Bhutan because I'd been told a Chinese visa for Tibet was unlikely, he continued:

"Do you have a visa?" he asked.

"Not yet," I told him.

He was quiet for a moment and surveyed the room.

"OK, you go to Chinese mission in Kathmandu. You tell them you go to Mount Kailash. Then you go quietly, and relax, and then get permission from authorities to go Lhasa."

He continued to stare at me through those iconic, thick glasses.

"When we have success, you come back. We have big welcome, I would like that. Then…" He paused for effect. "Maximum publicity. Till then, silent!"

So no meaning of life then, just some travel advice. Though, I suppose if there was anything I'd learned on this journey, it was to expect the unexpected.

I asked him if he had a message for the people of Tibet.

"No," he replied. "I don't think you mention to Tibetans that you meet me. For time being, no mention, or you'll risk work. Your work should be successful. Then after, we are quite free." He winked in a conspiratorial fashion.

All the while he'd never let go of my hand. "Then, I am awaiting your own return. Thank you." And with that, his secretary nodded, and I knew our time was up; it was our cue to leave.

I knew little about Buddhism and I'm not into hero worship, but I'll always remember that morning. I met a truly great man, whose genius lay not in his birthright, nor his religious standing. I think his genius was in his understanding of change in the modern world—particularly in the Himalayas—and the power of people to create change.

On a journey like this, there are people you meet every day who are story-worthy; some warrant a whole book in themselves. This little encounter didn't happen to make it into the television series—but with some 1,700 miles to cover, it's hardly surprising. That's the beauty of writing a book; I was lucky enough to explore these little-known corners of the Himalayas on foot, so it seems only appropriate to share the inspirational stories of the people who call these mountains home."

Questions and Answers

1. What compels you to walk?

I find that foot journeys enable you to interact on a human level with individuals and communities. It breaks down barriers and allows for real, authentic communication. People tend to view you less as a tourist and more as a fellow human being. You need to put yourself in the same vulnerable situations as the local people to begin to understand their lives. Moreover we walked out of Africa and as a species it's the mode of transport we are designed for, that we have undertaken walking expeditions for thousands of years and it's something we can all relate to on one level or another. Also, it's a great way to get fit, lose weight and see the country at ground level without the burden of a vehicle.

2. Do you experience instances while you are walking when your mind in somewhere off the trail and on its own journey?

Not really, I find that walking is a form of meditation—you have to live in the moment—surviving from hour to hour so you tend to mainly be thinking where the next meal or drink of water is coming from, and planning the route rather than thinking too deeply about things that don't matter.

3. How do you manage to stay physically and emotionally healthy during long and arduous journeys?

Keeping perspective helps- you're on a journey, that is all. Mentally no matter how hard it is, you're only there temporarily, and no matter how hard it can be, there are some communities that have to put up with the environmental and political hardships on a daily basis so it's best to be grateful. That keeps you grounded. In terms of Physically healthy, I don't do too much physical preparation, just best to take it easy the first few days until you're fit enough. I don't stress over nutrition or kit or routes. Eat what you can get your hands on, wear what you are given and follow the road wherever it may lead.

4. Please share a high and a low period that you experienced during your walkabouts.

There are so many! For me journeys are about people, so it's those that make the trip worthwhile and memorable. I've met all sorts; from cannibals, to warlords, to smugglers to the Dalai Lama—I always to try to take away some wisdom from the people I meet along the trail. The lows are when it gets lonely and you start to question yourself and your own motivation and capacity. Along the Nile I spend weeks at a time walking through deserts and I felt like I'd almost been exiled from the world, from life itself, and that is a pretty daunting prospect—watching as everyone leads their own lives from afar. It's the fear of missing out. Also, falling off a cliff in Nepal and breaking my arm was pretty terrifying, oh and getting shot at in South Sudan, but to be honest they weren't as bad as looking at my Facebook feed with six months left to walk.

5. Have you experienced an important Encounter that somehow changed the direction of your journey?

I think one of the most fateful events of my journeys was when I was nineteen, walking through Nepal. I met a youngster my own age who took me into the safety of the hills away from the fighting in the cities during the civil war. I had no money to pay him so made a promise to return one day. I did, 14 years later and Binod became my guide. Seeing his family after all that time was a real homecoming and I felt like I'd gone some way to repaying my debt of gratitude.

Photograph courtesy of Levison Wood.

Biography

Levison Wood is a former officer in the Parachute Regiment. He is best known for his extended walking expeditions in Africa and Asia. Over the course of nine months from 2013-2014, he undertook the first ever expedition to attempt to walk the entire length of the White Nile river from the Nyungwe Forest in Rwanda. The expedition took nine months and covered approximately 4000 miles. It was commissioned into a four-part documentary series for Channel 4 in the UK. He also wrote a *Sunday Times* bestselling book detailing the expedition *Walking the Nile*. In 2015, he walked the length of the Himalayas from Afghanistan in the west, to Bhutan in the east, totaling some 1,700 miles. He has undertaken numerous other overland journeys including a foot crossing of Madagascar and mountain climbing in Iraq and has walked across 13 countries. He documents his journeys through books, TV and photography.

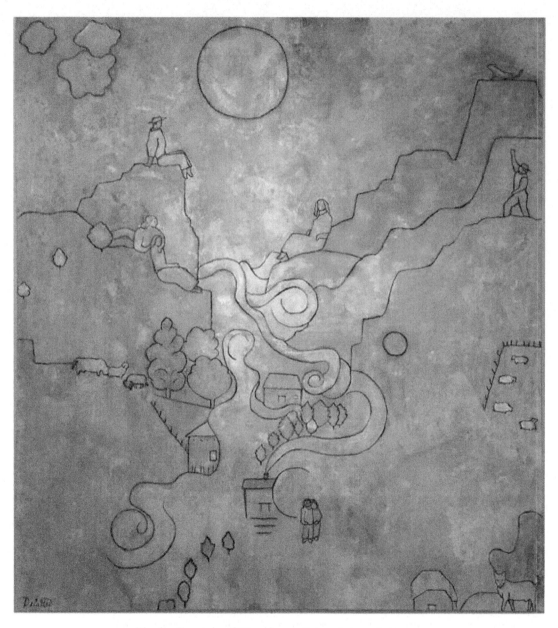

To the Summit of Happiness. *Painting by Pierre Delattre.*

Pierre Delattre

In a world of fugitives, a person going in the opposite direction appears to be running away.
T.S. Eliot

Breath, Trajectory, Spiral: Walking with the Motions of the Universe

Wherever I live, wandering the countryside in search of the most beautiful rock for that day's painting is what thrills me most, and what presents the greatest physical challenge because I have to carry it home or back to the car, sometimes for miles. The rock I seek often has a lot of heft, being about the size of my own head. But on my favorite hikes that rock I will paint and show in my gallery is my destination, the mystery that awaits me, and the public art offering I will most likely exchange for my daily bread. I will honor the beauty already there in the rock by not covering it with too much paint, but leaving much of the surface exposed, simply finding my image by following the lines in the folds, cracks, lines and colors evolved over centuries of its being broken off from larger chunks of stone, rolled up arroyos, rivers or ocean shores, wrapped in roots, moss and lichen, burrowed and scratched into by creatures, weathered, fired and finally brought to rest where I found it.

For eighty years now I've been wandering the countryside in search of rocks to paint. I've sent thousands out into the world, and though I love painting on canvas too, I love paintings rocks best of all since I live with rocks for a long time before I paint them. They are like friends I come to know well, though what they evoke is such a great mystery that I sometimes almost feel in terror of them, and I perfectly understand why an old guy once chewed me out for having the nerve to desecrate them with my art. I love the shapes, colors and striations of those I can pick up, turn in my hands and sometimes lug a long way home, cradled against my stomach as the art object I will give birth to. Yes, there is a kind of male pregnancy in bringing new life to rocks, though rocks have brought me to life as well. In more ways than one, rocks have literally saved my life.

It all began when at age four, I was climbing the big pile of boulders my grandfather had gathered to build the chimney of his farmhouse on the shore of a lake in the north woods of Wisconsin. When the rocks started to roll, I somehow got buried under them. My parents assumed I had been crushed and was probably dead. The question was how to move those big rocks off my body without the risk of crushing me even more. They found the rocks had formed an arch over my body and left me unscathed. My mother liked to tell of how the rocks almost killed me. But, young as I was, I knew the rocks had saved my life, and I was grateful to them. I was glad my name means rock. I became a kind of rock mystic. And I find it interesting that my son became a geologist, also making a living while uncovering the mysteries of rock.

As I see it, when I go wandering I participate in the three essential aspects of motion in this universe: breath, spiral and trajectory. Without them, life grows dull. We say farewell, spread out, expand away from each other so as to return to each other with greater joie de vivre: The more far out life is, the more pleasure in the places where we put up the tent and come close in. That's breath. Aesthetic arrest brings us to a stop. But we heavy breathers love to resume the trajectory; we move on in quest of the Great Mystery. We need to get away from a tight community into the far away, the spread out; eventually longing, of course, to come back, but not before communing with our solitude; in my case often sharing that solitude, both with the rock I'll bring home and this massive rock I sit and meditate upon while it travels spiraling through space. Like black holes, like stars that shine bright, collapse, and explode again into light, like comets broken loose from larger rocks, we practice the art of wandering off into vast spaces and coming back in our own good time. Because we move as we breathe, we spiral. As Lao-Tsu would say, "Whirl with the whirl and swirl with the swirl, and no bones shall break."

We move from community, from partnership, from being well known to being… too well known; then it's back to the trajectory of solitude, distance, abandoning ourselves more and more to the great unknown until we are once more blessedly stumbling over the rocks we have no impulse to pick up, bring home and paint. We're just glad we're, for some mysterious reason, still standing, taking in the view, then moving on. Instinctively we know that to find ourselves once more, once more we need to get lost.

PIERRE DELATTRE

Questions and Answers

1. What compels you to walk?

Though as an artist, I have a romantic feeling about urban 'watering holes' around the world where I have spent time among artists experimenting with new visions, I quickly grow tired of social clusters where artists and aficionados pack themselves into the same favorite bars, galleries, bookstores, etc. and debate the relative importance of their work. Something in me still feels the ancient DNA call of the hunter gatherer. That is why I live in the mountains on Picuris Indian reservation land with my studio out in the country a half hour drive from Taos. I like to set forth almost every day into the wilds in search of materials and inspiration for my art. So does my wife, the painter Nancy Ortenstone. Before we worked with acrylic on canvas, we were working with rock, earth, dried flowers and grasses. We can't imagine doing our art without first going out on what you might call a vision quest. This is characteristic of Taos painters, photographers and ceramicists. They do not stay in their studios, but go out almost daily, sometimes very far out for days, and then return to do their work.

Twenty-five years ago I heard about the cave digging artist Ra Paulette, saw one of his extraordinary shrines within the earth (see cavedigger.com for the short documentary) and sought him out in the mountains where he was practicing a dance vision he had for a cave where men would gather to explore new ways ceremonially protecting what he called "the great Mamma." We became close friends and spent many years walking across the northern New Mexico landscape, exploring for what would become his cave sites: fourteen at last count. With only hand tools and a wheelbarrow, he created the most beautiful works of art I, and many others, have ever seen. We always had time to sit looking out over vast landscapes while developing a new vision of art where people could actually or symbolically enter the earth and exit from it inspired, cleansed, transformed, reconnected to what has been so desecrated. He's still experimenting, currently with dance and song. I'm still searching for art materials and tagging along with Ra on his quests whenever I get a chance.

2. Do you experience instances while you are walking when your mind in somewhere off the trail and on its own journey?

For the sixteen years I lived in or near San Miguel de Allende in Mexico, I would stop at the market place for a bolillo, cheese and some fruit for my shoulder bag, then catch a third class bus and get off anywhere in the countryside to follow winding trails and river banks. The campesinos in their fields usually greeted me with a friendly "Adios" and sent me on my way with a blessing, sometimes insisting I come home with them or join them in one of their taverns for a drink. They weren't happy until I was so drunk I had to sleep at their house, which meant waking up to the wife and children, all eager for me to enjoy a good breakfast and share a few stories before I left. Once I woke up to find the wife had used her wedding dress as a sheet to keep me warm. I have always believed the Biblical admonition that 'there is no fear in love' and that perfect love 'casts out fear'. Fear, it seems to me, is always the weaker force. Every wanderer knows he or she has to master fear. Or else. Mexican country people make a game of this, trying to scare the shit out of you. But if you keep the love alive with all your heart, even when a guy is brandishing a machete and giving off threatening growls, or you find yourself out in the middle of nowhere passing a joint with a bunch of guys dropping strong hints that you're about to be robbed and left for dead, love prevails and you are soon shaking hands, even embracing. I know I'm a fool, but my mind comes most alive after one of these encounters where, once again, I find myself marveling at what it's all about to be a human being dancing the light fantastic. Why this game of good and evil? Life is a performance piece, I guess. Bravado, bragadaccio, just levels of fear acted out while secretly longing for love. You always know you could surrender to fear. But that's the challenge. To me, it always comes back to the polarities of love and fear, and which will prevail—the challenge to hold fast to love and not be shaken. Of course there have been some very close calls, so I won't say I haven't been lucky. At 85, I may be quivering in my boots during the next encounter. And then it would be, So long, dead ass. I know that. I'll take my chances. Or at least I imagine I will.

3. How do you manage to stay physically and emotionally healthy during long and arduous journeys?

My art journeys have not been long and arduous, so I can't answer this one except to say that here I am of sound mind and body when so many friends my age have lost it one way or another. And I attribute this to walking about in nature almost every day. I believe that we are here on earth to put as much beauty, happiness and love into the world as we can, from the ageless, timeless source of our being.

When we 'walkabout' we are harvesting these qualities into our souls to eventually offer them as spiritual nourishment for others.

4. Please share a high and a low period that you experienced during your walkabouts.

This quiet day on Quiet Hill was both a high and a low period:

My walkabout friend Ra Paulette found such a perfect spot, way up in the badlands beyond where anybody would ever find it, with just the right kind of carvable sandstone, that he secretly wrote out and staked "a beauty claim" on public land, burying the claim in a bottle under a rock. He called the cave site Quiet Hill. There, with mattock and wheelbarrow, he tunneled into the side of the hill to create the most awesome of his many shrines within the earth. The cave was ornamentally sculpted with meditation seats, a central circle for group sitting, shafts of light coming down from the top of the hill, a bed, kitchen, writing space, and an outdoor terrace. Ra wanted to offer it as a hermitage, possibly even to the Dalai Lama if he wanted to hide out for a time, escape from his public persona. (The cave has since been filled in.)

On the day when the Twin Towers went down, Ra, Doctor Wu (a Taoist sage from Stillpoint Colorado) and I… we decided we should convene a meeting of what we called The Ne'erdowellians. We took the long hike up to Quiet Hill, sat around the fire circle and tried to foresee the consequences of what had just happened in New York.

We knew the world would never be the same. Prolonged chaos, with more terrorism, was bound to ensue and spread across the globe. Explosions on earth, bombs, guided missiles raining from the sky, vast social upheavals. So why, we asked ourselves as we gazed out across the vastness, were we three humans suddenly so strangely elated?

Something wondrous was in the air.

It's the silence, whispered Dr. Wu. Why is everything so silent? Even the birds were silent.

Ra remarked on how serenely blank the sky looked. There was none of the usual scribbling from airplanes, not a single vapor trail. No rumblings up above.

We listened to the silence for a long time. On any other day, at least one or two airplanes could be seen from up here. There were none. Then we remembered. They had all been grounded. No planes were allowed in the sky for a day and a night.

We were amazed at how peaceful, how much more wondrous the world had become.

5. Have you experienced an important Encounter that somehow changed the direction of your journey?

I went through a crazy period, probably influenced by Milarepa, when I thought I could make such magic with my mind that I could actually alter the natural world, dissolve rain clouds, make fish jump and such. One day I was sitting meditating under a juniper tree when I looked down the slope and saw two beautiful daisies, about ten feet apart. A butterfly landed on one. In my mind, I told it to fly off and go land on the other. It did. I told it to go land on a rock and then fly back to the first daisy. It did. Wow! As I was marveling at my mental connection to this fluttering creature, my wife Nancy clambered down from where she had been hiking up above. She sat down beside me. "Watch this," I said. "See that butterfly on the daisy down there? I can make it leave the daisy and come land right here on this little spot of sunshine on my knee."

Straining my brain, I visualized this happening. But the butterfly, as if annoyed, flew off and away out of sight over the tree.

Nancy chuckled. "Maybe the creatures out there don't like you trying to control them. Maybe you should give this up and leave them be."

I decided she was right. In fact, I decided to abandon my brain game once and for all, and I felt much relieved.

We had been talking of other things for quite some time, the butterfly entirely forgotten, when lo! From around the far side of the tree it fluttered down and landed exactly there, on that little spot of sunshine of my knee.

That incident may not have changed the direction of my journey, but it changed the direction of my mind.

Photograph courtesy of Pierre Delattre.

Biography

Pierre Delattre recently published his fifth book, *Korrigan's Shadow*, a fictional journey about a young man and woman's journey toward artistic self-completion. He took his graduate degree in Sacred Arts at the University of Chicago, and since then has made the art life one of sacred explorations, both in creative solitude and in merging his life with 'bohemian' communities where new visual and literary expressions are conceived. During the beat era he ran a spiritual coffee house in San Francisco's North Beach, spent eighteen years writing and painting while exploring his theme in Mexico and Puerto Rico, has been living in the northern New Mexico countryside since 1986 while running an art gallery in Taos, New Mexico with his wife Nancy and daughter Carla, both fine artists. At 86 he continues to hit the trail almost every day, regarding art as a way of hunting, gathering and bringing home new vision.

"From wonder into wonder existence opens."
~Lao Tzu

Photograph courtesy of Mikael Strandberg.

Mikael Strandberg

Yemen- 126 degrees Fahrenheit in the Shade

"I have to get out of this heat!" screamed Tanya. "I can't stand it. I will die out here!"

My thermometer read 48 degrees Celsius. Our throats were sore, dry and hurting. Sweat was pouring down our bodies even when we were sitting dead still in the makeshift shadow we had created by hanging a blanket between two thorn trees.

It was 11 a.m., and it would get hotter by the hour until 3 p.m. when it would cool down enough for us to feel alive. I knew from experience, if we didn't drink 1.5 litres of water per hour during the hottest hours, cramps, sunstroke, and a gruesome death would eventually follow. We had to pump our water through a filter to be sure we wouldn't get ill. The night before, we had drawn our water from a dirty well; it took us 20 minutes of hard work to filter one liter of water.

Worst of all, the sun's intensity was so strong that it hurt Tanya's eyes and I knew that it could cause her permanent blindness. Early in the morning, I had taped her sunglasses with duct tape to keep the sunlight from reflecting off the sand and into her eyes.

Walking was out of question between 8 a.m. and 4 p.m. The brain stops to function when it reaches 45 degrees. In an hour, we would have problems just breathing; it would be impossible to think, and good decision-making was out of the question.

"You just have to accept it, Tanya," I told my partner, who was on her first expedition. "There's no other way, but to suffer and wait until it gets bearable."

For Mabkhout, this extreme heat was a part of life. He knew nothing else. This is the life of the Bedu; extreme, raw, and fragile. He didn't see any beauty in the landscape. For him, this was hell. But he was happy having a job, because he has been out of work for quite some time. His life wasn't easy. He currently had two wives, four children with each of them, and a few-months-old daughter.

He took the job to feed his family. He had been the only surviving child in his family. All his brothers and sisters were dead. The more we got to know him, the more we liked him, and I started to understand why he fought so hard for a raise. He needed the money to survive. I would have done the same.

Mabkhout was very open about the ups and downs of his life. He had been in prison in Oman for three years. He was tricked by a rich Omani to smuggle items across the border but had been caught. He wasn't welcome in Oman anymore and disliked the place. His dream was to invest in a car and drive professionally again. But, right now, life was hard. He hadn't bought a new futa (skirt-wrap) for almost a year, and it was even longer since he'd bought a new shirt.

We carried almost 40 kilograms of personal equipment, but Mabkhout brought only his Kalashnikov rifle. When he saw all our equipment the first day of packing, he wanted us to at least get rid of the tent. "Bedus don´t need a tent," he told us. We tried to convince him that it was necessary for keeping our equipment safe, and for our field "office."

Mabkhout dismissed the GPS as useless, because it could find neither water nor good grazing land. Yet, later he was impressed that I could pinpoint where we were on the map, even though it was in English. Evenings, around the campfire, he bragged to other locals about my map and the ability to give exact distances walked each day.

Once we got to know Mabkhout better, we began to like him. In turn, he became more comfortable with us. At the nomadic camps, he took over our difficult job for negotiating for the payment of food, grazing, water, and petrol for our stoves. Visits to the nomads' tents were the highlights of the trip. The Bedus were generous, friendly, charming and helpful people. Later in our expedition, we met Bedus who now lived in settlements, and the experience was not so good. Life as a nomad is far better than settled life.

Questions and Answers

1. What compels you to walk?

I walk at least 10 kilometers every day. For me, walking is important for two reasons. The first is to keep physically fit. Since I have spent thirty years of my life needing to be physically fit for my profession, I walk to stay in shape, and walking calms me. Second, walking gives me the time I need to think about everything, from my children to my work.

Professionally, my interest is learning about cultures and getting as close as possible to the people in the regions I explore. I have realized that if one travels in a simple way, with an animal, it is easier for the local people to open their doors to their homes and their hearts. I am not saying they understand what I am doing, but they respect it and feel some pity for the hard work involved. Traveling with a camel, for example, where they are important, gives me an immediate connection and topic of discussion with the local people.

I also like walking because it makes me part of my surroundings, which is impossible if you travel by vehicle or even on a bicycle. This is how humans left Africa—we stood up and walked. Walking is written in our genes, and I believe we feel our best when walking.

Walking makes you a better traveler because you are vulnerable all the time and have to open your heart and soul whenever you meet people. You have to ask for help. I like that. It keeps you honest, genuine, kind and level-headed.

Walking means happiness to me. I walk twelve kilometers to school with my children. It gives us time to discuss our lives. It is easier for us to solve problems while walking than at home.

2. Do you experience instances while you are walking when your mind is somewhere off the trail and on its own journey?

Most of the professional walking I have done lately has been in extreme heat, with only 2-3 hours a day of enjoyable walking. This is when I feel at one with my surroundings; happy and privileged to be there, and great thoughts turn up. The rest of the walking day is just pain, acute tiredness, longing for a shadow or a well or people, and the only thoughts are of food and water. There's a time when you don't think at all, only survive. On and off, those rare moments arrive, when your thoughts wander away on their own journey until they're brutally cut off by something happening in your surroundings: a predator bird shrieking or your partner says something unimportant. I believe these wandering thoughts are there to keep you sane and alive for the moment. Nothing else.

3. How do you manage to stay physically and emotionally healthy during long and arduous journeys?

I put on a lot of weight before I set off—up to 40 pounds. This keeps me strong for at least six weeks. Then I have to have to stop and load up on more fatty foods. This system works well in both extreme heat and cold. Because I love being an explorer, these are the best moments of my life, and being emotionally healthy is easy. But, of course, seeing suffering and pain, does affect you. When I don't travel, I exercise at least an hour a day, and I don't eat meat. The older I get, the more I have to take care of myself.

4. Please share a high and a low period that you experienced during your walkabouts.

I have had many highs. Most of them are when I meet people on my expeditions. In thirty years of exploring, I've found most people to be friendly. I have been scared. On my last journey, through the Al Mahra desert in Yemen, it was supposedly a haven for Al-Qaeda according to Western media. I didn't meet one of them.

The lows are few and as hard to define. The worst is coming across suffering people. These are mainly simple people living in areas, which in one way or another have been forgotten by the rulers. They have been thrown into poverty and wars by the surrounding world and are at times run by evil people. I come across these suffering people often. Seeing the effects of climate change also hurt, again due to decisions by people at the top who have no clue. Unfortunately, I also often see this.

5. Have you experienced an important Encounter that somehow changed the direction of your journey?

When I was younger I often felt that I came across special people who gave me direction, such as a Siberian shaman, but with age it is being with my children that I learn the most about myself and others—my children are my most important encounter.

Photograph courtesy of Mikael Strandberg.

Biography

Mikael Strandberg was born in 1962 in Dala-Järna, Sweden. He started his professional career as an explorer 28 years ago. He is currently working as a lecturer, film maker and as a writer. He has produced four documentaries, *Patagonia–3,000 Kilometres by Horse*, *The Masaai People–1,000 Kilometres by Foot*, *-58 Degrees–Exploring Siberia on Skis*, and *Expedition Yemen–126 degrees In The Shade*.

Mikael's expeditions include long distant bicycle trips from Chile to Alaska passing through the Darien Gap, Norway to South Africa passing through the Sahara Desert, New Zealand to Cairo traversing Asia. Other expeditions include Patagonia by horse through Chile and Argentina, a walk through Maasailand in eastern Africa to learn about the Maasai people, exploration of the Kolyma River in Siberia with Johan Ivarsson, 'Expedition Yemen' by camel from Zabid to Sanaa to show the world the real Yemen, and not what the media portrays it as. He crossed the sands of Al Mahra with Tanya Holm. Expedition Frozen Frontier—he travelled through Siberia with reindeer and sleds. Expedition England–with a pram (stroller), Georgia Villalobos, and Mikael´s daughter Sardana, going from Moss Side, Manchester to Buckingham Palace, London.

The Explorers Club in London awarded Mikael 'the Determination in the Face of Adversity' medal, 2005. The Travellers Club of Sweden awarded Mikael the silver medal, 2006. Travellers Club in Finland awarded Mikael the Mannerheim medal, 2006.

Colin Monteath

A Photographic Essay

I have spent all of my adult life undertaking expeditions in the polar and mountain regions of the globe…be they hard mountaineering or trans-alpine treks when I was younger or, more recently, ski traverses in places like Zanskar, Svalbard and Alaska where the secret was to keep heavy loads off one's back and knees, and pull a loaded sled. The important ingredient of any journey for me is to get away from the automobile. Of course, I use planes and vehicles to change environments, but then it is vital to walk or ski alone, or in a small team making use of local transport such as camels, yaks, dogs, or horses, and in the case of this trip in northern Mongolia, reindeer.

Only by slowing down to the 'pace of the land' and walking, is it possible to open the mind and senses to absorb important details of landscape, flora and fauna and culture…the essence and texture of the land.

I have a love/hate relationship with photography. I find it hard to intrude into people's lives, and yet, in places where I don't speak the language, by making an effort to communicate with my face and hands, many doors open, at times allowing the camera to catch a fleeting candid glimpse of the experience without causing offence. I know how hard it is to take meaningful images of a journey when it is paramount that I also pull my weight to do the necessary chores each day. Yet, by working harder to be out there at the start and end of the day, I feel I capture the spirit of a journey and often see things that others do not. Photography can energise me to find the extra drive or stamina on extended journeys.

Looks like Rain, Dear

In early March 2014, my Mongolian interpreter Saraa and I joined two Tsaatan reindeer herders and set off into the mountains and taiga forests of northern Mongolia on a journey to search for their herd. The reindeer had been out in the Hunkher mountains all winter, grazing on moss and lichen after scraping away the deep powder snow. Our group crossed several high passes and followed frozen river systems before we ended up almost on the Siberian border due west of Lake Baikal.

We had four reindeer for riding and four for baggage, though quite a bit of the trip had to be completed on foot, especially over the steeper icy sections. There are only 40 Tsaatan, or Dukha, families living west of Lake Khovsgol and between them, they have some 4000 reindeer. The Tsaatan originated in Siberia (near Tuva), however; they migrated over the border into Mongolia with their beloved animals after persecution during the Stalin era.

This image shows the first pass we crossed. The journey eventually reached the mountains on the horizon, effectively the border with Siberia.

Afternoon tea is served on the trail with pre-made rounds of doughy bread toasted in front of the fire. There is no shortage of firewood in the taiga forest, though sometimes we had to dig away a one-metre deep, powder snow layer to create a base for the fire and our teepee. Each night we cut eight long poles, tied three of them together to create a tripod, and then slotted the others into a circle. We wrapped the canvas saddle blankets around the poles to make the teepee before installing our tiny metal stove with its three-part chimney. Within 40 minutes of taking the saddles off the reindeer, we had a snug camp for the night.

A Tsaatan father and son cross a high pass to gain access to the next river system, close to the source of the mighty Yeninsei River. The river originates in Mongolia but eventually flows all the way through Siberia to enter the Arctic Ocean. At times, the snow was near the top of the chests of the reindeer, so it became easier for the animals to walk in front of the Tsaatan who broke trail.

We brought down some 400 reindeer out of the high mountains. The Tsaatan love their reindeer very much, and rarely kill them for meat; instead, they milk them to make yogurt and cheese after the herd is brought down to their summer camp beside a lake. The reindeer are salt-starved over the winter, so to control the animals during our round-up, all we had to do was rustle a cellophane salt packet, and they came running, fighting with each other to get a handful of salt.

It was not easy to go for a pee, for almost immediately you were encircled by reindeer, their antlers clicking and clacking together as they jostled for position to lick the yellow snow…and anything else that gets in the way.

From the outset, we knew this group of Tsaatan (including one 14 year old) was out on the trail ahead of us. By the time we caught up with them, they had been riding for 42 days and were totally out of food, apart from some tea. Despite having guns and traps, they hadn't caught any wolves or squirrels, so they were very pleased to be able to share our food as we spent time with them around the fire and in the teepees.

Far from the madding world of the automobile…resting our reindeer in the forest on the way home…a deep blanket of snow, utter silence.

Colin Monteath at the end of the journey. *Photograph courtesy of Colin Monteath.*

Colin Monteath is New Zealand's most widely published photographer and writer of polar, mountain travel and wilderness material. Colin has authored 10 books and contributed imagery for many others. Colin spent 31 seasons in the Antarctic, four in the Arctic and 22 expeditions to the Himalaya. Colin's images have been widely used in magazines such as GEO, *National Geographic*, and *Time*.

"As one looks across the barren stretches of the pack, it is sometimes difficult to realize that teeming life exists immediately beneath its surface."
~Robert Falcon Scott

"In every walk in nature one receives more than he seeks."
~John Muir

Dan Rubinstein

Walking, ideally, is a state in which the mind, the body, and the world are aligned, as though they were three characters finally in conversation together, three notes suddenly making a chord.
~Rebecca Solnit, *Wanderlust*

The Walking Cure
On the trail in a Canadian winter—
finding salvation, one step at a time

The late-afternoon late February sky is a flat grey, not the most flattering light in which to behold the muffled beauty of Quebec's boreal forest. The wind whips my face and erases the tracks of the pilgrims whose footsteps I am following across a frozen lake. Wet snow has been falling all day, weighing down the scraggy branches of the black spruce and balsam fir that crowd the blurry shoreline. Chin tucked into jacket collar, wool toque pulled low over forehead, I shield my eyes by studying my borrowed snowshoes, glancing up every few strides to gauge my bearings. A tedious way to move forward, to be sure, but it gives you plenty of time to think.

Lurching around the park down the street from my bungalow in semi-suburban Ottawa for an hour, I am now realizing, might not have been adequate preparation. My back aches from pulling a cheap plastic sled laden with twenty kilograms of warm clothing and camping gear. I'm sweaty, which can beget trouble on a winter expedition. I'm thirsty: more trouble. There is chafing. And it's only the first day of a seventeen-day trek. We have another 340 kilometres to cover.

The distance is daunting, but more so is the thought of doing this trip with roughly sixty strangers, all of whom are Aboriginal or francophone, or both. As a unilingual, urban Anglo-Ontarian more accustomed to solo hikes and car camping, I am apprehensive about such close quarters. It's not a paralyzing doubt, more of a gnawing anxiety. I know where I am and where we are going (more or less), but I'm not convinced I can reach the finish line—and, perhaps most worrisome, I have lost track of why I'm here.

The home stretch of today's route crosses the neck of a Y-shaped lake just southwest of Manawan, a small, isolated Atikamekw reserve about 250 kilometres north of Montreal. Dozens of others are traversing the same stretch of ice, but I cannot see another soul. They are out there in the squall somewhere, drawn to this trek, like me, by the vision of an Innu doctor who believes walking can help guide people toward well-being.

In the spring of 2008, depressed over the end of his second marriage and drained by an exhausting work schedule, Stanley Vollant, Quebec's first Aboriginal surgeon, set out to complete the Camino Francés pilgrimage into Spain at a marathon runner's pace. After twelve forty-two-kilometre days, stubbornly ignoring excruciating pain in his shin, he developed a serious infection that almost turned into necrotizing fasciitis—but his fainting spells and throbbing feet had an upside. One night in a mountain refuge, in a feverish dream, Vollant saw himself walking in the woods with Aboriginal youth and elders, away from alcohol and drugs, refreshing their bodies, minds, and spirits. Now he is in the middle of a six-year, 6,000-kilometre series of walks between every First Nations community in Quebec and Labrador and a few in Ontario and New Brunswick.

I first heard about the Innu Meshkenu (Innu Trail) project in 2010. Vollant and I spoke on the phone, and he invited me to join a walk. Then he returned to his busy life, lecturing at the Université de Montréal medical school, conducting clinics in remote Aboriginal communities, spending time with his three children, and walking more than 1,000 kilometres a year, while I got bogged down at my desk.

My dream job, editing a national magazine, was turning into a nightmare. The work—spinning stories for sponsors—felt increasingly dishonest, and the dissonance between what I believed in and what I was doing from nine to five spilled into my home life. My wife, daughters, friends, and family were losing patience with my broken-record complaints. For months, I had alleviated the stress by taking long lunch hour runs. Then I tore the meniscus of my right knee, painfully albeit comically, by sitting down on the ground awkwardly at a folk music festival. (It was noon; I hadn't been drinking.) On the cusp of forty, it was a sign of aging and, clearly, time for a different approach.

In search of direction, I meandered throughout Ottawa whenever I had downtime, following desire paths across railroad corridors and reedy creeks. I skipped sessions at conferences to roam around unfamiliar cities, and assigned myself travel articles anchored by hikes. Intent on following transects people seldom explore by foot, I walked from my childhood home in Toronto to my parents' cabin in Ontario's Muskoka region. Every time I walked, everywhere, everything seemed better. What's more, sitting at my computer, easily distracted from the task at hand, I began tripping over reams of clinical and academic research into the physiological and psychological benefits of walking. Was this a frequency illusion, triggered by my obsession, or a prescription for change?

My conversation with Vollant continued to resonate. "When you begin a journey, you don't know why," he had said sagely. "The trail will show you the way."

So I quit my job, assembled a pulk for hauling gear, and ventured off, well, not quite into the wild but certainly into the unknown.

Woodsmoke wafting skyward is a welcome sight. Even more welcoming, just a day's walk into my new mindset: bear hugs from brawny men I had met only this morning. I have arrived at camp one.

With help from the snowmobile-riding support crew (fourteen logisticians, whose job, one tells me, is to keep us alive), men set up small wood stoves inside canvas prospector tents. Women spread fir boughs over the snow for bedding. Vollant's winter 2013 expedition starts soft. On the first two nights, there are backcountry cabins for cooking and eating. The tea and soup are ready, I'm told, though I am cautioned not to take too much; we're having turkey fajitas for supper.

Jean-Alfred Flamand beckons me inside. I hang my wet layers by the fire, don down pants and a puffy parka my wife calls "Fleischman" (the Manhattan doctor who moves to Alaska in *Northern Exposure*), and follow Flamand back out. The grey-haired fifty-three-year-old moved and spoke slowly at the send-off feast last night in Manawan; he seemed tired, frail. Here, after setting a fast pace across the lake, the man everybody calls Napech—"youngest of the elders" in Atikamekw—is downing dead trees with a chainsaw and splitting rounds of wood with one hand.

The forty-five walkers range in age from thirteen to sixty-seven, and two-thirds are women. Most are from the Atikamekw nation. For centuries, their ancestors were semi-nomadic hunter-gatherers in Quebec's upper Saint-Maurice River basin. Manawan did not get year-round road access until 1973; another main village, Wemotaci, did not become a permanent settlement until the 1970s. Atikamekw culture remains strong: children learn their ancestral tongue before French, and hunting is a common activity among boys. Growing up on the reserve presents challenges, though, including an above-average risk of obesity and diabetes, and myriad other ailments associated with a sedentary lifestyle, poor diet, and poverty (which, in turn, can be linked to the educational and economic apartheid that defines the federal government's relationship with Aboriginal Canadians). "We want walking to become, again, a social norm in Native communities," says Jean-Charles Fortin, Innu Meshkenu's project manager and an instructor in the outdoor recreation and adventure tourism program at Université du Québec à Chicoutimi. "We want people who take their ATVs 300 metres to go to the grocery store to look stupid."

Walking was once, of course, the only way we went anywhere on land. Lacking speed and strength, humans had stamina, and that gave us an advantage over other species. But our big brains continued to evolve: we harnessed the power of horses, trains, cars. Today parents drive their children to the school bus stop half a block from home, while sidewalks are left to immigrants, the elderly, the poor. It is the destination, not the journey, that matters. Even though we say we want to slow down. Even though a solution is right there at the ends of our legs.

After day one's seventeen-kilometre slog, my legs feel heavy, and I don't know where to stow my pack. "Take a space in the reporters' tent," says Fortin, nodding toward an open flap. Inside, Mathieu-Robert Sauvé, a journalist from Montreal, is rubbing Vaseline on his feet, a veteran tactic. He joined last winter's walk and has been writing about Vollant in French since 2008; he smiles wearily and shuffles his duffel bag into the corner to make room.

"Who else is in here?" I ask, relieved to be bunking with somebody fluently bilingual, even if he is my rival (and has home ice advantage).

"Stanley's there," says Sauvé, pointing to a pile of gear right next to where my head will rest. "And Éric"—Vollant's police officer cousin, Éric Hervieux—"is against the far wall." Journalists are cautioned against sleeping with their subjects, but what about sleeping beside them, I wonder?

Hervieux—strong, stoic, and unintentionally intimidating—ducks into the tent, greets me with a silent nod, and lies down for a nap. Our chief is not in camp right now. Vollant took a motoneige (snowmobile) back to town to prepare for a phone call with the Canada Revenue Agency. He is so far behind on his spousal support that his passport was taken away. Since starting Innu Meshkenu in 2010, he has been trading shifts in the clinic for time on the trail, and his salary has plummeted. That has made it difficult to pay his bills, the kind of concern that tends to fade in the forest.

Broiling inside Fleischman, I leave the tent to seek out a chore. It doesn't seem to matter what kind of shape you are in or how tired you are—even if it's frying bannock or mending moccasins, when you get to camp you work. After taking a few ineffectual swipes at a log with a large axe, I settle into my five-foot-four city slicker niche, carrying branches to the women and distributing kindling to the men. The more I move, the more energy I feel. All of this communal bustle demonstrates a counterintuitive truth: one of the best treatments for fatigue is moderate exercise, and the easiest physical activity to encourage—so accessible and low impact that even toddlers and centenarians can do it—is walking.

The therapeutic properties of moving around on your feet are powerful, and backed by a growing mountain of data. Walking protects you from obesity, diabetes, heart attacks, and strokes. It lowers blood pressure, improves cholesterol, and builds bone mass. Walking improves your balance, preventing falls. It strengthens the muscles in your arms and legs, and gives your joints better range of motion. It eases back pain, and reduces the risk of glaucoma. In Japan, researchers studying Shinrin-yoku (forest bathing) have concluded that walking in the woods helps the body produce anti-cancer proteins. Walk for thirty minutes, five times a week, says an American educational alliance called Every Body Walk!, and the endorphin boost will ease stress, anger, and confusion. Scientists in Scotland believe walking could help stave off brain shrinkage and Alzheimer's disease. The Canadian Centre for Occupational Health and Safety counsels that walking "with good company and in pleasant surroundings" limits depression and anxiety, and leads to better sleep. The take-away: walking keeps you healthy and helps you live longer.

In 2011, exploring novel ways to speak directly to Canadians, Toronto physician Mike Evans made a whiteboard video called *23 and ½ Hours* that has hit more than five million views on YouTube. It argues that in that remaining half-hour each day, the single most constructive thing you can do for your health is to be active. That is a message one seldom hears in our siloed medical system, an incubator for the commercial industries that have developed around obesity, diabetes, and heart disease, with the quest for cures often driven by studies financed by pharmaceutical companies. Similarly, funders who donate millions of dollars to hospitals want to buy "fancy new machines," says Evans, not support workaday initiatives to get people moving. "I would do a walking intervention before anything else," he says. "Programs that get people active give you more bang for your buck. We need to create a Ministry of Habit."

Meanwhile, changing demographics and skyrocketing rates of chronic illness threaten to unleash a perfect storm on our cardiovascular care system, reports the Heart and Stroke Foundation of Canada. So many people will be so sick, hospitals and health care workers won't be able to keep up, and provincial governments won't be able to handle the bills. "The medical system is woefully out of touch," says Halifax psychologist Michael Vallis, a professor at Dalhousie University, and head of the Orwellian-sounding Behaviour Change Institute, which helps health care providers alter their patients' conduct. "It's geared toward acute problems, but lifestyle diseases are overwhelming the system."

Among Aboriginals, there is already an outright cardiovascular crisis, and because the population is so young and growing much faster than any other group in Canada, the social and financial costs will continue to balloon if precipitators are not addressed. "We're such a strong demographic force," Vollant says, "that if we do something positive to change things, we'll benefit the country as a whole." But when he holds clinics in Pessamit, the Innu village he comes from, on the north shore of the St. Lawrence River, patients often ask for pills or an operation to remedy their ailments.

Behaviour change is hard for pretty much everybody, everywhere. Often, we are prisoners of the patterns we establish, or the patterns others impose. A reimagined future can feel out of reach, which is why Vollant says, "You always have to concentrate on the next step, the next hill you're going to climb." This kind of counsel might sound cheap in an airport hotel banquet room, but not in these earthy surroundings: chickadees chirp, shafts of sunlight sparkle on the snow, and each fatigued step leads to another.

On day three of the expedition, Vollant and I are pulling our sleds up a slope on a snow-covered logging road in ZEC Mazana, part of Quebec's network of controlled hunting, fishing, and camping zones. Six feet tall and a little over his running weight at 195 pounds, our leader has light brown skin, a broad Roman nose, and kind eyes, and he keeps his long, greying hair tucked away in a bun. At forty-eight, he looks like a cross between Kobe Bryant and Mario Lemieux, and he speaks English with a warm French accent, like Roch Carrier in *The Sweater*. "These walks," he says, "are all about individual and community empowerment. People start to believe in their own dreams and become more of a presence in their own lives."

As befits a man with his feet in two worlds, Vollant wears merino wool and Gore-Tex layers under a hand-stitched jacket made from canvas, a technological revolution for the Innu when it was introduced by Europeans in the 1850s, because it enabled them to travel light. His gear, bungee wrapped under a blue tarp on a wooden toboggan like the one his grandfather used on hunting trips, includes a bulging forty-five-litre medical bag. He treats blisters during morning bush clinics and dispenses Motrin in the middle of the road. Stretching and meditation and traditional knowledge will only take you so far; sometimes, you need modern meds to keep moving.

"Don't fight with the pain," he says, stopping for a swig of water and a bite of moose jerky. "You have to feel some pain to know the meaning of a journey, but if there's too much pain, if you're stuck in the past, the bad memories will keep coming back. It's okay to have memories, to learn from them, but if you're too focused on the pain it's going to get worse."

For many of the walkers—residential school survivors, victims of domestic violence—that is critical advice. Feel the pain, understand it, then let it go. My demons are much less fierce. Yet, despite the strongest conviction that long walks could help me rekindle a sense of purpose, I had abandoned a pair of previous multi-day hikes (I called for a ride not a dozen kilometres from the family cottage in Muskoka), and the failure lingered. Heeding Vollant's wisdom, I painstakingly deconstruct the mistakes I made: poor planning, new boots, heavy loads. I mentally scan my aches (post-op right knee fine, left knee sore). Then I will my attention to the rolling road ahead.

Embrace the transitory nature of the universe, the Buddha said (more or less), and the moments of bliss can feel heavenly. Watch out for storms, though.

Night five. The barometer is falling.

Twice a day, after breakfast and before supper, we have formed a circle and held hands. There are prayers, technical briefings about our route, and then, finally, Vollant speaks. "We are bonding," he says each time, "like a big family."

Coming into this trek, I had never sung "Kumbaya." Never went to summer camp. Never said grace. Never gave props to the Creator. Last time I was in a synagogue, it was for a classmate's bar mitzvah, nearly thirty years ago. I was not called to that bar. Spirituality has never been a ritualized practice for me. But here in the forest, a natural temple, gloved fingers entwined with those of a pair of middle-aged women one day, two teenage boys the next, I have felt it: the kinship of a shared journey. Sauvé, who shares my secularism, tells me one day, "*Il n'y a pas de culture sans culte*," quoting Catholic French Canadian writer Jean-Paul Desbiens. There is no culture without cult.

In the 1960s, American psychologist Bruce Tuckman mapped out four stages of group development: forming, storming, norming, and performing. We have apparently entered stage two, and at tonight's circle Vollant calls us out sternly. There has been some bickering among the logisticians, and many of us, including a certain branch schlepper, are not lending a hand as quickly as before. Last winter's Innu Meshkenu expedition to Manawan almost broke apart on the fifth day, says Vollant, his voice rising. "You're tired of yourself, and we're tired of each other," he says. "But remember: we are one big family."

Yes, take care of your own needs, he says, but do not rest until everyone else is warm and comfortable. That is how Aboriginal people, and all Canadians, used to live. And that is why his grandfather—who took young Stanley hunting and fishing in the bush outside Pessamit—would be rolling over in his grave if he saw how greed and self-interest had supplanted the ethos of sharing and self-sufficiency among his people today.

"Your toboggan is an important symbol!" thunders Vollant, a preacher on the pulpit. He wants the walkers to stop asking logisticians to shuttle their sleds. "Your ancestors pulled 200 pounds in their toboggans. Without them, they would have died. Even if you only carry your water bottle in your sled, take it! We are proud people. We don't want snowmobilers passing by and saying, 'Look at those Indians. They're letting machines do their work.'"

Trouble is, we are hard wired to let machines do the heavy lifting. Michael Vallis blames three basic rules of our internal operating system: To save calories, we are programmed to choose the path of least resistance, which is why we stand on escalators and park close to the doors at the mall. Next, we are governed by the pleasure principle: avoid pain, seek pleasure. Our choices used to be run or get eaten by a bear, or eat some berries or starve. Now we can lie on the couch gorging on jelly doughnuts without fear of being attacked by so much as a mosquito. Finally, we go for instant gratification. We don't ask, "How will I feel tomorrow if I take a walk today?"

The Behaviour Change Institute equips health care workers with knowledge and techniques for encouraging people to get fit and eat healthy, but Vallis also wants to address the systemic causes of the sitting disease epidemic. We need to reimagine the built environment (don't widen roads; improve sidewalks), and remove the agricultural subsidies that support the proliferation of high-fructose corn syrup, which lights up the limbic system like cocaine. The media culture that has made "Go big or go home" a mantra is also to blame, argues Vallis. Television shows such as *The Biggest Loser* and programs like Weight Watchers, and a running craze in which ultra-marathons are the new marathons, set people up for failure. "We need to promote doable and sustainable activities," he says. "Slow and steady wins the race."

Amid this shift in medical thinking, however, University of Toronto health communication specialist Margaret MacNeill issues a cautionary note. Arthritic knees respond well to a strict workout schedule; post-heart attack exercise regimes are curative. "But if you medicalize exercise, you make it a dose," she says, "full of little formulas, measures you might not achieve.

"With medicalization, we narrowly construct the problem and narrowly search for solutions. We lose touch with what physical activity should be: social and fun. You know the phrase 'Exercise is medicine'? It can be, but not for everybody. Walking is more than exercise. It is life."

The evening of Vollant's sermon, the mood in camp is dour, so I hide away, sequestering Napech for an interview in the cook tent. Sitting on an overturned plastic bucket, he is quiet after each of my questions: eyes closed, sometimes nodding, uttering the occasional sigh. "I'm here to spend time in nature, with the children," he says finally, through a translator. "It makes me feel younger." More silence. Then, when I wonder whether he is dozing off, he adds, "Life is like an arrow. You have the tip, the shaft, the feathers. The tip represents the youth, the shaft represents the adults, the feathers are the elders. The arrow is balanced when all of the parts come together. That's why it flies so well."

I have a flash of my wife and girls, then others I am close to, and the roles we all need to play to make our families and communities work. Back at the tent, Vollant needs me. The wood is wet, I am told, so we'll be staying up in shifts to keep the fire burning and avoid getting smoked out. "If I die before I wake," he says, rolling into his sleeping bag, "pray the Lord my soul to take."

"The Bible?" I ask.

"No, Metallica. 'Enter Sandman.' I'm a big heavy metal guy."

Sauvé takes the first watch, waking me at midnight. I stoke the stove, then slip outside to pee. The night is still, clear. A row of ten smoking chimneys. Snoring muffled by canvas. Half a dozen snowmobiles parked in a jumble on the logging road. It resembles a roadblock.

Vollant calls this walk, which follows a route the Innu traditionally travelled to recruit allies for their fights against the English, a mission of peace. Since he started Innu Meshkenu in October 2010, walking 620 kilometres, mostly alone, from Natashquan, Quebec, to Baie-Comeau, near Pessamit, in twenty-three days, he has completed seven treks, with more people joining each expedition. This winter's walk is the largest yet. It is like *Survivor*, only the goal is to get everybody to stay on the island. Vollant has seven additional legs planned. He has been asked by the New Democrats and the Liberals to run for federal and provincial office (and has his eyes on a health minister's portfolio), but he is a decade away from even considering such a shift. "For me, it's important to finish things before starting new ones. Finishing Innu Meshkenu will give me better knowledge of my country, of my people, and of the real challenges people are facing."

Wandering through the encampment, I think about the men and women inside each tent, and the stories they have told me on this trip. Nathalie Dubé started drinking heavily while living with her abusive husband; now separated and on her second walk with Vollant, she is sober and 100 pounds lighter. Daven Petiquay, seventeen, is the type of tough-looking, long-haired teen I would dodge in the city; he didn't say much to me initially, but yesterday we fell into the same rhythm on the road and talked for three hours, about hockey and his plan to become a wilderness guide. Alexandra Awashish, thirty-eight, a former band council adviser in Wemotaci, has four kids and lives on social assistance; her feet are sore, her body hurts, but in her head "everything is going into the right place." She often wears a Superman cape when she walks and says she plans to run for chief.

Things are starting to feel right for me, too. I started the journey as a mildly neurotic urban professional, but as the days beat on, the lines blur. I leave Fleischman in its stuff sack, join men hunting partridge and foraging for firewood, and crack jokes in halting grade nine French, at one point pantomiming Hervieux using his police badge to confiscate a box of fried chicken: "*Venir avec moi, poulet frit!*" I am the one initiating bear hugs now.

After Vollant's pep talk, despite a smoky night (and a reprimand from my tent mates), the 5 a.m. reveille sparks a resilient energy. Breakfast and teardown proceed with cheerful efficiency, and I cover two dozen kilometres like an arrow, pulling my sled the entire distance, except on downhills, where I unbuckle my waist belt, hop on the back, and rumble down at speeds reaching forty kilometres an hour, whooping wildly.

Tonight's destination is the community hall in the village of Lac-Saint-Paul, where for the first time on this trip there will be a pay phone for calling home, a depanneur, indoor plumbing, and a dry floor for us to sleep on—all crammed together, a jumble of bodies, like in some kind of emergency shelter. A week ago, this scenario would have sent me fleeing, but ascending the next snowy hill, undeterred by what might be around the corner, I grasp at last that walking is a way to push toward change at a moderate pace, to leave one comfort zone and begin to forge another.

The next morning, fuelled by rabbit pie and spaghetti with moose sauce, we cross frozen Lac-Saint-Paul and zigzag along a series of secondary highways, leaving behind Atikamekw territory and moving deeper into Anishinabe land. Pulks don't glide well on gravel shoulders, so the logisticians load our sleds into a cube van, and we average twenty-seven kilometres a day for five days.

Fortin's trailer blows an axle, which breaks just outside the town of Mont-Laurier, a snowmobile touring mecca that may have more welders per capita, he posits, than anywhere else in Canada; the unit is roadworthy again in a few hours. Near the tiny village of Montcerf-Lytton, the proprietor of Fromagerie la Cabriole chases a couple of walkers (he had read about the project in a local newspaper) and hands over a sack of chèvre made with port. A stray dog, a dead ringer for the Littlest Hobo, joins the expedition that day, staying with us throughout the final week. These are random occurrences, of course, but stringing them together, like stones leading across a river, it is hard not to ascribe meaning to them.

After a one-day break on the Kitigan Zibi reserve, we have permission from Quebec's Fédération des clubs de motoneigistes to travel along one of the province's main snowmobile routes for the last few days, through a wildlife reserve, to the Anishinabe village of Rapid Lake. We number fewer at this point; not even Vollant's toenail removal operations could keep some walkers on their feet. Those of us who continue struggle after the break. There are long, steep hills to climb, and though some rare bright sunshine allows us to strip down to T-shirts, it also makes the snow soggy and the pulks harder to pull.

We have been at this for two weeks now, and every morning still brings a new series of challenges. At one stop, a wet, weary evening when the temptation to huddle in my sleeping bag with a book grows strong, I find myself at the woodpile amid a ring of shining headlamps, where Super Alexandra shows me how to rotate a log to find the grain and strike hard with a heavy axe blade at a slight angle. I misfire a few times, then find the sweet spot and start splitting rounds with one swing. "You," she says, "would make a good Indian."

On our final night together, we gather around a bonfire in the middle of the circle. As semis roar past on Highway 117, just beyond the edge of camp, Napech and the other elders recite prayers in Atikamekw and French. Then a logistician from Manawan drums and sings a rousing song, his metronomic strokes and gruff, undulating falsetto—"Ya hey-ya-hey hey-ya, ya hey-ya-hey hey-ya"—rising above the crackling of dry, dead branches. Vollant nods to the beat, arms crossed, head down. When the song ends, he asks everyone to take a turn speaking. For my part, I thank my fellow marcheurs for sharing their land and culture, for overturning stereotypes I had harboured, for helping me learn a few things about myself. Fortin translates my final words: more Canadians should have an experience like this.

"Listen to me," Vollant then says quietly, peering around the circle, looking everybody in the eyes, the firelight reflecting off his bright yellow parka. "I'm speaking as a physician.

"Right now, we feel really good because of the endorphins we've generated. This sense of well-being can last for three or four weeks, but then you can fall into a deep depression. It happens to Olympic athletes, to people who climb Mount Everest. It's normal, not a sign of weakness."

Heads hang down, boots kick at the snow. Hours away from our triumphant walk into Rapid Lake, this is not what we want to hear. But most of us are starting to figure out that on its own, the act of putting one foot in front of the other cannot solve anything. That this walk does not really have a finish line. When you get home, rest for a couple of days, recommends Vollant. Drink lots of water; wean yourself off high-carb meals. Talk to people if you feel troubled. Then, when your blisters have healed, he says, keep on walking.

Originally published in *The Walrus*. © Dan Rubinstein. Reprinted by permission of the author.

Questions and Answers

1. What compels you to walk?

I walk because it makes my body, mind and spirit feel whole, and because it connects me to the natural and human ecosystem that surrounds me, wherever I happen to be.

2. Do you experience instances while you are walking when your mind is somewhere off the trail and on its own journey?

Inevitably, during most walks, my thoughts will wander. The physical movement and the stimulation and serenity of my surroundings inspire a surge of creativity, whether it's figuring out a solution to a problem I've been struggling with, or a fresh idea or perspective.

3. How do you manage to stay physically and emotionally healthy during long and arduous journeys?

Although my body gets weary, and my feet and knees often ache, the next morning I feel refreshed—it's the momentum of the journey carrying me forward, constant progress toward a distant goal. I get emotionally weary too, but have done enough long walks to know that this moment's worries and fears will fade, that a rest, a cup of coffee or a good conversation will give me a boost and the mental energy to keep going, one step at a time.

4. Please share a high and a low period that you experienced during your walkabouts.

On one hike, which was supposed to be a week-long 300-kilometre loop from and back to my home in Edmonton, Alberta, through the province's central plains—parks, farms, river valleys, small towns—my body broke down just a day and a half and 65 kilometres into the journey. I felt like a failure, that poor planning and an overly ambitious daily mileage had done me in. But later that night, back home in the bathtub, soaking my aching body, I decided to complete the hike in a series of two-day stages, relying on family and friends to drop me off and pick me up. There were many high points as a I completed the walk, especially when I was climbing out of Edmonton's deep river valley at sunset, the final leg of the trip, just a few minutes from home.

5. Have you experienced an important Encounter that somehow changed the direction of your journey?

This sounds like a copout, but on just about every walk I do, everywhere, I meet people who, even if our time together is brief, change the experience—and almost always for the better.

Photograph courtesy of Dan Rubinstein.

Biography

Canadian writer and editor Dan Rubinstein is the author of *Born to Walk: The Transformative Power of a Pedestrian Act* (ECW Press, 2015). He is a *National Magazine* award-winning writer and editor. He has hiked atop mountains and along coastlines throughout North America and Europe, and written about these experiences for publications such as *The Walrus*, *The Economist* and *Canadian Geographic*, but his favourite walking route is from the place where he is to the place he has to go. borntowalk.org

Photograph courtesy of Maria Coffey.

Maria Coffey

If I could not walk far and fast, I think I should just explode and perish.
~Charles Dickens (who regularly walked 20 miles day.)

Miles for Elephants

We gathered in a circle, the camels behind us. The men took turns to say prayers: Abdi and Ahmed in Arabic, Lemukan in Samburu, Njoroge and Machairia in Kikuyu. They asked for protection on the way to the Kirisia Hills, protection for the black people, for the white people, for the camels. They held out their hands, palms up, fingers curled, and at the end of each prayer called out to the god who dwells on Mount Kenya: N'Gai, N'Gai, N'Gai.

The sun was climbing into the sky and warming the air. Our six camels stood patiently, jaws working from side to side as they ruminated, tails flicking away flies. Ahmed, the head camel trainer, had brought them to Laikipia, in Northern Kenya, from Somalia; he had walked with them the entire way. To him the safari we were about to embark on must have seemed like a stroll in the park, yet he prayed devoutly.

It occurred to me that I should send up a few prayers of my own. Plans for this journey had evolved fast. Our friend Anne Powys contacted us about a group of community scouts she knew in the Kirisia Hills. They were trying to protect their forest and stop elephant poaching in the area. They had never accepted outside help, but now they realized the problem was becoming too big for them. Anne knew we were on our way to Kenya for some elephant work. Would we be interested in getting involved? The Kirisia Hills lie about 80 miles from where Anne has a small eco-camp for tourists. I had presumed we would drive there in her jeep. Then she mentioned her camels, and how she wanted to train them for walking safaris. So why didn't we walk with the camels to Kirisia and back again? A two-week round trip, including a couple of days in the hills? She hardly needed to ask. Trekking across the high plains of Kenya with camel support, for an important mission—it was the kind of adventure we relished and we said yes to everything.

Anne's camp, Suyian Soul, was tucked away in a remote corner of her father's sprawling ranchlands. This was our third visit, and it felt like coming home. The night before we set off on the walk, we had dinner under a huge acacia tree, its spreading branches festooned with weaverbird nests. Darkness descended fast, and we sat by the fire pit, gazing up at an impossibly dense Milky Way. Anne refilled our wine glasses, then told us she had just had an unexpected booking for the camp, one she couldn't afford to turn down. She needed to be back in just over a week, so the 160 mile safari would be 'a bit faster' than expected. Oh, and she had just the right tent for us, a mesh contraption that she called a *meat safe*. Our team was still praying. I turned my hands palm upwards and chimed in with them: N'Gai, N'Gai, N'Gai.

And then, simply, we set off. One foot after another, winding through rocky outcrops on red soil. Three camels ahead and three behind, swaying like ships, our bags strapped to frames set over thick mattresses on their backs. We climbed up and up, to the edge of the Leroghi Plateau. It was vast and golden, stretching in all directions. The grasses were thigh high, the ground was dry and hard and we had to watch out for ankle-turning holes, the dens of aardvarks. I walked behind the last camel in the lead group, putting my feet where his had been, keeping pace with his steady plodding. Groups of zebras stood stock-still to watch us pass, giraffe loped away, gazelles quivered then turned tail. This was mesmerizing, this was right in every way. And this went on for hours. The equatorial sun was unforgiving. My trainers filled with dust and little stones. My socks got covered with tiny sharp grass seeds that stuck into my skin. During one brief stop Anne pointed to a low blue smudge on the horizon. The Kirisia Hills. Our destination. "See that white stripe? That's where we're headed." I could barely see the stripe. The smudge seemed impossibly far away. And we had just three days to get there.

From the edge of the plateau, we dropped down to a valley and stopped for lunch in a grove of low acacia trees. The camels grazed around us, their loose leathery lips closing around the spiny branches. We ate cheese, salami and soda bread, and drank sweet milky tea. I sat in the dappled shade, grateful for the rest, and gazed at my companions. Ahmed, slim and fine featured, was showing Dag how to wrap his keffiyeh scarf into a turban. Abdi and Machairia were keeping an eye on the camels. Lemukan flicked a cloth over the food to keep away flies. Njoroge stood with his legs crossed, his staff between his knees, gazing into the distance. Anne, their boss, was chatting with them in fluent Swahili, the common language among East African tribes. She cut a striking figure in loose cottons, a flowing scarf and lots of silver jewelry, her shock of long blond curls topped by a wide brimmed felt hat adorned with feathers and beads. Raised in the Kenyan bush by eccentric parents who had allowed her to run wild, she was totally at home in this landscape, and she knew it as intimately as the men on her team. And, I soon learned, she knew how to think like an elephant.

On the way to our lunch spot, we'd seen signs of elephants: huge footprints in the dust and a trail of fresh dung. Less than half an hour into the afternoon's walk, Ahmed's keen eyes spotted the flap of an ear and a boulder-like torso between some trees. Through binoculars we saw that the elephant was part of a family group: Dag identified an old matriarch, a mother and baby, some aunties and a couple of young males. They were feeding, reaching up their trunks and ripping off branches. Changing course, we skirted around them, keeping downwind and at a safe distance. My heart was pounding and the muscle stiffness I had felt on setting off again was gone, chased away by adrenaline. Much as we wanted to save these beautiful creatures, being close to them while on foot in the wilds was not on our wish list. It was a dangerous situation, completely different from being in a vehicle with a fast means of escape.

There were more groups of elephants on our path. For two hours we zigzagged across the valley to avoid them. Finally we seemed to be in the clear, until the large, solitary bull elephant turned up. Unlike the other elephants, who were busy foraging and simply watched our progress, he was on the move—towards us. When we switched direction to avoid him, he also changed tack. It was soon apparent that he was following us, getting steadily closer. Tension spread through our group. We were unarmed, and while the camels offered a barrier against wildlife, if a 12,000-pound elephant decided to charge us we would have little chance. Anne brought us all to halt, and for a minute she studied the bull through her binoculars.

"I think he's just curious," she said. "He can't work out what we are. We have to do something he understands."

Following her directions, the team got the camels sitting in a circle, and Ahmed lit a grass fire in the middle, creating a pretend campsite. Smoke curled up. The bull came closer, and stopped. He lifted his trunk to smell what was on the air. Then he turned to one side and pulled at some grass, watching us from one eye. He took a few steps away then turned back and smelt the air again. We waited; he waited. Finally he began to sidle off. Anne pointed to a rise, with a group of trees, in the opposite direction to the bull. "We'll head there quickly," she said. "I think he's lost interest in us, but if he starts to follow us again we'll do this again."

By sundown we had found a campsite, and lost all sight of the bull. Sitting around the fire, eating soup and pasta, we watched a bush baby jumping through the branches above us, and discussed the events of the afternoon. Not long after Dag and I had settled into our tent, a lion started roaring—a series of deep, long, hoarse grunts. We were too enthralled to be worried. Then sleep born of physical exhaustion overtook us and the stars wheeled across the sky, unseen.

We crossed the valley next morning with no more elephant encounters, and were soon back on the Leroghi Plateau. It was an ocean of waving grasses. Anne pointed to our route—straight across the plain, towards two spindly trees in the far distance. Behind them was the blue smudge, not noticeably bigger than yesterday. We walked without a break until almost noon. I had swapped my trainers for sandals, which felt far more comfortable. Our pace was steady and we spoke little; moving through this vast landscape on foot was a perfect form of meditation, and I felt a quiet and profound happiness settle over me.

Halfway through the morning I eased my day pack off my tired shoulders and gave it to Ahmed, who attached it to the carrying frame of the lead camel, Dege. Inside the pack was my precious stuff–passport, wallet, laptop, iPhone, Kindle, spare glasses. Tucked away at the bottom was my mascot, a little stuffed monkey I bought after my father died, because its bright eyes, sticking out ears and bald head reminded me of him. Since then it had accompanied me on every journey. I rarely let that pack out of my sight and I was reassured to see it rocking slightly from side to side with Dege's swaying motion.

I'd become very fond of the camels. I liked their gargling sounds in the mornings, their arch expressions, their glamorous eyelashes, their two-toed flat feet. Ahmed had named most of them after their physical attributes. Dege meant big ears, Gedu was long neck, Gazle was hairy and Kabari was small. Then there was Ico, named after his previous owner, and Pakistan, just because Ahmed liked that name.

We had almost reached our lunch tree when Dege spooked. There seemed to be no apparent cause—later Anne said he may have been stung by a bee—but with sudden force he ripped the lead out of Ahmed's hand and bolted. Gedu and Gazle were tied in a line to him, and the three of them took off at speed across the plateau, bucking wildly, luggage flying off the frames on their backs. In disbelief, I stared at the animals doing their mad dance. I watched bags and boxes tumble down into the tall grasses. And I thought: *My daypack*. Ahmed and Abdi were chasing after the camels. Eventually they all disappeared over the horizon. Njoroge and Lemukan started looking for the discarded luggage. Njoroge found Dag's big grey waterproof bag and carried it to the tree where Anne had instructed me to sit in the shade. Lemukan retrieved a box of food. They ran back and forth, finding more things, but not my daypack. Anne pulled out her cell phone. We'd been out of coverage since yesterday morning, but now, amazingly, she had a signal. She called the owners of a ranch some miles away to ask if they had spotted the camels. No luck. About half an hour later her phone buzzed. She had a long conversation in Swahili, then turned to me.

"That was Ahmed. They've caught the camels. Your pack is still on Dege's frame."

I jumped to my feet, grinning in relief.

"But I'm afraid it's empty."

"Empty?"

"It turned upside down and got caught beneath the frame. The zips must have burst. Everything fell out."

I stared at her, aghast. "My computer...." I said weakly.

Dag put his arm around my shoulders. "Maria, it's gone," he said. "All the stuff is gone. We'll never find it. You just have to accept that. "

Anne thought differently.

'Tell me exactly what was in the pack," she said. "We'll start looking at this end, and Ahmed and Abdi will search on their way back."

I listed the contents, and she relayed these by phone to Ahmed. When I mentioned my mascot, she gave me a bemused look.

"*Tumbili kidogo*," she told Ahmed. "*Ndiyo, ndiyo, tumbili.*" A little monkey. Yes, yes, a monkey.

Looking carefully for broken grass stalks, Njoroge, Lemukan and Anne began tracking the trajectory of the camels, with Dag and I behind them. An hour or so in, they started to find things. First, my Kindle, which was smashed. Next my local cell phone, also broken beyond repair. Then Anne caught side of my Mac Air computer. I picked it up—there was a dint in the bottom, where a hoof had caught it.

"It will be toast, Maria," warned Dag.

I sat down, opened the lid, pressed the start button—and the screen came to life. I turned it off and on again. It worked perfectly.

Ahmed kept calling Anne to report what he had found—my wallet, the pouch with my passport, my glasses, as well as some things I'd forgotten were in the pack. Eventually we met up. In one hand he held Dege's lead. And in other, a small black stuffed toy. "*Tumbili mama ya!*" he cried. "Mama's monkey!"

After a late, quick lunch under the tree, we were walking again by mid afternoon. In the far distance two specks appeared, gradually growing into people: the chief of this area, Panta, and Julius, a member of the group organizing the community scouts in the Kirisia Hills. Anne had previously contacted them about permission to walk through these lands, with our approximate time of arrival. They had been waiting patiently for hours to greet us. Apologies and explanations followed, with lots of laugher about *tumbili mama ya*. Panta was dressed up for the occasion in smart green army pants and a pressed shirt with epaulettes. Proudly he told us he had been chief of this area for twenty four years. There were three thousand people in his community, spread across many *manyattas*, small enclosures with low wattle and daub houses where extended families lived. Julius was dressed in traditional Samburu garb—a *kikoi* around his waist and a red *shuka* draping his chest. He told us about a good camping site near his *manyatta*, an hour's walk away, and he and Panta offered to accompany us. The sun dropped to the horizon and darkness wrapped around us as we wound our way through low croton bushes and across a stream towards a massive fig tree. One side of its trunk had a big hollow where, Julius announced, Mama could bathe in private. He was concerned about the noise from the *manyatta*. A group of young Samburu men had been circumcised that day, becoming *moranis* or warriors, and there was a big celebration underway. We weren't concerned; we lay awake for as long as we could, enjoying the whoops and the breathy rhythmic singing. And when we opened our eyes at dawn, the party was still going on.

Njoroge heated a bucket of water over the fire, and I had my promised wash in the hollow of the fig tree. Then we walked for three hours straight, past big herds of Grevvy zebra and oryx, only stopping briefly to chat to a Samburu herder who spoke good English. His goats and sheep were friendly and relaxed around us; Dag commented on how well they must be treated to have such little fear of humans. Lunch was in a shady spot by a river. Young *morani* came strutting by, decked out in their warrior gear of fancy headdresses, armloads of bracelets and beaded necklaces. Their ochre dyed hair was elaborately braided with extensions and hung half way down their backs. At the riverbank they stripped off their *kikoi* and waded into the water to wash, sleek as otters and naked apart from their 'bling'. Young Samburu girls, also weighed down with heavy necklaces, herded small flocks of sheep and goats past us, shyly returning our smiles and waves.

The Kirisia Hills seemed to have suddenly grown; they rose up from the plain like an island, their soft green folds contrasting starkly with the yellow plains. To keep on schedule, by that evening we needed to reach our basecamp at the foot of hills. We left the river and walked for six more hours. The white streak Anne had pointed out on our first day transformed into a massive metamorphic outcrop, upended on one side with sheer cliffs. On and on we walked. During yesterday's big chase, Ahmed had strained a muscle in his leg, and he was limping. Everyone was tired, including the camels. We walked by goats and sheep grazing among zebra, along a narrow dusty road and past small settlements where children stared at us through prickly fences. At the edge of a village we were welcomed by Michael, Anne's main contact in the community group, and Tena, a young *morani* who was one of the volunteer scouts. They led us into the forest. It was pitch dark by the time we crossed a river on stepping-stones and walked along a rough path between tall trees. We shone flashlights, looking for potholes. Ahmed was cross—he complained to Anne that the camels couldn't see well, that they were tired, that it wasn't fair to push them like this. I was moving on autopilot, my back, hips and legs aching. The last half an hour seemed endless, but finally we reached a clearing with a fire pit and a rudimentary table and benches—our home for the next three nights.

Dag and I had just snuggled into our sleeping bag when elephants started crashing round in the bushes behind us. We heard the squeaks of a baby, the rumbles of adults. We spoke quietly to each other; Dag reminded me about the time hippos grazed right around our tent on the shores of Lake Malawi and that we were safe as long as we were inside the tent. "Just don't go outside for a pee," he said—an unnecessary warning.

Arriving by night, we had only sensed the scale of the forest. Now, in the light of a new day, we were amazed. It was dense and lush, with huge yellowwood, juniper and iron trees, their branches hung with mosses. This forest cloaked the entire hills, turning them into a vast water tower for the surrounding plains. And it was a sanctuary for elephants, until the poachers turned up. In recent years there had been a big spike in the killings for ivory. Soon after breakfast, the leaders of the Kirisia Community Forestry Association arrived to meet us. They explained that the scouts were local men, most of them herders, who did the job on a voluntary, rotating basis. They were the eyes and ears on the ground, the first line of defense against poachers. But they needed equipment. They needed training. And we, suggested, stipends for their work. Everything was quickly agreed upon. Back in Canada we would go on a speaking tour to raise both awareness about the poaching crisis and funds to support the community scouts. We settled on an initial sum, to be sent by the end of the year. Then, based on the results of this, we would look at the possibility of ongoing support. There were handshakes all round, I was presented with a beautiful beaded necklace, and the promise was sealed.

Anne made arrangements for us to purchase a sheep. A *morani* brought it into basecamp, and handed me the end of the rope around its neck. I felt badly for the poor animal, knowing its fate, but I led it across to where our team were camped and formally presented it to Ahmed, with thanks from Mama and her *tumbili kidogo*. A whole sheep was a big deal for them; that evening they roasted it, and brought me a plate of chops, burned on the outside, raw within, which I accepted with grace, and passed to Dag.

Dag and Anne went hiking up into the hills, accompanied by a scout carrying a rifle in case of encounters with the notoriously dangerous Cape buffalo that roamed the forest. They returned with ecstatic accounts of the amazing trees and plants higher up, the stupendous views from lookouts. But I was happy to relax at basecamp, and gather my strength for the long return march. Ahmed brewed me endless cups of the sweet milky tea he knew I relished. Machairia brought me bowls of warm water for me to soak my sore feet. And a young *morani* bedecked in feathers and beads shadowed me, a throwing stick tucked into his *kikoi* to fend off any wildlife that might wander by.

When we walked out of the forest, the local shaman came to meet us. He was small and bent, wrapped in a blanket, hobbling with a staff made from an acacia branch. He gazed up at Dag and me. Eyes whitened by cataracts. Fingers knarled by arthritis, soil beneath his nails. He smelled of smoke and milk. He spoke at length with Anne.

"He heard that you came to offer help," she said. "He's going to close the forest behind you and keep it safe until you return."

He held out one hand, palm up, fingers curled and began a long intonation. I closed my eyes. Birds sang in the canopy, and our team chimed in with the shaman: 'N'Gai, N'Gai, N'Gai.

I didn't want to cry. I knew it would embarrass and confuse everyone. But the tears came, and with them the realization that we had to return here. We'd walked for three long days and 80 miles to reach this pristine place. Now we were heading back to Anne's camp, and my muscles had been rebelling at the thought of another tough march across the high plains. But suddenly I felt new strength. And new resolve. As we set off, past the last settlements and onto the sweep of the Leroghi Plateau, Dag and I talked and planned. We would return. We would bring others with us on this walk. Together we would continue to help these scouts save elephants and the land they shared. The shaman would open up the forest for us and we would walk back in.

©Maria Coffey

Photograph courtesy of Maria Coffey.

A Pilgrimage to Everest

The rain fell relentlessly through the night and into the morning, turning to snow as we crested the valley and moved into a landscape of rock and sparse vegetation. I walked alone, locked into private thoughts and listening to the sounds of my own body moving through the silent surroundings.

Hilary's footsteps were ahead of me in the snow and I found her waiting in a small cave on the edge of a lake of the clearest blue that reflected the rocky slopes above it. A thermos flask and food stood ready; since our little expedition in the Alps her sense of when my energy was about to flag was uncannily accurate and she would always be there with supplies. Our trekking team was spread out as we moved along at individual paces, each reacting differently to the altitude. Hilary and I had been first away that morning, carrying packs in case we reached the next campsite long before everyone else and wanted to put up our tents. The track was easy to follow and Dong had given Hilary careful instructions. It was good to feel so independent and to realize we had gained the trust of our Chinese guides.

We set off again after our snack and I hung back until Hilary was out of sight, reassured by her tracks but wanting to feel the solitude and remoteness of the place keenly around me once more. My pace settled into a regular plod and I moved slowly and easily, feeling warm and comfortable despite the low temperature. Wet snow fell around me, flakes landed on my face and immediately dissolved. The protective clothing was a cocoon; my breathing was amplified inside the jacket hood. A sense of peace settled over me. Suddenly and unexpectedly, I felt Joe's presence. I have no explanation for this; what happened on those high slopes in Tibet may have been generated by my own mind or may have been a manifestation of some form of energy from Joe. I really do not know, but I had experienced this awareness of him before. Shortly after learning of his disappearance, I had asked Sarah to drive me to his house in Derbyshire. I wanted badly to be in the house and among his things again, yet it was a dreadful journey, knowing that I would not find him at home then, or ever again. I sat in the car, distraught, unable to speak to Sarah, feeling sucked towards a horrible finality. And then, as we left the outskirts of the city and headed towards open country, I felt him there, all around me, comforting and reassuring. Sarah got out at her cabin and I slid over into the driver's seat. I wanted to go to the house alone.

"Are you sure you're alright?"

She bent down to look through the open window. Her face was concerned.

"Yes, I'm fine now, it's not far. I'll see you in a while."

I drove along a back lane, and experienced the same heightened awareness as when Dick first told me about Joe's disappearance. The afternoon was vibrant, trees reached out their branches towards the car, and the leaves on them shimmered. Joe's presence was still there when I arrived and unlocked the house. I had been too preoccupied with work on my own place to visit it while he was away. It felt like minutes since the day we had left. I wandered around inside, soaking in the familiarity. On the bed I wrapped myself in the duvet, my nostrils filled with his smell and I felt him about me then most powerfully. I cried, talked aloud like a child and finally slept. A deep dreamless peaceful sleep. When I awoke the sun was still streaming through the window. Leaving the house was difficult. My impulse was to stay there, and wait. Only when I parked the car at the bottom of the track leading to Sarah's cabin did the feeling of Joe gradually fade.

She was standing in the garden among long grasses, shading her eyes against the sun to watch my approach. The scene was uncannily still, as if she was a figure in a painting. I began to tell her.

"I know," she said. "He was in the car when I was driving. I felt him. It was really strong. I wasn't going to say anything in case it upset you."

It has happened several times, only infrequently but always intensely and without warning. And so, in Tibet, heading towards the Langma La Pass from where I hoped to glimpse the Kangshung Face, I did not try to block the feeling but allowed it to flow. Without knowing how or why, I felt infused by Joe as I plodded along. I listened to him talking to me, encouraging me. He was all around. I felt the gentle pressure of his hand on the back of my neck. This was utter contentment, a sense of rightness as I headed up the wintry slopes.

Joe, or whatever the sensation had been, ebbed away, leaving me relaxed and smiling and still walking at a measured pace. A dog bounded into sight, ahead of a herd of yak driven by a preoccupied man. Fifty beasts lumbered by, their shaggy coats brushing the snow. They were rounded up by a wide-eyed child who had already, I later discovered, been scared witless by an initial encounter with Hilary. Straggling along at the end was a baby yak, which stopped in its tracks, refusing to pass me. The little boy, frightened anew by the sight of another strange woman, could not pluck up the courage to urge the animal. My attempts to walk past them only caused the yak to scamper about in terror, and for a few minutes we executed an impromptu matador scene until the boy suddenly made a break for it and drove the yak past me with a switch.

The track became very narrow, cutting through a steep scree slope along a valley side. Far below me lay a long, densely gray lake with no reflection. Snow fell lightly, the air was damp and the cloud cover so low that mist swirled around me from time to time. My boots crunching on the loose rock broke the silence. In the distance, where the track curved and was swallowed by mist, some shapes took form. Several scrawny cattle swayed along the track until I had to scramble up the slope and make way for them. Behind the animals, carrying staffs and walking slowly, were an old man and a young boy. The man was slight, his face narrow, wrinkled and serene, and from his chin a long white beard fell in two strands. Their gray woolen blankets and felt boots seemed insubstantial against the snow and rocks. They stopped and regarded me curiously. "Chomolungma?"

The old man pointed to where he had come from, towards the Langma La Pass. I nodded, and waited. All morning I had felt a stillness within me, a tenuous but undeniable link to a dimension outside the well known and understood parameters of my world. Being high in the Himalayas, sensing the solidity, force and sheer permanence of the environment, as against human transience and fragility, was opening up my mind and allowing in a chink of awareness of the full scope and mystery of existence. The man and boy seemed creatures wholly connected to the mountain they stood upon. The child gazed up at me, unsmiling, with an air of wisdom and experience far beyond his years. His companion shook his head gravely. "Chomolungma, Chomolungma," he repeated and taking my hands in his he intoned a prayer, perhaps a blessing. I welcomed this: I wanted to draw from the knowledge of ages he surely possessed. He raised his hand in farewell and moved past me with the boy, towards their cattle. I watched until they went out of sight and imagined how we must have looked from above, three tiny figures passing through a vast and unmoving landscape.

Beyond the prayer flags of the Langma La Pass a bank of thick cloud lay over the Kangshung Face. Hilary sat very still, gazing towards it. I put my hand on her should.

"The man and boy—did you meet them? Did he bless you?"

She nodded. We waited together, silently wiling the mountain to reveal itself, until the rest of our team arrived.

Chomolungma kept her Eastern Face shrouded for the next two days as we moved closer to the mountain across dramatically changing terrain. Moonlike landscapes on the high plains transmuted to muddy trails through lush vegetation in the valleys. We pressed on, crossing and recrossing rivers by rickety bridges or by precariously hopping from stone to stone, trudging through mud, willing the clouds to lift. I remembered Chris and Charlie's prediction that there would be little chance of good weather on east side of the mountain, but I was still convinced we would be lucky. The feeling of drawing so close was intense. Hilary was voluble in her grief, she talked and cried openly. I became increasingly withdrawn, conscious of tension building inside me. If Chris was right, if Joe and Pete had fallen down the Kangshung Face, then they were not far away, they were somewhere in crevasses at the foot of Chomolungma. I immersed myself in an awareness of Joe's proximity, allowing it to override my loneliness and the reality of the loss. Asleep and awake I dreamed of somehow getting to his body, wrapping myself around his frozen form and breathing warmth and life back into him. It was an illusion, born out of hopeless desperation.

Drying out around the stove at the end of the fourth day of trekking, we made a group decision to turn back. Going further towards the Face meant crossing a glacial moraine that could be unstable after so much rain, and there was no indication of the weather clearing. Early the next morning, Hilary and I walked up to a rocky knoll to make our private goodbyes. The Kangshung Face was ahead of us, hidden by the heavy mist that clung to it so resolutely, but I could feel its presence. Joe could be nearly, held somewhere within its folds. Perhaps this was as close to him as I would ever be again. With that thought the illusion snapped. There were no miracles to be had; the relationship was over, except what I could cling to in memory. Chomolungma could not give him back to life. I sat down and began to weep, heaving sobs that bent me double as in the early days of grief. Hilary held me until I quieted and then I leaned on her tried, brokenly, to express my thoughts. She looked over my head.

"Zhaing is coming."

He walked slowly by, placed something on the cairn at the very top of the knoll, then stood and looked towards the cloud-covered mountain. When he returned his face was set tight as if holding in his feelings, and he did not glance in our direction. We went up to the cairn. Two cans of beer were there, and a small posy of flowers lay between them. An offering to the mountain and a sign of respect to Joe and Pete.

"That was more apt than any church service," said Hilary.

It was a gesture that helped me to walk away from the knoll towards the waiting yaks.

We retraced our steps, back through the dense vegetation, up the muddy slopes and onto the windy plain. As night fell the mist rolled in around the campsite. In the big wigwam I chopped vegetables, drank whisky and tried to socialize, but I couldn't concentrate on conversation. My mind was outside, in the mist and heading towards the mountain. After dinner I walked through the fog until I was out of earshot of the camp and away from its light. Squatting on my haunches I felt the cloud close in and I imagined Joe walking towards me with his long relaxed stride, dressed in his usual garb of jeans, boots and sweater that varied little with the seasons. Had his ghost emerged from the mist I would hardly have been surprised, but nothing moved, there was no sound. I remembered an American girl I had met years before, in Patagonia. I had just arrived at Fitzroy National Park and she and her team of Italian climbers were preparing to leave. Her boyfriend had died on a nearby mountain the year before, and she had travelled to South America to find his body and bury it. One of the climbers was a priest. They had reached the point on the glacier where her boyfriend and his companion had landed after the fall, said Mass and lowered the bodies into a crevasse. She was young, in her twenties. As we talked she was using an ice axe to hammer nails into the wall of the wooden hut that was at the 'road head' of the park.

"This was his," she said, waving the axe.

"You mean...."

"We found it beside him. I may as well use it. These nails will be good for hanging stuff on. And who knows, I might come back one day."

"Are you glad you came?"

"Sure I am. Now I can really believe he's dead. Now I have a picture of him. Now-" She stopped for a second, her voice caught. "It was good to at least be able to say goodbye."

That girl....I couldn't remember her name, or what part of America she was from, or why she was with the Italian climbers. But the feeling I had had on that day came back clearly, my admiration of her composure, and my wonder at her strength. I could never have foreseen it then, but now I was envious of her, for her chance to say goodbye.

The sharp frost of the morning gave us hope the mountain would appear. The clouds were playing a teasing game, allowing a glimpse of a peak then covering it up again. Makalu appeared for a time and there was confusion over whether or not it was Chomolungma. We ran up a slope for a better view, our lungs heaving and burning in the thin air. The face we saw was massive, spectacular and terrifying, but it was not the Kangshung.

As I plodded up snow covered slopes behind a yak, past tiny blue lakes, with the sun breaking through and snow peaks appearing, the loveliness would send a shiver through me and I would be glad to be alive and be there. Hilary and I hung back at the

Langma La Pass, watching the clouds around Chomolungma, wiling the curtain to open and show us the awesome vista behind. Three times the mist rolled back to reveal the summit, but the Face stayed shrouded. Zhiang was hovering anxiously, wanting us to leave and follow the others, but we needed the steadying of those minutes, letting our thoughts settle before heading down the mountain. It occurred to me that perhaps it was no coincidence that the Kangshung Face was not being revealed to us. Perhaps it was, after all, easier for us this way. I blew a kiss to the east side of Everest and turned away.

Verdant hillsides pungent with juniper and the gentle colours of the irrigated fields and villages: after the landscapes of the high passes I felt I was seeing the lower Kharta Valley with new eyes. And as we began the drive to the northern side of Chomolungma I was calm, almost happy. Two eagles hovered above us on the air currents. Joe and Pete, I thought, watching us leave. It was a fine place to spend eternity.

Excerpted and adapted from *Fragile Edge: A Personal Portrait of Loss on Everest*, Mountaineers Books, 2000. Reprinted by permission of the author.

Question and Answers

1. What compels you to walk?

I wish I could remember learning how to walk: the excitement of the moment when I finally found my balance and took my first steps. While the memory isn't there, I believe the joy of that discovery runs cell-deep. Walking is the purest form of exercise, because it is how we were built to transport ourselves. When I walk I feel connected to the earth, to the environment I'm moving through. I love—and I need—that sense of my body being strong and efficient, doing what it is meant to do.

2. Do you experience instances while you are walking when your mind in somewhere off the trail and on its own journey?

Of course! When I'm walking I write chunks of books, I compose long letters, I hatch new plans, I replay difficult situations and solve problems. Walking is like dreaming, a process that allows the mind to sift through life events and make sense of them.

3. How do you manage to stay physically and emotionally healthy during long and arduous journeys?

For physical health I get lots of sleep, drink no alcohol and eat at regular intervals. I have a humming bird's metabolism, so sugar snacks are a must for me.

For emotional health, I never consider the whole journey ahead. Instead I break it down into chunks, setting myself short-term goals: getting over the next pass, or as far as the riverbank where we will take a break, or to the acacia tree I can see on the horizon. Once I've reached that goal, I set the next one…and so on and so on….

4. Please share a high and a low period that you experienced during your walkabouts.

When the camels bolted on our Kenya trek this was both a low and a high in one day—read about it my essay "Miles for Elephants."

5. Have you experienced an important Encounter that somehow changed the direction of your journey?

My meeting with a shepherd high in the Himalaya—read about it in my essay "A Pilgrimage to Everest."

Photograph courtesy of Maria Coffey.

Biography

Maria Coffey is the author of 12 internationally published and award winning books. Based on Vancouver Island, BC, Canada, she is married to the photographer and veterinarian Dag Goering. The couple have co-founded Hidden Places, an adventure travel company, its conservation branch Elephant Earth and, most recently, Adventures for a Cause. Their 100 Miles for Elephants fundraising treks in Kenya won an award from *National Geographic Traveler Magazine*, and to date have brought donations of over US$100,000 to anti-poaching efforts in Laikipia. For more information, see http://hiddenplaces.net/walking-safari.php

The biggest walks of my life have been in response to big issues. In 1982 I walked to 21,000 feet on the north side of Everest in an attempt to come to terms with the death of my partner on the mountain. For the past few years I have been walking across the high plains of Kenya to raise funds that help stop the slaughter of elephants. Soon I will walk over high passes in the Kumaon Himalayas, assisting a grassroots organization in their efforts to mitigate human–snow leopard conflict.

But walking is also a huge part of my daily life. At home, I walk to do my chores, to visit friends, to go out for dinner. When Dag and I travel, we explore the new places we land on foot.

Walking is one of forms of self-propulsion that gives me joy and satisfaction. Over the last thirty years, with Dag I have also embarked on long expeditions by kayak, bicycle and sail boat. Along the way we've published twelve books, had a number of photo exhibits and founded an adventure travel company, Hidden Places, which has a conservation fundraising branch.

I like to say we walk our talk. And we definitely talk when we walk—it's when our very best ideas are born!

Copyright © Helen Thayer.

Helen Thayer

Age is no barrier to your dreams and goals.

Excerpt from Polar Dream

By four o'clock an enormous wall of blue-black clouds stretching miles across was building up and moving in from the south. The uninterrupted horizon allowed me to see an entire storm-front in one overwhelming view. The wind gusted strongly at times, swirling snow high into the air. The sun disappeared behind the mass of clouds, but before it did, I checked its direction and that, combined with various directional checks all day, told me the wind was still southeast and I was steering a straight course due south. The wind continued to increase but not enough to stop travel. The great ugly mass of black clouds in the distance appeared to be moving closer, but sideways to my path. It looked as if I would catch only the extreme edge of the storm as it went by.

Skiing at a two-mile-per-hour pace, I was closing in on the Pole. But sometime after four o'clock, I saw to my horror that the boiling mass of thick clouds from the far distance was racing low across the ice behind a great wall of wind-driven snow straight at us. I stopped and, grabbing the bag of ice screws, I quickly anchored everything securely to the ice, starting with Charlie on his chain, then his sled, then my larger, higher sled anchored at both ends. It would be our only protection from the full blast of the wind. I shoved my arms into my down parka, and stuffed my overmitts into the pockets. Then, with everything as ready and as secure as it could be, I hurriedly took the tent out. There was no time to put it up, but I knew I could wrap it around me as I sheltered with Charlie behind my sled.

Pulling the sled bag zipper closed, I was about to tighten a tie down rope when I heard a sound like an approaching jet as the wind bore down on us with maniacal force. I raced toward the sheltered side of the sled, clutching the tent to my chest, but had only taken a stride or two when the wind plowed into my body, throwing me off my feet and down onto the ice with such a bone-jarring thud that my goggles were knocked off. As I slithered to a stop, still clutching the tent to my chest, my bare face and eyes were blasted and stung by particles of flying ice. Hardly able to see or breathe in the violence of the storm that seemed to suck the air out of my lungs, I looked across to Charlie, dreading that I might see him airborne. But I had anchored him well and he was crouched down, protected by my sled. I scrambled to my sled, half crawling in the hellish wind that was blowing gear away into the unknown. The loose tie-down rope had allowed the zipper to be blasted open and the wind was tearing at the contents of the sled bag, almost ripping it off the sled. Grabbing the zipper I yanked it shut, pulled the tie-down rope tight, then dove over the top of the sled to join Charlie on the other side.

Suddenly there was a pause. The first gust had passed by, but away in the distance I could hear more jetlike gusts coming. Then I noticed blood trickling down my face. Blinking my eyes to clear away the blood I felt my forehead and around my eyes. When my goggles were knocked off, the exposed upper half of my face had been cut by ice. I couldn't keep my right eye open. I was terrified that it was seriously hurt. I stood up to look for the first-aid kit but immediately saw another blast of wind-driven snow and ice bearing down on us. I ducked just as it hit the sled and, in a sitting position, I pulled Charlie close to me and spread the tent tightly over and around us. A boiling mass of clouds hung over us as if trying to crush us into the ice. The sled took the full force of the blast, but the wind in its fury was not to be denied its victims as it reached over and around the sled, swirling snow and ice, pulling, tugging, and slamming at our bodies, trying to rip the tent away.

With my head on bent knees and blood trickling from my face and eye, I sat close to Charlie, hanging onto the tent. I could feel the wind slamming into the sled, jarring it into my back. The jetlike noise was deafening. I worried about the gear the wind might have carried away when the sled zipper had been torn open and I worried about my eye. I couldn't see out of it. It seemed impossible to survive the hole in hell I found myself in. A few tears mixed with blood trickled down my face. Then I suddenly realized what I was doing. I was allowing the storm to take over my life, allowing it to dictate the terms of my existence. "Damn it," I said aloud to Charlie who couldn't possibly have heard over the din, "The Arctic has rammed everything down my throat from polar bears, to storms, to weird ice and now this. I'll sit this storm out and beat it."

Charlie showed no sign of being impressed, but for me the whole situation changed from fateful submission to a fighting attack. I needed a plan of action. Without one my mind would only drift without positive direction. Just before I was forced to stop, I had checked my mileage at eleven miles for the last southerly leg. That meant I now sat only two miles from the pole. All I had to do after the storm was ski those two miles, then head for land and the prearranged aircraft pickup spot. I was almost there. Not even this fiendish storm was going to stop me now.

But first I had to stay warm. I couldn't stand up in the wind and inactivity was allowing the cold to sink its sharp teeth into my body. I zipped up my jacket as far as it would go. I put my overmitts on and slid the end of the tent fabric under me so that I wasn't sitting on bare ice. From an inside pocket I took the last two peanut butter cups of my day's supply, ate one and gave Charlie the other. Then, smoothing one of the wrappers, I placed it over my right eye and tied a drawstring cord taken from the inside of my jacket around my head and over the wrapper to hold it in place, allowing my eye to remain closed more comfortably. Then, pulling the tent fabric closer around Charlie and me, I prepared to sit out the storm.

Charlie was curled up at my side. I couldn't believe he was sleeping in all that screaming chaos. The cold grew worse and I had to do something to keep hypothermia away. I worked to stay warm with isometric exercises, tensing one set of muscles for twenty seconds, then shifting to the next group. I moved fingers, toes, ankles, shoulders, arms and legs as much as possible in the confines of my tiny, sheltered space. My face and eye stopped bleeding. The blood had frozen on my face. But now that I had a plan for survival, I felt in control in spite of my precarious position. Optimism flooded my mind, leaving no space for negative thoughts.

Time crawled by. After an hour I was still pinned down behind the sled by the howling gale. The cold marched onward throughout my body. My hands and feet were cold but not frozen, while the rest of my body was shivering trying to stay warm. I pressed close to Charlie, who remained curled with his nose hidden in his tail. I was hungry, which didn't help with the warmth problem. I did not dare try to stand up, much less look for food in my sled. Food would have to wait. Occasionally I peeked out from beneath the tent fabric and saw a still chaotic storm hurling ice and snow horizontally across my world, engulfing me and reducing visibility to a few feet. My joints were cramped and feeling stiff and sore. The cold was unbearable and began to lull my mind. I did mental arithmetic to stay alert, but nothing seemed to stop the slow progress of creeping cold. As the wind continued to scream its fury, my mental arithmetic trailed off and I had to forcefully bring myself back to it, trying to keep alert. But the cold came on and on, and I became more sluggish.

Finally, after another hour the wind slowed and the screaming howl quieted. When it dawned on me that the storm had paused at least for now, I tried to stand up, but I was so cold and stiff I could only get to my knees then haul myself up slowly. Every joint protested. It was as if the cold had welded my joints together. There was still a strong wind but it wasn't blowing me over, and I sluggishly thought that if I could get my body moving I would put the tent up. But first of all I had to warm up. So I stuffed the tent safely into the sled, then I wind-milled my arms while I walked in circles. It was a pathetic slow-motion effort, but I kept at it, feeling the warmth slowly inching back. It took some time but at last my body, although not really warm, was an immensely improved version of the cold, stiff bundle that had huddled desperately behind the sled.

Once more I took the tent out and began putting it up, at the same time noticing that the wind was gradually increasing. I tried to hurry, but my fingers were still slow and my body, which seemed burdened by an extraordinary weight, wouldn't listen to my mind urging it on. Snow picked up by the increasing wind billowed into the air. Afraid that I wouldn't get the tent up in time, my body at last kicked in, warming as I shook the great weight off and regained strength. Now pure raw desire to survive took over. I had already anchored one end of the tent, even before beginning to erect it to prevent a possible untimely exit. Now I shoved poles into the tent sleeves, working furiously to beat the wind. One blast almost turned the tent inside out and I was afraid a pole would break, sending its sharp end through the thin nylon fabric and destroying my only protection in this hostile world.

Finally a combination of poles, ice screws and tie down ropes anchored the tent to the ice. I could hear far off the approach of another screaming torrent, and as I prayed that the tent would be strong enough to withstand the full fury of the next round of wind, I ran around adding as many tie-downs as there were places to attach them, then invented more until I had no more rope. I dragged my sled into the tent and propped it against one wall to help brace against the wind, then attached Charlie's sled to an ice screw just outside.

As the high-pitched scream of the wind drew closer, I ran to Charlie, rushing him into the back of the tent. After one last check that all was secure, I dove through the doorway and with a belay rope that I carried in my sled for emergencies, tying one end around my waist and the other to Charlie's harness. Then as fast as I could I hooked the rope to an ice screw just outside the doorway so that if the tent was swept away Charlie and I wouldn't go tumbling across the ice after it. Zipping the door closed as much as the rope allowed, I leaned against the tent wall to brace for the blast I could hear coming.

It hit with a thunderous roar, throwing me forward and snapping the tent upright. With feet braced against the sled I leaned back again, stretching my arms along the walls to take the next mad blast. The tent walls vibrated and heaved as if they would burst. The storm had engulfed us again but each blast was repelled, as I fought with all my strength to brace the windward wall. It was too wild for Charlie to lie down, so he unwittingly fought the storm as he leaned calmly against the narrower back wall, his weight helping to anchor the floor. He was unruffled by the fury that raged about us.

After struggling against the wind for about an hour or so, I detected a slight pause now and then that grew more apparent until there were lulls in which I could catch my breath. Then finally there were only stray gusts that snapped at us as if reluctant to leave. The main force of the wind had passed, but the tent still flapped in the swirling snow. I looked out to see that the clouds were still heavy overhead, blocking the light, leaving only a solid grayness. My inspection of the tent showed the only damage to be a torn out tie down grommet. The low profile and modern design had won through. I put the antenna up to call base camp. There were worried inquiries about the weather. After giving a description of the storm and my location, I signed off, anxious to take inventory of my sled's contents.

It was with a certain amount of dread that I unzipped the sled bag. My worse fears were realized. All my food, except one small bag of walnuts in my day food bag tucked down in the front of the sled, had been blown away, along with most of the fuel, a pair of crampons, two fuel bottles, the spare stove, a few items of clothing and assorted odds and ends. I went outside to check Charlie's sled. It was covered with drifted snow but still tied securely to the ice screw. It had flipped upside down, jarring a rope loose and allowing several sacks of food to be blown away.

It would take seven more days to reach the pole and then get to the pick up point at Helena Island. I figured Charlie had enough food left for half rations for eight days. It was one thing for me to go hungry and thirsty, but a food shortage for Charlie was a different matter. However, he was in better shape, with more weight on him than when we left base camp. I had fed him well and he had learned to drink more water, so I reasoned he would be alright on half rations and could go back to eating ice for the seven days. Inuit dogs are used to frequent periods of starvation and have learned over many generations to survive under conditions much harsher than the ones we faced now. I hated to ask Charlie to go to half rations, but I knew that he would endure it, just as he had endured so much else on this journey.

Having assured myself that Charlie would be safe, I turned to my remaining food supply. I counted out five handfuls of walnuts. Not enough. I divided them again and came up with seven handfuls. Perfect. There was enough fuel to melt ice for one pint of water per day, not much compared to the two quarts I had been used to, but it would have to do. The next question was could I survive with so little food and water in this cold, extremely dry climate? I knew that women, due to their physiological makeup can live off their bodies quite well in times of starvation, so I reasoned that I would survive. I understood the realities of going from five thousand calories a day to one hundred calories, and from two quarts of water a day, which is minimal, to only one pint per day while working hard in a cold dry climate. I would be fighting hunger, thirst and weakness, which would make it difficult to travel the remaining miles, but I knew it could be done. To help the fluid problem I could chew ice and snow. I was confident that I could finish my journey. I knew I would be in for some hard times but they weren't enough to make me quit.

As I sat there planning, I wasn't despondent. This was the Arctic, after all, and I knew that among the many hazards I might face, there could be problems at any time that would change the entire logistical picture of the expedition. I would never have begun if I hadn't thought of these problems and if I hadn't the confidence that I could handle them. There was something else that spurred me on, something deep down that I would understand better later on when I was able to reflect upon my feelings at this moment. There was a core in me that wanted to jump out and face this new challenge, give it a good shake and win.

I took out the signal mirror and first-aid kit to inspect my face and eyes. My reflection showed numerous small cuts on the upper half of my face, above the area my face mask had covered. My right eyelid was cut and one corner of the eye was very tender. Both eyes were bloodshot, swollen and bruised but my left was not cut. I looked like a prizefighter who had gone too many rounds. "I'm glad I've got a few days to heal," I told Charlie, "I would hate anyone to see me like this." I then thought, "What a dumb remark." Vanity seemed so out of place here. My eyesight was fuzzy in the right eye and less so in my left. I covered my right eye with an eye patch to keep it closed and hoped a good night's sleep would heal everything.

I unloaded my sleeping gear and threw it in the tent. I fed Charlie in the tent and let him sleep there. He had been all that I could have asked of him that day, calm and obedient. I was hungry, but I would have to wait until tomorrow to eat and drink. The temperature had climbed to plus 16 degrees, an incredible change and no doubt a large factor in the storm. The wind was calming down and it began to snow. "If there are any bears around out there," I told Charlie, "they'll have to wait until morning." He was curled up asleep alongside my sleeping bag and didn't hear me. It wasn't long before I, too, fell asleep, glad to have got through that hellish day in one piece.

Excerpt from *Polar Dream: The First Solo Expedition by a Woman and Her Dog to the Magnetic North Pole*. Starpath Publications. Reprinted by permission of the author.

Questions and Answers

1. What compels you to walk?

I have never had any desire to use mechanization or animals as a means of transportation. Whether I'm skiing to the Poles, walking across vast deserts or walking in the Amazon, I believe that the only way to immerse myself into the surrounding natural environment I'm traveling through is one step at a time. My senses are sharper, ready for any emergency. I absorb details that could easily be missed, such as that tiny insect, obscure plants, and the sky overhead. The desert that most would describe as empty and dead, I find as I walk teems with life. At journey's end I have a deep sense of having truly connected, absorbed and be absorbed by the environment through which I have traveled. Walking among indigenous people gives me a fuller sense of sharing and learning their lifestyles and traditions. Walking gives me a sense of joy at just being there and being alive.

2. Do you experience instances while you are walking when your mind is somewhere off the trail and on its own journey?

Many times over the years I have actually planned the next expedition in my mind. In the uncluttered world of the wide-open spaces of the Sahara, Gobi or Polar regions my mind is free of the demands of society, and the need for correctness. I can allow my mind to take me to far off places and figure out how I can make it all come to reality. My sense of true freedom in such places also allows me freedom of thought.

3. How do you manage to stay physically and emotionally healthy during long and arduous journeys?

As most of my long journeys have taken me to places where I have no outside contact for long periods of time I am careful to take care of myself in every detail. At home I am conscientious concerning physical and mental preparation. I try to be prepared in every way I can think of. I regard this as similar to having money in the bank. In times of stress or emergency I draw off my physical and mental resources to get me through so that I remain self-reliant and safe.

4. Please share a high and a low period that you experienced during your walkabouts.

A few days into my solo ski journey to the magnetic North Pole I allowed myself to think of home, and my family who had given me so much support. It suddenly hit me that all those people were at home worrying themselves half to death about my safety among the polar bears and other arctic hazards of a lone woman traveling across the ocean ice. It took me two days to straighten out my thoughts and put my mind back onto a positive track again.

I have experienced many highs, e.g. when the polar bear standing six feet in front of me finally turned away, the firing squad that allowed me to go on living, and to finally get through a mine field alive.

5. Have you experienced an important Encounter that somehow changed the direction of your journey?

I am very focused and disciplined during my journeys. Even frostbite, standing in front of a firing squad, crossing through land mines and facing polar bears have not turned me away from my goal of completing the journey.

Helen with a camel in the Sahara. *Copyright © Helen Thayer.*

Biography

I began climbing mountains when I was nine years old when I climbed Mount Taranaki in New Zealand (the country of my birth) with my parents and Sir Edmund Hillary. He was a close family friend and one of my childhood mentors. On that climb I knew that an outdoor life was the only one for me. Over the years I have climbed mountains all over the world, represented three countries on their national track and field teams and became the USA national luge champion. But walking long distances was and is my first love. I am 78 years old and am still a work in progress. So far I am living the same active lifestyle I lived in my twenties. (Hopefully with a bit more mature sense.) I have several thousand more miles and more expeditions to walk yet. I continue to be motivated by my desire to produce ever more programs through my walking adventures for Adventure Classroom. I am Founder and President and I work to motivate students, kindergarten through grade 12 to set goals, plan for success and believe in themselves. I have so far spoken in schools to over one million students since 1988 when I became the first woman to travel solo to any of the world's Poles.

French Alps. *Photograph by Brandon Wilson.*

Brandon Wilson

Travel is like a mirror held up against the world. It gives us a different perspective on life. And if we hold it just right, we might catch a glimmer of our own soul.
~from Dead Men Don't Leave Tips

Over the Top & Back Again: Hiking X the Alps

Strange things go through your mind when you're dangling by a thin blue rope in the pelting rain, hanging on in a white-knuckled grip as a freezing wind pushes you back and forth like a pendulum over a 1000-meter chasm. Unlike a Hollywood movie, my life didn't flash before me. Oddly enough, one thing came to mind: Ötzi. Who? Ötzi the Iceman, the Alpine hunter who disappeared high in the Alps some 5300 years ago. Only recently did a hapless hiker discover his mummified body, freeze-dried with a grimace on his face. If anything, I sure didn't want to end up like him. Did he know that fateful day of marmot hunting would be his last? Of course not. Likewise, we had no clear-cut idea what we were getting ourselves into. We took a leap of faith. That's like a leap into the abyss; only with that, the outcome's more certain. And just like that thin blue rope that now kept us connected to life, an equally fine line separates "adventure" from sheer madness. This time, we'd stepped over that line. Let me explain…

As with past adventures, once again, it all started innocently enough. My ever-trusting wife, Cheryl, and I had heard about a new hiking path called the Via Alpina that connects eight countries and covers 200,000 square kilometers. Its five trails run some 5000 kilometers or 3100 miles across the length of the Alps connecting existing long distance trails. Many date back to the days of the Romans, pilgrims and traders. I truly hoped some improvements had been made since then. Five variations on the route come in a variety of colors: red, green, blue, purple and yellow. The longest, the red route, consists of 161 stages and runs from Trieste, Italy on the Adriatic Sea through Slovenia, Austria, Germany, Liechtenstein, Switzerland, and France to finish in Monaco on the Mediterranean Sea. Although geographically separated by mountains, these trails occasionally intersect, allowing a hiker to hop from one to the other to explore Alpine areas you like. Exciting, right?

Yes, but trekking it was not a challenge to take lightly.

Even so, it was especially appealing, masochist that I am, since it's still fairly unknown to hard-core North American thru-hikers who're busy trekking the popular Appalachian Trail from Georgia to Maine or the Pacific Crest Trail from British Columbia to Mexico. It's one of the newer faces in the trekking world. It was just 2002 when partners from the Alpine countries founded the Via Alpina to promote sustainable green development.

The Via Alpina's different, I kept telling myself, a road truly less traveled. If we accept the challenge to hike its length, maybe we won't be the first, but we could be among the first handful to complete it. And, Ötzi aside, who knew what we'd discover up there?

Okay, I admit I've long been fascinated by the Alps. Each snowcapped mountain has a tale and personality all its own. It holds an inexplicable magic that we've forgotten in our lives today. It's a place of legend, of monsters, both real and imagined. The range is home to wild creatures like the steinbok, golden eagle, mouflon, marmots, the Alpine version of our groundhogs, and hundreds of plants like the edelweiss and alpenrose. It's a traditional abode to kings and knights in castles, to dark forests with tiny gnomes. It's a region full of history and culture, as each passing civilization left their mark over millennia. It's also the center of a fiercely independent lifestyle that's becoming as threatened as the melting glaciers on its highest peaks. Finally, and how could I forget, it's home to blonde, pigtailed, rosy-cheeked Heidi, my first boyhood crush. For a young guy in those days before Lara Croft, she was as sexy as it got. I just knew there had to be something special in the alpine cheese.

Then again, I knew the region's much more than stereotypes, more than cheese and gnomes. I wanted to discover the real Alps, to share it with others who've never ventured far off the beaten path, or who view Europe with a jaundiced "been there, done that" eye. Wild paths take you far beyond the staid museums and cathedrals, bridges and bars found on the city-a-day tour circuit. Then again, it's more than simply "bagging peaks." It's the unique people, culture and unforgettable experiences along the way.

What an adventure, I thought. If we trek the red route, we'll be in the high Alps moving from hut-to-hut for more than five months—and that's not even taking into account any time off. Given the narrow window of opportunity in the high country between first and last snows, June-October, we'll be pressed for time. It'll be similar to the challenge Cheryl and I faced when trekking across Tibet in '92, always wondering when the first blizzard would hit and the passes became blocked until springtime thaw. Even though this isn't the Himalayas, it's far from a walk in the park.

Back in Tibet, we'd discovered the beauty of "slow deliberate travel" as we hiked the high Himalayan Plains from Lhasa to Kathmandu with Sadhu, our Tibetan horse. Besides witnessing the endangered Tibet lifestyle as we spent evenings chewing the yak with former monks and farming families around their fire each night, we found an added bonus. Total immersion. Something happens to your perspective when you slow life down, when you wallow in your surroundings. You eat where locals eat. Sleep where they sleep. You see a side of their life that others miss. Plus, there's a beauty to simplifying your own. Forced to carry everything you need for months on your back, your oozing blisters and aching muscles quickly convince you to travel lightly; that's an important lesson on the trail and in life.

I'd taken that style of travel to heart. It was my passion; you might say, "a sweet addiction." Over the next decade, I'd spent a month or more nearly each year trekking across Europe with a backpack, including the Via de la Plata and Camino de Santiago (once with Cheryl) through Spain, the Via Francigena from England to Rome, St. Olav's Way across Norway, and then again a long-distance trail from the Italian

Dolomites to Prague. Probably the most difficult was in 2006 when a French friend and I set off hiking 4500 kilometers on a peace trek from France to Jerusalem. Walked by those who became the first Knights Templar, we re-blazed what I called the Templar Trail, narrowly dodging missiles and jihadist rage. We survived, but just barely. Still, I was hooked and after two years of facing the scary sameness of a so-called normal life, I was itching for a new challenge. And something told me this Via Alpina would be like none of the others.

After doing a little research, it was obvious to me that it'd be necessary for us to apply for visas, if for no other reason than to be able to attempt to complete the vast trail in five months. Nowadays with the Schengen Agreement, many travelers can only stay in the entire European Union for ninety days at a time—not ninety per country, as in the days of francs, liras and marks. And stretching it into two seasons, a *hikus interruptus*, was out of the question.

Why not, I figured, use this opportunity to experience the Alps more fully? Why not live there? That's the ultimate in immersion. Besides, after living off and on in Hawaii for decades, a change of scene was overdue. Mountains, fresh air, four seasons, and evergreen were sure to be balm for the tropical soul. But where? Ah, Grasshopper, that was the question.

Thinking back on all our travels, I remembered September 11, 2001, that day of infamy. With no idea of what had just happened in New York, we'd landed in Milan, Italy and promptly caught a train to visit Siegi, a friend I'd met on the Camino de Santiago. He lives in Brixen, a tranquil Alpine village in the Südtirol or Alto Adige region. Although now part of northern Italy, it was Austrian until the end of World War I. I enjoyed the way its mixed culture combines a bit of Tyrolean Alpine practicality with a refreshing sense of Italian *la dolce vita*. (Besides, I'd secretly hankered after a cool pair of *lederhosen*, or leather pants, to complement my annual Oktoberfest chicken dance.)

Brixen, or Bressanone, as it's known in Italian, is a valley village of 20,000 in a storybook setting. Once it had been the center of the south Tyrol bishopric, and its low skyline is still dominated by an imposing cathedral, Gothic archways, oriel windows and Middle Age towers. Yet despite its 1100-year history, it has an air of normalcy. It's not some fabricated, fantasy Tyrol-land. You sense the contentment as couples walk hand-in-hand down traffic-free, cobblestoned streets. Folks watch the world go by in outdoor cafés, while reading their newspaper over morning cappuccinos. People casually bike along the tree-lined Eisack and Rienz Rivers offering a "*Hoi, Gruezi*" or "*Buongiorno*" as they pass friends and neighbors in this bilingual community. Why, even at the market, you can overhear one clerk gossiping to another in Italian, who answers in German.

Here in the shadow of the legendary Dolomites, the crisp mountain air invites you to breathe deep. It's the ideal spot for hardcore trekkers. Locals take to the surrounding mountains for relaxing weekend hikes on well-groomed trails, while winter is anxiously awaited for the chance to ski, sled, and snowboard the Plose. Even Brixen's indoor pool and spa seem more designed for locals than visitors.

Then there's the food, equally super-natural. The valley's vineyards and apple orchards offer fruit straight from their trees, as well as an autumnal blast of color.

Their water was the sweetest I've ever tasted. Dairy farms produce fresh hormone-free milk, cheese and yoghurt, and the valley celebrates its abundance with festivals that feature their tasty smoked ham, apple strudel, breads, beer and wine served to an oompah beat.

Ultimately, something impressed us even more. During that time of turmoil in 2001, we could never forget how sympathetic Brixners had been, welcoming two strangers far from home with open arms. Consequently, it seemed like a logical (and delicious) choice. Besides, its central location in Europe would make it so much easier for us to plan our annual treks without having to take out a second mortgage to fly halfway around the world. That never makes much sense when you're trying to live simply and lessen your carbon footprint.

Our decision opened the floodgates on what could have been a logistical nightmare. Soon we were swamped with the details of applying for an elective residency visa and all its various stamps. Siegi came through for us in Italy, as he knows everyone and greased the wheels. I also contacted Nathalie, the Association Via Alpina network's go-to person, explaining that we were interested in hiking their trail and in writing a book about our experiences. Even though I vowed to write my usual warts and all account (bound to offend everyone in some small way), they made us official partners and even provided a letter of introduction for officialdom. Why not? I figured every little bit might help our case.

While the consulate deliberated on whether to let us stay for a year, there was no time to waste. We switched into phase two: gearing up and finding the absolute best and lightest equipment available. There's an old Swiss joke that every day the TV weather forecaster calls for the same thing: "Sunny with rain and a chance of snow." True. That makes it especially tricky to plan for all Alpine weather contingencies. Given the distance and workout of climbing 1000 meters (3200+ feet) up (and then back down) mountains every day, we knew it'd be suicide to carry more than seven or eight kilos (15-16 pounds) each. So after careful deliberation, we decided to pack just the essentials: one change of clothes, extra socks, rain ponchos and pants, running shoes, lightweight hiking boots, gaiters to keep snow or gravel from our boots, hats, down jackets and sleeping bags, digital cameras, soap, LEKI Nordic poles, Swiss Army knives, and sachets of Zip-Fizz, a powdered energy drink. We'd split a basic medical kit, compass, maps, and power cords among us. Cheryl would also bring her trusty compact Mac iTouch that'd allow us to read a Via Alpina PDF for directions, since there was no English guidebook available then, and to possibly check our emails—if or when we ever found Wi-Fi coverage in the Alps. That was a huge unknown. I also took a GPS backtrack gizmo that'd allow us to retrace our steps if (when) we became lost, if nothing else.

After hours of research into a dizzying number of innovative designs, we contacted GoLite to get their new lightweight backpacks, sleeping bags and clothing. I'd carried their gear on two former expeditions. Gossamer Gear supplied a miracle tent weighing a kilo, handy in case of an emergency or if we were ever stuck in a blizzard between villages, while Omni Resources provided thirty topographic maps that we'd carry a few at a time.

To physically prepare, a local health club beat our flabby office bodies into submission with three months of strength and aerobic training. I have to admit, their treadmill incline worked wonders. Cheryl transformed from desk jockey to mountain diva. Better still, I could see that this challenge of trekking across the Alps appealed to her inner jockette. There was a little-disguised bounce to her step and sparkle in her hazel eyes.

Finally, we picked up our visa-required health insurance policy, which I saw as little more than a security blanket. If we slipped off a 4000-meter peak, there wouldn't be much left to ship off to a hospital emergency room. We were on our own.

Speaking of which, let me make this positively clear right up front: I have great respect for mountains. It doesn't take much for them to shake you off, like a dog ridding itself of pesky fleas. Unlike some, I'm convinced that there's no such thing as "conquering" mountains. You can merely hope to survive them. That said, the enormity of our journey didn't fully register until those topo maps arrived. One evening, Cheryl and I sat surrounded by them sprawled across the living room rug. As she called out each village name, I carefully traced a line between our daily stages. My orange marker went from valley to mountain summit and back down again, sometimes several times a day before we reached a cabin. It wound around glaciers. It looped entire regions in crazy mandala circles, only to come back again.

We didn't say much, didn't have to. We'd been together long enough. One look said it all. Dammit. Just what have we gotten ourselves into this time? We aren't mountain climbers, just trekkers. Sure, my last hike was across eleven countries. But as you know, it's not length that counts; it's the ups and downs, the backs and forths. A thousand-meter climb and descent each and every day, for months on end, would be harder than we've ever done before.

Still, it was meant to be. The stars came into alignment. The mail arrived one afternoon and we were so startled to receive our Italian visas that our screams left the bananas outside shaking from their stalks. Yet with one major hurdle crossed, leaving Hawaii was another challenge altogether. How do you sort through a lifetime of possessions to lighten your load?

Did you know that kitchen cups multiply like bunnies when left alone in dark cupboards? True. Fortunately, about this same time, Cheryl was laid off her job, so she came to my rescue and pulled me out from under the boxes. Plants, cars and appliances all eventually found new homes, as well as our furniture and far too many accumulated things. Our shedding continued right down to the garden gnome who was left, still smiling, at the cottage. At long last, we carted our remaining worldly possessions to a shipping company. Our boxes were so tightly packed within a single wooden crate that a feather couldn't fit between them. Looking at it, we beamed like proud parents, satisfied to see our lives reduced to a more manageable size—yet shocked at the implications.

This time we'd definitely burned a bridge.

The days flew off the calendar like in one of those cheesy black-and-white films as we set off on a new chapter, the start of another trail. This one just happened to also be an exciting new path in life we'd chosen—for better or worse. We flew high on a surge of adrenaline. Mentally we were eager to escape paradise for a while, although I admit we were touched by sadness at leaving our circle of friends and family. After saying *aloha* to them in Hawaii and on both coasts, Cheryl and I nervously flew to Munich and then connected by train to Brixen.

Unfortunately, our arrival didn't provide the "whew" moment we'd long anticipated. With the clock ticking loudly in our ears, we faced a deluge of last minute details, especially applying for what they called our *permesso di soggiorno* with all its various stamps and processing at the local INAS (National Institute for Social Assistance), then the police station and post office. Although we already had visas, the *permesso* was our permission to actually live there. We'd heard it might take months for them to schedule our personal appearance, at which time we had to produce more documents and have our fingerprints taken. By then, with any luck, I figured our trek would be completed and we'd be back in our Tyrolean hideaway.

In one final stroke of genius, Siegi signed us up for the *Alpenverein Südtirol*. As members of the regional mountaineering association, we'd save 20-30% for a bunk bed at the alpine huts. Since this expedition was entirely self-funded, we needed to make every euro count. Unlike previous treks, we couldn't depend on staying in inexpensive *refugios* and hostels, plus the anemic American dollar was bound to put our budgets to the supreme test. Then again, I thought, this is hiking. It's about as Everyman an activity as you can find. How much could it possibly cost to hike?

We did take time to mix a little pleasure with last-minute errands. Why not? On the way home from neighboring Bolzano, Siegi drove us to a quiet, shady park for a brisk walk in a sluice flowing with icy water. *Kneipping*, named after the Bavarian priest with the same name, is a teeth-chattering naturopathic treatment—perfect for returning plane-swollen feet to almost normal size. Too bad I couldn't fit my entire body in the channel.

Ultimately, our endless checklist was completed. The evening before we left for Trieste to begin our trek from the Adriatic Sea, we drove to a neighboring village to launch our great upcoming journey. The restaurant was traditionally Tyrolean from its sturdy handcrafted rustic furniture to the ceramic-tiled woodstove, from its unpronounceable menu down to the apple-cheeked waitress in her poofy *dirndl* dress and checkered apron. It was perfect, just as I'd always imagined. We ate in near silence, overwhelmed by the journey ahead, but I still remember that meal. Cheryl savored the *speckknöderl* soup, featuring giant doughy baseballs of ham and flour that taste like Thanksgiving dressing, while I dug into the spinach ravioli and Siegi had spinach gnocchi, all washed down with a local Magdalena red wine served in an earthenware jug. Afterward, we shuffled out to the sun terrace just in time to catch an ethereal pumpkin light illuminating the jagged, snowcapped Dolomites towering above us. At last, we relished our long awaited "whew" moment, a delicious dollop of Alpenglow for dessert. Funny, I optimistically took that as a good sign; there'd be clear sailing ahead. The Universe, well, had other plans.

Excerpt from Chapter One, *Over the Top & Back Again: Hiking X the Alps* by Brandon Wilson © Reprinted by permission of the author.

In Quest of Mount Everest

November 13

A buzz rose throughout the compound, as everyone made last minute preparations for their odyssey. Billie, Marley and Cheryl ran to the store, while Hans and Jacob stowed bikes and gear in an outdoor meat locker. Tanji, our Japanese snowman, purchased one of those brilliant red liter thermoses for the expedition. He had arrived without a canteen, cook kit, tent or utensils and, confidentially, I wondered how he'd made it that far.

Amid the bustle, I rushed among our companions collecting half of Mr. Big's fee to be paid in advance, the rest upon our safe return.

"Don't forget to take care of [our horse] Sadhu," I reminded him, as I counted it into his callused hand. "Remember, for that price he gets both hay and barley."

"Do not worry, sir," he replied, smiling. "I will take good care of your, your…brother."

It was noon by the time we'd loaded supplies and packs onto the awaiting donkey cart. As two gaunt Tibetan teens led our anxious procession through that settlement in Everest's shadow, villagers craned their heads and unabashedly stared from tri-striped windows and cloth cloaked doorways. There was no awe, only wonder. They knew where we were headed. Maybe they only wondered, "Why?"

For nearly an hour, we tumbled across a marshy open plain at a relaxed, steady pace. Along the way, as if meant to confuse us, narrow dirt trails, no more pronounced than goat paths, crossed and headed off aimlessly in different directions. Ignoring these, we continued tagging behind the creaking supply wagon. Until finally, we dragged into the open courtyard of an even smaller hamlet known as Ra Chhu, hewn into the hillside overlooking Tingri Valley.

To welcome our arrival, swarms of curious, irresistible kids mobbed us, giggling and yanking at our sleeves. We loved the attention. Marley swung several in the air. Jacob, growling like a crazed yeti, chased others. While a few more brazen fellas even mugged for Tanji who swooped and circled like a persistent *paparazzi*.

After everything had been unloaded from the cart, our two guides, "Don Juan" and "Ugly" finally made their debut and began strapping supplies onto four stout, black yaks.

Now, just to set the record straight, Don Juan and Ugly weren't uncomplimentary nicknames we'd given them. On the contrary. Those were their actual Tibetan names just mangled into English.

Don Juan was tall and muscular for a Tibetan, perhaps in his mid-twenties, although it was difficult to tell. His thick, black hair was slicked straight back with yak butter pomade. His teeth were stained ochre, the patina of a crumbling Italian facade; his face, slightly pitted to match.

Ugly, his shorter, more reticent partner was perhaps a little younger. The herder was reed thin with slightly effeminate features. Laughing, almond eyes framed an angular nose, while long black hair was carefully wrapped with a braided red rope and wound around his crown.

At first, it looked like they had yak packing down to a fine art. Employing a well-honed system, the first three yaks were easily loaded. While Ugly steadied them by holding their braided yak hair bridles, Don Juan saddled and cinched them. Then effortlessly, he tied packs, their bulky wall tent and sacks of supplies onto sturdy wooden saddles.

Everyone watched with a curious fascination. From a distance, whenever we'd encountered them, yaks looked affable in an oafish sort of way. They were Tibetan cartoon caricatures of hyperthyroid sheepdogs. But looks can be deceiving.

Our guides left the most recalcitrant one, an ornery, bucking black brute weighing nearly a ton for their grand finale. First, eluding the saddle, the mad yak ran wide circles around the courtyard, chasing and inciting the others into a mad frenzy. Sensing an uncontrollable chain reaction, the herders quickly jumped into the fray. Ugly dove and caught the ivory-tailed behemoth's bridle, like some Tibetan cowpuncher. Then Don Juan cautiously placed a wooden saddle on the unyielding yak's hunched, shaggy back, carefully cinching the wide girth strap.

That was the easy part. Now, the beast simmered on a slow boil.

Pressing their luck, the guides gingerly eased the first two packs across his saddle. Well, the monster no sooner felt the weight than he lunged and bucked, sending the bags sailing! Unflinching, the guides regrouped and tried again. Then again. Each time with the same disastrous result. At last, exasperated, Don Juan carefully looped a yak hair rope around the obstinate yak's horns. Then grabbing him in a tenuous headlock, he tried to muscle him into submission—about as easy as flipping an SUV with a spatula. Well, that certainly didn't help the yak's disposition. This time, as soon as the bags touched the saddle, Don Juan himself was thrown airborne.

Watching those escapades, it didn't take long to realize how lucky we were to find our over aged wander horse.

"Imagine us," I thought, "struggling to load him everyday?"

Finally, in a stroke of engineering genius, Don Juan tightened his rope around the animal's razor-sharp, gnarled horns. Then yanking it down, he looped it around the yak's front hoofs, tying it off at the head. The demon glared with rage, steamed with fury. But convinced he was safely hobbled, at least momentarily, our guides moved quickly, tightening four packs against his sides. Then, loosening restraints, they sprung out of his path.

The shaggy dervish tossed back his head, bucked and furiously stomped around the courtyard for a few tense minutes, a furious thousand pounds of steaming revenge. But the packs refused to fly.

In homage to that behemoth's noble defiance, it only seemed right to give him a name. So we dubbed him, "Bad Ass." And although it had taken Don Juan and Ugly nearly forty minutes to load him, we were finally off.

Tingri quickly became a speck on the horizon as we set an energetic pace, slogging through soggy tundra, crossing scorched gravel patches, and leaping frigid streams and flooded irrigation ditches. Still, as much as we pushed, we struggled just to keep up with the yaks and guides.

For hours, the plain was barren, except for a lone adobe hut.

"Look, Cheryl," I gasped, pointing fifty yards ahead. "There's another one of those houses like the others we've seen with rivers running through them." We'd wondered whether they were badly designed, or if someone just wanted a place with cold running water?

Vaulting over a stream, we approached a startled teenager leaning against the open front door. Bewildered by our request to peek inside, he obligingly led our group into his family's tiny, lightless room. Two massive stone wheels powered by the stream rhythmically turned around a rock basin, grinding barley into *tsampa*. So, that's what they are! The miller family's beds, cradled between bulging barley sacks, were just meters away.

Curiosity satisfied, it took our ragged procession nearly three more hours of grass "muffin" hummock hopping before arriving in Lungjhang.

Reverently, as though intruding, our group ceremoniously circled the village *chorten* and its stack of *mani* or prayer stones. Making the rounds, I was surprised to see their carved Sanskrit inscription, "*Om Mani Padme Hum*," was identical to those painted on hillsides outside Lhasa, on the giant prayer wheel, and on other indelible holy billboards across the plains.

I, too, whispered a silent prayer. "On this part of our journey," I reckoned, "we'll need all the help we can get."

After advancing through the nearly deserted settlement, the last on the plain, we paused at a mud brick enclosure. While Don Juan disappeared to find the corral's keeper, we had a spare moment to study the bleak graveled terrain that started its stratospheric wind upward.

"Already, we're at 4,511 meters (14,800 feet)," I thought. "My God, there's another 610 meters (2,000 feet) to climb over the next two days just to reach base camp!"

As my mind staggered with those implications, an attractive village girl appeared, smiled bashfully and unlocked the gate to our dung-scattered animal pen.

Stepping in, we tried to avoid the more obvious piles, while surveying our home for the night. For once, I could really sympathize with Sadhu.

"At least it's empty," I thought. "We don't have any goats to contend with. Plus, we'll be sheltered from this wind."

As if on cue, our breeze quickly grew into a howling tempest, plunging the tundra's frigid 30°F at least 10°F lower within seconds.

With growing urgency, we pitched our nylon two-person tent atop a flattened hay bin, as Marley and Billie unfolded theirs next to Jacob and Hans's inside the main corral. Tanji, since he had no equipment except the ever-present multitude of cameras bandoleered about his small frame like some Nipponese bandito, was forced to share our guides' tent.

After unloading our contrary yaks, a chore much easier than saddling them, Don Juan and Ugly unfolded their enormous, tattered canvas sheet. While Don Juan hoisted its center with a wooden pole, Ugly stretched yak hair ropes tight from each corner. Tying them off to nearby rocks, he sealed its sides with other stones. Then, while we methodically unrolled our modern, self-inflating foam sleep pads, down bags and nylon bivy sacks, the guides scattered tattered blankets and hides across the dirt inside their primitive shelter, leaving a narrow gap in between. There, sheltered between two rocks, they started a dung fire.

First, Don Juan drew a homemade goatskin bellows from his sack. Then, he lit a handful of slender juniper branches, toted all the way from town. Once ignited, inside that ring of stone, those fragrant needles crackled and burned intensely for seconds. As he feverishly pumped the swollen, wombat-like bellows, Ugly carefully fed the flames, breaking dried yak dung patties in half until a light glowed brightly.

It quickly boiled one pot of *chu*, another of *cha*. By then, our group had joined the hardy herders under their canvas. Realizing we were novices at the fine art of dung cooking, Don Juan and Ugly gently pumped and stoked the temperamental flames, while we wasted no effort in cooking pasta for seven, wolfed it down, and drowned our carb-fest with *chang* and tea. Finally satiated, we relaxed shoulder to shoulder, butt to butt, in the cramped quarters.

With us out of their way, our guides contentedly guzzled liters of yak butter tea and cups of *tsampa*, first alone, then blended together in a pag, kneaded with their fingers.

Frequently as they ate, the fire threatened to sputter out. That's when Don Juan, setting his wooden *tsampa* bowl aside, would rhythmically embrace the bloated bellows again with Jacob chanting, "Pump, pump the jam, pump it up, pump it up!"

Don Juan let loose a hearty guffaw. Then, like some Tibetan rapper, he sang along, pumping to his beat. "Pump, pump da jam, pump eet up, pump eet up."

Within seconds, a blinding, choking cloud of dung smoke ballooned, throwing everyone hacking onto their backs and our devious guide into delirious laughter. He continued with renewed vigor. "Pump, pump da jam, pump eet up, pump eet up." Again, black smoke streamed from the fire, flooding the snug tent, stinging eyes and singeing lungs.

Enough! We couldn't stand it any longer. Staggering from their toasty tent, we laughed and shivered back to our flimsy shelters.

"He only…had to ask us…to leave," I coughed, struggling with numb fingers to unzip our frozen tent fly.

November 14

It was late morning by the time we'd *tsampa*-ed, *cha*-ed, struck camp, and loaded the cranky yaks. Remembering Don Juan and Ugly's heated battle the day before, Marley, Jacob and I offered to help load Bad Ass.

"Sure!" Don Juan pantomimed. "Surround him in a circle."

So, standing guard, each armed with only a handful of measly rocks, we watched for any sign the unwieldy two-ton beast was ready to break for the freedom of the open plain. Well, it didn't take long. As soon as Don Juan approached with his saddle, Bad Ass sprung with a furious lunge in Marley's direction.

"Watch him! Watch!" I screamed.

Marley loped ten steps to his right. The angry creature swerved and spun the other direction. Jacob jogged to his left to cut him off. But the yak poured on speed like a charging bull. He paused. Then lurched toward me. I fired off a rock just in front of his flaring nose. He stopped in his tracks, spun, whipped around and charged back the other way. Marley cocked his arm and let a missile sail, SMACKING the beast on the side of his great shaggy head. He glared, but didn't attack again. Fierce, still fuming, he stood stock still while Ugly and Don Juan finished their task.

After the last packs were loaded and cinches tightened, Don Juan glanced over at us, obviously amused by our first awkward attempt at yak herding. Then, to our surprise, he sheepishly pulled open his jacket. Pointing first to his side then to Bad Ass, he made a horn-like gesture, hands atop his yak-greased head. Marley and I stared in wide-eyed disbelief at a grotesquely purple scar, zigzagging ragged down his side.

"He's already been gored?" Marley sighed.

"Now, he tells us…"

All day long, we slogged through a bog-like tundra, trekked over rocky plains and trudged through stream-fed marsh. Occasionally, we'd spot the ruins of a crumbling dzong on a distant mountainside or a herder's stone corral enveloped in solitude. Otherwise, there was little evidence that humanity ever invaded that lonesome end of the world.

For hours, Billie and I scampered ahead, scouts tracing the narrow dirt path that wound endlessly through those hills. After a while, as one of us ran out of conversation, we'd drop behind, striking up a new topic with another companion. As we barely knew the other five, any subject was fair game. And since I'd nearly perfected reading Cheryl's mind, having traveled together so long, it was refreshing to inject a little new blood into our pilgrimage.

Yet, no matter what any of us mindlessly gabbed about, everyone's rapt attention ultimately remained focused on the mountains and unknown challenge looming ahead.

For twenty-five kilometers (15.5 miles), we huffed and struggled up bone-wrenching slopes or were challenged to jump thawing, crystalline rivulets in the valley below. Only too soon, we'd resume our dogged ascent along the vaguest of steep dirt tracks. Frequently, other trails would appear, merge, and then splinter off in different directions. Confused, I'd pause, turn, and crane my head for some reassuring sign from the diligent Don Juan, pulling up the flank with his yaks. Invariably, he'd signal to continue straight ahead, usually up another heart-thumping incline.

We seldom stopped, nibbling on puny cooked potatoes and roasted barley as we hiked. Breaks were brief, just long enough to catch a miserly measured sip from water jugs. Everyone knew their scant, one-liter canteen had to last 'til sunset. Each trekker carried their own, buckled to belts or strapped across chests.

Tanji was the only exception. His huge crimson thermos, too bulky for any sensible trekker to lug, was lashed to the side of one of the yaks.

In early afternoon, just we crested a summit overlooking a breathtaking gorge, Bad Ass spotted the crimson tempting gleam of Tanji's shiny thermos out of the corner of his eye. Magically, he was drawn to it, like a bull to a matador's sanguine cape. Sharply swerving to his left, he caught the other yak totally by surprise. As he gored its hairy side, there was a loud "POP!" and Tanji's glass jug cascaded in shimmering mirrored fragments over the cliff.

"What a hoot! Only now," I thought, "he'll be more dependent than ever on the rest of us."

We made good time considering our various physical conditions. It was no race, but pacing was just as vital. Air became as precious as food. Supplies were limited, water rationed. We knew there'd be no more villages until we reached Rongbuk Monastery, and everyone expected near-freezing days, arctic nights, dwindling sunlight and heavenly altitudes to take their toll and test our very resolve.

Just that evening, as the sun escaped behind the snowcapped impasse before us, the day's greatest challenge soared overhead.

"Why couldn't this have come earlier?" I fretted, staring at the immense visage of Pang La, towering to 5212 meters (17,100 feet) ahead.

With intense, gut-wrenching deliberation, our very survival seemingly in the balance, the group made one last painful push up the vertical naked slope. Wind slashed across our half-frozen eyes. We trembled with inconceivable cold as sweat froze to our backs. Stumbling in the fading light, sharp slag slid and shifted below our feet. Lungs burned. Hearts erupted. Heads throbbed louder than thoughts. Until finally, as the last whisper of strength was sucked from shivering, expended bodies, we crawled to the crest.

There, joined by bemused guides and hungry yaks, we shuffled in twilight haze across its bleak plateau, sliding down the opposite side to where an empty drogpa, or nomad's camp, awaited amid the fury of arctic gales.

Although we pitched our tents inside the protection of the stone ring, for hours, whipped by that relentless tempest, our tents shook with a fury and life all their own. We were famished. Yet, our meager meal of ramen noodles did little but brightly stoke our fires, soon fizzling to ash, like juniper needles upon dung flames.

Silently suffering from complete and undisguised exhaustion, everyone turned-in early. Alone, snuggled deep within the privacy of our down bags, we uncontrollably shook, struggling to keep warm. Our breaths rose and froze above us. Only the promise of reaching the Mother Goddess kept us going.

November 15

We awoke the next morning still shivering, wrapped in a wet shroud. Our breaths, at night a frozen mist lining the tent walls, had thawed, showering rain and drenching our sleeping bags. Normally, that would be no major problem. We'd simply stretch them out in the sun to dry, as we had back in that potato patch.

"But today," I thought, "today there is no sun."

After a futile attempt to dry them in the still gusting, freezing wind, we reluctantly stuffed them back in our stuff sacks. Realizing these down bags were worthless when wet, reaching Rongbuk Monastery and its heated rooms before sundown became more crucial than ever.

However, it was nearly 11 a.m. by the time we broke camp. Everyone was hesitant to leave that stone corral, reluctant to tackle the pass that had drained so much from them the day before. Don Juan and Ugly lingered a little longer over *tsampa* and *po-cha*. Hans and Jacob milked a third bowl of java. Cheryl and I savored a precious, withered apple squirreled away from Tingri. Tanji, as usual, contentedly shared everyone else's larder. Like clockwork, the yaks stamped and stalled, throwing their usual conniptions.

Once we setoff our pace was brisk, as though to compensate for the late hour and temperature. In actuality, it was as lively as could be expected, considering the altitude of more than 16,000 feet.

Unfortunately, my breath was more labored than ever. Sucking noxious fumes from the dung fire morning and night for two days had wreaked havoc on my bronchitis.

By mid-afternoon we reached several deserted stone corrals and decided to take a breather. From that pristine, rolling alpine pasture, we gazed down 300 meters to the valley and meandering river far below. Surveying our route, at first it appeared an insurmountable granite wall blocked our path.

"Wait a second. We don't have to actually climb that," I thought, "do we?"

Then, upon closer inspection, I could barely detect a faint path winding down the mountainside. Turning south, it seemed to skirt the shimmering river.

"*Kaaaputh! Chugrath, chugrath!*" Suddenly, there was maniacal snorting and rambunctious thunder behind me. I spun around. Bad Ass had thrown my bag into the air and Don Juan and Ugly were frantically barreling after him across the meadow.

"Stop! Stop him!" they bellowed, as the beast galloped full tilt up the embankment!

Snatching rocks with both hands, Marley, Jacob, Hans and I joined in that frenzied chase. As Marley whizzed stones across the beast's blazing eyes, the rest of us circled our prey like Neanderthals. The creature charged then slammed to a stop. Spinning 180°, he blustered off in the opposite direction. Then the demon madly galloped right at us threatening to ram us head-on. But we stood our ground. Until finally, nearly able to feel his foul breath, we shot off rockets, sending him spinning in another direction like some crazed fur ball. This mayhem persisted for at least twenty minutes until, at last, Don Juan and Ugly were able to sneak up behind winded Bad Ass, lassoing his horns and tying them again to his front legs. Safely hobbled, they loaded my bag back onto him.

Hoping everything was still in one piece, I ran through a quick inventory of breakables while negotiating a gravel switchback down the slippery slope.

For twenty minutes we edged the water's path, until reaching a broad, well-constructed wooden bridge festooned with gaily-colored prayer flags. Crossing halfway across the ice-choked, glacier-fed river, I abruptly stopped and gazed upstream. Mount Everest, home of the Mother Goddess, shone and sparkled on the snowy horizon with all the intensity of a million Hope Diamonds. Then, for the first time since leaving, I knew we'd make it. At last, success was within our grasp.

For three more hours, we wound along the dizzying, scraggy shore led by Chomolongma's lifeblood. Frequently, tidy rock mounds cropped up on the rugged hillside. Stacked by pilgrims throughout the centuries, they reminded me of home in Hawai'i and of offerings to the goddess Pele, who lives inside the now-erupting Kilauea Volcano on the Big Island.

As I became lost in memories of home, for once, like horses returning to the paddock, both guides and yaks shot past us.

What secrets did they know? Were we that close?

Walking hand-in-hand, Ugly sang a sweet Tibetan ditty in a high-pitched, falsetto voice, while Don Juan danced a jig. We were just content to stumble along in pious exhaustion, anxious to find our own respite in a valley once famous as a Buddhist retreat.

In the past, hermits sequestered themselves in hillside huts or caves for years or a lifetime. There in reverent meditation they lived in humble seclusion. For some, food and water was even slipped to them through chinks in their cell walls. Sadly, although there'd once been as many as six active monasteries in the valley known as "Sanctuary of the Birds," since the Cultural Demolition, only one remained. That lone survivor was Rongbuk Monastery.

Perhaps in joyful celebration by those long-solitary monks, the moment of our own arrival was brilliantly auspicious. We gazed upon the reassuring glow of Rongbuk *stupa's* golden spire at 4983 meters (16,350 feet) just as the sun embraced the rooftop of Mount Cho Oyu. And although I'd heard there is actually a pass just up the valley called Changri La, between Mount Cho Oyu and Mount Everest, we were pleased to stumble upon our own private paradise.

Wandering inside the temple's gates, our group was hailed by a young, exuberant monk with short-cropped hair. He wore a traditional maroon Buddhist robe, covered by an untraditional high-tech fleece jacket.

Whispering, "Follow me," in perfect English, the holy man glided past and led us up a flight of creaking wooden stairs to a five-bed dorm beside the temple, or *lhakhang*.

Although it was hardly a place snooty travel editors would rave about, its rug-shrouded beds, broken window panes stuffed with wadded newspapers and potbellied stove protected us from howling Himalayan winds, much more than any four-star monstrosity's complimentary shower cap ever would.

November 16

Hans, Jacob, Marley and I departed the following morning, bound for Mount Everest. Each harbored his own private reason. Hans hankered to reach the advance base camp at the edge of the East Rongbuk Glacier at over 6400 meters (21,000 feet). Jacob seemed content to just explore its glacier, realizing the limitations of his equipment only too well, having already worn out one pair of cheap Chinese hiking boots on the trail from Tingri. While Marley and I were in it for the "experience," just wanting to get as close as we could and live to tell the tale.

Of their own choosing, Cheryl, Billie and Tanji stayed behind, basking in the warmth of the dorm's dung fire. They'd reluctantly decided it was better to recoup before starting our arduous two-day trek back to Tingri West.

For the better part of an hour, our foursome battled the frigid wind, as we inched our way up the vast valley. The mountain, itself, served as our guiding beacon. Each step drew us closer to that extraordinary source of power.

For a while, Heinrich, a lanky Austrian wayfarer whom we'd met back at that Tingri inn and again at the monastery, joined us. Fueling our imaginations with a vivid tale of his trek to Rongbuk Glacier the day before, he convinced us it could, in fact, be done. For an instant, I chewed over the possibility again in my mind. But before I'd committed to brave it, he directed us to the best glacier viewing point, then scrambled a nearby path to explore the ruins of Sherab Chholing Nunnery.

Over the next hour, we beat a furious pace toward the peak that had already brought us halfway around the world.

Like a beautiful woman, a "Lady of the Lake," she was elusive. For a while, her snowy shawl rose almost close enough to grasp. Then, as we'd head back down into a gravel valley, she was totally obscured. Until finally, running over a craggy knoll, I stopped short in awe. Mount Everest sparkled ahead, flooding the horizon.

"Magnificent!" I whispered to the wind.

Similar, meaningless epithets were all the others could sigh in quiet chorus of praise, disbelief and wonderment.

Since I was a child, I'd fantasized about what it'd be like to gaze upon the world's highest peak; to feel the same air brush past my cheek that rushed along her ivory face. To me, it was one of those sites I had to see in the world—more than any Taj Mahal, Eiffel Tower or Great Pyramid, all monuments sculpted by human hands. Chomolongma humbles them all.

We crouched on that rise in silent, reverent appreciation of the unblemished beauty enveloping us. The aqua ice fields of Rongbuk Glacier flowed like a cape to her right. Her jagged toothed, snow draped crown, for once free from any cloud, glistened against a royal sapphire sky. And her precious gilt-edged peaks radiated a pureness, twinkling in stark contrast to the slate gray glacial path of the ancient ocean floor below.

In her regal presence, I was disappointed that our pilgrimage, the season, or my own sensibility, prevented me from climbing with the others farther into her lap. Although they planned on trekking another two days, I still wasn't convinced, especially with their lack of winter gear, that it was wise.

"Maybe," I mused, "just maybe, I'm getting too old, or too practical for all this?"

But as the others, fifteen years younger, stared at the dangerous passage ahead, they, too, questioned their sanity.

"I know Hans is crazy," Marley confided, lowering his telephoto lens for an instant. "And Jacob's got his moments. But this mountain and what it's capable of doing has me scared dungless!"

"Well," I thought, "that's a healthy attitude for this altitude in mid-November."

"Just don't do anything too stupid," I warned the ill-equipped musketeers. "We expect to see you guys back in Kathmandu!"

As I slid down the steep, slippery descent to the 16,900- foot (5,150-meter) base camp, and the world's highest concrete toilet, my companions soon were reduced to mere specks on the gravel overlook. I was content with my decision. Feeling that merciless wind slap across my chapped cheeks and sweep down my back once more, there was no doubt I'd made the right choice.

On the way back to Rongbuk, I paused to explore the crumbled nunnery ruins, Heinrich had diverted to earlier. Missing the path, I scaled a treacherous rockslide, then wove through a cavernous maze, unearthly in its silence. A miniature deserted village of stone huts was tucked deep within. Tattered strands of prayer flags fluttered mutely atop bamboo poles, while holy chortens sheltered pilgrim's tsha-tshas, clay offerings to the gods.

And for one strange moment, I swear I heard chanting; the echoes of a hundred thousand mantras wafting through the ruins, droning down deserted corridors, pounding with an eternal pulse over impenetrable boulders. A thousand sighs and heartbeats passed into another dimension.

THE WALKABOUT CHRONICLES

Chapter XIII
A Simple Act of Defiance

November 17-18

It was a grueling two-day trudge back to Tingri with Billie, Tanji and Cheryl. At first, we were forced to face dreaded Pang La again. What was merely exhausting on the hike there, became nearly bone-crunchingly impassable on our return. Yet, that night we safely returned to the abandoned stone corral. This time, in hopes of relishing the added warmth, everyone, even Tanji, huddled together under our guides' heavy canvas shelter.

Since Bad Ass had crushed our short-wave radio during his earlier mountaintop tantrum, for once in our lives we were completely out of touch with the world, left to our own vacant stares and banal mumblings.

After fixing an early dinner of (what else?) ramen, we were ready to call it a night when Tanji shocked our band into a sensory overload, nonchalantly tugging hoarded treasures from his pack. And what rare morsels they were. Corned beef and real honey! We'd had very little meat in weeks and the mere thought of sweets set our mouths trembling. Every delicacy, each bite sized victory was slowly savored, as the scrumptious flavors exploded upon our long forgotten taste buds. But even that small delirious pleasure was short-lived.

Once the sun set, even with Don Juan's furious "pumping up the jam," it remained well below freezing inside. Smoke from the dung fire blackened our already grungy faces and noxious clouds flooded every inch of the shelter.

Until finally, unable to breath, I flew into an irrepressible coughing fit which only ended after I felt a "snap" and searing pain between my now cracked ribs.

Still, our tent flaps remained closed. Heat was too precious to waste. Dung equaled life.

Though our sleeping bags had dried at Rongbuk, near zero temperatures pushed them, and us, to absolute limits. The only way to get any sleep required scrunching into a fetal position deep within our mummy cocoons.

Although uncomfortable, that seemed to be just the solution until, sometime in the middle of the night, I bolted up screaming, "Ahhh! Ah yuchh!" Like some maniac shampooing with fire ants, I flung my head in fits and feverishly ran fingers through matted hair.

"Whazza matta?" Cheryl mumbled, cocking a groggy eye and propping herself up on one elbow.

"Something just ran across my head!"

"You're dreaming," she sighed. "Go back to sleep." And with that she rolled over.

"No, I swear. It was mice!" I flopped back down, drawing the bag's hood about my face. Then I tightly cinched it, until only a tiny opening remained around my mouth. That's when a horrible thought crossed my mind.

"What if the mice find the hole and hop right in? Ahhh! Into my mouth?"

The following morning we made fast progress to Tingri with its promise of hot momos and a good night's sleep spurring us on. For hours, everything went smoothly until we reached the lower plains. Abruptly, Don Juan and Ugly whistled, barked and began herding the yaks toward Ra Chhu where we'd left the donkey cart. Trouble was, that slight detour would send us hours out of our way.

Hey, wait a minute… "We are goin' to town, aren't we?" I shouted over to Cheryl.

"Yo, Don Juan," my partner yelled, "you're taking us back to Tingri, aren't you?"

"No," he screamed, smiling, just eager just to get home. "Village."

"Wrong!" I reminded him. "You're supposed to take us all the way back to town!"

Unmoved, he just shook his yak butter slicked head. "No. Village."

Just as dead tired, Billie finally entered the debate. Cooing, "Come on now, Don Juan," she gushed, "You don't want me to carry ma pack all the way to Tingri now, do you?"

Ever since we'd met him, everyone suspected Don Juan had a soft spot for her, and now that twinkle in his soulful eyes betrayed his secret. Sneaking one glance at her pixie face, he melted, shrugging, "Okay. Tingri."

Now that the plans were in motion, Don Juan and Ugly joined an old buddy for a swig of chang out on those plains while, for some reason, Billie set-off trekking on her own toward town which rose on the horizon. She didn't seem to notice or care that we were still bound for Ra Chhu to drop off the yaks and pick up the cart. It wasn't until we pulled into that tranquil settlement that Don Juan even realized she was missing.

"Where Billie?" he cried, flustered. "Where Billie?"

"Don't know?" Cheryl replied. "Must have gone straight to town."

A look of disappointment, or was it concern, crossed his face. Swiftly piling everything from the four yaks plus the five of us onto one cramped, wobbly donkey cart, we set off trotting down the bumpy trail to Tingri. As we bounced and jiggled along at double time, I figured our Tibetan Casanova was making that special trip just to see Billie one last time. But everywhere we looked, there was no sign of our friend.

As we grew nearer the village, Don Juan became more and more frantic, crying, "Billie? Where Billie?" as he craned his head, scanning the wild tundra.

Cheryl, her motherly instincts kicking in, grew worried as well. "Wonder if she's lost? Maybe she couldn't make it across one of these streams?"

They did etch a hazardous, steel blue, meshed net of freezing water across the boggy landscape.

"Maybe she's stuck in one!"

For the next hour, all the way back to the village, we fruitlessly scoured desolate plains. It was if she'd simply fallen off the edge of the earth. That is, until we trotted into the inn's courtyard and spotted her, demurely relaxing in the shade as she sipped jasmine tea.

Greatly relieved, yet a little upset at her game of tundra hide-and-seek, Cheryl confronted our companion.

"Hey, thanks for leaving us behind…to handle all the details with your friend."

I wasn't sure if she referred to the budding romance, or the money everyone still owed the guides that she assumed Billie carried.

"Sorry," she sighed. "Just thought ya'll were headed straight back. So I walked on ahead. Unfortunately, I ended up gettin' lost and havin' to cross a stream up to my waist. Boy, talk 'bout yer instant karma!"

To complicate matters, Billie couldn't pay our patient guide after he'd ridden so far out of his way. Hans didn't give her any money and Jacob didn't give her enough. Ultimately, she borrowed the balance and paid her ardent admirer without even an appreciative, "Ghale phay!"

A jilted Don Juan mounted his wagon seat, snapped his reins and clopped into the darkness.

November 19

Tingri quickly vanished the next day, soon reduced to a distant, dusty blur shadowed beneath a pristine panorama of frosted peaks. After six days under the innkeeper's watchful eye, our wandering Sadhu was a round, brown blimp. Unless it was my imagination, a long absent bounce had returned to his step.

Cheryl, however, was less enthusiastic about leaving. Suffering aches, pains and a throbbing head from the past few days, she was contrary as a yak. Although I, too, was physically worn out, I was determined to maintain our race to the last pass before those pure snows created an ugly impasse.

"It'll soon be December," I fretted, and shuddered at the implications.

For several hours, we continued west, hobbling across arid, scrubby flatlands toward Gutsuo, a day away. Having passed up Tingri's heinous selection of black dace or mystery meat, our supplies reached a critical stage. Since Gutsuo had a military base, we counted on them to have more food to spare. Any hope of finding supplies or rest before then was pointless.

There were few villages and even fewer people—except for the two Chinese soldiers toting an automatic weapon who lurked up ahead, right in the middle of the road.

"Oh, no. They've heard what you did last night!" I half-joked. "The Colonel's sent them to bring you in!"

"What I did?" Cheryl laughed. "Everybody else was in on it, too!"

Everyone was hostile to the five Chinese soldiers at the hotel's restaurant. However, it all started innocently enough.

When we first walked in, we were a little surprised to see Billie "chatting up" the troops. She tittered and flirted with smiles and long glances exchanged on both sides of the table. She was eating up all the attention. But one thing really caught my eye. Those fellows seemed all too eager to share beers with her and it didn't take a mind reader to figure out they were seriously trying to get her drunk.

"Billie?" Cheryl whispered, "How can you act like that with them."

"Like what?" she replied, becoming defensive.

"Making 'nice-nice' with these fools."

"I am not. They jest wanna buy me a beer," she coquettishly replied. "That's all."

"But," Cheryl reminded her, "you don't drink."

"So?" she giggled, with a lighthearted toss of shoulder length hair.

"So?" I reminded her, scanning the soldiers' hungry smiles. "So what do you think these guys expect in return?"

Her jaw went slack. "Oh…"

"There must be a way we can douse water on their plans," I figured. "I owe it to Marley. If we join them, at least, Billie won't be alone. Who knows? Maybe Cheryl and I can even drink them under the table. Hey, it was worth a try."

"Say, can we buy one of those beers from you?" I cordially asked one smirking soldier. He looked over to his comrades, who nodded. So, pulling a Pi Jiu from the wooden box behind them, he passed the cool bottle to Cheryl.

"How much?" I asked, knowing ours wouldn't be free.

"It'll probably be three yuan," I figured, "the same as in that Shigatse restaurant."

Glancing toward his friends again, there was a short animated discussion. Then chuckling over their decision, he faced me and announced, "Six yuan!"

"Six?" Why, in that land of constant negotiation, that was an insult!

"Keep your beer then," Cheryl insisted.

As the bottle was pushed back and forth several times, the friendly banter soon ended and the scene grew ugly. The soldiers kept demanding yuan and we kept refusing to be taken for naive tourists.

"Well, this is one sure way to disrupt their plans," I thought.

The whole episode dragged on several tense minutes. Until finally, frustrated, the troops screeched back their chairs and stood up en masse to retreat. As if that wasn't victory enough, Cheryl stubbornly refused to move her seat and allow their officer past.

"Why should I move for him?" she quipped. "I'm tired of always having to kowtow to the army here."

There was a hush throughout the room. Then, all of a sudden, the scene took a startling, more defiant turn. Tibetan waiters and cooks, encouraged by our simple act of resistance, joined in. They made playful, mocking faces behind the backs of the hated troops and even flashed that all-too-familiar crooked little finger indiscreetly in their direction. The only thing missing was the singing of "La Marseillaise," à la Casablanca.

The soldiers had taken all they could stand. At last, both humiliated and infuriated, the Colonel and his drunken troops grabbed what was left of their Chinese beer (and honor) and slinked out of the cafe.

As soon as they were out the door, the room erupted with glee and we were treated to a fountain of Tibetan chang by a victorious kitchen staff.

As we approached the young soldiers, we forced a smile. They grinned back and waved their rifle in the air as we marched by.

"That's a good sign," I kidded. "You're lucky. They didn't recognize us." Then, casually glancing over my shoulder, I was chagrined to report, "They're following."

Figuring maybe there is something to our suspicions, we walked a little faster. They marched quicker. We picked up the cadence. The duo matched our pace. This tit-for-tat continued for several kilometers, until finally, they drew alongside. For a few tense moments, we pretended to ignore them. Then, realizing that made us seem even more suspect, I ventured to say, "Hello."

"Hello," they snickered back. At first, only that one word was uttered. Then for several frustrating kilometers, as we reluctantly kept them company, one soldier haltingly tried to communicate. Asking nearly unintelligible questions, in turn, I offered vague answers.

"Where you go?"

"Down the road."

"Where you come from?"

"That way."

"What village?"

"Very far."

The other soldier just nervously fingered his rifle.

Eventually, weary of the suspense, I whispered to Cheryl, "Let's take Sadhu over there for some water."

"But he just had some…"

"He's…thirsty…again!" I announced, winking. "Bye now!" I shouted with false bravado, waving to the troops.

Well, of all days to be contrary, our horse just stood beside that stream, which only proves you can lead a Sadhu to water but you can't make him drink.

Meanwhile, our two unwelcome companions marched two hundred meters ahead. Then halting, one fell down on one knee and began shooting at some distant, unknown target.

As usual, that only spooked Sadhu more and we had to virtually drag our gun-shy gelding up the road past the gunfire.

"At least," I reminded Cheryl as we neared, "they're not shooting at us."

Reaching them, they ceased fire and resumed their uneasy, uninvited armed escort. One fellow, the soldier shouldering the automatic, marched on our right flank while the other brought up the rear. As we drew closer to the military barracks ahead, we grew queasier with each step. Conversation died. Our guards became sullen. And the suspense built.

We stopped to pull water bottles from our saddle net. They waited. We paused to tie boots. They stopped. It was unnerving. That cat and mouse game continued for two…long…hours while we sweated bullets, concocting any reason to stop. We hoped to God, for once, they'd continue without us.

Until finally, we paused to study our useless map one last time, to stall, to secretly wish them away.

Call it magic, call it fate, or call it that mysterious force that had watched over us since our odyssey began. But when we eventually, cautiously, glanced up, I swear the two had simply vanished.

By late afternoon, just as we passed the ghostly ruins of an ancient, once palatial city on the windswept plain, a shout rang out from behind. "Oh no, not again!" I cringed.

Startled, wheeling around, we detected a surreal image silently bobbing up and down the road. Experience told us it could only be one thing. Nearing, the vision glided to a halt.

"Hey, ya'll!" Billie coughed.

"What are you doing here?" Cheryl asked, knowing she had planned to wait at the Tingri hotel for Marley to come down off the mountain.

The capricious cyclist pulled off her dusty goggles. "Well, I started thinkin'," she wheezed. "Why stick around till the 25th when I can be relaxin' in Kathmandu in three days?"

"Three days?" I mused... "It'll take us another week or more at this rate."

"What about Tanji? Did he leave too?"

"Did he pay for another oxcart ride?" is what my partner meant to say.

"Get this...Tanji actually refused a ride in a truck all the way back to Lhasa!" Billie exclaimed, shaking her head. "Ya'll believe it?"

"Incredible!" Free truck rides were as rare as free Pi Jius, and no amount of smiling and flirting would help.

"Yea," Billie smirked, "he said he was too tired to ride!"

"Too tired?" Cheryl groaned in disbelief. "He should try walking."

"Well, I gotta go, ya'll," Billie declared, remounting her well-worn seat. "But I'm sure we'll run into each other in Kathmandu."

"Right!" I was anxious to find shelter before it got too late. Then, remembering N.D., I reminded our buddy, "Hey, don't forget to deliver that letter, all right?"

"Don't worry!" she assured me, pedaling off.

Turning, we continued our forced march into the wind, just as the predictable, sandblasting mid-afternoon squalls surfaced.

Unlike other days, I had this intense feeling of dread, like something horrible was about to happen. Looking out to the horizon, my fears were easily confirmed. Ominously black, snow-bulging clouds gathered and headed straight for us; apocalyptic horsemen galloping down off the icy mountains.

"Time's run out," I thought. "And it's more than the weather. It's us. Our systems are shutting down. We haven't had more than a taste of protein in weeks. Diarrhea drains my energy. Every day, it gets harder to hit the trail. Harder to hobble another thirty-five kilometers (twenty-two miles) on aching knees. Harder to choke on dust through sun-scabbed noses and peeling lips. Harder to sleep on stranger's floors. Harder to pantomime and deal with rejection one more time. Harder to stay disgustingly filthy. Harder to remain positive about what we're doing..."

While I privately wallowed in my own self-doubts, Cheryl toppled by the roadside. "Damn you! I told you I didn't want to hike today!"

Why was her pain always my fault?

"Look," I reasoned, trying to stay calm, "as I explained before, we have to keep movin'." Couldn't she see it? Couldn't she see what was moving in, right now? Losing my patience, I screamed back, "We're runnin' out of time!"

"I'm so tired of bein' miserable."

For the first time in our arduous journey, overcome with acute exhaustion, hunger and fear, Cheryl sobbed.

"I know," I whispered, trying to comfort her without breaking down myself. "I know how you feel."

"What are we doing?" she whimpered. "Why are we out here?"

I'd asked myself those very same questions so many times. Yet only one thing could ease her pain; that same word she'd reminded me of so frequently before.

"Faith," I whispered, gazing into her mournful eyes. "We must have faith."

Gently gathering her fragile body in my arms, I pulled her up as together we stumbled toward a cluster of buildings a kilometer ahead, hoping to God that it was either a road crew house or hotel.

Spotting the building's imposing facade, Cheryl quipped, "What do you think? Holiday Inn?" as she smeared tears in charcoal trails across her dirt crusted face.

"Laughter's always a good sign," I thought. "She's already seeing the humor in our desperation."

"I don't know? Maybe Motel 6, " I replied. "Are the lights on?"

It was obvious that the stark complex squatting beneath the stark hill was neither. "More likely," I thought, "it's a military base since twin scarlet flags framed its gateway."

Squinting, we detected a delegation standing in the middle of the road across from the compound. A road block?

However, drawing nearer, we were relieved to discover our welcoming committee was just a group of kids playing and a plump Tibetan lady personally enticing guests to stay in her lodge. A hand-lettered sign, in three languages, dubbed the concrete bunker, "The New Restaurant and Hotel."

"When it's old," I wondered, "will they change the name? To what? 'The Old New Restaurant and Hotel?'"

Our timing couldn't have been better. With little ceremony or the usual meddling, we settled into another brightly daubed, concrete room boasting standard Spartan amenities.

Later, while Cheryl contentedly dozed off and our candle melted, forming a milky pool on the cold stone floor, I offered a silent prayer for strength…since we, too, were fading, weak as our candle's dying light.

From *Yak Butter Blues: A Tibetan Trek of Faith* by Brandon Wilson © Reprinted by permission of the author.

Questions and Answers

1. What compels you to walk?

It is my passion. For me, walking is reconnecting with the earth, letting go, discovering, and in truth be found. It is a chance to reconnect with nature, your soul and the universe. Like Henry David Thoreau's noble quest to "live life deliberately," walking forces me to slow down and reduce life to its essentials.

The ultimate beauty of walking, of "traveling deliberately" one foot in front of the other, is the opportunity to observe and wallow in the minute details of everyday life surrounding us. Trekking is time devoted purely to the present. There is no past, no future, only now. Your world is your breath, a heartbeat reverberating in your ears; a Zen-like placing of each footstep along a well-trod path others have walked over the centuries. It is the heady aroma drifting from fields of thyme; the drone of bees in a sun-dappled forest. It is autumn frost blanketing a multi-hued trail; the rough grain of your walking stick rubbing against your palm.

By traveling one step at a time, we can revel in the life surrounding us, the gritty beauty others miss by barreling through. There's time to share a moment in peoples' lives, their hopes, their triumphs, their fears, and to truly live the path leading to the destination.

Hiking is traveling lightly. Just as you leave worldly belongings behind, on the trail there is a gentle unraveling of fears, emotions, desires and demons as you surrender unwanted psychic baggage to the universe.

Walking is a purging of the soul. It is a thousand small moments. It is unexpected acts of kindness and fleeting revelations. It is surrendering to fate, spontaneity, absolute unknowns, and small arrows that mark your way.

"Maybe we're all Forest Gumps in life, running away from demons in our past that are chasing us until we rid ourselves of our braces or chains that bind us. Only then can we sail on down the road." ~ from *Along the Templar Trail*

2. Do you experience instances while you are walking when your mind is somewhere off the trail and on its own journey?

Constantly. I call it "traveling outside while traveling within." Walking is a solitary journey through a portal of perception. It is a chance to reconnect, to listen, to face your inner self, to actively commune with a greater power. It is a refuge from the din and clutter of the outside world. It is a unique dimension to appreciate life's wonder. Alone on a trail, I have time to deal with my thoughts, to listen, and then to accept, validate, reject, or re-think my reasoning objectively from a distance. It's often a series of meditative moments. It's also my most creative time. For me, walking becomes "a trampoline for the mind," allowing it to bounce unfettered from thought to feeling. It enables a psychological cleansing and healing—and promotes inner peace.

"The peaceful Kirsch Way (Bavaria) was Ronald Reagan-straight and we followed it until we reached Lager Allee. Conifers lined both sides of the dirt trail and only two cyclists passed in as many hours. Isolated, I wore the solitude like a comfortable cloak. It was a primeval sanctuary, the most holy of cathedrals. I embraced its cool darkness and wrapped its filtered light around me like a shroud. It was perfection. Allowing introspection and quiet contemplation, it reminded me of an omnipresent magic in the world, a force of never-ending birth and death, creation and destruction." ~ from *Along the Templar Trail*

3. How do you manage to stay physically and emotionally healthy during long and arduous journeys?

Health on the trail, often elusive, depends on conditioning, planning and a certain amount of luck. Physical conditioning is certainly essential. I don't hope to advance from couch potato to happy wanderer overnight—no matter how mentally motivated I am. I hit the gym or take off frequently across nearby terrain that's as similar as possible to where I'm trekking. I start slowly and then increase the distance, speed and the amount I carry. An hour on the trail at home does little to prepare for eight to ten hours carrying a full pack over mountains. Next, I practice packing light, carrying no more than 10% my body weight. I carry the load. Then I pack lighter. This is essential to creating a successful (and enjoyable) expedition. Next, I plan as much as possible. Nothing spoils a long-distance trek faster than getting lost due to bad maps, non-waterproof waterproof gear, running out of supplies, unanticipated severe weather—or gun-toting soldiers). Eventually, once on the trail, I become more in tune with my body. Although each day brings uncertainties and changes in weather and terrain, I remind myself to adapt to these and resist giving it 110% every moment. Remaining healthy requires flexibility. Although tenacity is a treasured asset, the western practice of forcing my way through challenges can get in the way of sound judgment and very survival. Pacing is everything. Finally, I save room in my pack for an extra amount of humor and optimism, my most useful tools. In some ways, each day I create my own reality.

More than anything: "Long thru-treks are much more than climbing another mountain. They're an exercise in concentration, focus, and a chance to re-affirm your own worth and sense of self. They're empowering. Each day is a challenge. Some days, every step is one. As in life, it's mentally important to celebrate the triumphs of the little steps—and not to hold ourselves back waiting for the big victories." ~ from *Over the Top & Back Again: Hiking X the Alps*

4. Please share a high and a low period that you experienced during your walkabouts.

High: One of the highest moments I've experienced trekking began as one of the lowest. To recreate the route of the First Crusades, my friend "Emile" and I had set out to establish the 4500-kilometer Templar Trail on a trek from France to Jerusalem. Although well-marked paths already existed to two of the most important pilgrimage sites in Christendom, Santiago de Compostella in Spain and to Rome, Jerusalem needed an established route for future pilgrims to walk in peace, regardless of nationality, culture or religion. We left in April as we at first followed French canals until we connected with the source of the Danube in Bavaria and then traced it via the

Danube Radweg all the way to Budapest. Quite unexpectedly, by the time we reached Belgrade, Serbia, all hell broke loose in the Middle East. Hezbollah sent missiles across the border into Israel, bombing the airport. Lebanese civilians were being evacuated to Cyprus. Folks whispered it might be the beginning of World War Three.

Adventure is one thing. But to deliberately meander across a war zone where there's a price on westerner's heads borders on lunacy. For one long day, we debated whether to postpone our journey. Finally, after painful deliberation, we decided to continue as far as Istanbul and reassess our chances and the world situation then. Much unlike the original thousands of troops of the First Crusades, we traveled alone. Two fellows with backpacks and unsupported in any visible way, we'd planned to continue trekking more than a thousand kilometers across Turkey, Syria and Jordan to the Holy City. How would the locals see us? Would they greet us as two peace pilgrims—or as an infidel threat?

By the time we reached Istanbul, the conflict in Israel was far from resolved but we'd reached a decision. Emile, already suffering from his diabetes and dehydration, would return to France. I'd press on—alone.

As I wandered closely observed through Turkish villages, miraculously, my initial fear of violence disappeared with each frequent cup of tea offered by curious locals.

My most surprising experience was on a particularly tough day while trudging thru the desert plains of central Turkey. It had been more than ninety degrees since dawn. I was down to one cup of water with no village in sight. Just as life appeared bleakest, I spotted a cattle trough. A couple of men stood nearby. So, I decided to fill my water bottle, just in case. I figured contracting giardia was better than dying from dehydration.

Approaching, I asked, "Can you drink this water?" They shrugged. "Well, can you please tell me if there's a restaurant or petrol station nearby?"

"Why, are you hungry?"

"More thirsty than hungry," I admitted, dipping my red bandana into the foul water.

"Come, follow us," one replied, and they led me to some olive trees where four other men of varying ages and two boys sat around a virtual banquet. They motioned me to join them, and then presented me with half a watermelon and plastic fork. I was bowled over. I'd fantasized about melon for days. Still, this was just the beginning of a feast for a man literally starving in the desert. Bread, feta cheese, olives, tomatoes and cucumbers all filled my plate. Meanwhile, the men were interested in hearing what brought me to the middle of nowhere. I was happy to fill them in on all the details of my peace walk between bites.

As my story was translated from man to man, a couple exclaimed "Bravo," while others grinned and enthusiastically applauded. I felt embarrassed, humbled, and yet pleased my message of peace stuck home.

We chatted an hour in broken English until eventually they loaded cups, plates and silverware into their van. I stood to shake hands with each of them and asked, "What about this food?"

The father calmly replied, "We leave it here."

"Why, I couldn't eat all this." It was more than I'd eaten all week.

"No, it is for you," he said with finality.

Once strangers, we solemnly shook hands as friends and wished each other "Salaam," or "Peace," before they piled into their van and headed down the road.

I was like the family dog left alone at the Thanksgiving Day table. I didn't know what to eat first, but after thirty minutes in the shade of that olive grove, I did a decent job—and never feared Muslim hospitality again.

Low: Often when traveling, you have the false impression of existing within a protective bubble. Nothing could possibly happen to you because, well, you've come so far. That can be fatal. In 1992, when we trekked across Tibet from Lhasa to Kathmandu on an ancient pilgrimage route, everything was an unknown. The Chinese called it an "impossible" journey from the start. The border had been closed to independent travelers for decades. It only opened briefly just the day before we arrived in Kathmandu and then in the opposite direction. Perhaps this serendipity was the first sign our journey was meant to be. Per their requirements, we flew to Lhasa, took their propaganda-laden tour, and then started the long 1100-kilometer trek back to Nepal. Over the next thirty-five days with Sadhu, our tsampa-munching Tibetan packhorse, we progressed slowly. Relying on outdated maps, we hobbled from village to village, begging like monks for places to sleep with local families, scavenging food, and fearing entrapment by the authorities or impending November snows.

Although reaching Kathmandu and presenting our Lhasa prayer flags to the King of Nepal was our ultimate goal, climbing to Mt. Everest was sure tempting. Who could resist? We'd run into four younger bicyclists en route from Chengdu to Kathmandu. One evening as we shared steaming momos at Tingri's rugged roadside inn, they mentioned a hike they'd planned to Mt. Everest. Would we like to join them?

Half of me leapt at the prospect. That was a dream trek. However, my more sensible side weighed our options. If we diverted four days to Rongbuk Monastery and basecamp, we risked the possibility of running out of time. Already snow blanketed the surrounding Himalayan peaks. Would we have time to hike there and back to Tingri? And would we then have another two weeks to reach the lower elevations of Nepal before a blizzard hit and closed the road and trails until spring?

Cheryl and I decided to meditate on an answer—and what better place than a 14,000' Tingri hilltop festooned with colorful prayer flags. Transfixed as we faced Chomolungma, the Mother Goddess, we were afraid to speak, reluctant to break her spell.

Suddenly, there was a sharp "PING!" Then another "PING!" whizzed by. Still another whistled past. Someone was shooting at us! We both lay frozen a few seconds, an eternity. Then we realized whoever was firing hopefully had no idea we were up there. We screamed and hurled rocks over the crest until the bullets ceased. Crawling to the mountain's edge, we spotted two armed Chinese soldiers scrambling up the hill toward us. Frantic, we looked at each other. As improbable as it might sound now, we calmly sat back down in lotus position and stared at Mt. Everest, meditating on its strength. Its image was the one I most wanted etched in my mind, if the worst happened.

Within seconds, a panting Chinese officer approached stuttering, "Sorry, I shoot at birds. Many birds," he giggled. "Sport." That great barren plain was once alive with antelopes, gazelles, blue sheep and wild asses. Today, pilgrims and birds (and one ass) was all that remained. But we had our answer. We'd risk it all to trek to Mt. Everest.

5. Have you experienced an important Encounter that somehow changed the direction of your journey?

While in Tibet, one of our few luxuries was a small propane stove used to heat water for tea or tsampa, a barley flour gruel, each morning. After a particularly strenuous day at nearly 14,000 feet, choked in dust, with thin air and freezing temperatures, we finally stumbled into a roadside guesthouse.

Wary, not quite knowing what to expect, the innkeeper led us to a room garishly bathed in bright reddish orange paint, ringed by a band of cosmology symbols. A welcoming statue of the Chinese goddess of mercy greeted us from a bureau; a dour portrait of Mao, father of the genocidal Cultural Revolution, glared from a distant corner.

"Famished, Cheryl began to unpack while I started fixing a simple dinner of dehydrated burritos.

"Hey, have you seen our fuel bottle?" I routinely asked.

"No, isn't it strapped to your pack?"

"No, not here…"

"Well, then it must have fallen off," she sighed, unfazed, pulling out our cook kit. "That's okay. We still have a spare." Then she realized the real problem. "Oh, no!"

"Yeah, our only fuel pump's on that bottle. We're sunk!"

With its loss, there was no way to cook food for the rest of our journey. We couldn't even boil water to drink or add to our remaining foil dehydrated food pouches. Of all the things we could have lost, that hurt us the most. It was a blow at our very survival.

"From now on," I lamented, "we'll be even more dependent on the kindness of our hosts."

At just that moment, there was a hesitant rap at the door. As I stood to answer, it swung open and the manager's shy wife shuffled in, carrying a thermos of boiling water.

"Our luck, our lives, had become just that magical." ~ from *Yak Butter Blues*

This was a brick-to-the-head moment for us. We were meant to be there.

Brandon and Mount Everest. *Photograph courtesy of Brandon Wilson.*

Biography

Brandon Wilson is long distance trekker, Lowell Thomas Gold Award-winning author/photographer, explorer, and peace pilgrim. He has explored nearly 100 countries, including making an African transect from London to Cape Town. However, over decades, he's been especially passionate about hiking historic long-distance pilgrim trails. In 1992, Brandon and his wife Cheryl became the first Western couple to trek the 1100-kilometer trail from Lhasa, Tibet to Kathmandu. Then he focused on Europe, trekking the Camino de Santiago Frances (twice) across northern Spain, then the Via de la Plata from Seville, and next the Camino Catalan and Camino Aragonés from Barcelona. Brandon was the first American to traverse the 1850-kilometer Via Francigena from Canterbury, England to Rome. In 2006, he hiked and founded the 4500-kilometer Templar Trail, recreating the route of the First Crusades as a path of peace from France to Jerusalem. Later, in 2009, Brandon and Cheryl trekked the Via Alpina along the backbone of the Alps across eight countries from Trieste to Monaco, climbing the equivalent of 12 Mt. Everests. Most recently, he hiked the ancient St. Olav's Way for the second time across Norway and Sweden on an Explorers Club Flag expedition. Brandon is a Fellow of The Explorers Club and was recently knighted by the Sovereign Hospitaller Order of St. John of Jerusalem/Knights of Malta.

"After I view the moon my departing shadow followed me home."
~Basho

"People do no decide to become extraordinary.
They decide to accomplish extraordinary things."
~Sir Edmund Hillary

Erin McKittrick

A man on foot, on horseback or on a bicycle will see more, feel more, enjoy more in one mile than the motorized tourists can in a hundred miles.
~ Edward Abbey

Umnak Island

Waves of wind rippled silver-green as we strolled away from Nikolski's scant cluster of buildings, setting cottongrass tufts head-banging to its rhythm. A small lake blew sideways across our path. A small bird blew sideways between my son's legs. Sand stung our eyelids.

But this was a warmish summer day. The wind was nothing any resident would notice. It was as mild an introduction as you get, in the Aleutians. So I told my daughter she shouldn't walk in the lake if she wanted warm feet. And I told my son to turn his face from the blowing sand. And I told myself this was only day one of forty-nine—surely we'd soon be transformed into a well-oiled expedition machine.

Umnak Island is part of the Fox Islands in the Aleutian chain, one step farther west than Unalaska. I'd flown to its southwestern end from Dutch Harbor, with my husband, kids, and mother (expedition age range: 4-61), planning to paddle and hike our way back to Dutch on a meandering 300 mile path.

Why? Because it's the Aleutians! Because I feel an irresistible pull to glaciers and volcanoes, to storm-washed coasts and tumultuous pasts, to shifting climates and shifting seasons. A pull to places that transform. My son Katmai shares his name with a famous volcanic eruption. My daughter Lituya shares hers with a famous tsunami. So we embraced our small disasters—and set out to traverse the island.

Umnak Island smells like the salty decay of washed up kelp. It smells like sweet flowers and crushed grass. It smells like cow piss. It smells like a wild 700 square mile barnyard. A dozen cows had staked out a lee on the beach, behind cliffs painted monkey flower yellow. Their brown and white hides rippled with muscle as they pounded away, leaving us their campsite. The cows honked like geese with bronchitis. The kids mistook Hig's snoring for a cow.

There were twenty-two villages on Umnak Island when the Russians arrived in the middle of the 1700s, home to some portion of the Aleutians' 15,000-18,000 Unangan people. There are twenty-two people now, in the single village of Nikolski. There are somewhere around 7,500 cows.

The trails we followed were nearly all theirs. Hoof-terraced switchbacks cut into a sandy slope, leaving archaeological history crumbling out beside them. Sea urchin spines poured into my hand, layer upon layer of fragile green shards, shot through with fish bones, charcoal, and a bone harpoon. Whale bones stuck out. A layer of pumice sliced through the center of the midden—one tumultuous interruption in those layers of life.

Umnak is a place of tumultuous interruptions. It was hard to imagine this hoof-pocked island before the cows got to it in the late 1940s. It was just as hard to imagine the 12,000 sheep that preceded the cows, and the bustle of WWII military life that sprawled across the island in roads and airports and quonset huts, shipping out the people who were here before them. All those sheep are gone now, disappeared along with the military as the cows spread out across their former range, as the ranchers set up shop in the former Fort Glenn, and as some of the people made it back.

Of course the volcanoes were building and transforming Umnak long before the Unangan people arrived 9,000 years ago. A few days from Nikolski, we climbed through the fog that spilled from Mt. Recheschnoi, where a scant cover of plants crept across a black stubble of lava rock. In the distance, the hills steamed. Our route traced a dot-to-dot path between the geothermal vents and springs that dotted the middle of the island.

Geyser Bight:
Sulfurous steam shrouded my family, revealing them in foggy and discontinuous pieces—two tiny silhouettes linked hand in hand with Hig's larger form. He guided them carefully. It was easy to imagine that a wrong step here could send you to the center of the earth. In the middle of Umnak, the ground roared. Hissing jets of steam, spat from puddles and flowed away in searing streams, past cauldrons of bubbling red mud. Geysers erupted every minute or two, then gulped their boiling water back down. The mountainside around them was an unbound riot of energy and color—of lush ferns and tall grass and sphagnum so thick that when I plunged in my hands they were swallowed nearly to my elbows. In the threads of that moss I could feel the heat of the earth.

Geyser Bight has the only geysers in Alaska, and some of the hottest and most extensive geothermal springs in the state. Cow bones turned to chalky dust in a crusted white pool. In another, we placed our pot of couscous, boiling dinner with five minutes of geothermal energy. Handy, on an island with no trees for firewood. In a milder pool, the kids and I wriggled on our elbows, dragging naked bellies across the smooth slimy mats of green and brown algae, like we were ancient creatures wallowing in the primordial ooze.

Volcanoes remake the world. When you walk over them, you can't help imagining how everything transforms, your mind swooping through past and future. Their bulk seems so imposing, but their skin—that rough unvegetated rock—so naked and brand new. Compared to most mountains, volcanoes are babies.

Okmok Volcano:
Grayish water sliced through shelves of black scoria, and shot down waterfalls of gray. I clutched Lituya's hand, holding on to the stretched out cuff of her too-big long johns. She was my baby cow, pretend-munching the last of the grass on the volcano, well above where the real cows traveled. We'd gone nearly six and a half miles already

that day. At four years old, after a week and a half of travel, she had suddenly transformed into a fast and capable hiker. We crunched over dirty snow. We crunched over hills of volcanic rocks spit over the 3000 foot rim of Okmok caldera, until we stood at the top, socked by the cold wet wind and by the prospect of the fifty foot cliff interrupting the long slope between us and the crater floor.

The mist was so thick that it swirled in the beam of my headlamp, forming veils of tiny white droplets. Our paddles became shovels, digging a flattish square through hills of sharp black scoria on the slope below the crater rim because it was late and we couldn't descend in time, and we had to sleep somewhere. The rocks covered snow left over from before the 2008 eruption of Okmok. The snow was older than my kids.

I crawled into my sleeping bag, balancing on a sleeping pad blown into an awkward balloon from a strange manufacturing defect, and scanning a blown up map of topo lines on a tiny phone screen. Is it even possible to get down?

The kids giggled from their sleeping bags. That was when I knew we really had transformed into a well-oiled expedition machine. Not because we could suddenly descend cliffs or hike twenty miles in a day (we couldn't), but because every one of us took the uncomfortable uncertainty in stride.

We found a way around the cliff the next morning. Crater lakes glowed milky turquoise under a glowering gray sky, as we scrambled through a maze of badlands and gullies—ash made solid, rivers made dry, monster-shaped lava boulders set on hills of sand. It looked like a cross between the desert southwest and Mordor.

Around 8,000 years ago, Okmok spewed out cubic kilometers of molten material, destroying all life to the coast and burying one of the islands oldest village sites. 2400 years ago it did it again. 1000 years ago a giant crater lake overflowed, wiping out everything downstream in an apocalyptic flood. Seven years ago, it turned the green caldera floor to an ashy badlands, sending the cattle ranchers scrambling to flee by helicopter.

As we reached the end of Umnak Island, we visited the ranch, where they were preparing to round up thousands of cows by helicopter. They gave us a long 2x4, and we prepared to transform a trio of packrafts into a nearly-untippable tied-together contraption that would take us through the four miles of currents and rips between Umnak and Unalaska Islands. Transformation, and adventure, continued.

Questions and Answers

1. What compels you to walk?

In the 21st century, we have maps, GPS, and satellite photos where you can pick out your own house from space. There's nothing new to explore. That's fine. There never was. Humans have been wandering since humans evolved, and the European explorers of a few hundred years ago rarely found any "new lands." They went out to discover what they didn't know before—what they didn't even know was out there to learn.

I am a modern explorer. I usually devise my expeditions as a long, bold (often wiggly) line across the map, where I start at point A and end up, some number of months later, at point B. This is, on the face of it, a silly and pointless exercise. First I have to arrange travel to point A, then home again from point B, neither of which are places I particularly need to go. No one pays me to do it, and when I arrive, I have won no race, set no record, or achieved any particular glory. The reward is in the places in between.

I am careful to see them all. I never skip over the places in between. Not the ugly ones, the hard ones, or the boring ones. I walk, or paddle, every step of the way, even if those steps take me through an urban strip mall or a hellacious devils' club bushwhack. At that human speed, I notice things. At human speed, I meet people. At human speed, I learn.

I learn where the bears walk, how the winds blow, when the alders died, or when the king salmon stopped running. I learn archaeology, history, ecology, geology, and politics. My role is to be a scientist and a storyteller. To go out there with as open a mind as possible, learn what I can, and come back and share it with the world.

2. Do you experience instances while you are walking when your mind in somewhere off the trail and on its own journey?

I travel with saber-toothed tigers, magical fairies, and improbable flying machines. I travel with children. And while a solo walker might have a large space of time just to think, a parent walker spends a lot of time talking—and even more time listening. Sometimes it's practical. I'll coax the kids along, or give tips about the best way to negotiate a creek crossing or a stretch of slippery boulders. Sometimes it's educational. Each of us will point out interesting pieces of the natural world, and our discussions will range across the expanse of all our knowledge. Other times it's imaginative. I'll pretend with the kids, listen to their monologues about castles and fairies, or tell a story from my own imagination.

When we walk, all we have is our minds. No books, no internet, no way to look up a fact or escape into someone else's world. It makes our own mental worlds—the independent world of daydreaming, or the shared world of games and stories and passed-down facts—richer.

3. How do you manage to stay physically and emotionally healthy during long and arduous journeys?

More than ten thousand of years ago, people sewed themselves clothes that could withstand an Alaskan climate, carried all the tools they really needed, and headed out across the land. People did this all over the world, with old folks and little kids included, across all of human history. In the grand scheme of things, our long and arduous journeys are normal. My body is better adapted to walk hundreds or thousands of miles than it is to type this essay. I try to remember that, when my shoulders ache and my knuckles fester with devils club spines, and my feet are cold soggy lumps.

We move slowly. It's one of the best protections—against accident, injury, or plain old overuse. It's an even better protection against stupid or dangerous mistakes. Our journeys sound extreme to some folks, but we are not record-setters, nor elite athletes. We give ourselves time, so we can think things through.

With caution and luck, no one in my family has ever had a serious injury in the wilderness, in sixteen years of wandering. With less caution and less luck, we have scraped or poked many knees and fingers, and caught many mild communicable diseases. The latter is especially a problem in the winter, when we visit small villages, give talks in the school, and catch every cold in the entire school district before we head out again. I have no recourse for this, other than to be patient, wait it out, and know that the human connection is worth the sneezing.

4. Please share a high and a low period that you experienced during your walkabouts.

Picture snow-capped volcanoes, and long grassy hills, sloping down to broad sandy beach. The beach is steaming. You take off your torn, worn, hiking shoe, and dip a toe in. This is the Bering Sea—a pool of cold that reaches almost to the Arctic Circle, and brings a wash of frigid water down to the Aleutian Islands, where you are standing. But it feels warm. Hot springs bubble up beneath the sand. You lay in a hot-tub tidepool, eye level with the ocean swells, lounging and soaking and listening to your kids giggle. You wonder how many years it has been since another human was here. The geology seems almost like magic.

Picture the wind, screaming out of a long bay, white-capped and wild. Picture the misty rain, sneaking through the gaps in your worn-out raingear. You eat, as slowly as you can manage, your lunch of a single pilot bread cracker. You are almost out of food, and there is no way to get more without launching into that splashing surf, struggling against that windswept ocean, camping in a downpour, and then walking miles through belly-high grass the following day.

Those two scenes were part of the same journey. And while they were weeks apart, they could have easily happened a day apart. A journey is built of wonder and challenge, and the mood rockets back and forth like a ping pong ball, bouncing between highs and lows. You can't have one without the other. I don't think you'd appreciate the high points nearly as much without the challenge of reaching them. I regret the occasional stupid or dangerous mistake, but I don't regret the low points. Discomfort is part of the deal.

5. Have you experienced an important Encounter that somehow changed the direction of your journey?

In 2008, my husband and I set our packrafts in the muddy swirls of Cook Inlet, Alaska, and jumped in. Ice floes spun in the rushing tidal currents, crashing together, crumbling around us, closing off any hope of a way through. It was well below zero, and ice formed on our paddles as we struggled through the maze. We encountered the ice. So much ice that we feared we'd be trapped—frozen into it in our tiny rubber boats. We turned around, paddled back out of Knik Arm, landed in Anchorage, and changed direction. The new direction took us several days skiing up the coast to a better crossing point, and several days skiing back down to reconnect with our original plan.

That wasn't the first time I've encountered crushing ice that forced me to change my direction. I've also encountered, and deviated to avoid, cliffs, rapids, thin ice, thick brush, precarious rock piles, bears, and any number of other obstacles. Changing direction has to be part of the plan.

Yet the most important encounters are those we've had with people. Hundreds of them, all over Alaska, in every stage and circumstance of life. These encounters rarely change a trip plan. I leave someone's house, and generally continue walking in the exact same direction I was before. In total, however, they have shifted the direction of my life.

In the dark fall and winter of 2007, when Hig and I were walking to Alaska, we spent time in the little towns of Gustavus and Cordova, and the hospitality of those communities made me realize I could live in a small off-the-road-system town myself. Across all our years of walking, I've met a lot of people very different than me, with very different beliefs. Meeting them in person (as opposed to just reading or watching a media caricature) makes me realize that most people I disagree with are smart and thoughtful—worth reaching out to and worth learning from.

Photograph courtesy of Erin McKittrick.

Biography

Erin McKittrick grew up hiking the trails of Washington State's Cascade Mountains with her family, swimming in icy alpine lakes, catching newts, and fashioning dolls from sticks and lichen. Maybe she was crazy even then, but insanity needs good company. In college, she met her husband Hig (Bretwood Higman), and together their dreams grew wild. When Erin graduated from college in 2001, the pair hiked 800 miles down the Alaska Peninsula. In 2007, 24 hours after Hig finished graduate school, they handed the key to their landlord, left their Seattle apartment, and spent the next year walking, paddling, and skiing 4000 miles to the Aleutian Islands. By the end of the journey, Erin was one month pregnant with her first child.

Her son Katmai was born in 2009, followed by a daughter Lituya in 2011. They hiked the arctic coast, spent two months on the icy expanse of Malaspina glacier, and traced the 800 mile coastline of Alaska's Cook Inlet, all by human power. They skied the sea ice of the Seward Peninsula, as winter was breaking into spring, and as summer was turning into fall, they paddled current-swirled passes in the Aleutian Islands. By the time the kids were six and four years old they were veterans of five wilderness expeditions across Alaska, ranging from one to four months each. The kids traveled over 2000 miles themselves—strapped to a parent's back, paddled in a packraft, pulled in a sled, and finally skiing and hiking on their own two feet. Erin's journeys have been chronicled in three books: *A Long Trek Home, 4000 Miles by Boot, Raft, and Ski*, *Small Feet, Big Land: Adventure, Home, and Family on the Edge of Alaska*, and *Mud Flats and Fish Camps: 800 Miles around Alaska's Cook Inlet* (Mountaineers Books, due out in Spring 2017) as well as a children's picture book *My Coyote Nose and Ptarmigan Toes: An Almost-True Alaskan Adventure*.

"...it occurred to me that every single road in the world is somebody's neighborhood, part of somebody's everyday routine and comfort zone. Why, I then reasoned, couldn't I be perfectly comfortable walking down their road?"
~Polly Letofsky

Polly Letofsky

Be yourself; who else is better qualified?

Photograph courtesy of Polly Letofsky.

3mph: The Adventures of One Woman's Walk Around the World

It was March 28, 2002, a typical one-hundred-ten degree day near Kondhali, India, when Shankar, the temporary crew support I'd hired to help me survive the last half of India, pulled up next to me. He said he'd be right back, he was just going to go fill up the car with petrol. "Please, please, don't go," I begged, leaning through his window. "Whenever you leave me, the men harass me and chase me and hassle me. Please don't go!"

"Oh stop, you are being silly. They are very friendly to you. You will be fine. I will be five minutes."

"Hurry!" I yelled after him as he disappeared around the bend.

At that moment, a truck roared around the same corner and headed in my direction. The truck was so overloaded with its cargo of oranges that its burlap tarp was bulging over the sides. When he hit that curve it sent him into a wobble that caught him up on two wheels and sent him careening out of control. I stopped walking and watched as he skidded to the left, to the right, to the left and SMACK into a cow. The cow came flyyyyyying through the air right toward me.

Oh good God, I thought. Please don't let me die like this! How will my parents take the news that I was killed by a flying cow? I threw my hands over my eyes and ducked.

The cow dropped a few yards ahead of me and bounced on the blacktop.

Dead.

I stood with my mouth agape, unable to move, though grateful that my obituary didn't include farm animals.

Within seconds I watched as the Hindus raced out of the village to the dead cow, weeping, praying, grieving over Her Holiness.

The Muslims were right behind them brandishing butcher knives, and I watched as they tore into the cow, blood pouring into the street. Don't look, don't look, don't look! I told myself. But I had to look, and I watched the Muslims lifting slabs of cow onto the backs of their bikes and strapping them down with bungee cords. My stomach came up to my throat and I started gagging.

I tiptoed through the blood puddles dry heaving past the dead cow and made my way into the village. Immediately on my left was a group of women holding down a goat by all four limbs, and I started talking out loud to myself, Don't look, don't look, don't look! But I had to look, and at that very moment, a woman cut the throat of the poor goat in what appeared to be a religious sacrificial goat killing.

The shock of it, while still in the throes of hurling from the cow, launched me into another bout of dry heaves, but I didn't have a moment to recover. A group of men had just spotted me and started yelling, "Madam! Madam! One moment, please, Madam!" Now all the men in the village knew there was an unaccompanied woman in their midst and sprang out of the woodwork. I picked up my pace, burst into a sprint, running through the village, gagging, blood on my shoes, the dead cow, the poor goat, I might faint, oh God, don't let me faint. I turned around to judge my progress and saw what appeared to be every male in the village—along with a parade of goats, cows, chickens and stray dogs too—running after me, "Madam! Madam! One moment, please, Madam!"

At the far end of the village a truck had just plunged off a bridge. Its two back tires caught the railing, leaving it swinging above the creek below. The men (and ensuing goats, cows, chickens, and stray dogs) immediately changed their focus and ran down to the riverbank to assist the driver as I continued running/heaving/puking out of town and finally slowed to catch my breath.

Within seconds Shankar drove up beside me, "You see?" he said, oblivious. "You are just fine."

Had this happened to me at the very beginning of my five-year journey, I would have cried uncle: "All right! All right! Never mind! I'll take that job back, please, and the condo too!" and would've found a way to live happily beneath the weight of a dream unfulfilled. But by that day in March, 2002, I had been on the road for two and a half years. Though I was unaware of it at the time, it was exactly to the mile, (mile 7,062) halfway through my walk around the world, and I had come to accept, even expect, the loony and exasperating demands of the road. Heck, even the good times were demanding. But when people ask, "Did you ever feel like quitting?" I can honestly say no. Not once. Not ever. Not even the time I was nearly killed by a flying cow.

Prologue from Polly's book, *3mph: The Adventures of One Woman's Walk Around the World* Reprinted by permission of the author.

Questions and Answers

1. What compels you to walk?

I was always a walker. Primarily because I was too poor to buy a car. The first time I noticed that walking was much more than a poor man's mode of transportation was when I had a corporate job in a downtown Boston. I took the commuter train to work, and walked the final half-mile through a crowd of people on bustling sidewalks to get to my high-rise corporate American cubicle. In an effort to find a balance, I ditched the commuter train and opted to slip on my walking shoes at five-thirty in the morning and hike nine miles to get to work by eight. It was the medicine I needed to help control stress levels and arrive to work with a glow instead of a growl.

2. Do you experience instances while you are walking when your mind in somewhere off the trail and on its own journey?

Years after my walk around the world a friend, who is a therapist, observed that my nightly walks were serving as a form of meditation for me. It struck me as a big duh. Of course, I thought to myself. Some people do yoga, others do meditation, and apparently I have found walking to serve the same objective—to destress, get clarity, and percolate on creative endeavors.

Walking is my secret weapon to happiness. Nature's medicine. It's also a great social hour with friends, and more recently I've taken it up with clients as we do "walking meetings". Frankly, it's a big duh.

3. How do you manage to stay physically and emotionally healthy during long and arduous journeys?

I have a playlist on my iPod of music that I simply cannot sit still to. Music is scientifically proven to lower cortisol, which helps lower anxiety levels. And a whole lot less money and healthier than any drug on the market! So when I am in a grumpy mood or wound up from a work related drama, I put on my walking shoes, stick on my playlist entitled "Get Your Groove on" and that mood disappears inside a mile. It's true!

4. Please share a high and a low period that you experienced during your walkabouts.

There were big milestones: meeting Gandhi's granddaughter, meeting the first man to walk around the world, a city in Thailand threw me a parade. But those gigantic moments are so filled with being "on", that you can't be in the moment and simply enjoy it.

One of my highlight moments came at six o'clock on a Thursday night as I strolled into bustling nighttime London. Nine-to-fivers were hustling through the streets lugging briefcases, talking on their mobile phones, racing for the tube, living busy lives. I stood in the middle of the bustle hovering over my map, studying the maze of streets to Trafalgar Square, where I was meeting a man from the London Lions Club who would be my host for the night. The map indicated that to get into city center I had my choice of crossing the London Bridge, Waterloo Bridge, Southwark Bridge or Westminster Bridge. Since I didn't know one from another I took a stab in the dark—Westminster Bridge, just because.

I strolled over the bridge, pushing my buggy Bob slowly amid the grandeur of the historic Thames glowing in a nighttime London. The lights of the city surrounded me. I felt swept up in the energy of millions of people scurrying to friends and pubs and parties and families. Suddenly I was hit with a moment—the kind of moment you can't explain when people ask about your favorite moments—when the light is just right; when there's a magic, an energy in the air, that hits you suddenly, centers you in the here and now and swallows you whole. A moment I'd thought about years before when I had maps spread all over the floor and wondered about the day I'd walk into London after years on the road. Now here I was, walking over the Westminster Bridge into London with Big Ben greeting me in all his glory. And all the city bustlers were oblivious to the girl pushing her three-wheeled buggy Bob over the Westminster Bridge having a moment.

****

A low point on my walk was after the 9/11 events. It was my first twinge of understanding the tribal nature of human beings, wanting to be among our own people during tragedy.

I was in Malaysia at the time, and overnight I became keenly aware that I was no longer a woman walking for women. Clearly now I was an American woman with a Jewish last name walking through a Muslim country during holy jihad, talking about breasts.

Friends and family called and emailed with urgency in their tone, "What's your escape plan? Do you have an emergency plane ticket back to the U.S.?"

But there was no escape plan. Even when I was 12 and got this idea in my head for the very first time, I knew I couldn't embark on this journey if I couldn't accept the tough times. I always knew that there were going to be tough times, situations I could never plan for or predict. This was one of them. I expected, and accepted these setbacks as part of the journey.

These are our times of growth. Our times of challenge. And unfortunately we don't always get to choose them. Instead, sometimes we're thrown into that painful discomfort zone where we're forced to reevaluate, restructure, reach out.

The Lions Clubs had taken me under their wing since the early days of Australia, and in Malaysia I was surrounded by them every morning, noon, and night. These were highly connected, well-respected, highly influential men and women. So one morning, shortly after 9/11 I reached out to the Lions and asked them if they would consider helping me contact the President of the International Lions Club and ask him if they would consider an official international sponsorship—and they agreed.

So with the Lions as a solid foundation under my feet while these global events started swirling on around me, the Lions Clubs took care of me from village to village through Malaysia, and carried on through Thailand and into India.

5. Have you experienced an important Encounter that somehow changed the direction of your journey?

Prior to leaving on my walk around the world I remember thinking that this was so crazy, silly, some might even say irresponsible, and I didn't really have an answer to "Why?" so I probably wouldn't talk about it much. And who would care?

But that vision changed with a seemingly insignificant encounter on the side of the round in a small farming community in Australia.

It was my fourth night in Australia when I walked into a little town at dusk. There was no place to stay—no campground or youth hostel—so I had the great idea that I'd find the town park and camp out for the night. So there I was standing on a street corner waiting for a light to change, looking at my map trying to find my way to the town park for the night, when a woman came up behind me. "You look lost. Can I help you find something?"

"I was looking for the town park if you have one."

At that point she heard my funny accent she asked who I was and what I was doing. When I told her she said, "Well, I'll be! Let me introduce myself. My name is Margaret and I'm the President of the local Lions Club. The Lions Clubs have got to get involved with this. Why don't you come home with me tonight?!"

Margaret got me organized with the warm bed and big meal, and then began to call all her Lions buddies. "Meet us at the pub!" Now, if you don't know the pub culture in rural Australia—the pubs are the gathering points for everything from the 4-year old's birthday party to date-night, 50th anniversaries to guys-night-out, everything happens at the pub. It's sort of a community center—with beer.

So we weren't there five minutes when Margaret stood up on a stool and told the crowd what I was doing, and "all the funds for breast cancer stayed right here in Australia, so let's show her a little Aussie spirit." She then plucked a hat right off a guy's head and started passing it around. I watched as the hat traveled through the front of the bar, the restaurant, the pool hall, and within fifteen minutes the hat made its way back to the bar where the barkeeper counted the money and announced to the cheering crowd that we had just raised $332 for the Breast Cancer Network Australia!"

The next morning Margaret called the Lions Club in the next town and introduced me and could they help. They said, sure, send her on up. And in 15 miles there they were waiting for me and said, "Let's go to the pub!" They called the next club, and they called the next club….and now I was doing a 2000-mile pub crawl up the east coast of Australia!

The Lions Clubs not only helped me stay safe by providing a warm place to stay every night, but with the press coverage that the Lions Clubs were now generating across the country it was as if an entire nation started rallying behind me, assuring I would make it through their country safe, and fat without spending a dime.

The snowball of support from the Lions Clubs grew stronger and stronger up the east coast of Australia and eventually blossomed into an international sponsorship where the Lions passed me village to village around the world.

Who knew that standing on a street corner in a town where I knew no one, could be such a game changer. Certainly for my walk, if not my life.

Photograph courtesy of Polly Letofsky.

Biography

On August 1, 1999, Polly Letofsky left her Colorado home and headed west. She traveled across four continents, 22 countries, and over 14,000 miles—by foot—to become the first woman to walk around the world.

As an awareness campaign for breast cancer, survivors and well-wishers around the world came out to walk with her. Every day strangers welcomed her into their homes and shared meals. Across four continents she had dinner conversations with poets, politicians, country singers, olive growers, pig farmers and the female bomb maker in Australia. The world had embraced her.

But in the middle of Polly's five-year journey, the world suddenly shifted on its axis when September 11 flung us all into a crossroads in world history and she found herself navigating a vastly changing world.

Her journey became much more than a fundraising event. It became a journey personifying the spirit of commitment and perseverance that will compel us all to conquer life's biggest challenges—one step at a time.

Photograph by Jerry Kobalenko.

Jerry Kobalenko

The worse, the better.
~Russian explorer

Excerpt from Horizontal Everest

"Sledding is monotonous work, but it complements the lure of those glaciers. I sometimes feel that this is what I was born to do, haul a sled over Eureka Sound for 8 to 12 hours a day, temperature -20°F, snow hard, winds calm, trudging "like a camel, which is said to be the only beast which ruminates when walking." (Thoreau) In April, the sledder doesn't stop much—five minutes or so every hour and a half to rest the legs and fuel up. Longer than that, and the body cools down and it takes thirty minutes to feel your fingers again. In good conditions, sledding can continue for twelve hours in this vein. Hours eleven and twelve are the most revealing: They are like the final rounds in great championship fights, when all the bullshit and grey areas of the personality sluff away, and only strength and weakness remain…

Manhauling has been described as "about the hardest work to which free men have been put in modern times." Victorian geographical societies rightly saw arctic exploration as less dangerous but more arduous than the tropical variety. Arctic travelers didn't die from malaria or native spears or endure the frustrating laziness of local porters who for some reason didn't want to kill themselves for the Empire. On the other hand, they often had to haul their own gear on foot.

It's a lovely occupation, if you like walking. Coleridge considered a twenty-mile hike in the mountains nothing special. Beethoven composed while trekking in the Alps. Nietzsche wrote that "only thoughts reached by walking have value." Bertrand Russell claimed that war would end if every young man walked twenty miles a day.

But not all cultured Europeans understood activity. In *Journey to the Center of the Earth*, Jules Verne's heros endured "three hours of terrible fatigue, walking incessantly." Jean Malaurie, modern author of *The Last Kings of Thule*, that wonderful study of the Polar Inuit, makes a big deal of walking six miles per day and—whoopee-do—"penetrating inland to a depth of nineteen miles." Even Mark Twain, that vigorous traveler from the vigorous New World, believed that walking was "merely a lubricant" for good conversation.

In his essay on walking, Thoreau writes that the origin of the word "saunter" may derive from the medieval peripatetics who claimed to be going to the Holy Land, "la Sainte Terre." Sledding is, in this sense, a lot like sauntering. An imitation of Christ whose Golgotha is healthy exhaustion. For the Western soul, exertion may do what fasting does in the East."

Excerpt from *Horizontal Everest*, by Jerry Kobalenko. Reprinted by permission of the author.

Questions and Answers

1. What compels you to walk?

Physical restlessness. I've always sympathized with the zoo wolf, pacing back and forth all day. Wrangy to move, by its very nature. Also, walking is natural for me: It's a nontechnical activity that frees a daydreaming mind to wander. When you have to concentrate to stay safe, as in downhill skiing or climbing or even inline skating, the mind is grounded in the dreary present, it can't achieve lift.

2. Do you experience instances while you are walking when your mind in somewhere off the trail and on its own journey?

All the time, every day, every hour. See previous answer.

3. How do you manage to stay physically and emotionally healthy during long and arduous journeys?

All athletes listen carefully to their bodies. On long-distance treks, if you need a rest day or two, you take them. If you feel a tweak somewhere, you monitor it carefully to determine whether it is a warning bell, a temporary sign of fatigue, or a phantom ailment, usually worry manifesting itself physically. Because this sort of travel involves neither speed nor explosiveness, the main danger is repetitive stress injury. But I've been lucky, am active and careful, and train judiciously for every long-distance trek, that I've managed to avoid these. If I'm training and I feel a tweak, I immediately back off and keep up fitness through a different activity. Mental stuff has never been a problem; either I'm emotionally solid or too far gone to notice what a basket case I've become.

4. Please share a high and a low period that you experienced during your walkabouts.

Low: some trips turn out to be boring or you're simply not into them, but this isn't the place's or the activity's fault. Bad experiences are an occasional part of long-distance travel, and nothing to get too bummed about, just like disagreements are part of a couple living together and not automatically a sign of incompatibility. High: Joy is the rarest and most intense form of happiness, but it is a frequent visitor on long-distance trips.

5. Have you experienced an important Encounter that somehow changed the direction of your journey?

No, although every partner leaves his or her indelible imprint on a trek. In retrospect, the partnership is what you remember most vividly, not the physical effort or the landscape. On solo trips, the encounter is with oneself and with the land. In arctic travel, chance encounters with other people simply don't occur.

Photograph courtesy of Jerry Kobalenko.

Biography

Jerry's writing and photography have appeared in hundreds of publications around the world, including *National Geographic, Conde Nast Traveler, Canadian Geographic* and *Time.* His books *Arctic Eden* and *The Horizontal Everest* recount the author's lifelong love affair with the Canadian High Arctic. The New York Times Book Review writes that "The *Horizontal Everest* is refreshingly free of the hubris that marks much adventure writing, and the reader never feels assaulted by Kobalenko's daring, only inspired by it."

THE WALKABOUT CHRONICLES

Wade Davis and Sebastian Snow, the Darian Gap, 1974. *Photograph courtesy of Wade Davis.*

"Wade Davis was a shrewd choice for our trip, for this young, very tough Canadian was not only conversant in Spanish, but he was also a competent photographer, when his Pentax functioned properly, which it sometimes did. He could read a compass and a map and could charm the Noble Savage with his long red flute and was good at whittling things with his buck knife, some of the many vital attributes I lack, to my undying shame." Sebastian Snow.

Wade Davis

Wade was a gentle giant with very broad shoulders; a strong walker, loose limbed and long legged with kind, blue, wide-apart eyes, capped by a rumpled mop of hair.
He had a penchant for adventure and was a very courageous person indeed.
~Sebastian Snow, *The Rucksack Man*

One River: Explorations and Discoveries in the Amazon Rain Forest

The wind in the evening runs away from the shores of Panama. An hour or two after sunset, when the sparkling cruise ships waiting at the mouth of the canal light up like carnival tents, the fishermen at the settlement of Veracruz drag their skiffs across the beach and into the sea. Those with small motors disappear quickly into the night. The others have to row, struggling through the surf and then pulling away from the shore and each other with long, smooth strokes of the oars. Their destination is the edge of a coastal shelf where the shallow seabed falls away and the deep, cold waters of the Pacific rise, bringing schools of fish to the surface. They know they are there when they can no longer smell the land or distinguish the lights on the horizon from the stars in the sky.

In the short time that I stayed in Veracruz I often went out at night with one of the fishermen, a young man named Ohilio. He was a gentle person, a mixture of a dozen races, short and thin, with the rough hands of one who had worked the nets for years. Unable to hear or speak since birth, Ohilio had found in fishing the perfect vocation. On land he had the look of someone who had spent his life shying away from people. On the water at night, with quiet all around and the darkness broken only by the dazzling phosphorescence in the sea, he was completely at ease.

Ohilio rowed by choice, not necessity, for he always caught fish. He believed that the fish found him and that it was God's way of compensating for his misfortune. And so it seemed. For while the others labored at their nets, pulling them in and letting them out many times a night, shifting locations, chasing the fish, Ohilio would set a single net and then, as his boat drifted in the current, curl up in a bundle in the bow and go to sleep. Generally he woke up only once during the night to check his net. Sometimes in the cold hours before dawn he got up a second time to relieve himself, casually straddling the forward thwart, pissing over the bow as the skiff pitched and rolled precariously in the waves. He was completely fearless. Once at dawn as we pulled in the net, killing the fish we could sell with a swift blow to the head and throwing the others back into the sea, an enormous shark suddenly broke the surface just beside the boat. In an instant I found myself tossing a large fish past rows of teeth into a gaping jaw. The shark swallowed the fish sideways and then fell back into the water with a crash that nearly swamped us. Its tail struck the side of the skiff, the planks by the keel shuddered, and the entire boat spun violently. Stunned, I looked to Ohilio, whose eyes were gleaming and whose mouth was shaking with the laughter of the mute.

Most of our outings were less eventful, of course, and the quiet hours of the night were rare moments of peace and forgetfulness. Free of language, with no friction to our thoughts, we shared a strange solitude, a life momentarily drained of volition, as elemental as the sea. At the time I had little energy for new sensations. For a month or more I had been in the forests of the Darien, a difficult passage that had begun, perhaps predictably, with a contact provided by Professor Schultes. Eight weeks before, shortly after we left the Sierra Nevada and Tim returned for a month to Harvard, an old crony of Schultes, a geographer and explorer attached to the Botanical Garden in Medellín, invited me to join a British expedition intent on traversing the Darien Gap, a broad expanse of roadless swamp and rain forest that separates Colombia from Panama. The expedition turned out to be one man, Sebastian Snow, an English adventurer who, having just walked from Tierra del Fuego at the tip of South America, intended to continue north as far as Alaska. It was June, the height of the rainy season, and the Darien was said to be impassable.

Our route from Colombia had taken us on foot from Barranquillita; a ramshackle settlement just off the Medellín-Turbo road, sixty miles west across the Tumaradó swamp to Puerto Libre, a row of huts strung out along the banks of the Río Atrato. The Atrato runs four hundred miles south to north, draining the Chocó, the wettest region of South America, thirty thousand square miles of forgotten rain forest cut off from the Amazon millions of years ago by the rise of the Andean Cordillera. Downstream from Puerto Libre is the Gulf of Urabá and the Caribbean. Upstream is more swamp and forest, and a land that for Colombians is synonymous with disease and disappointment.

Like so many lowland settlements Puerto Libre was a place of lassitude strangely at odds with the intensity of life that surrounded it in the forest. It consisted of ten sun-bleached shacks and three floating outhouses, each with three holes in the floor—one to relieve oneself in, one to wash in, and a third to draw water. The lives of the local women revolved around these riverfront latrines. They were there with the children at dawn, and they remained for much of the day, washing clothes or idly gossiping. In the evening, when the night air finally offered some relief from the heat, mosquitoes rose from the river like a miasma, driving everyone indoors to the isolation of their netted hammocks. Once it was dark, caiman came ashore by the score and for the rest of the night sprawled on the grassy slopes leading up to the shacks or lay about on the wooden landings where so few hours before children and infants had bathed.

> "Wade saw a chimpanzee as big as himself and then suddenly got stung very badly by seven hornets. As he dashed, yelling, past me I Thought he had gone beserk, run amok or something. He was that sort of man. As a result of Wade's Quixotic action I was the recipient of only one hornet sting under the neck, not very painful." Sebastian Snow.

After three miserable days, including a morning when I awoke on the floor to discover that a dog had given birth on my foot, a local skin trader ferried our party upriver to a place called La Loma. There we hired mules to carry our gear beyond the Atrato up a narrow track that crisscrossed the Río Cacarica and rose toward the Darien. Three days later, having abandoned the mules and engaged three Emberá Indians as guides, we reached the height of land at Palo de Letras, the border between Colombia and Panama that, as the name suggests, is marked only by a pair of letters carved into the bark of a tree. Once beyond the frontier we entered a world of plants, water, and silence. For the next ten days we moved from one Emberá or Kuna village to the next, soliciting new guides and obtaining provisions as we went along. Nowhere did we stop long enough to understand the lives that we drifted through, but each day became part of a veil that gradually enveloped us as the forest closed in, absorbing our party as the ocean swallows a diver.

> "Wade's clothes I noted, were visibly rotting on his body, as were mine, because of the mildew and fungus mould." Sebastian Snow.

It was during those days that I first experienced the overwhelming grandeur of the tropical rain forest. It is a subtle thing. There are no herds of ungulates as on the Serengeti plain, no cascades of orchids—just a thousand shades of green, an infinitude of shape, form, and texture that so clearly mocks the terminology of temperate botany. It is almost as if you have to close your eyes to behold the constant hum of biological activity—evolution, if you will—working in overdrive. From the edge of trails creepers lash at the base of trees, and herbaceous heliconias and calatheas give way to broad-leafed aroids that climb into the shadows. Overhead, lianas drape from immense trees binding the canopy of the forest into a single interwoven fabric of life. There are no flowers, at least few that can be readily seen, and with the blazing sun hovering motionless at midday there are few sounds. In the air is a fluid heaviness, a weight of centuries, of years without seasons, of life without rebirth. One can walk for hours yet remain convinced that not a mile has been gained.

Then toward dusk everything changes: The air cools, the light becomes amber, and the open sky above the rivers and swamps fills with darting swallows and swifts, kiskadees and flycatchers. The hawks, herons, jacanas, and kingfishers of the river margins give way to flights of cackling parrots, sungrebes, and nunbirds, and spectacular displays of toucans and scarlet macaws. Squirrel monkeys appear, and from the riverbanks emerge caiman, eyes poking out of the water, tails and bodies as still and dull as driftwood. In the light of dusk one can finally discern shapes in the forest, sloths clinging to the limbs of cecropia trees, vipers entwined in branches, tapir wallowing in distant sloughs. For a brief moment at twilight the forest seems of a human scale and somehow manageable. But then with the night comes the rain and later the sound of insects running wild through the trees until, with the dawn, once again silence: The air becomes still, and steam rises from the cool earth. White fog lies all about like something solid, all-consuming.

After just a fortnight on the trail, our passage began to take on the tone of a dream. In part this was because we rarely slept. With the rain sleep was not often possible. At the end of long days we simply lay in our hammocks in an unnatural rest, like a state of trance, dulled by exhaustion and insulated from the night by mosquito netting and the smoke of a smoldering fire. But mostly we became infected by the spirit of the place. The Darien turned out to be less a piece of terrain than a state of mind, a wild frontier utterly divorced from the moral inhibitions of ordinary human society.

In each of the small villages—Paya, Capeti, Yape, El Común—that marked the route from the frontier to the main settlement at Yavisa, there was a recent story of murder or death. On the Río Cacarica five men had fought and wounded one another with machetes. In Capeti a black Colombian thief known as Mentiroso Serio, the Serious Liar, killed a woman and was himself hunted down, shot, and strung up in the forest beyond Paya, just short of the Colombian frontier. Seven Indians were murdered on the Río Chico; a Colombian was killed for his cooking utensils on the trail to Tigre; a man and his wife were fatally tortured near Yavisa. Those investigating these crimes, or at least responsible for recording them in their moldy logbooks, were the Guardia Civil, a clumsy and corrupt paramilitary force then under the command of a young Manuel Noriega.

Midway through our journey trouble with the Guardia Civil at Yavisa forced us to change our route. Stripped of most of our gear and driven away from the settlement, we followed three Kuna guides up a series of rock falls and cascades, a serpentine route designed to evade pursuit. In the process the Kuna themselves became disoriented, and for the next week we wandered through the forest lost or, at best, only vaguely aware of where we were. Free of distractions, one became honed by life in the forest—the howler monkeys overhead, the incessant streams of ants, chance encounters with snakes and jaguar, the haunting cries of harpy eagles; iridescent butterflies, teasing with their delicate beauty, while at one's feet bronze and purple frogs, poisonous to the touch. In my journal I noted the simple luxuries of forest life: "the smoke of a fire that chases away the insects, a rainless night, a thatch hut found in the woods, a banana almost gone bad found lying in a trough, abandoned plantings of manioc, a fresh kill, whatever it may be, water deep enough to bathe in, a hint of a solid shit, a full night's sleep, a lemon tree found in the forest."

By the time we came upon the road head some twenty miles east of Santa Fe, the cumulative effects of two years on the road had physically broken my English companion. In all he had lost fifty pounds. Leaving him with one of the Kuna, the remainder of our party went ahead to seek help. Several miles on, we came upon the right-of-way of the Pan American Highway, a cleared and flattened corridor that stretched to the horizon. We hesitated, momentarily confounded by so much space. Then we began to walk past the charred silhouettes of trees and onto a beaten track that meandered through the slash. It was several hours before we heard the sound of machinery—chain saws at first and then the dull roar of diesel trucks. We walked for another mile or two before coming upon a D-9 cat, the largest bulldozer made, buried up to its cab in mud. A second bulldozer, snorting and belching smoke, tore into the ground with its blade while two others, attached to the trapped machine with thick cables, attempted to haul it out of the mud. None of the workmen noticed us. The sound was deafening: the hiss and moan of hydraulics, the iron cables snapping like strings, and the smell of grease and oil.

The Kuna had never seen machinery of such a scale. Clinging to their rifles, struggling through the cloying mud, they walked past the bulldozers and gravitated toward a small work gang clustered at a bridge site half a mile beyond. It was dusk and the crew had broken for dinner, served by Kuna kitchen boys from a mobile canteen. The foreman asked where we had come from. When I said Colombia, the workers in a single gesture leaned forward to offer us their plates of food. I looked about, invited my companions to eat, and then glanced past the foreman to the road ahead, a scene of desolation that ran north as far as one could see. He followed my gaze. "The civilization of nature," he said, "is never pretty."

> "Suddenly out front there was a terrific war whoop from Wade. Sebastian, Sebastian, Sebastian, we are through…we are through…through the Darien Gap; here's the road! The Road!" Sebastian Snow.

Four days later, having successfully crossed the Darien, I abandoned Sebastian to his walk and at Santa Fe climbed aboard a small plane for the short hop to Panama City. A last-minute addition to the passenger list, I was squeezed into the rear seat, my knees pushed up to my chest, unable to move and scarcely free to breathe. The pilot led us immediately into a tremendous tropical storm. Visibility dropped to nil. The woman beside me threw up on my lap. Her mother, a corpulent black merchant, turned to offer consolation and promptly threw up herself. For an anxious few moments, as the winds buffeted the plane, I feared that having survived the Darien, I was about to die ignominiously. When finally we landed at Panama City, I walked off the plane drenched in vomit, with only two dollars to my name. As for Sebastian, the last I heard he made it as far as Costa Rica before being admitted to a hospital. In the middle of the night he awoke and left the hospital in his pajamas, starting to walk north. He was arrested and spent a delirious week in jail before being rescued by a staff member at the British embassy who bundled him back to England.

> "Wade's last words to me were, 'What an adventure crossing the Darien Gap without maps or compass and in the rainy season too. The greatest adventure of my life.'" Sebastian Snow.

Excerpt from: Davis, Wade. *One River: Explorations and Discoveries in the Amazon Rain Forest* Simon & Schuster. Reprinted by permission of the author.

Biography

Wade Davis is Professor of Anthropology and the BC Leadership Chair in Cultures and Ecosystems at Risk at the University of British Columbia. Between 1999 and 2013 he served as Explorer-in-Residence at the National Geographic Society and is currently a member of the NGS Explorers Council and Honorary Vice-President of the Royal Canadian Geographical Society. Named by the NGS as one of the Explorers for the Millennium, he has been described as "a rare combination of scientist, scholar, poet and passionate defender of all of life's diversity."

An ethnographer, writer, photographer and filmmaker, Davis holds degrees in anthropology and biology and received his Ph.D. in ethnobotany, all from Harvard University. Mostly through the Harvard Botanical Museum, he spent over three years in the Amazon and Andes as a plant explorer, living among fifteen indigenous groups in eight Latin American nations while making some 6000 botanical collections. His work later took him to Haiti to investigate folk preparations implicated in the creation of zombies, an assignment that led to his writing *The Serpent and the Rainbow* (1986), an international best seller later released by Universal as a motion picture. In recent years his work has taken him to East Africa, Borneo, Nepal, Peru, Polynesia, Tibet, Mali, Benin, Togo, New Guinea, Australia, Colombia, Vanuatu, Mongolia and the high Arctic of Nunuvut and Greenland.

Davis is the author of 265 scientific and popular articles and 19 books including *One River* (1996), *The Wayfinders (2009)*, *The Sacred Headwaters* (2011), *Into the Silence* (2011) and *River Notes* (2012). His photographs have been widely exhibited and have appeared in 30 books and 100 magazines, including *National Geographic, Time, Geo, People, Men's Journal,* and *Outside*. He was the co-curator of *The Lost Amazon: The Photographic Journey of Richard Evans Schultes*, first exhibited at the National Museum of Natural History, Smithsonian Institution, and currently touring Latin America. In 2012 he served as guest curator of *No Strangers: Ancient Wisdom in the Modern World*, an exhibit at the Annenberg Space for Photography in Los Angeles.

His many film credits include *Light at the Edge of the World*, an eight-hour documentary series written and produced for the National Geographic. A professional speaker for 30 years, Davis has lectured at over 200 universities and 250 corporations and professional associations. In 2009 he delivered the CBC Massey Lectures. He has spoken from the main stage at TED five times, and his three posted talks have been viewed by 3 million. His books have appeared in 19 languages and sold approximately one million copies.

Davis is the recipient of 11 honorary degrees, as well as the 2009 Gold Medal from the Royal Canadian Geographical Society for his contributions to anthropology and conservation, the 2011 Explorers Medal, the highest award of the Explorers Club, the 2012 David Fairchild Medal for botanical exploration, the 2013 Ness Medal for geography education from the Royal Geographical Society, and the 2015 Centennial

Medal of the Graduate School of Arts and Sciences, Harvard University. His recent book, *Into the Silence*, received the 2012 Samuel Johnson prize, the top award for literary nonfiction in the English language. In 2016 he was made a Member of the Order of Canada.

Johan Reinhard examining the cloth that covered the face of a young female mummy found on the summit of Llullaillaco (6,739 meters). The girl's head cloth had been damaged. *Photograph by Johan Reinhard, 1999.*

Johan Reinhard

Experience is only half of experience
~Johann Wolfgang von Goethe

A Discovery in the Andes

When my flight landed in the Peruvian city of Arequipa late in August 1995, I thought my research in the Andes had ended for the summer. Discoveries of Inca ruins in eastern Peru had been followed by more in Bolivia—it had been one of my best field seasons ever. Even my visit to Arequipa was happenchance, only being possible when a trip to Tibet had been cancelled at the last minute. Nothing gave the slightest hint that a short expedition would lead to my life being changed forever.

I had spent the previous fifteen years working as an archaeologist in the Andes, climbing over a hundred mountains in the process. A new field had developed called "high-altitude archaeology" (over 5,200 m) with its focus on the Inca culture of 500 years ago. Within a vast area of the Andes, encompassing the countries of Chile, Argentina, Bolivia, Ecuador, and Peru, the Incas had built stone structures on mountains as high as 6,739 meters. Such heights were not even reached—let alone structures built on—until some 400 years after the Incas. Taken together, these sites must constitute one of the most awesome achievements known to us from ancient times.

As a climber and anthropologist, I had long been fascinated with mountains and mountain cultures. I had been conducting anthropological research in Nepal since 1968 and had participated in traditional mountain worship practices during some Himalayan expeditions, including one to Mt. Everest in 1976. However, it was not until I reached the Andes in 1980 that I learned that archaeological sites existed at such high altitudes, much less that they had involved the Incas undertaking some of the longest and most difficult walks known to us from ancient times. There were no animals to ride and no wheeled vehicles existed in the Andes. The Incas not only had to walk to the mountains—some of them nearly 2,000 km away—they had to climb to their summits once they arrived!

In 1980 it was a mystery why the high-altitude sites had been built, and it was not clear who had made them nor how far they extended in the Andes. Yet discoveries had been made on a couple of the mountains that were among the most spectacular in archaeology: perfectly frozen mummies and Inca objects that looked like new. It is rare indeed to find a project that could involve discoveries of importance and the opportunity to gain information that could change how an ancient culture was understood. Finally, it allowed me to combine "tools," such as mountain climbing and scuba diving (yes, underwater research was also involved—even to 5,850 m), with archaeology and ethnohistory. This made for a combining of science and exploration that I had longed for since I began my university studies in 1962, and it made for an irresistible research project.

I was met in Arequipa by the Peruvian archaeologist José Antonio Chávez. We had worked together on several mountain summits during the 1980s, but had not been to a peak together since 1991. Reports of looting on the nearby mountain of Chachani only weeks before meant that he was as keen as I was on our continuing with our excavations of high-altitude sites. We immediately began listing the mountains we hoped to investigate in 1996.

Unfortunately, José Antonio couldn't get free due to his obligations at the university and none of the other archaeologists and climbers I had worked with in the past was available. Then by chance I ran into Miguel Zárate, who had just returned from a job working on the coast. He had been my assistant on some previous expeditions and had both climbing experience and a strong interest in archaeology, a rare combination.

Several of the peaks close to Arequipa had Inca sites on them, but we had already done preliminary investigations of them. Now those bordering the more distant Colca Canyon, twice as deep as the Grand Canyon, were among the ones that most attracted our interest. The inhabitants of the Colca Canyon had worshiped mountains long before the arrival of the Incas, especially Hualca Hualca, Sabancaya and Ampato, the latter being the highest in the region at 6,312 m. Miguel and I had climbed Hualca Hualca's easternmost summit in 1982, but it was westernmost peak that had most caught my attention. It stood out by itself from the rest of the long, flat-topped massif and had vertical walls surrounding it. It was interesting from a climber's perspective, but it remained to be seen if the Incas had reached its summit. And there was something else that drew me to the region.

Ampato was not only the most prominent mountain, it was also one of the most sacred in Inca times. Nonetheless, I thought that Ampato was the peak with the least likelihood of finding anything on its summit, since it was permanently covered in ice and snow. However, I wanted to photograph its lower neighbor Sabancaya, because it was still an active volcano—indeed it had been erupting daily for several years. Ampato was perfectly positioned for this, and so I decided to try to take photos from the slopes of Ampato and then attempt Hualca Hualca, making a walking loop back to the Colca Canyon. It wasn't long before Miguel and I were on our way out of the town of Cabanaconde on a two day hike to the base of Ampato, along with a man and his two donkeys carrying our supplies.

We set up our base camp at 4,900 m in a sunken, dried-out streambed, where we were protected from the wind. Before noon the next day we had reached 6,100 m on Ampato's north ridge. By taking this route I was guaranteed to get the photos I wanted of the eruptions, but not Ampato's summit, which was now a long way off. Worse, we were confronted with an ice field full of ice pinnacles that extended in an upward jumble for over a kilometer to the mountain's highest point. To our amazement the summit appeared to be free of snow for this first time in recorded history. We laboriously worked our way through the ice field until we came to a hilltop covered with hundreds of square meters of thick grass that must have been brought up from lower elevations over a dozen kilometers away. Scattered on top of the grass were pieces of Inca pottery and clothing, sections of ropes, chunks of wood, and even leather and wool sandals. The grass must have been used for insulation, and the Incas had likely used llamas to help carry up material weighing over a ton. It seemed likely that the site had been utilized as a resting place before attempting the steep, final section to the summit, still nearly a kilometer distant.

We could not reach the summit before dark, so I went over alternatives in my mind. If we carried up a tent and food to a plateau on the ridge below us, the following day we would have time to search around the summit. The conditions at the time of the Incas must have been similar to the relatively snow-free terrain we were observing now, since otherwise the Incas couldn't have built the site at 6,100 m the way they had.

Once we had reached the plateau at 5,800m the next day, we surveyed structures we found scattered around it. Now that we knew of Inca structures at 5,800 m and 6,100 m, it only remained for us to see if the Incas had actually reached Ampato's highest point. On September 8 we made our way past the 6,100 meter site. Thanks to having left behind our rope and crampons, we had some scrambling to do before we could reach the summit. To our surprise its normal 10-meter-wide ridge now barely measured a meter. A large section had to have collapsed since the last known ascent of 1993. Within minutes we were stunned to find Inca statues sticking out of the exposed slope where a platform had been built five centuries ago. It was obvious to us that artifacts must have fallen inside the crater when the ridge collapsed. After climbing down into the crater, we spotted what looked like a mummy bundle lying on the ice. I had been to dozens of sites on mountain summits over the years and found skeletal remains at one of them, but I had never even seen a mummy bundle on a mountain, let alone one lying out in the open.

"Maybe it's a climber's backpack," said Miguel. "Maybe it's a climber," I replied, only half joking. As we drew closer to the bundle, my pulse quickened. Given the other items we had found, it seemed certain that it would contain a mummy or at least something of value to the Incas. Miguel moved it on its side for a better grip, and, as he did so, it turned in his hands. Suddenly, time seemed to stop. We were looking straight into the face of an Inca.

I soon realized that the mummy's face must have become exposed after a cloth covering had ripped open during the bundle's fall down the gully. The face was thus dried out, and our hopes of a frozen body evaporated. But when we tried to lift the bundle we were surprised at how heavy it was. The thought struck me that there wasn't enough ice to make it so heavy, and I felt a surge of adrenaline as I realized what this meant—most of the body had to be still frozen.

Few frozen mummies had been found anywhere in the Andes and none in Peru, close to the heart of the Inca Empire. Although little showed but the face, it seemed clear to me that the mummy was a female, and, if so, we had found the first frozen female in the Andes. Inca female clothing had never been found in such good condition while still being worn. Aside from the value of the clothing and any artifacts found together with it, the mummy's intact body tissues and organs would allow for complex DNA and pathological studies to be undertaken that had never been done on an Inca mummy before. Our accidental discovery would provide information unique in our knowledge of the Incas.

My mind raced with the implications. If we left the mummy behind, the sun and volcanic ash would further damage it. It was impossible to bury the mummy in the rocky, frozen ground, and covering it with ice could only be a temporary solution. The warmer weather of the coming months meant that the mummy would suffer more from exposure, which could be surprisingly warm when the sun hit and reflected off the ice. Even in the best conditions the mummy would continue to deteriorate. Obtaining an archaeological permit could take weeks, if not months, as could obtaining the funding to organize a scientific expedition—and we were fast approaching the snow season. And if the mummy became snow covered, it would be hard to locate inside the crater. I also knew that we could not save time by flying in with a helicopter. Most helicopters could not land safely even at the altitude of our base camp.

It would have been impossible for us to lug the mummy on our backs from the base of the mountain to the closest town of Cabanaconde in a single day, but we could make it if one of the donkey's that we had waiting at base camp carried it. We could pack the mummy in ice, wrap it in the insulated pads we used to sleep on, and return to the town the way we had come. The pads would protect the mummy from the sun, and most of the trip across the plateau would take place in the chilly temperatures at 4,300 m.

I knew there was no telephone in Cabanaconde and that no freezer would be available to store the mummy. However, I also knew there was a bus leaving the night we planned to arrive, and it would reach Arequipa around 6:00 the following morning. We would be able to have the mummy in a freezer not long after sunrise.

In the fading light the volcano's cloud of ash seemed to take on a sinister aspect. Having a dead body on my back added to the surreal scene. Images of Incas struggling through the same terrain ran through my mind. For a moment I was transported back in time, and I had the eerie feeling that I was rescuing someone who was alive. Although I do not personally believe in mountain gods, I can easily understand why many people in the Andes do. You can't spend years in the mountains without gaining respect for them, and often they seem to take on personalities of their own.

I remembered that during the dry season many Andean peoples believe the mountain gods provide "gifts" to those who they feel merit them. We were in the height of the dry season, and some villagers would be searching the mountain slopes in search of stones that have the shape of animals, such as llamas and alpacas, which are thought to increase the fertility of herds. But the gifts can take other forms—including a mummy. In other words, some villagers would believe that we had not "found" the mummy, but that the mountain god had given it to us. In truth, the circumstances were so unusual, I began to feel this way myself.

There was still one problem: Miguel was not feeling well and thus wouldn't be able to help carry the mummy. I wasn't sure I could do it either, despite being well acclimatized and in shape from recent climbs, since when I tried to get up with it tied to my pack, it was so heavy Miguel had to help pull me to my feet. (We learned later that it weighed over 40 kg.) "I'll be lucky to make it to the crater rim," I told him. Although a relatively horizontal hike of about a kilometer to the rim, I had to climb around strips of ice that zigzagged vertically up and down along the slope. A vertical ascent of only fifty meters required an effort that left me exhausted.

Worst were the repeated falls. Each one knocked the wind out of me, and I cursed myself for not bringing crampons. Once at the rim and heading downward, it got dark and instead of getting easier, the way became worse and at times dangerous. Part of the slope inclined at 50°, which would seem nearly vertical to a non-climber. Meanwhile the batteries in our headlamps were giving out and falling rocks whizzed by us in the dark. Cutting footholds with his ice axe immediately below, Miguel pleaded with me to leave the mummy behind. It was obvious that it would take a long time to cross the slope with the load on my back and thus there was a high risk that one of us could be hit by a rock. So I eventually agreed to leave the bundle firmly lodged among ice pinnacles at 6,000 m. Without the weight, we quickly crossed the slope and descended to our tent in the dark. We collapsed inside, too exhausted to eat.

The next morning dawned clear and sunny. I returned alone to carry the mummy the rest of the way down to our high camp. While I started up, Miguel set off down a steep scree slope, which allowed for a fast descent. He reached the foot of the mountain in only half an hour and arrived in base camp soon after. This was vital. Before we had started our ascent of Ampato, the donkeys' owner had taken them from base camp down to a stream at the foot of the mountain, so that they could graze and have water. We had arranged with him that he could return to Cabanaconde, if we weren't back in base camp that morning. We thought we could just head straight to Hualca Hualca via a higher route, if we changed our mind about staying on Ampato. Fortunately, Miguel reached the camp just in time to keep the man from leaving with the donkeys.

Unaware of what was happening below, I reached the mummy an hour and a half after beginning the ascent. Once again I fit the bundle onto my pack, dreading what was to come. As soon as I had it tied firmly, I pushed the load up the side of an ice block. I gritted my teeth as I slowly rose up and away from the ice, finding the pack just as onerous and bulky as before. I wobbled a bit, but with a wonderful sense of relief, I realized that I wouldn't fall. The memory of last night's ordeal had been so strong that this was the first time I felt certain I would be able to carry it the rest of the way down. I started the descent, slowly working my way over, around, and through the edge of the ice that protruded into the scree-covered slope. Difficult, at times exhausting, the trip nonetheless seemed like a cakewalk in the daylight and after a night's rest.

Suddenly I sensed someone coming along beside me. Who could it be? The hood of my parka blocked my peripheral view, but I could swear I caught a glimpse of movement. Had Miguel climbed up for some reason? Or had a climber descended from the summit having reached it by a different route? I quickly turned, but no one was there. The second time I turned, I knew what was happening. I was experiencing an illusion that other climbers have described, when they were convinced of the presence of someone beside them. I read of one climber having gone so far as to pull out food to offer his newfound companion! Even the knowledge that it was an illusion did not stop me from a subconscious conviction that I had a companion by my side. In a way, it was oddly reassuring—I felt I was not alone.

I decided to cross the exposed slope higher up than we had last night. I soon realized that descending at night would have had one advantage. The number of rocks falling had been less frequent, because more of the rocks were frozen due to the night cold. Now rocks were regularly bouncing down by me on all sides. I looked up trying to estimate their paths, but a bad bounce could send a stone in any direction, including mine, and it was usually too late to step out of the way in any event. I felt like a moving bowling pin avoiding a series of balls. I soon stopped looking up and worked my way down and across the slope as fast I could. Just before the ordeal ended, Sabancaya erupted. The wind carried the ash overhead, and soon I felt it striking my face in hundreds of tiny needles. "Yes, mountains do seem to have personalities—and this one is a bastard," I thought to myself. Once I was across, I caught my breath as I rested amidst some boulders. What remained was an easy downhill stroll, and a half hour later I was back at our tent. "I did it" I thought with relief, even though I knew it was still a long way to Cabanaconde.

Miguel had climbed back up to help with carrying the mummy and our equipment the rest of the way down, and before long we were reunited with the donkeys and on our way to the foot of the mountain. The next day we reached Cabanaconde in the dark after walking for over 13 hours with only a ten minute stop to share a tin of sardines. Later that night (and unbeknownst to the passengers) a plastic-covered bundle tied up with rope was placed in the undercarriage of a bus. Hours later the mummy reached Arequipa in the early morning and was rushed off to be placed in a freezer arranged by Prof. Chávez. We later anxiously watched as the plastic covering and insulated pads were removed to reveal pieces of ice still adhering to the mummy bundle. The Inca girl, soon nicknamed the "Ice Maiden" by some and "Juanita" by others, had made the journey from the mountain to the city and arrived in the same state as we had found her.

It seemed ironic, yet appropriate: Five hundred years ago the Ampato Ice maiden was a young girl whose destiny was to be sacrificed to the gods, and for centuries she had lain forgotten. Then in 1995 the eruption of a nearby volcano had caused her to appear from the ice. After news of her discovery was made public, she once again became renowned and honored. By a strange twist of fate, the children that were discovered frozen on mountain summits have become wider known than they were in the time of the Incas. More than a billion people were estimated to have heard of the Ice Maiden. For many people, mummies make the past become real by being individuals, sharing in our common humanity. True time capsules, these frozen bodies allow a view into the past that cannot be obtained through any other means, including that of the best-preserved mummies found in other conditions, including those preserved in the deserts of Egypt and coastal South America. Due to their excellent preservation, finds made at high altitudes enable unique opportunities for studies ranging from the biological (such as intact DNA, ancient diseases, nutrition, etc.) to the archaeological (e.g., rare Inca offerings looking pristine and, especially important, being found in context). Unlike most finds from the past, frozen mummies will never stop adding to our knowledge, since technology is constantly evolving. Ironically, scientific research, rather than denying the mummies' humanity, allows for their personal stories to be revealed. Whatever the reasons for our fascination with them, they will always remain stunningly unique windows into the past.

Once a villager said to me, "You need to understand. For us the Incas are still alive. They are hiding inside the mountains, waiting for the right time to return." His expression turned somber. "For us they will never die." I looked at him and smiled. "You are right. They never will."

Adapted from Johan's book *The Ice Maiden: Inca Mummies, Mountain Gods and Sacred Sites in the Andes* published by the National Geographic Society. Reprinted by permission of the author.

Peruvian villagers combine worship of the cross with that of sacred mountains during the festival of Qoyllur Riti near Cuzco, the center of the Inca Empire. *Photograph by Johan Reinhard, 1985.*

A view from the highest point of Llullaillaco's summit (6,739 m) over the world's highest archaeological site. Team members can be seen near Inca structures, and three frozen mummies were found in the ceremonial platform (upper left). Our high camp is visible at lower right. *Photograph by Johan Reinhard, 1999.*

Team members survey a site on Llullaillaco's summit. *Photograph by Johan Reinhard, 1999.*

Questions and Answers

1. What compels you to walk?

Walking works at so many levels, and for me, it can be a form of meditation, a way to feel in attune with my surroundings, a way to have direct, personal experiences that enrich my life, a way to help me maintain mental and physical health, and a way to search for answers to mysteries by taking me to places where I can gain a deeper understanding of past and present-day peoples and cultures.

2. Do you experience instances while you are walking when your mind in somewhere off the trail and on its own journey?

The most pleasant time I recall of my mind going off on its own was while solo climbing the last of four 6,400 m peaks in a week. Never before (or after) have I laughed all the way up a mountain. Indeed, at times I had to rest due to my side aching so much from laughing. I couldn't stop visualizing scenes from "Raiders of the Lost Ark," but ones based on my own experiences, presented in the same over-the-top (so to speak) style of "Raiders." OK, I knew the altitude was getting to me—but that didn't make the experience any less enjoyable.

3. How do you manage to stay physically and emotionally healthy during long and arduous journeys?

I've never been much for hard exercising before long walks, rather I just try to maintain enough conditioning to help me through the first days on the trail. In the Himalayas it often took several days and sometimes weeks to reach a destination, so I could slowly get into shape in the course of the trip. In the Andes my work means that I often have to make several carries on a mountain to get equipment and supplies to the summit, in order to remain there for the days needed to carry out research. So once again there is time to get into shape. The hardest part of high altitude archaeology is not physical, but psychological. Long periods without results can be debilitating, so varying the work to maintain interest is key. However, once a discovery is made, there is no problem…at least not for another couple of days.

    For long walks of over of a few weeks, I mainly live off what the local people eat, figuring a little weight loss never hurt anyone. Of course, there are walks and there are "walks." I once spent a year and a half—a good chunk of it walking—doing research in West Nepal without returning to Kathmandu. Nothing could have prepared me psychologically for the return to a city with people speaking English and the disorientation I was to experience passing between two completely different worlds.

4. Please share a high and a low period that you experienced during your walkabouts.

<u>High</u>: In March 1999 the team had descended to Base Camp and I sat alone on the summit of Llullaillaco, letting my thoughts roam. At 6,700 m we had completed the excavation of the world's highest archaeological site. More importantly, we had found

three frozen Inca mummies that were among the best preserved in the world. At the same time we had recovered dozens of rare, intact Inca artifacts. Llullaillaco had provided us with some of the most important Inca finds ever made—and all were in their original contexts. We were especially relieved that we had managed to do this before looters had destroyed the site, such as had already occurred at over a dozen burials lower on the mountain and as we had seen only weeks before at 6,100 m on Quehuar, where looters had used dynamite and blown apart a frozen Inca mummy.

However, the sense of accomplishment I felt stretched well beyond this expedition. I thought back over the twenty years I had spent in the Andes, including three previous expeditions to this very peak. Memories of storms, hunger, pain, and close calls were mixed with the joys of companionship and discoveries—mental as well as material. And then something dawned on me. Events on the summit had happened so quickly that only now did I realize my Andean research had not been the new stage in my life that I had once believed.

While still in my teens, I had set out to acquire a variety of "tools" to help make my mark as an anthropologist and explorer—and to use in a lifelong pursuit of a deeper understanding of the world around me. In the Andes and Himalayas I had been able to combine such academic disciplines as archaeology, linguistics and ethnography with everything from cinematography to mountaineering and scuba diving. Now I realized that my Andean project was the continuation of a course I had chosen while still a boy and stood as a metaphor for all that I had been trying to do with my life. I felt the powerful tug of destiny, not in the sense of being programmed since birth, but as the culminating point in the life that had emerged while I followed my dreams. So many climbs, so many people's lives changed—especially my own. I looked to the dozens of snow-capped peaks on the horizon, many of which I had climbed. I took my hat off, slowly gave my thanks, and then, with a strange mixture of gratitude and sadness, I started down.

Low: It was a hot July day in 1976 when I picked up my mail at the US Embassy in Kathmandu. I opened a notice from a district court informing me of the date for a reading of my mother's will. "Why am I being informed of what is in a will," I wondered? Then I read the bottom of the notice. My mother had passed away three weeks before, and it had taken that long for the letter to reach me. I was just a few days away from leaving with the American Everest Expedition. In those days only two expeditions a year were allowed to climb Everest from Nepal, and ours was the first to follow the 1963 climb American ascent. Entire countries had been waiting for years to obtain a permit. It was too late for me to attend my mother's funeral, and, as we left for the mountain, I had no word on how she died or what would happen to the only home I had known. I had been extraordinarily fortunate to be part of the expedition, likely a once in a lifetime opportunity, and for months I had been looking forward to it. Now I was overwhelmed with grief and thoughts that couldn't have been more removed from the daily progress we made walking to the mountain. What was to become one of my most memorable experiences had at the same time turned into being one of the most emotionally difficult.

5. Have you experienced an important Encounter that somehow changed the direction of your journey?

When I was 16 I leaped at the chance for a job working on the Rock Island Railroad traveling throughout the Midwest. This was a way to earn money that would allow me to begin expeditions that I'd long been dreaming of. During the summers of 1960, 1961 and 1963 I worked with southerners on a railroad line gang. Our main job was to dig holes by hand, put up telegraph poles, and then climb up them to add cross arms and telegraph lines. The men were all at least four years older than I and, being from the Deep South, came from much different backgrounds—to put it mildly. To me they were like people from another world and in a way they were. As a northerner I had to act and talk like they did in order to become accepted. Without knowing it, I had begun to behave like an ethnographer (doing what in anthropological jargon is called "participant observation"), constantly learning more about how these strange men thought.

I had my share of "learning experiences" during those summers, but one would dramatically affect me for the remainder of my life. One day in 1961 I climbed up a 10 meter pole that was in bad shape and needed to be replaced. My job was to untie the lines from their insulators so that the pole could be cut down and a new one put in its place. I strapped myself in and leaned out to undo the last wire on a cross-arm, watching as it dropped below. The next thing I knew I was falling straight back—the termite-eaten pole had snapped off and was falling down with me dangling under it. Ironically, the belt that had kept me from falling, also kept me from throwing myself off the pole. I knew I was dead.

The fall must have taken only a couple of seconds, but I wasn't counting. Scenes went slowly through my mind taking me back to early childhood. A few of them stuck in my mind at the time, but days later I could only remember details of the last one. I have never forgotten it. I was on my mother's lap in a rocking chair in front of our home's Dutch bay windows. Later my mother calculated that she had gotten rid of that rocking chair before I was two and a half years old. All the scenes I recalled had been peaceful ones. None dealt with anything dramatic in my life. Although I have had other close calls, this is the only one that I had where my life (or rather scenes from it) passed before my eyes.

I survived because, although the wires had dropped down, they were still hanging above the ground and attached to the telegraph poles on both sides of me. The cross arms on my pole caught in the wires, and there was a "bwang" as the pole bounced up. It quickly fell back down, and I found myself dangling only a few feet off the ground. Once my mind had cleared enough for me to realize what had happened, I slowly undid the belt. With a quick push, I threw myself off to the side, hoping the pole wouldn't somehow spring out and follow on top of me. I lay there shaking for several minutes, until I finally got enough strength to stand up. I walked slowly over to the pole and shoved it free of the wires. It landed with a loud thud, bounced a few inches, then lay still.

As paradoxical as it may seem, the experience underscored to me the importance of living life the way I wanted to. It crystallized in my mind, like nothing else could at that age, the reality that one day I would be dead, and I should not let my life be wasted on doing things I did not find interesting. In the years to come whenever I was in a difficult situation and asked myself the question, "Why am I doing this?" that last scene on the telegraph pole would replay itself in my mind's eye…and I would know.

Biography

Born in Illinois, Johan Reinhard received his Ph.D. in Anthropology from the University of Vienna, Austria. He has undertaken walks and climbs in the Andes that have involved over 200 ascents above 17,000 ft and the discovery of Inca mummies on five mountains, including perfectly preserved mummies at 22,000 ft on Llullaillaco, the world's highest archaeological site. In 1995 and 1999 *Time* selected his mummy finds as among "the world's ten most important scientific discoveries" for each of those years. Museums have been built in three countries to exhibit his archeological discoveries. His on-the-ground explorations of the landscapes surrounding Andean ceremonial centers have led him to present new theories to explain the mystery of the Nazca Lines (giant desert drawings) and the ancient sites of Machu Picchu, Chavín, and Tiahuanaco. He was a member of a team that made a crossing of the Llanganatis mountain range in Ecuador to reach the Amazon and has trekked through Tierra del Fuego. He has been involved in underwater archaeology expeditions in Bolivia, Chile, Peru, Ecuador, Mexico, Austria, Italy, and Kyrgyzstan.

During his ten years living in the Himalayas, he has hiked throughout most of Nepal and was the first to contact two of the world's last nomadic hunting and gathering tribes, while also exploring seven of the sacred "hidden lands" of Tibetan Buddhism and being a member of several climbing expeditions, including the 1976 American Everest Expedition. He participated in some of the first descents of Himalayan rivers (Trisuli, Sun Kosi) in the mid-1970's. He has explored much of the Himalayan range, including isolated regions in the Hindu Kush, Garhwal (NW India), western Tibet, and Bhutan. Elsewhere in Asia he was a member of one of the first camel crossings by westerners of the Great Indian (Thar) Desert, conducted ethnographic research on Muslim fishermen in the Maldive Islands, and investigated traditional religious beliefs in Mongolia, Bali, Israel, and Turkey.

His explorations have taken him around the world and also involve records made while not walking: scuba diving, sky diving, and rafting. His research has been featured in several TV documentaries and books. He has received the Explorers Medal of the Explorers Club of New York, the Rolex Award, and the Puma de Oro (Bolivia's highest distinction for archaeological research). *Outside* selected him as one of "today's 25 most extraordinary explorers" and the Ford Motor Company chose him as one of the "Heroes for the Planet." He is currently affiliated as an Explorer of the National Geographic Society and as a Senior Fellow of The Mountain Institute.

JOHAN REINHARD

A Special Tribute

Sacred World Explorations
Alaska

We would like to pay special tribute to these epic and inspirational walkers who are not in the book. Thousands of people have climbed Mount Everest, hundreds have been to the Poles, yet only a handful of people have walked around the world.

George M. Schilling – He walked around the world from 1897–1904 on a wager. In nine years he circumnavigated the globe, walking 55,000 miles, having left New York penniless and wearing a suit made out of newspapers. The conditions of the wager dictated that he leave with no money and return with $5,000. There is no doubt in my mind that George was a real character.

Dumitru Dan – In 1908, the Touring Club de France announced a contest for walking around the world, with a prize of 100,000 francs. Dumitru Dan, a Romanian, and his countrymen Paul Parvu, George Negranu and Alexander Pascu, were all students in Paris at the time, and they decided to take up the challenge. The group returned to Romania to prepare, learning languages, cartography, and weight training and exercising for two hours a day. They also walked 45 km per day and slept outdoors in all weather conditions. In 1910, wearing native Romanian garb and walking in sandals, the group set out to walk around the world with their dog, Harp. They performed traditional Romanian folk music to finance their way. In 1916, Dumitru Dan completed the journey alone. He had crossed ficve continents, three oceans, walked through 76 countries, and visited more than 1,500 cities, wearing out 497 pairs of shoes.

Dumitru and friend.

David Kunst – He is the first person independently verified to have walked around the earth, between 1970 and 1974. The walk was intended to be achieved along with his brother John; however, John was killed by bandits, and David was wounded. David resumed the walk, and completed the walk with his other brother, Peter. He walked for four years, three months, 16 days, and 14,452 km with his mule, Willie-Make-It II. David said that he took 20 million steps and wore out 21 pairs of shoes.

I will never forget reading David's book entitled, *The Man Who Walked around the World*. The book fueled my imagination, and from age 16 onward there has rarely been a day when I haven't dreamed of walking around the world like David. He broke a barrier with his walk around the world and set the standard for the few that would follow in his footsteps.

Sebastian Snow – In 1973 this eccentric English adventurer set out to walk the length of the Americas. With a young Canadian, Wade Davis, he managed to make his way through the notorious Darien Gap. He later fell ill, and never completed his journey to Alaska. He wrote a fantastic book entitled, *The Rucksack Man*, and would go on to influence future walkers such as George Meegan.

George Meegan – He is a British adventurer, born in 1952, and alternative educator known for his unbroken walk of the Western Hemisphere from the southern tip of South America to the northernmost part of Alaska at Prudhoe Bay. He covered 19,019 miles from 1977-1983 and wrote a book, *The Longest Walk* (1988), about his experience.

Peace Pilgrim – Born Mildred Norma in 1908, Peace Pilgrim was an American spiritual teacher and extraordinary walker. In 1952, she became the first woman to walk the entire length of the Appalachian Trail in one season. Then she walked over 25,000 miles across the United States back and forth for 28 years until her death in 1981. She wrote that she would "Remain a wanderer until mankind has learned the way of peace, walking until given shelter and fasting until given food."

Karl Bushby – He is a former British paratrooper attempting to be the first person to completely walk an unbroken path around the world. Bushy's trek is known as the Goliath Expedition. He was last seen walking in Russia.

Rosie Swale Pope – She is an adventurer, marathon runner, and one amazing human being. She is the only person in history to run solo and unsupported around-the-world. She ran 20,000 miles facing extreme danger, bitter Siberian and Alaskan winters, ax men, and desolate loneliness. She wrote a wonderful account in her book, *Just a Little Run Around the World*. Siffy and I spent time with her on Skype one evening, and her positive energy surged through the computer. Rosie told us that she is now going to walk around the world, slow down, and enjoy everything along the way. We are inspired by this brave woman.

"I used to think determination was the key. Now I know it is love. Also, when struggling, not to be battering at the obstacle, but to try to be like the sweet wild river water, and just find the Way." Rosie Swale Pope.

Rosie on the road.

Jean Béliveau – He is possibly the greatest walker of all time. Paul walked 75,554 kilometers during his eleven-year-odyssey, crossing six continents, 64 countries, and wore out 54 pairs of shoes. He stayed in temples, jails, parks, and ditches, during his uninterrupted circumnavigation of the world, which is considered to be the longest ever achieved in history. And…his wife waited in Canada for him!

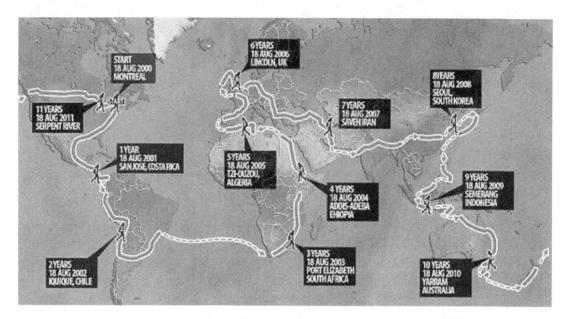

Jean's route

Masahito Yoshida –Not only has Masahito already officially walked around-the-world in four and a half years, he keeps going. More than 60,000 km have passed under his feet. He was last seen in South America. We are impressed by his top-notch photography from the road. As they say in Japanese, *Ganbatte Kudasai* (Do your best), Masahito.

Tom Turcich – On April 2nd, 2015, he left his home in New Jersey to embark on a five-year trek across the seven continents. His dream of walking around the world formed at age seventeen after his friend Anne Marie passed away. Since her death he decided to make the most of each day. He wants to walk the world and become immersed in unknown places and be forced into adventure day after day. In Texas, he adopted a dog, Savannah, and they have crossed every border together ever since. He writes and takes photos, and hopes to get better at both with each passing day.

Photograph by Masahito Yoshida

Photograph by Tom Turcich.

Nacho Dean – Twenty-five year old malagueño publicist quit his job in 2013 to embark on a world walk, and hopes to become the first Spaniard to walk around the world. He has walked over 33,000 kilometers and worn out 12 pairs of boots, as he has traveled across four continents, 31 countries, and deserts. He has slept on the roof of a police station, in churches and temples, and sometimes his only shelter was the stars.

Paul Salopek – He started his walk at the birthplace of humanity, in 2013, in Ethiopia. He is retracing the diaspora across the Middle East, Asia and then across the Bering Strait to the Americas and he will end at the tip of South America. He walks as a journalist, writing about climate change, survival, mass migration, and technological innovation. Moving to the slow beat of his footsteps, Paul is seeking the quieter, hidden stories of people who rarely make the news.

Ade Summers – He has climbed, trekked and traveled on all seven continents. Highlights include leading the first trek into Afghanistan's Wakhan Corridor, developing new routes in Mongolia, and leading a trek up the frozen Zanskar River. Ade grew up in Wales. One day he decided he was bored with this engineering job so he quit and spent the next 14 months travelling overland from Cardiff to Australia where he began his new life. Ade is a guide's guide and travels to places remote and off the beaten path. He is a wonderful photographer and we are honored to include several of his photographs in this book from Pakistan and the region.
www.ade-summers-photography.com

Keep on walking on!

Tor Torkildson

Ade Summers. *Photograph courtesy of Ade Summers.*

Photograph by Ade Summers.

Photograph by Ade Summers.

Photographs by Ade Summers.

Photograph by Ade Summers.

Circumnavigating the World on Foot

A basic definition of a world circumnavigation is an around the world journey on a route which:
- begins and ends at the same location,
- travels in one general direction, and
- reaches a pair of antipodes.

The implications from the above descriptions are that a true circumnavigation route:
- must cross the equator at a minimum of two points,
- must touch at least one pair of antipodes, and
- must travel a distance that is equal to or more than the length of the Equator.

According to *Merriam-Webster*, the word circumnavigation dates back to 1634, meaning "to go completely around" or to navigate the circumference. The world is a sphere. Going around a sphere entails great circles, and a circumnavigation route must approximate a great circle. Given the above gentlemen's rules, it is understood that when a route is laid out to travel only in one hemisphere, northern or southern, without even touching the equator, such a route becomes a polar circumnavigation at best. Any alleged circumnavigation route which does not include a pair of antipodes cannot be called a circumnavigation. This is the only way to ensure that one's travels go "to the ends of the earth" or "to the farthest possible location on earth" or "beyond the horizon" and that no shortcuts are taken.

Antipodes: Pairs of points on earth which are antipodes, are located diametrically opposite of each other. Every point on earth has its own antipode. The North Pole, for example, is the natural antipode of the South Pole.

Great Circle: The center of a great circle is the same as that of the earth. For example, the longitudes are great circles, and the equator is the latitude which defines the longest great circle given the earth's shape. Other lines of latitude which are shorter are not great circles because their centers do not match that of the earth. Great circles divide the earth into two equal hemispheres. Following a great circle path is not practical for surface journeys, thus; a true circumnavigation will approximate a great circle by complying with the antipodal requirement.

Guinness World Records, which is an independent arbiter of all records, requires that a human powered around-the-world surface journey must:
- start and finish at the same location,
- cross the Equator,
- cross all lines of longitude,
- resume each leg of the journey from the exact point at which the last one ended,

- cover a minimum distance equal to that of the Tropic of Capricorn, which is 36,788 km/22,859 miles and
- proceed in one direction, east or west, any distance doubled back must be deducted from the total.

Afterward

When I began working on this book, I had no idea how it would come to consume my life and the summer of 2016. What started out as a fun project for friends, quickly escalated into a major book publication endeavor. I made a closed Facebook group to create a tribe-like feel. This sucked me in for two to three hours a day as I researched walk related articles, books, stories, and shared posts by the group members. The group grew to over a hundred members, and I started to develop friendships with many of the participants. The essays started to roll in, at first a trickle, then a constant flow. People asked if they could join the group or share their walkabout story. In four short months, I had enough material for two books.

Early on, I thought *The Walkabout Chronicles* would be about epic walkers: the type that walk around the world, the length of the Nile, or across the Himalaya. My goal was to learn from these walkers and share their experiences. But the project soon became much more, as I began to realize how broad a subject walking is. I had a collection of walkers who were diverse, had a multi-faceted view of the world, and had pushed the ordinary to the extraordinary. Despite our differences, we all shared the love of walking.

By mid-summer, I had enough material to hand over to Siffy, the format wizard, to take the book to its fruition. With 35 essays, I felt a great sense of satisfaction and bewilderment. Did I actually have this stack of brilliant essays and photographs, without a single major crux in the process? There were no ego-maniacs to deal with despite the all-star line-up.

The essays in this book became my friends, the kind that inspire you to your greater self. I was surprised with the wide-ranging diversity of the answers I received to the identical questions that I presented. For me, the most enjoyable aspect of this book project was getting to know the authors. What a wild, intelligent, brave, and positive tribe.

I will always cherish the get-togethers, Facebook and email chats, and Skype conversations. It was also enjoyable and affirming to work on this project with my wife, Siffy. We didn't have a single argument throughout the entire process, and I believe our relationship grew deeper as a result of this shared endeavor.

Tor Torkildson

Author Resources

Bernbaum, Edwin
www.peakparadigms.com

The Way to Shambhala, three editions published by Anchor Doubleday, Jeremy P. Tarcher, and Shambhala Publications.
Sacred Mountains of the World, two editions published by Sierra Club Books and University of California Press.

Coffey, Maria
www.hiddenplaces.net
www.adventuresforacause.org

Davis, Wade
www.wadedavis.com

Delattre, Pierre
www.pierredelattre.com
www.ortenstonedelattre.com

Dorsey, James
www.jamesdorsey.com,
Twitter, @Agingexplorer
www.linkedin.com/in/jamesdorsey9149559?trk=nav_responsive_tab_profile_pic

Downie, David
www.daviddownie.com

Francis, John
www.planetwalk.org

Fuchs, Jeff
www.jefffuchs.com

The Ancient Tea Horse Road (ebook) - www.amazon.com/The-Ancient-Tea-Horse-Road-ebook/dp/B008T8P7S0
The Ancient Tea Horse Road (hardcover limited edition) – Viking-Penguin
www.amazon.com/Ancient-Tea-Horse-Road-Himalayan/dp/0670066117/ref=sr_1_cc_3?s=aps&ie=UTF8&qid=14605596 04&sr=1-3-catcorr&keywords=the+ancient+tea+horse+road
Upcoming feature length *Tea Horse Road Documentary* teaser: vimeo.com/131565614
Blog: www.tea-and-mountain-journals.com
Facebook: www.facebook.com/Jeff-Fuchs-Tea-and-Mountain-Journals-152840281433111/

George, Don
  www.don-george.com

Gyangen Tsumba, Dhawa
  www.asiakhamsang.wordpress.com

Ibbotson, Sophie
  Afghanistan: Beyond the Wars Facebook: Maximum Exposure PR
  Instagram: @maximum_exposure_pr
  Bradt Travel Guides: Kashmir, South Sudan, Sudan, Tajikistan, Uzbekistan.
  Insight Guides: China, Silk Road.
  Panorama Journal: www.panoramajournal.org

Karnath, Lorie
  www.huffingtonpost.com/lorie-karnath/
  www.loriekarnath.info
  www.amazon.com/Lorie-Karnath/e/B0045B3XCW
  www.facebook.com/lorie.karnath
  www.facebook.com/explorersmuseum
  www.explorersmuseum.org/

Kirtley, Ariane
  Amman Imman: Water is Life: www.ammanimman.org ;
  www.facebook.com/AmmanImmanWaterisLife/

Books and articles:

"Water for Life Voices." *UN News Center*. UN, 2015. Web. 03 July 2016.
Houston, Jean. "The Heart of the Matter." *The Wizard of Us: Transformational Lessons from Oz*. New York: Atria, 2012. 86-90.
'Chimpanzees in Uganda, An Unforgettable African Adventure!" *Trunkline* (1999): 8-10. *Part II*, 24-27.
"Providing water, sustaining life." *Yale Public Health Magazine* (2016): 36-39.
"Water Is Life, a Letter from Niger." *Yale Medicine* (2007): 24-29.
Kottler, Jeffrey A., and Mike Marriner. "International Jetsetters." *Changing People's Lives While Transforming Your Own: Paths to Social Justice and Global Human Rights*. Hoboken, NJ: John Wiley & Sons, 2009. 176-79.
Menouna, Olivier. "Ariane Kirtley Chercheuse D'eau." *Africa International* (2007): 37.

Kirtley, Michael and Aubine
 The World Memory Film Project: www.worldmemoryfilmproject.org

 Pertinent books and articles:

 Kirtley, Michael and Aubine. *Côte d'Ivoire, Révélations en terre d'ivoire*, Les Editions du Jaguar (2014) (Photography)
 Kirtley, Michael and Aubine. *Côte d'Ivoire, Les Racines de la Sagesse*, Grand Livre Les Editions Jeune Afrique (1981) (Photography)
 Reed, Billy. "Michael Kirtley's Sahara", *The Courier-Journal and Times* (February 13, 1977): Cover Story, Accent Section
 Kirtley, Michael and Aubine. "The Inadan, Artisans of the Sahara," *National Geographic Magazine* (August 1979): pp282-298 (Text and Photography)
 Kirtley, Michael and Aubine. "The Ivory Coast, African Success Story," *National Geographic Magazine* (July 1982): pp94-125 (Text and Photography)
 Kirtley, Michael and Aubine. "Finding Jenné-Jeno, West Africa's Oldest City", *National Geographic Magazine* (September 1982): pp396-418 (Photography)
 Kirtley, Michael and Aubine. "Senegambia, A Now and Future Nation," *National Geographic Magazine* (August 1985): pp224-250 (Text and Photography)
 Kirtley, Michael and Aubine. "Interview of Libyan Leader Muammar Gaddafi", *LIFE Magazine* (February 1980) (Interview and Photography)
 Kirtley, Michael and Aubine. "Les Derniers Seigneurs du Désert", *GEO Magazine* (June 1985): pp206-226 (Text and Photography)
 Upcoming novel: *The Lakmy Tale*

Kobalenko, Jerry
 kobalenko.com
 Twitter: @JerryKobalenko
 Facebook: Jerry Kobalenko

Leftofsky, Polly
 www.PollyLetofsky.com
 Facebook: www.facebook.com/pollysglobalwalk

 Book: *3mph: The Adventures of One Woman's Walk Around the World*
  https://amzn.com/0983208506

Maxwell, Angela
 www.shewalkstheearth.com

Mangan, Tony
 World walk website: www.myworldwalk.com
 World run website: www.theworldjog.com
 Facebook: www.facebook.com/tony.mangan.14

McKittrick, Erin
www.GroundTruthTrekking.org
Facebiook: https://www.facebook.com/Ground-Truth-Trekking-316861406084/
Twitter: https://twitter.com/Erin_McKittrick

Books:
A Long Trek Home, 4000 Miles by Boot, Raft
Ski, Small Feet, Big Land: Adventure, Home, and Family on the Edge of Alaska
Mud Flats and Fish Camps: 800 Miles around Alaska's Cook Inlet (Mountaineers Books, due out in Spring 2017)
My Coyote Nose and Ptarmigan Toes: An Almost-True Alaskan Adventure. (Children's book)

Newman, Steven
Steven's two books from his solo walk around the world are no longer being printed in hardcover or paperback. However, the most popular of the two books, *Worldwalk*, is available in e-book format at Amazon.com. To follow Steven's latest travels and adventures, be sure to befriend him on Facebook.

O'Donnell, Francis
www.wliw.org/marcopolo is the link to my Emmy nominated PBS Documentary *In the Footsteps of Marco Polo*.

If you would like to purchase the book or a DVD of the film, please do so directly from me, via Pay Pal, you can email me at: franc.is.marcopolo@gmail.com

www.facebook.com/inthefootstepsofmarcopolo/ -The official Facebook Movie page.

www.facebook.com/Francis-Daniel-ODonnell-1571958456467850/
   The link above is to my author's page.

www.facebook.com/Francis-ODonnell-118137955249749/

This link is to my art page:
www.smithsonianmag.com/travel/marco-polos-guide-to-afghanistan-57650764/?no-ist

mongolschinaandthesilkroad.blogspot.com/2015/03/paperback-reprint-just-out-in-footsteps.html

Rardon, Candace Rose
http://www.candaceroserardon.com/

Reinhard, Johan
www.johanreinhard.net
Photo Gallery: http://picasaweb.google.com/johan.reinhard

The Ice Maiden: Inca Mummies, Mountain Gods, and Sacred Sites in the Andes (2005)
Machu Picchu: Exploring an Ancient Sacred Center (2007)
Inca Rituals and Sacred Mountains: A Study of the World's Highest Archaeological Sites (2010) (with Constanza Ceruti).

Rubenstein, Dan
borntowalk.org
Twitter: @dan_rube
My book's web page with the publisher: ecwpress.com/products/born-to-walk

Saunders, Robb
www.robbsaunders.com

Strandberg, Mikael
www.mikaelstrandberg.com

Thayer, Helen
www.helenthayer.com
www.adventureclassroom.org

Torkildson, Siffy
www.sacredworldexplorations.com
www.darksky.org
Facebook: SiffyandTor Torkildson, Sacredworldexplorations

Torkildson, Tor
www.sacredworldexplorations.com
Facebook: SiffyandTor Torkildson, Sacredworldexplorations
www.amazon.com:
Encounters-With Remarkable People and Extreme Landscapes
Elbow Room-Wanderings and Musing in the Aleutian Islands
Cloud Wanderer
Agadir Dreaming

Turk, Jon
www.jonturk.net
@Deepwilderness

The Raven's Gift: A Scientist, a Shaman, and their Remarkable Journey Across the Siberian Tundra
Crocodiles and Ice: A Journey into Deep Wild.

Wilson, Brandon
www.pilgrimstales.com

Books:
Over the Top & Back Again: Hiking X the Alps, a ForeWord Magazine Bronze Award-winner
Along the Templar Trail: Seven Million Steps for Peace, Lowell Thomas Gold Award-winner for Best Travel Book; ForeWord Book of the Year finalist
Auf dem Templerweg: Sieben Millionen Schritte für den Frieden (German translation)
Yak Butter Blues: A Tibetan Trek of Faith, an IPPY Award-winner
Yak Butter Blues: Una Caminata de Fe Por El Tibet (Spanish translation)
Dead Men Don't Leave Tips: Adventures X Africa
On a Donkey's Back; wrote introduction to a collection of poetry and paintings by and about Nepalese Sherpas
Naïve & Abroad: Spain, Limping 600 Miles Through History by Marcus Wilder; fifty photos with essay on the Via de la Plata
Stories: "*Life When Hell Freezes Over*," about a year of surviving life in an Arctic Inupiat village, appears in They Lived to Tell the Tale: True Stories of Adventure from the Legendary Explorers Club
"*Along Life's Trail: War and the Environment Within*," appears in the anthology Wounds of War: Poets for Peace
Wilson's photos have won awards from *National Geographic Traveler* and *Islands* magazines. His travel articles have appeared in many publications worldwide and on the internet.

Facebook:
Brandon Wilson Adventure Travel Author
Facebook: Explore pages with book excerpts, hiking tips and photos:
Templar Trail
Along the Templar Trail
Yak Butter Blues
Over the Top & Back Again
Dead Men Don't Leave Tips
Amazon: www.amazon.com/Brandon-Wilson/e/B001JS4J0O

Wood, Levison
www.levisonwood.com

Sacred World Explorations
Alaska

Sacred World Explorations is a small publishing company. We publish articles on adventure travel, the environment, spirituality, food and wine, sacredness, and far flung journeys around the world. Guiding and consulting upon request.

Our destination is, in a sense, sacred, with the belief that certain voyages out, might become voyages in. Think of it as a sort of geo-poetic quest; the glint of an outer light reflected or of an inner light revealed. Through our memory maps, we will navigate the sacred world, creating a web of connections from everywhere to everywhere.

"Wandering re-establishes the original harmony that once existed between humans and the universe" Anatole France.

Books from Sacred World Explorations:

Korrigan's Shadow by Pierre Delattre
Agadir Dreaming by Tor Torkildson
A Wild Hare by Siffy Torkildson
Cloud Wanderer by Tor Torkildson

Made in the USA
Monee, IL
12 December 2020